AF675135

SAAKSHI

SAAKSHI

THE WITNESS

S.L. BHYRAPPA

TRANSLATED FROM THE KANNADA ORIGINAL BY

LV Shanthakumari

NIYOGI
BOOKS

Published by
NIYOGI BOOKS
Block D, Building No. 77,
Okhla Industrial Area, Phase-I,
New Delhi-110 020, INDIA
Tel: 91-11-26816301, 26818960
Email: niyogibooks@gmail.com
Website: www.niyogibooksindia.com

Editor: Gita Rajan
Cover design: Misha Oberoi
Layout: Shashi Bhushan Prasad

ISBN: 978-81-933935-5-0
Publication: 2017
Reprint: 2025

Printed at: Niyogi Offset Pvt. Ltd., New Delhi, India

A different light, altogether unfamiliar. Entirely different to the light which co-operates with the function of sight or vision. Not that such light was not seen in the past. How can the entire countenance be visualised in a brightness that flashes and vanishes in a moment and the source of light becomes dark even before comprehension?

The thumb-sized *preta* looked around and wondered, could this be Yamaloka? Or could it be somewhere in between? Despite these doubts, the *preta* felt neither fear, nor anxiety nor excitement. Just a curiosity whether this pervading mass of light that encircled it from ten directions was external or internal. Perplexed, the *preta* stood still. Quite a lot of time was spent in that state in which memory, thought and expectations were unable to be expressed and mobilised. The *preta* looked around and the doubt resurfaced – is this yamaloka or a world prior to it. Nothing other than this strange light to suggest an answer.

And then, a voice: 'Are you the *preta* of a person known as Parameshwarayya?'

It was a voice clear, soft and emotionless, without a bit of noise, without cadences, inflections or modulations, without a definite direction of origin. It seemed to come simultaneously from all around.

But whom should the *preta* respond to; when nobody was visible, none present. How could the *preta* talk about itself? Wondering thus, the *preta* realised, that its other state was a person called Parameshwarayya; it was the minute thumb-sized *preta* of that person; and it was the receptacle of that person's thoughts, behaviour and actions. When viewed through the slit of this knowledge, Parameshwarayya's physical form began to appear in the light that was needed for the external eyes. Nevertheless, he was conscious that he now stood in an altogether different light, the glow of the world of darkness.

'*Preta*s in the presence of Yamadharma are not questioned directly. According to the rules here, Chitraguptas are asked to narrate the good and evil deeds committed by the *preta*s, while they lived on earth. When they arrive here, the *preta*s cry, beg humbly, lie, say they have not committed any sin, request for pardon or sympathy, for deeds committed unknowingly. Therefore two Chitraguptas, who dwell inside the body of every being, are ordered to note down everything and report it here. These reporters are free from anger, envy, distress and jealousy. It is their duty to narrate everything that happened there, to keep it in memory and report it. As they never lie, their version alone is considered the truth. In the end, the *preta* is asked whether there is any falsehood or discrepancy in the Chitragupta's narration.'

The eyes and ears of Parameshwarayya's *preta* were searching for the speaker. None was visible. A firm voice devoid of feeling, soft and clear, without consolation or condemnation, echoed from all around. 'We are departing from procedure in your case. You have suffered unbearable agony, felt remorse and dejection and decided not to carry on living for having told a single lie during your entire life on earth; have come here by committing suicide. We think you won't lie and we have decided that you yourself should present your report. But if you slip from the truth and start weaving lies, either because of forgetfulness, shyness or fear, then the Chitraguptas will step in and set right the report. Realise that this opportunity of presenting your own report is a special favour offered to you by Yamadharma.'

The voice stopped. The *preta* was engaged in recalling clearly the memory associated with Parameshwarayya, the person. The *preta* was ordered to recount the entire life of Parameshwarayya. But, the person he should address was not to be seen. How could one talk to an invisible being, talk to someone not before us? Moreover, what all was supposed to be narrated if Parameshwarayya's life was to be reported? Where should one begin? What details were to be included and which ones omitted, where should it conclude? Is it ever possible to narrate the entire life of a man? While the *preta* pondered, the voice was heard saying:

'Common people find it difficult to speak in the absence of a form – either gentle or rough. Should you too feel so, tell me, I'll appear in any form you like.'

The *preta* travelled down memory lane and dredged out the routine of Parameshwarayya. He thought: Most of the time I used to be silent. I would speak only as much as was needed for the transaction of day to day activities. All other speech was happening within me. I would present a lengthy report to my inner-self, would contradict, approve and work out the pros and cons of situations. I would walk far up to the top of the hill touching the clouds, look down and evaluate whatever I spoke. It was my practice and it was easy. Now in this world of Yama also, I can present my report without any visible form.

While the *preta* thought so, the voice was heard.

'Do you want to know where to start? What details should be included? Well, why did you lie and what for? Why did you commit suicide for telling a single lie? First answer these two questions in detail.'

'*Niyantru*, you are Yamadharma, the lord of right and wrong, of righteousness. Before answering your question, I want to confess the change taking place inside me at this moment. Prior to your speaking, I had thought that there was no relation between the life I left on earth and my present state as *preta*. Then I felt there was only a relation of memory between them. But now I feel that I still bear the moral and ethical responsibility for the life I left behind. This is the responsibility that has given the authority of questioning to you and the duty of answering to me. Am I right?'

'Yes, absolutely. You need have no doubt on that score.'

It was now easy for the *preta* to continue. Moreover the *preta* got the precise background that it was Parameshwarayya who committed suicide and came here and now it could answer easily and started its narration:

'What I said was not merely a lie. It was a false testimony. It was a lie told after swearing before the judge in the witness box that I would invoke my inner conscience and make it speak. I had lied before all the people assembled in court and through this, it was a lie that I had told in the scope of the knowledge of myself, the accused, other witnesses and all other beings of the world. Now I'll answer the question why I lied. If I answer briefly without explaining, why, for whom and in what context I lied, it will not amount to putting the whole truth before you. But I hesitate because listening to all those details might seem unnecessary to you. Perhaps just a summary of the right and wrong would suffice.'

'There will be no essence of truth in a barren summary. Tell me all.' No cadence in the voice. By now the *preta* had understood that the voice had the quality of an ethical maxim, the manner of a disinterested and impartial narrator, without cadence, pressure or emotion. The *preta* felt a growing intimacy with the voice and was weighing itself against that benchmark. Its self-confidence was growing. It felt certain of visualising and narrating with detachment, untinged by self-pity or self-justification.

'*Niyantru*, I did not and will not blame Manjayya for this incident. He put before me the temptation to lie. But he did not force me nor did he use physical strength. He ended our meeting in the coconut grove, clearly stating that it was up to me to be or not to be a witness in his favour. Everyone says that lawyers on earth are liars and they coach others to lie. I too knew this. So, I do not feel like blaming advocate Venkataramayya, for his clever manipulation of words in making Manjayya's temptation seem agreeable, legally sound and above board. It is true whoever tempts is a liar, but he who falls for that temptation is a greater liar. Only after I was clear on this score, I thought of committing suicide. Kanchi did not die accidentally by slipping and falling from the coconut tree when he went into the grove in the night for his usual round of thieving. I never had any doubt that it was Manjayya who had murdered Kanchi. People say that a liar is neither courageous, nor fearless, nor a truthful man. Perhaps it is true generally.

'But on that day at sunset, when I was near the well in my grove, Manjayya walked in with a guilt-free, fearless air, as if nothing had happened! He came near me, looked me straight in the eye and talked. There was neither humility nor pleading. His manner clearly proclaimed: "If you want, you may do so, if not it is your wish, there's no force or pressure." What self-confidence, despite knowing that he would be sentenced to at least ten years of hard labour! The very first words he uttered were about farming. "You see, tender and twisted leaves are sprouting in some six trees on that side of your fence. You must fill it with two seers of salt and pour plenty of water on the tree bed." His words confounded me. Before I could recover, he continued, "A new type of pesticide is available in the market. If you spray it on the saplings, those damned insects that destroy coconut trees will never hover near.

I'll bring it for you the next time I go to Hassan or Tiptur," and sat on the stone slab. I was standing. My mind ruminated. He had married my daughter, deserted her and left her to eke out her living as a teacher in Channarayapattana. He had distanced himself from her and from us. Now, pretending as if nothing had happened, he squatted casually on the stone slab near the pond. It was a suggestion for me also to sit. Then he started off: "Look here, I am rushed for time. The whole village knows Kanchi is a thief. From morning to evening people toil in the sun, cultivate, plant saplings, water them and tend them carefully, so that they grow into fruit-bearing trees. Then Kanchi comes and lowers down the bunches and makes off with them as though he is the owner of all the groves in the village. Not a single man caught him red-handed. The police who display their power and authority and brag about their exploits sitting in Channarayapattana have never warned him. They neither listen to our problems nor help us. How long should this injustice have continued unchecked? It is true that I removed Kanchi and it is also true that the police are looking for me. But before they catch me, I will surrender myself in Channarayapattana police station. You come to the court and bear witness in my favour and save me from this charge. After I am acquitted, I promise to come to your home, confess my wrongdoings to Savitri before you, take her home and be an honest husband. I'll never behave as I did earlier." He grew silent. His eyes confronted mine, and were firm, as if they held my sight in a wrestler's grip. I thought, has he already caught the pulse of my innermost being, my Achilles' heel? He had tried to, but I was not weak. I laughed within myself. There was no reaction from me, or perhaps, without my knowledge, my face might have betrayed some reaction that I myself was not aware of. He continued speaking: "I have decided to surrender. Is it not your moral duty to save me? Not merely from the point of your daughter's family life but from the point of rescuing a person who has removed a wicked worm, a thorn, a peril to the villagers. It is enough if you state in court: 'that night you had gone with me to Tiptur on some business. You and I stayed over at your *sambandhi* Nagappa's house until next evening. Then I left for Arsikere on business and you returned to your village.' It is enough if you come to court and say this much. Nagappa, too will confirm this statement." I was troubled. Nagappa may commit perjury, but how could Manjayya think I too will commit perjury? He continued: "Nagappa will come as a witness in any case. The lawyer said that your statement as a witness will strengthen the case. Why should I hide anything? The lawyer opined that even the judge believes your words and regards them as words from the scriptures. It seems the judge knows your name and feels your witness is equal to that of ten other witnesses. Do you think it is fair that I should be jailed or do you feel it right to protect me, I, who removed that thief who was swallowing other people's property every night? I need not teach you the nuances of dharma. I agree I've committed wicked deeds. But removing Kanchi was not one such deed. He might not have stolen from your grove," he concluded and fell silent. His bold stare stated clearly that he did not care. Manjayya continued, "Listen, Malali Venkataramayya, the lawyer said, 'This is not a premeditated murder, nor is it committed with past animosity. It is an accidental death, occurred while preventing a theft from a grove, a theft of crop grown with labour and love. Instead of him, I too could have died. So, even if I am found guilty, I will be sentenced to only five years.' Instead of living here, I'll stay in prison. But the question is, what is your moral duty? Whether to protect me or to leave a thief like Kanchi on the loose, scot-free? Have you ever, even for a day, confronted Kanchi, advised him that what he was doing was wrong, was not dharma and tried to reform him? You did not. Or given your nature and inclination, you should have destroyed the thief in him, destroyed that thieving tendency. I destroyed the thief. If you do not protect me, it is as good as justifying Kanchi's deeds." Manjayya got up, said arrogantly, "I haven't come to request you or plead my cause. You may decide, what your moral duty is. I'm committed to my word." With firm, bold strides, he walked off on the ridge between lines of coconut trees, towards the gate of the grove.

'*Niyantru*, I must narrate a bit more in detail the dilemma that arose within me, in what directions my mind sought true dharma and how I suffered from that day onwards. I very well remember that it was a Thursday of the new-moon. Manjayya threw before me two dazzling temptations, with the clear intention that I should stoop to pick them up. One, the form of righteous temptation: that is, his killing of Kanchi was for common welfare. The second was stimulating filial affection, that is, after he would be acquitted of charges, he would come to my home, beg my daughter's pardon before me, take her home and lead a decent family life. The next day, Friday that is, he strode majestically to Channarayapattana Police Station, brimming with self-confidence and said: "I learnt you were looking for me. As soon as I heard of it, I have come here. Proceed with your legal action. Let the wheel of justice start rolling. But follow the law to the letter. Don't forget, I am *Manjayya*."

'Two weeks later, again a Thursday, Malali Venkataramayya, the famous advocate of our district, came to our village. It seems, he had inspected Manjayya's grove, the spot where Kanchi was murdered, for more than two hours. Then he went to the house of Kanchi's widow Lakkoo and had a meeting with her in private. He came to our house for lunch. My son Ramakrishna treated him with respect and sent word to me through the servant, as I was working in the grove. My daughter-in-law Sukanya cooked special dishes to honour the guest – rice, rasam, lentils, curry, other side dishes and curds. But there were no ragi-balls. After lunch, when we were chewing betel leaves and areca nuts sitting on the mat, the advocate added another temptation to the list that Manjayya had already put forth. This was in the form of justification of falsehood. Ramakrishna was also there. The advocate's lowered voice to convey what was supposedly secret was so loud that it could be heard by Sukanya in the kitchen. He said: "It is true that Manjayya is a lewd person, a rake. How can a wife tolerate such a person, that too how can your daughter, born of a decent family, beautiful as Goddess Mahalakshmi, put up with him. As an advocate I question, why should she? If my son-in-law had done this, I would have never let him get away. But, look here, Parameshwarayya, understand one thing. Even the vilest person introspects while undergoing terrible grief and misfortune. He sincerely desires to rinse his filth. I visited Manjayya five times in jail. He was in tears all five times. Not with any intention that I should save him, but those were burning tears of heartfelt penitence. He felt that his disloyalty to a good wife, a godly father-in-law and a friendly brother-in-law, was the root cause of his mind turning wicked enough to commit murder. He said he deserved to be punished. He held my hands and pleaded, 'Please don't try for my acquittal.' You see until he went into custody, he was the Manjayya of earlier days. Now, the atmosphere of prison and the experience he underwent there has brought in him a moral transformation." These words had an effect on Ramakrishna. I knew when I spoke with Sukanya later, those words had the desired effect on her also. But it was highly impossible for me to believe the recommendation of the advocate regarding Manjayya.

Then the advocate started on his second point: "You know, I've been in this profession for over forty years. Advocates not only from this district, but from different session courts come to me for advice, if there are tough murder cases. If the cases are very important, they request me to handle those cases and they call for me from far off places. I tell you from these experiences: you see, murders do happen and ninety percent of them would be justifiable. If a person decides to commit a murder, knowing fully well the rigorous punishment or death sentence awaiting him, he must have suffered severe injustice, isn't it? People decide to inflict punishment and take law into their hands when they feel it impossible to solve injustice legally. You yourself know that Kanchi was stealing coconuts from everybody's grove. Suppose the villagers had lodged a complaint against him in the police station, the police ask umpteen questions, like, 'what is the evidence for his stealing, have you ever caught him red-handed, and so on.' If this is the case, how can this thief be reformed? Moreover there is another question here, regarding psychology. It will not be such a great loss if only fifty coconuts are stolen from your grove. Any owner would feel it an insult that a fellow like this trespassed his land, inside a locked and fenced grove. He would feel he had become impotent. It is not merely the loss of fifty-sixty worthless coconuts, it is the insult for which a thief is killed. Manjayya as you know, is hot-headed. Two days before this incident, it seems Kanchi broke into Manjayya's grove and stole coconuts. That day, that amavasya Thursday, Manjayya was waiting in his grove. Thinking Manjayya was out of station, Kanchi entered the grove, and was confronted by Manjayya. In that thick, dark midnight, in the grove outside the village, a fight ensued. Who else had the courage in this village to fight a man like Kanchi? In this confrontation, Manjayya himself could have died instead of Kanchi. So, how can you call it a murder?"

'The third point that the advocate mentioned concerned our legal system. "If you lodge a complaint against Kanchi and say that he is a thief, the police ask for proof. But what details do they know about the background or the spot? I don't say that there shouldn't be any enquiry. But I feel, proper enquiry should be conducted here, in this village, Bilikere, in the vast compound of Lord Shiva's temple, before the village elders and under the leadership of honest, righteous people like you who have not uttered a single lie to date. Any punishment which takes into consideration the crime committed, degree of the crime, the circumstances, the context and the balance between crime and punishment, would be acceptable. If you decide that Manjayya should be hanged on the branch of the big banyan tree opposite Lord Shiva's temple, that too would be right. Courts that dispense justice sitting in distant cities and looking into records without knowing facts, were established by Englishmen who came from across the seas. Truth uttered there is not the truth and a lie is not a lie. It is only a means of livelihood for lawyers like me. What Mahatma Gandhi called native truth was this kind of inquiry."

'Then I noticed. This eminent advocate wore a white khadi dhoti and a white khadi shirt. Though I was not a follower of Gandhi, I knew he was a truthful man. If my eldest son-in-law, Satyanarayana of Mattikere, is leading a virtuous life by restraining his sensual desires, it is only due to Mahatma Gandhi's influence. Anyway, the advocate said this much, sat in the rear seat of his shining black car and drove away. After he left, this dilemma started inside me: was Manjayya guilty of Kanchi's murder? Was the murder right or wrong? It is true that I have not done anything to reform Kanchi. I had not thought of avoiding the loss that the other grove-owners were suffering on account of Kanchi. Mattikere Satyanarayana would have tried. He would have visited Kanchi's house and advised his wife or would have gone to Kanchi's house on a hot afternoon, sat before Kanchi while he took his meals and would have said, "Look here Kanchi, what you are doing is injustice, adharma. Until you swear on the food in your hand and say, 'I give up thieving,' I will fast," and he would have started satyagraha. But me? I lived by myself not even aware that a thief named Kanchi lived amidst us in our village. Perhaps he never stepped into our grove, as I used to spend the whole day in my grove. So, how could Kanchi come in the nights for thieving, unless he could visit the grove during daytime and had a chance of marking trees with fully ripe bunches of coconuts? That's why he had not entered my grove. All in all, I lived like a frog in a well, not coming out of my self-absorption, not trying to understand the problems and miseries of my neighbours. But Manjayya solved everybody's problem. Perhaps his method was wrong. With this thought, the scale of my sense of justice was tilting in favour of Manjayya for four or five days. I felt Satyanarayana was leading a more virtuous life than I. Very rarely he comes to visit me after the death of my daughter Seetha. Moreover, we belong to different taluks.

'I suffered a sense of moral lapse that I did not do anything to reform Kanchi. Now what could be done to Manjayya who solved the problem in his own way? This question tormented me; if I do not help in Manjayya's acquittal and let him suffer imprisonment or death sentence, would it not amount to falling into the abyss of revenge? He has wronged my family and ruined my daughter's life. At the same time, it was not possible for my conscience to give false evidence in court. Didn't I know that truth and falsehood are not words decided by justice or injustice? They are facts that show the light shining in the depth beyond conscience. If I keep quiet and remain unconcerned even if Manjayya meets with injustice, what then would be the value of my truth? This thought also was churning inside me, that I was giving supremacy to my own truth and falsehood. By nature, I was reticent. I became more of an introvert ever since the death of my wife thirty years ago. With whom could I confer? To whom should I have confessed to lessen my grief? Even God cannot perform the surgery for removing the thorn of pain that pierces within. As such, I used to be on my own. All sorrows of my life revolved around the question 'What is meant by truth?' and took form around it. All those years, the only support found for living, was to realise the truth and practise it. But after this advocate spoke, I was remembering Satyanarayana. I began to feel that instead of withdrawing into my inner-self because of personal grief, if I had engaged myself in philanthropic activities, I would have found a sense of fulfilment, if not the realisation of truth. I became progressively depressed thinking that the silence and withdrawal of all these years were meaningless, wasteful. Sleep left my side completely. Peaceful sleep had already been ruined after the death of my wife. Since then, there had not been a single night of undisturbed sleep. There would only be a semblance of sleep after tossing in the bed for hours on end or sleep would be in snatches. When I was too tired, I would fall asleep early. But by midnight, I would be wide awake, without even the sound of wind blowing on the flax tree in the backyard or of the buzzing, biting mosquitoes. In such peaceful silence spread all around, I would wake up as if I received a sharp kick from within. No matter what I did, sleep would never hover anywhere near me. Should it be so from one's fortieth year itself? It was not with the sexual urge of a widower that I suffered. My sex drive was burnt to ashes on my wife's pyre. It did not bother me either awake or asleep. What then was the reason for this sleeplessness? What was the origin of truth and falsehood? Why and from which source did falsehood originate? Was it the pain of not finding an adequate answer to this eternal question? In this distracted and withdrawn state of mind, I brought up my children. I married off my daughter Seetha to Satyanarayana and I witnessed her death. I sent Ramakrishna to Hassan to get educated and I saw to it that Savitri too got education.

'Whether the harvests were good or bad, it was a tradition in our family, since the days of my ancestors, not to send back anyone who came to our door on an empty stomach. Only recently have all the roads to our village become gravel-based and buses reach our villages. Earlier if people from the east and north-east wanted to go to Hassan, Belur, Sakaleshapura in the western direction they had to travel via Bilikere. It was our family tradition to bring home any traveller sitting near Lord Shiva's temple in the afternoon and serve him food. Only after the guest was fed, would we partake lunch. My father on his deathbed had asked me to swear upon him, my hand on his, a solemn sign of affirmation of the vow. He said, "See, my son, I don't ask you anything except to keep up this tradition of offering food to the guests and continuing our tradition of hospitality." He breathed his last only after I promised that I would do so. I maintained this *annadaana* as a vow, with faith and devotion. Now, after the buses started to ply, there were hardly any who travelled on foot. People who stayed on for lunch were also very few. Yet my son Ramakrishna too is continuing with this tradition with the same amount of faith and devotion. I understood by my experience that maintaining that one needs a wife to cook and serve food was merely an excuse. If I did not have the support of practising this *annadaana*, what refuge would I have had after my wife's death? When my wife died, Ramakrishna was nineteen and Seetha fifteen. Savitri, the last one, was only five. Not counting the two children who were born after Savitri but died soon thereafter. I used to do all household chores and finish cooking for guests too; but I didn't stop my children's education. I would cook food with a rough estimate about the number of guests sitting at the Shivaalaya. I would cover the pots of food, bolt the door and go to the temple. Some days there would be quite a few people. I would bring them home, feed them and if the food ran out, I would cook again for myself and the children. I would rustle up something like tamarind rasam. This made me happy. It gave me a sense of meaning and purpose. Even after such hard work, I couldn't get undisturbed sleep at night. Ramakrishna and Seetha, after finishing their homework, would sleep in one part of the hall and I would sleep in another part with Savitri next to me.

'Five or six days after the advocate Malali Venkataramayya had visited us, Ramakrishna said to me, "If we think of that wicked, unworthy Manjayya alone, it is right that he must either be hanged or be sentenced to severe imprisonment. But this is the only chance to bring together Savitri and Manjayya. If he is punished, there is no question of uniting them. Anyway he is now mellowed with penitence. Even though his words cannot be believed, that eminent advocate supports his words."

'While Ramakrishna spoke, fear tinged his face, eyes and voice. His words had the oblique suggestion that I should commit perjury. It was tantamount to asking me to give up the righteous practice of my whole life. I did not answer him. When I lifted my eyes and looked at him straight in the eye, his head drooped down as if he had been hanged. Contrite, he said, "I spoke these words for the sake of our Savitri's happiness, nothing else."

'It was really Savitri who had exhausted and enfeebled me. From her very childhood, she was a stubborn girl. Ramakrishna was fourteen years older than her and Seetha ten. After the death of their mother, these two had pampered and spoilt this little girl. I too did not refuse any of her demands. I don't know whether it was pampering or carefulness but I thought that there should not be an imbalance in the scale of my emotion. It is certainly not true that children become stubborn and self-assertive because parents fulfil all their demands. Anyway, it was Savitri's nature. If not, why would she be so adamant to marry Manjayya who was seventeen years older than her, a man more immoral than a street dog? However, this moral should not be applied to dogs. By the time I returned home from the grove, Ramakrishna had beaten the seventeen year old Savitri black and blue. There were welts on her cheeks, shoulders and back. I took him near the haystack in the backyard and asked: "We may restrict her. We may punish and advise, but should we give in to violence?" Ramakrishna answered: "Can we bow down to the stubbornness of her immature mind and agree to marry her off to *Manjayya*? You are a detached person. Being the elder brother, is it not I who has to perform the *kanyadaana*? Is not this beating her better than the sin of giving her away to such a person?" I did not speak further. Somehow it was not in my nature to lift my hand and strike. I felt as if weakness entrapped me and I could not decide anything. My son had called me a detached person. He was looking at my face. I recovered from the jolt and said: "Not just four, slap her ten times. If this marriage can be averted, will there be anyone happier than me? But, this obstinacy seems to be her *praarabhda-karma*. I shall not interfere. You are the head of the family as far as this matter is concerned." I came inside, but did not look at Savitri. Ramakrishna and I had our dinner. Then I heard Sukanya coaxing Savitri who was lying down on the mat in the room to have her dinner. Savitri did not budge, even though her sister-in-law pleaded, cajoled in many ways and said she too would starve if Savitri did not take food. I heard Savitri telling her sister-in-law "Don't touch me!" and pushing Sukanya's hand away again and again. Was it detachment? Or...? I, who sat leaning on a pillar in the hall, at once got up, rushed into the room and told Sukanya, "You leave this room, child. I'll teach her a lesson." Saying so, I started thrashing Savitri hitting her on the shoulders and back. I don't know when I started kicking her, on the waist, back, hip – one kick with my right foot, the other with the left, repeatedly. If Ramakrishna had not intervened and pulled me away, I would not have stopped kicking her. If that sort of non-stop beating and kicking had continued for some more time, certainly Savitri would have died. Ramakrishna held my hands and dragged me into the hall. Sukanya bolted the room from the inside, as if she was scared of me breaking free of Ramakrishna's hold, rushing into the room and start thrashing Savitri again.

'That night I couldn't even get my usual snatch of sleep. It was clear that Ramakrishna too had not slept. If he was asleep, he would snore like the roaring of waves. Once you heard the roar of waves inside, it meant Ramakrishna was asleep. A deadly silence squeezed the whole night inside and outside the house, in the village, the fields outside, the grove, the tank and the sky. As usual at cockcrow, I rose and went to the grove. I did not feel like doing any work. I quietly sat on the stone slab near the pond. For hours together, I was caught in the dilemma – whether I should stop this marriage or accept this also as another trial, as an act of *praarabdha-leela* and remain detached. By eleven, Ramakrishna came into the grove. Usually he wouldn't come into the grove, as he supervised the wet-lands and dry-fields. Tiredness and weariness oozed out of every pore of his face and his sleep-starved eyes. He too sat on the edge of that stone slab and said: "Appa, I have thought about it the whole night. Savitri is not the sort of girl to give up her stubbornness. Whole of yesterday, she did not touch a morsel of food. Till I left home, she had not touched anything. Sukanya too forced her many a times and now she has given up her efforts. It is altogether a different matter whether we agree to the marriage or not. You leave the decision to me. If you participate in making the decision and involve yourself in it, you will certainly be furious. You will beat her and kick her. As far as I remember, you had never given your mind to anger. You had never lifted your hand even to beat cattle. In spite of it, yesterday night you kicked Savitri brutally, without restraint. If I had not pulled you away, you would have surely killed her. I know you love her very much and it is quite natural that you got terribly angry when she chose a ruinous path. But if you get angry, and even for a moment your mind is subjugated by anger, I feel the very foundation of our family will collapse. So, if Savitri is to be punished, you please leave it to me in future. Whether we agree to her demand and marry her off to Manjayya is another matter. You entrust me with complete responsibility of it. Leave it to me, whether it is for better or for worse. I won't inform you about what I do or I do not. Only finally, I'll inform you about my decision. If you don't feel like talking, you need not say 'yes' or 'no.'"

'It was true that Ramakrishna took this responsibility off my shoulders, but did my responsibility really end? What action could I have taken in this state of dilemma? He too loved Savitri as intensely as a father. When their mother died, Ramakrishna was nineteen. He cajoled and consoled his five year old sister. Both he and Seetha called Savitri *amma*, for, she was the true replica of her mother in grace and facial features, fair complexion, shape of nose, chin, sharply bent eyebrows and height. Ramakrishna resembled me, had a masculine build, was tall and serious by nature. Seetha was a mixture of some aspects of both of us. She had a broad forehead like her maternal uncle. But do physical resemblances go with the characteristics of a person? Savitri's mother did not have this stubbornness. Yet, how did Savitri get this? Ramakrishna returned home. After midday I went to the Shivaalaya as usual. There were four travellers. Taking them home and offering lunch gave me satisfaction. What else was there to sustain me in life except this tradition, passed down to me through generations? I didn't enquire whether Savitri had eaten or not. Three days later, Ramakrishna came to the grove by the evening and said that he had decided to give Savitri in marriage to Manjayya. I kept quiet. Everyone in the village knew about Manjayya. He was thirty-four years of age. He could have got married twelve years back. His parents died when he was still young, but he was well off and had enough property. He was very handsome. His face and physique were suitable to play the role of Arjuna in dramas. Long hair, curling at the ends. He was so attractive that any girl would fall for him. When he was still young, he became a rake and fell into bad ways. Who would give his daughter to such a man? Moreover, he did not have any necessity of marriage. To him, who sought unlimited pleasure without any rule, regulation or binding, this limited pleasure of a family man and marriage was only an obstacle. Knowing fully well about Manjayya's history, how did Savitri agree to marry him? How did she become so adamant that she would marry only him and went to the extent of starving herself to death? One day when Savitri went to the village tank to wash her clothes, it seems, Manjayya was swimming near the boulder that juts out from the deep water in the tank. For three to four days, she went to the same place to wash her clothes when nobody was there. He came for swimming. They met, spoke and from there it all started. Ramakrishna had asked her. "Look here, his conduct in the past is such. What is the guarantee that he would be decent and virtuous in future?" Savitri said that Manjayya had sworn to be good. When Ramakrishna asked, "Does the oath of such a fellow have any value or meaning?" she had retorted, "If you start with suspicion from the very beginning, nothing can be achieved." It seems she consoled her brother: "Let him be whatever sort of man, I am confident of mending him. These scandalmongers of Middle-Street – Channammatte, Puttanamma and Venkatalakshamma – have blown things up and concocted exaggerated stories out of jealousy for he wouldn't marry girls from their families."

'The wedding took place. Who could say that Manjayya was a man of thirty-four? Guests who attended the marriage from the neighbouring villages thought he was a youth of twenty-two or twenty-three. Even today, while he is over fifty-two, anybody would say he is a young man of twenty-five. His personality and physical attributes conceal his real age.

'Anyway it turned out just as we feared. After the marriage, for three months, Manjayya did not leave his home and the newly married wife. Afterwards his old habit of philandering resurfaced. In about six months Savitri came to know about it. She did all she could for a couple of months to restrain him. Finally, she left him and one evening walked back to our house. For about a year she did not speak with anyone and lived here with a sense of guilt. Like a maidservant, she would do household chores from morning till night, even though her sister-in-law did not ask her to. She then insisted on getting a job for her livelihood at any place. Ramakrishna and I tried to persuade her and told her that this was her home too and she had every right to live here. But she was adamant, as usual. Ramakrishna contacted Chalapathi Shetty of Channarayapattana and with his influence, Ramakrishna could get Savitri a teacher's post in the local Middle School. Savitri went there, rented a two-room house and started living there. *Niyantru*, in my effort to tell you the background of my suicide, I have brought up other things before you. But, not a word of what I am saying is a lie. I do not know the absolute form of truth and falsehood. But I can say it with confidence that there is certainly no difference between my knowledge and what I am saying,' said the thumb-sized *preta* and stopped speaking.

'If falsehood creeps into your statement, the Chitraguptas will intervene and correct. Continue,' the voice ordered in the same detached manner.

'No matter how stubborn Savitri was, Ramakrishna's affection for his little sister never diminished. Otherwise could he have suggested that I should commit perjury for her sake? He said, "Appa, before I spoke with you, I went to Channarayapattana and talked with Savitri. I had a doubt if she would agree to live with him again, even if we save Manjayya from punishment. When I raised the matter, she said, 'If Appa's mind doesn't permit this, I don't want it,' but tears streamed from her eyes."

'Two weeks later, I got summons from the court in Hassan. That meant that I had to appear in court. That could not be avoided. When you stand before a judge, you only have the choice of either telling the truth or lying. But if you evade the choice and not attend the court, that too, I felt, would be a lie of sorts. As the day of hearing approached, I felt I was losing my innate strength. My daily sleep reduced to just half an hour at night. I thought of going to Channarayapattana and meeting Savitri. But a second thought occurred: it was I who had to decide and act. By seeing her, I would be burdening her with an obligation to do what I wanted her to. So I kept quiet. Ramakrishna said: "Appa, not even a coconut or a coconut frond has been stolen in any grove since Kanchi's murder." On my way to the grove, Baanappa, Chigarigowda, Chikkegowda, Kengayya and many others came to me and spoke of their own accord: "Your son-in-law may be a lech, but he is a *man*. Who else would have the courage to remove Kanchi? Now our crops are safe." All this justified my leaning towards lying in court. Ramakrishna and I reached Hassan in the evening by bus through Channarayapattana. I told Ramakrishna I didn't want to see Savitri. We went to the advocate Venkataramayya's house to stay there in the night. My *sambandhi* Nagappa, owner of copra warehouse, had also come there. The advocate explained the manner of the next day's trial and taught us what we had to answer, how careful we should be in the cross-examination. Nagappa was sharp witted. He would answer even before the advocate briefed us. That night Nagappa, Ramakrishna and I were accommodated in the hall upstairs. Ramakrishna was tossing and turning. He did not snore at all. Wasn't he suffering pain for making his father lie? Nagappa too did not sleep immediately and said to me. "You don't have the experience of going to a court. Do not forget to put your signature on both the forms. You should collect your expenses for being a witness, to and fro fare, lodging and boarding charges, etc. If you forget, you won't get anything. Anyway we are going together so I'll remind you."

'I did not reply, as I knew that Nagappa's existence was always ruled by money. I lay down quietly. The next morning I got up and had my bath. The advocate was busy looking at files and records in his room on the platform of that big house. I prayed to God in my mind to help out in the test of that day. By ten, Nagappa, Ramakrishna and I went to the court. I was called first. Trembling, I walked up the steps to the witness box and looked at the judge. Oh Lord,' saying so, that thumb-sized *preta* started laughing so loudly, that his laughter resounded everywhere inside Yamaloka. It seemed that the *preta* had suddenly forgotten the majestic, imposing presence of Yamadharma and the seriousness of the manner in which the decision about its good and bad deeds was being taken. The *preta*, as if it was a trivial situation, started to explode in peals of laughter as though it was vomit bursting out, refusing to stay in. Though the *preta* tried to control its laughter in the beginning, it thought it wise to give up that useless effort, and roared with unobstructed laughter that reverberated through hell, the netherworld and all territories inhabited by *preta*s.

The voice was then heard. '*Preta*, whether it is laughter or crying or narration, the rule here is it should come out in a soft and controlled voice. By now, you should have understood this. Stop laughing, tell us the reason for your laughter.'

The *preta* at once became serious. It composed itself in a moment and then said: 'I told you how I entered the court hall. As I started narrating that, I remembered the manner of dispensing justice, the whole set up and the judge sitting on the seat with a serious face and I felt like laughing. When a rhythm different to the strain of the serious vein of thought occurs, belly-shaking laughter is produced, isn't it so? And the judge sitting there, lies in ambush to see whether the lightning of truth flashes, when two lies collide with each other. His plight calls for pity. Moreover, he doesn't have the help of Chitraguptas, or Shraavanas and Shraavanis, like you have here. And there the defendant and accused present their demands and cases in the form of lies only ...'

And here the voice intervened: '*Preta-kaayaas* that come here also lie. That is why I have entrusted the job of reporting to the Chitraguptas. Chitraguptas have neither love, enmity nor hatred towards anybody. Their duty is only to make note of what actually happened and in the end, to report everything here and become silent.'

'But *Niyantru*, is lying an innate disposition of human beings? Shastras prevalent there say that before his birth, during his lifetime and after death, a man lies. And lie is the cause of birth. Is it true?'

'Let philosophical discussions be for later. Your report is not yet complete. Recount what happened in the court.' The voice was calm, serious and soft. Now, the thumb-sized *preta* fully understood that the voice was the power which controlled and commanded the direction of its speech.

'Manjayya stood in another box meant for the accused. The judge sat on a high chair on the platform behind the huge table. He wore a black gown. Below the platform, in the place meant for advocate, sat Venkataramayya, Manjayya's advocate. He behaved as though we had never met before, and even had we met, we had not spoken about this matter. The judge asked me to take the oath: In this procedure of legal decision, I promise to tell the truth only, I shall tell the complete truth. Except truth, I will utter nothing else. I swear in the name of God above, and on my inner conscience – whatever I tell is only the truth – after the judge made me repeat the last sentence of the oath, he slanted a glance at Venkataramayya. As soon as my tongue uttered the oath, a sort of burning started inside me. It was the feeling of a mildly shining light, becoming a thick blaze and beginning to burn all other things. But Venkataramayya had already begun the script of the drama he had written, tutored and made me practise. The style of a drama would have the power of making other characters pick up the cue and rattle on immediately after the first character speaks. Venkataramayya pointed towards Manjayya and started the first dialogue of the drama. 'Do you recognise this man?', 'Who else in this world knows him better than I do?', though details began to unfurl like a whirlpool inside me, I said only what I had been crammed with: 'Yes I can. His name is Manjayya. He is from my village, Bilikere.' Then, many questions followed: Where were you in the night on Saturday, the thirteenth? Who were you staying with in Tiptur? Why had Manjayya come there? I don't know how all these ended! He was the speaker on my part. I just delivered the dialogue he had taught me to cram. Then I heard Venkataramayya saying, 'That's all Your Honour' in English and he moved behind the curtain. Now the advocate for the prosecution came, stood before me and questioned. "You have sworn before this seat of justice, in the name of the omnipresent God and your conscience that you will speak only complete truth and would not utter the slightest falsehood. Is that right?" *Niyantru*, as soon as the advocate uttered the words 'the seat of justice,' somewhere in my inner being, I remembered you. Not that I had ever seen you before. But I had heard about you, who dwells deep inside every human being. I had tried to awaken and activate you, from the very moment I learned to think and more so from the day my wife died. I told you when the seat of justice administered the oath in the name of my conscience, there was a feeling that the mildly shining light became a blowtorch starting to burn up every other thing. Actually what happened was this: When the judge invoked my conscience, heat covered me inside and smoke began to envelop me. When the prosecution advocate aimed again at my conscience and addressed it directly, at once it was re-ignited. I felt like swooning. I leaned on the witness box, held on to it tightly and supported myself. I felt as if cold water filled my ears, and I could not hear a thing. When I recovered a little, I felt an intense desire to run away from there. But once caught up before the presence of justice, how was it possible to run away? Who had the strength to go out? *Niyantru*, once one enters your periphery, can one go out? Have you appointed any sentry at the door so that people inside should not escape? In that state in which I felt my conscience was drowned and completely drenched, I did not know whether the advocate for prosecution asked any questions or the seat of justice asked any searching or piercing questions. Once the judge said, 'You may go now,' but when he saw that I did not hear it, he repeated it again. I felt as if I was released. I quickly climbed down from the witness box and strode through the main door. Nagappa came running up and asked me: 'Did you sign the form of travelling expenses and daily allowance?' Lakkoo, the widow of murdered Kanchi, sat crosslegged and was chewing betel leaves and nuts. I came out of the court precinct and began to run, as one chased by a dog, and lost direction. I was continuously running, not being aware of the sweat, of my panting breath or my thumping heart. When I was extremely tired and could not run, I walked fast and when that too was not possible, I turned into slow steps. When I felt that my heart and legs were tied together and strained, I lied down on the grass under the shade of the tree. I slept. Oh! what a sleep that was! A sound and lengthy sleep that I had not had since my wife's death. The sleep in which external scenes did not hover in the form of dreams. It made me feel I was completely within myself.

'When I woke up, it was already dark. I didn't feel alert enough to get up and kept tossing for a while. Then I got up. I came out from the cover of the banyan tree and looked for the position of

Orion in the star-studded sky. When I found it, I guessed it was about two o' clock in the morning. I was in a dense, dark and lonely place and didn't have a clue to which town this hillock was near or in which direction, at what distance. There was only perfect silence, without even the sound of dry leaves, like when squirrels, lizards or chameleons move about, or the sound of wolf, jackal or a flock of sheep. I squatted there on the ground. In a short while, a slight wind began to blow. Then I heard the rustling sound of dry leaves on the ground, in the dense darkness where nothing was visible to the eyes. Branches of the banyan tree were still. They did not sway, so slight was that breeze. But I couldn't bear even that. I felt as if I was falling down where I sat and was actually falling down and floating like a dry leaf. I had lost my weight. I had lost that central gravity which controlled and sustained the balance of my personality. I stretched my hand, groped around to see if I could get a firm rock to hold and sit. But I found nothing. I felt if I dare to place my body directly across the wind that whipped the dry leaves, I would be buffeted around, tossed somewhere and fall down. Being cautious about the safety of my body, I lay down on the ground on my back. Immediately, anger raged within me like a fire. I felt furious about Ramakrishna, advocate Venkataramayya and Savitri. I thought of putting these three, especially Savitri into the fire and burn them into ashes. When I opened my eyes, I found that the dark sky with millions of twinkling stars had become a red burning orb. The blowing wind and the banyan trees growing there, that stood dark, also burned with a crackling sound. Savitri screamed from the burns in that inferno. But Manjayya was not found anywhere. I brought him to mind and conjured up his figure. However much I tried, it was not possible for my mind to push him also into that blazing fire and burn him to ashes. My anger was reserved only for members of my own family: especially for my daughter Savitri. Finally I closed my eyes, frightened by the cruel immensity of that fire impossible even to imagine. But that fire wouldn't vanish and the burning wouldn't stop.

'I slept again. Such a sound sleep, the likes of which was hiding and troubling since my wife's death. Oh! Such a sound sleep I got again. But this time it was not a deep sleep and external scenes took the form of dreams. The immense fire with crackling sound continuously burning within me was the dream in my sleep. There was nobody. Nobody was being roasted there in that fire. It was only I who was being burnt. But there was no pain. There was no groaning, no screaming. No fear or anxiety of the dream vanishing or breaking. It is true that the duration of sleep and the duration of a dream are different. But for the whole duration of my sleep, I was dreaming. That too might not be precise. Before I slept, I was looking at the earth and the sky blazing with fire. But before I slept, I myself was not burning in that fire. That was the main difference.

'When I woke up, it was noon. I had slept for such a long time despite the searing heat that pierced my face, eyes and body. There were three dogs around me and fifteen to twenty crows were hopping nearby on the ground, biding their time. A couple of vultures sat on the top of the banyan tree on this side. But luckily, no animal or bird had come near me and pecked or bitten me while I was asleep. Had they understood that I was not yet dead or were they waiting for me to die? I got up and sat down. The dogs and crows were disappointed and withdrew slowly. But far-sighted vultures still sat on the branch. I felt hungry. I thought of getting up and going to any village, asking for a couple of tender coconuts, if there was a grove. I felt like drinking tender coconut water and eating the pulp. When I looked around, I saw a village at some distance. I could not know the direction of the village as the sun blazed directly overhead. However, when I started walking, I remembered the anger I felt towards Ramakrishna, Savitri and the advocate and felt sad. If I had flatly refused to tell a lie, would they have used force and made me lie? Though I lied only for the sake of other people, it was I who lied. Thinking so, my mind felt better. I found peace that was gained by introspection. If our minds are freed from shifting the burden of faults to others and getting angry with them, we may find peace. Though I carried the burden of my fault, it was not possible to regain the loss of my original, essential power and the quality of goodness caused by it. There was no avenue available to regain it.

'I walked eight miles to the west from Hassan, through interior village roads. That village was to the south. I went up to the first house and asked for food. They gave me two handfuls of flour. I baked four rotis, ate two and wrapped the remaining rotis in a towel, tied it and started towards my village. It took two days of walking. Ramakrishna had reached the village. He was worried about my delay in returning home. He had rushed back to Channarayapattana by bus and again went to Hassan, enquired in the advocate's house, instructed his son Ganesha who was studying in Hassan to look for his grandfather, returned home and was restless. As soon as he saw me, he was about to ask me "where had you gone?" but, bit his tongue and stopped mid-sentence. I don't know what expression I had on my face.

'It was not in my nature to look around while walking on the road. My habit was to go to the grove and return from there with head downcast, my eyes on my feet. I would not notice things like who walked on the street, who was standing or who sat on the front platform of whose house. But the day after I returned from Hassan, as I was heading towards the grove, I felt as if I heard a crowd on the street, as if all the villagers lined up on both sides of the road saying among themselves, 'There goes Parameshwarayya the liar, Parameshwarayya who committed perjury." Many a time I would raise my head and look around. But there would be no one. Thinking it was only an illusion, I would avert my eyes and keep walking. *Niyantru*, in that context, I had opened up my inner-self and was critically examining whether I was afraid of people's opinion that Parameshwarayya lied or of my conscience. Not that I didn't care a bit for people's opinion. There were a number of people who sympathised with me saying, "Poor fellow, even he had to lie for the sake of his daughter." Especially senior women of the village I knew liked my act, approved it and were sympathising with me and quite a few men also favoured me. But is it possible to decide the right and wrong of our deeds according to approval or disapproval of others? Chiefly, truth was the firm foundation and support of my life; in my feeling, thought and conduct with others, there was no smear of lie. I used to weigh and decide every act of mine with this criterion. I was taking care so that my conscience grew sharp day by day, and it did not become dim with soot, or become dull and filled with smoke. As months and years passed, I would do work that enhanced its brightness without any inner struggle. I would snub any deeds that dimmed its brightness. That was the haven of my peace. If not, what support was there for me in life after my wife died? Routines like bringing up children and working for their progress may give an impetus: but they do not justify my life. What I needed was not to be obtained from anyone, nor could it be entrusted to any, it had to be delivered only to my inner light; it was not a mere flesh and blood related motivation. Now, by going to court, committing perjury, I myself have destroyed that justification. I have broken down the very foundation of my life. Now, where was the necessity to live? Why should I live? Nothing was more appropriate than ending my life; and the thought of suicide took a clear form.

'*Niyantru*, during this period I didn't lose appetite and did not suffer from sleeplessness. I started getting the same sort of sleep. The judge told me, "You may go." I rushed out of the witness box, ran out of the court premises, ran and ran and fell asleep beneath a big banyan tree; that deep, lengthy sleep, I didn't have since thirty years. Now I would have such undisturbed sleep that I wouldn't wake up even after sunrise. There was inner peace only when I was asleep. The burden of a life that had no justification would weigh on my shoulders the moment I woke up. A similar thing happened with food also. I lost the sense of proportion – whether what I ate was enough for me or I needed more. Daily ritual of going to Shivaalaya at noon to see whether there were guests had become meaningless. I returned home straight from the grove at lunch time. Ramakrishna noticed this and he himself started to continue that tradition. Even though I slept so much, ate well, day by day I became weaker and emaciated. Ramakrishna took me to Bilikere hospital. I had lost four kilograms in a week. By the following week, I had lost four more kilos. The doctor could not diagnose what the problem was but prescribed a tonic. One evening, when I was sitting near the well in the grove, the thought of suicide crystallised into a precise form. I slept too much. There was no dichotomy or sadness in sleep and there was no need for justification. But when I was awake, the lack of justification haunted. The only solution to this haunting nothingness was to go back to sleep. So, why should I not enter into the final sleep where there would be no choice of waking up at all. The moment this resolve took form, I thought of the method as well. Since we were agriculturists, we had plenty of rope in our house. I chose one smooth and shiny jute rope that would easily slide into a noose and put it under my pillow. As I myself used to roll up my bed in the morning, nobody would suspect the presence of the rope. But the surprising thing was, after my decision of committing suicide and hiding the rope, I lost my sleep. As in the past, I couldn't get even a couple of hours of sleep at night. Until then, I wouldn't be aware of anything during that profound sleep. Now, the pain of being awake the whole night was haunting me. Death was frightening me. Committing suicide seemed a terribly violent step. One day, I got up, hid the roll of rope under my arm, wrapped a shawl around me, went to the Shivaalaya in front of the village, quietly sat on the stone slab there for two hours and returned home. After I came back and lied down, I felt peaceful for a moment. I felt light, thinking that the danger was past. But it was only for a moment. Again I felt life to be a dead weight while remembering that I was deprived of justification. I thought I was a coward and felt disgusted with myself. Though I decided to go back immediately, I heard a cock crow in some street in the border of the village and I knew that people would get up, go to work in their fields and groves and I dropped that thought. After a little while, I thought: why should suicide be committed secretly? Why do people who commit suicide, do so in a lonely and deserted place? Perhaps with the precaution that other people might try to prevent them from this deed. But who had any right to stop me and force me to live without any support or justification? Some more time was spent in this thought. Crows cawed. As soon as I heard the sound of the crow, I felt the enclosing proximity of death. I got up, put the rope under the pillow, rolled up my bed and walked towards the grove. My mind was completely detached and still the whole day. This was the last day of my life, of my body and of this world. But I did not feel like looking around with fond memories as if it was the last time, at all these – the grove, swaying coconut trees, the bank of the pond that I daily used to sit on, the fragrant yellow flowers growing near the fence or the moon who moves from the east, rises to the top and slides towards the western valley with silent brightness. The meal didn't have any special taste either though it was my last supper. As usual I finished my meal. I wrote on a paper: "As I have lost the meaning in life, I have committed suicide. No one else is responsible for this deed." I tied that piece of paper to the edge of my dhoti. I spread my bed in the hall and lay down. I was waiting as a traveller waits for his departure time. The moment I felt it was past midnight, I got up silently, put the rope under my arm, wrapped myself with a shawl, opened the door silently, came out and shut the door. Since we returned from the court, the roars of Ramakrishna's snore had become very feeble. On my way, no stray dogs barked. I crossed the Middle Street, passed the street in front of the village and after the fort lane, I came to the Shivaalaya outside the village. The banyan tree opposite the temple stood like a mound in the dim light. Without delay, I started climbing the tree. As I was out of practice, I began panting and felt giddy. I crawled on the thick forked branch that had stretched towards the Shivaalaya and tied tightly one end of the rope to the branch, made a noose with the other end, put it around my neck, tied the shawl around both my hands and jumped down the branch. As I had expected, the noose tightened. As a reflex action, though, the hands started to untie the knot in the first few seconds, but the tight knot got in their way. I did not feel either sadness or grief even when I was choking and my consciousness was swaying between two edges of life and death. I did not get angry so as to blame or curse anybody. It was true that my body and legs were writhing in pain for a few seconds, and it was quite natural. But I ended with a firm mind this bubble of life which had no justification. I don't know what happened thereafter. *Niyantru*, I've answered your question.' The thumb-sized *preta* became silent.

Silence enveloped, profound silence, solid, palpable silence not found even in the womb of the deepest cave. It was that encircled silence, in which the report of the *preta* could be substantiated and could be distinguished into crystals of truth and lies. In a while a voice came out:

'*Niyantru*, this report is true only to the effect of what this *preta* has said. But it is incomplete. Incomplete truth will produce the effect of untruth. This man, instead of being present in the court and trying to be acquainted with the happenings thereafter, ran away. In fact, it was not with this man's witness that Manjayya was acquitted. Indeed his witness caused a little trouble for Manjayya's release.' The *preta* immediately identified that it was not the voice of Yamadharma, the *Niyantru*. The voice of Yama was all pervading and of the final power beyond which there was no pleading, it was emotionless and controlling. But the voice that was being heard now had neither that pervasiveness nor that magisterial quality. It was soft, humble and submissive. It was careful not to allow any emotion to disrupt the balance of the reporting. The thumb-sized *preta* understood that it was the submission of the Chitraguptas. But the *preta* could not understand, or distinguish, whether it was the voice of Chitra or Gupta or of both, though it heard with great attention. The submission continued: 'Yet, he feels a sense of regret that only because of his perjury, Manjayya was acquitted.'

Again there was a silence that anticipated speech. The thumb-sized *preta* did not know whether to deny this charge or clarify itself further. After a while, the voice of Yamadharma, now familiar to the *preta* was heard:

'For thirty years you lived a withdrawn and introverted life. After you gave evidence and came out of the court, except for knowing the news of Manjayya's release, you lived without showing any zeal or curiosity to know how and why he was acquitted. Even the words of Ramakrishna, your son did not touch your mind. Is it not so?'

The *preta* thought for a while and agreed that it was true.

'There will be several people involved in an action. The action cannot be understood until the thoughts of those people are known. We should not make any decision or judge any action without taking into consideration both the cause and the effect, the east as well as the west. Chitraguptas say that it was not because of your witness that Manjayya was acquitted. Their statement is the final truth. I will give you an opportunity. Do you desire to know the complete truth?' *Niyantru* asked.

The thumb-sized *preta* could think of nothing. What *Niyantru* said was true. It was also true that I had lived without any inclination to know the truth. Why should I know the complete truth now? The *preta* said, '*Niyantru*, what should I gain by knowing all those filthy disgusting things? I reported all these, for you ordered me to report whatever I knew instead of the Chitraguptas. With the help of Chitra-Gupta's report, please judge my rights and wrongs, give the verdict and end this matter, please.'

Niyantru said, 'Chitraguptas are *saakshis*, absolute witnesses. Prior to your suicide, you struggled to be a pure *saakshi*. You tried to lead your life with complete detachment after the death of your wife. You thought to live only as a *saakshi*, devoid of any contact with action. Now I give you the special power of knowing the inner thoughts of everybody without having any contact with action. This is the power that Chitraguptas have. Receiving that power, will you gather the truth and then report it? This is a special opportunity that is not available to all. Think about it and tell me.'

There was silence for a while. Finally, the *preta* accepted the offer.

Niyantru said, 'I will send you back to your former world in this state of a thumb-sized *preta*. There, you may enter into the minds of several persons and be a witness to their thoughts simultaneously. But you do not have the power either to influence or change their thoughts and feelings. The function of a *saakshi* is only to know. Nobody would know about your presence in his or her mind. As such, you need not feel fear, shyness or embarrassment. My Chitraguptas also function similarly. But, as they are not related to the characters, they are free from the burden of introspection. As you have to report the thoughts and deeds of persons closely related to you, there is no harm if introspection and comparisons rise in your mind. You may leave now. At the end of your visit, come back and report to me.'

The voice stopped.

Lakkoo lay on the bed resting her head on Manjayya's left arm in a hotel room in Tiptur, a small town. The fragrance of Mysore Sandal soap still lingered on her body. She scrubbed and washed herself three times with the soap, which was given to her by Manjayya. She wore the new sari that he had brought for her. He had ordered two full meals to be brought up to the room. After finishing lunch, they had sex and now were lying next to each other in silence. Lakkoo could never have imagined that the union between man and woman would be so delightful and pleasant with sweet-talk, just as in the films. Though she tended to be shy and withdrawing at times, she had expressed the desire that Manjayya remove her inhibitions by compelling her. She thought this pleasure would continue thus till her death. Hereafter, it was her fortune to enjoy this. But along with this desire for pleasure, a feeling of guilt pierced her mind for a second: whether what she was doing was right. She remembered: this is the second time I've slept with this man. The very memory of that first time, oh ma, makes my heart race. Catching me unawares, this fellow cast a spell on me. What magical power he has, he turns a woman into a bitch in heat running after him. Once I had asked Naagi of Fort-Street, 'What have you found in the fellow that you have tied yourself to him so strongly?' She had said, 'Oh akka, you don't know. If you sleep with him once, you will feel like living with him for seven births continuous, even if you have to do so as a bonded slave.' I did not know then that it would be so enthralling. I should keep him tied to me and see that he does not stray. If the man tied to a woman seeks happiness with others, how can she tolerate? Lakkoo thus decided to keep Manjayya tied to herself.

Lying on his back, Manjayya was comparing Lakkoo's sexuality with that of other women he had enjoyed. He had arrived at the decision that the build of her body was attractive but she lacked the sex appeal which a man craved for. He had realised years ago, given his experience, that it was not something that could be taught or cultivated but an inherent fragrance that rose and spread on its own. He thought, then, why did I bring her here today? Not because she was a new one. No, that night underneath the Indian beech tree behind the fort, after I saw her in the darkness .... no, no, I had not seen her properly in my fear and anxiety. I had merely shown my strength. Yes it is true that there was curiosity and a desire to experience someone anew; besides, shouldn't I show gratitude to the woman who helped me in getting acquitted? This Manjayya is never an ungrateful man. Along with this justification, he found that the bigger reason for this was to overwhelm in this manner, the wife of the man he had murdered. She was already conquered, subjugated. He knew that from now on she would obey him blindly. Even as he was thinking so, he turned to his left and opened her lips with his tongue, kissed her deeply and searchingly, whispered in her ears three times, 'Oh, my rani, my rani, my rani.' Lakkoo was intoxicated. Suddenly she remembered her husband Kanchi. She understood the difference between him and this Manjayya. 'Bronze' was Kanchi's nickname, his title. If you hit him on his thighs or arms, it would sound like bronze. His build was like that of a hound, long arms and legs, body ramrod straight. He could run faster than a horse, could climb a coconut tree as nimbly as a monkey. However tall the tree might be, he would climb it rapidly in one breath, pluck the bunch, slide down with the coconuts in hand, come home and snore. But Manjayya was different.

He would slide in, engage in various sorts of play, swim with the waves, measure the depths, would plunge deeper and deeper, and stay there playing ... oh, he was strong but not as rough as sandpaper, a man's shoulders must be like this – hard and strong but smooth; he should have the staying-power: What pleasure would there be in shoulders rendered rough and insensitive by carrying coconut bunches? When Lakkoo was comparing Kanchi with Manjayya, the fear crept in suddenly – what if Kanchi's ghost attacked her? Still she had not realised that it was she who sent him to his death. Kanchi had never gone out in the night without telling her to which grove he would go to steal coconuts. But that day, Kanchi who had never entered Manjayya's grove, had gone there without even telling her and had brought down three bunches. Lakkoo too did not feel like questioning him. She kept quiet thinking why should she enquire every night about thieving? It was her husband's lookout. What else could she have done? Manjayya was not in the village when the theft took place. On the fourth day, he came to Lakkoo's house at midday. She spread a mat and brought him betel leaves, areca nuts, lime and tobacco in a brass plate. Kanchi had gone out to wash the buffaloes. Manjayya looked at the plate and said, 'Oh betel leaves! I love them, but I don't know how to remove the stalk and apply lime. What should I do Lakkoo?' He looked into her eyes as if he was delving deep into her mind with his eyes and planting his seed. By then Kanchi had tied the buffaloes in the cowshed. He came inside and sat leaning on the pillar. When Lakkoo remembered this, Kanchi's figure and the contours of his body came before her eyes clearly. He sat like a hound ready to pounce. The very build of his body was angular. Nose, curved edges of eyebrows, eyes, mouth and moustache with pointed ends, all were sharp like arrows.

Manjayya asked: 'How dare you be brazen enough to trespass into my grove?' Though Kanchi's body was agile and active, the idiot's mind was slow and blunt. If only he had even a quarter of her intelligence or her brains, why would she allow herself to fall for Manjayya? He did not know what to answer and sat staring like a hound. Manjayya insisted, 'Come on, speak up.' Not knowing what to answer, how to defend himself, he blurted out, 'Well, at least, I don't invite every other woman from the village to my hut in the grove.' Why did this fellow speak so without rhyme or reason? Did he somehow know that Manjayya had met her and spoken to her in Tiptur. She had not told this to anybody. Had Manjayya told him? But, what had happened then? She had gone to Tiptur to sell copra. After her business was over, she was going to a hotel to have some dosas and there she met Manjayya. He called her, 'Come on Lakkoo, let us have some snacks together,' and made her sit opposite him in the chair. She felt shy, that too to eat dosa sitting before him. Though she declined and said she didn't want them, he ordered mysore-pak, coconut burfi, vadas, masala dosa and made her eat all those. After they came out of the hotel, Manjayya said, 'Look here Lakkoo, if you won't misunderstand, I would like to ask you one thing.' From the way he had looked at her, the meaning was clear. Yet as if she did not understand, she said, 'Ask me, please.' He said, 'Listen Lakkoo, since you came to our village after your marriage, I haven't had a wink of sleep. God should have made you my wife. But we can do nothing to change our fate. Anyway, you stay on in Tiptur tonight, I'll manage a room in a hotel. Nobody will know.' She was enraged and said, 'What, what the hell do you take me for? I haven't looked at a man since I married and will never look at anyone. I am a chaste woman.' Then he asked, 'What about before marriage?' How did this person know what she had been doing in Hassan before seventeen years? Had he come to her any day as one of her clients?

She came to Bilikere after her marriage and she was considered a chaste woman. If she had strayed a little, Kanchi would never have allowed her to live unharmed. She was almost shouting at Manjayya, 'What's it you are saying about before marriage? What's in your mind? What have you seen of me?' But Puttegowda of Channenahalli came at that moment and asked this man about the auction of copra and Lakkoo walked away from that place. From that day onwards, Manjayya had not spoken to her. But he would look at her with desire filled eyes and ask, 'Oh how are you?' But, now, when Kanchi blurted out, 'Well, I don't take all sorts of women from the village to my hut,' Manjayya at once said, 'Lakkoo you are the witness. Have I ever made a pass at his wife?? Have I spoken to her? Tell us, come on tell us.' My face turned as red as the hibiscus. I stared at Manjayya with steely eyes. He stared back, as if piercing them. After the spark he found in my eyes, he said, 'Understand one thing clearly! This man should never set eyes on my grove or take anything that belongs to me. With me it is an eye for an eye. Teach your husband justice. You're a clever woman. You better understand,' Issuing this threat, he left. But this donkey, her husband, could not understand anything. If she had not sent Kanchi, he would not have stepped into Manjayya's grove that day. Lakkoo was enraged. Her husband had trespassed, and pushed into Manjayya's grove, so this fellow was speaking of trespassing and pushing into her and this still enraged her. This fool, her husband, could not understand. Why did this idiot answer, 'Well I don't take all sort of women into my hut in the grove,' when Manjayya asked, 'Why did you step into my grove?' What connection was there between the two? After dinner, when they went to bed, Lakkoo felt a sort of obstinacy. How suddenly that man had said, 'I've not come to take your wife.' Lakkoo decided, at any cost she would make her husband step into Manjayya's grove. This fool, Kanchi, would fall asleep as soon as his head touched the pillow and would wake up at midnight to go out to steal coconuts. She also slept during those hours. But on that day, she did not close her eyes. She decided to show Manjayya what sort of a woman Lakkoo was, and resolved to ask Kanchi to trespass into Manjayya's grove. It was midnight and Kanchi suddenly got up. Lakkoo asked, 'Well, which grove are you going to, today?' He said, 'Vadera Siddalingayya's grove near the sand-pit.' She said, 'No, go to Manjayya's grove.' Kanchi answered, 'I had gone there four days back. Moreover that guy had come here and threatened. I've not marked trees in his grove, while I have marked Siddalingayya's trees! But she provoked him, 'If there are no ripe coconut bunches, cut a few unripe ones. Go into Manjayya's grove, let Manjayya understand what sort of a man Kanchi is.' Kanchi did not have the mind to do so. Yet, he agreed and headed off with a length of rope, a torch and a sickle.

Lakkoo and Manjayya had decided to start living together in a relationship instead of marrying and now Lakkoo felt like hearing the truth about the manner of Kanchi's death from Manjayya himself. She knew that it was not possible to change the manner of his death, yet an irrepressible curiosity raised its head. She turned to her right, put her left arm on his chest and said: 'Tell me something. Swear on God, that you will tell me the truth.'

'Why should I swear on God?'

'I took an oath in the name of God and gave witness in the court that Kanchi accidentally slipped, fell off from the coconut tree and died. Whether it was a sin or a good deed, I swore so, because I wanted to save you and live with you. At least now, tell me the truth, how did he die? In whatever manner he might have died, he's not my husband anymore, you're my husband.' Lakkoo stretched her hand that was on Manjayya's chest, groped and held his hand.

'Listen Lakkoo, Manjayya has only one tongue. I swear on you, that day I had slept in my house. But if I had said the truth that I was in the village on that day, those bastard police would twist the matter. So, I stated that I was in Tiptur, you realise this.' Then he squeezed her hands and said: 'You see Lakkoo, if it was not true that Kanchi really slipped and fell off the tree, wouldn't the judge know? What do you know about judges? They do have an all-seeing divine vision, just like Shiva with the third eye on his forehead.'

Whether Lakkoo believed him or not, her question was put to rest. Then Manjayya started caressing her erotic zones, arousing her and said. 'You sleep for a while Lakkoo.' She had got used, since the last fifteen years, to go to bed early, wake up by midnight, and be awake until Kanchi returned with stolen coconut bunches, open the door silently and after the bunches were lowered, again go to sleep. Now she felt sleepy and in a little while she was fast asleep and began breathing through her mouth. Manjayya's mind went back, recalling events. It was true that he had killed Kanchi. He had explained the details about how he killed only to the advocate Venkataramayya. Though he had said this to Nagappa of Tiptur and Parameshwarayya of Bilikere, he had not divulged the details. And thankfully they did not ask him. In his confusion, anxiety and haste, even he too could not remember every detail about the murder later on. Even when he was in jail, his mind was engaged only in planning and speculations about the future. It did not go back to the memory of how the murder had taken place. When he was recalling to mind his rule that a person who drowns himself in memory would never succeed in his work, all the details of how he killed Kanchi came to his mind. Manjayya enjoyed the pleasure of his achievement when he remembered the tricks he played to be acquitted of murder, and the thrill of removing Kanchi, that too, now, while Kanchi's wife was subjugated and was sleeping next to him with his left arm around her neck. Manjayya recalled: He had gone to Kanchi's house, had spoken in the language that at least Lakkoo had understood, returned home and had dinner. After ten in the night, he asked his servant Puttellayya to close the door and await his return. He stuck a sickle at his waist, took a torch in one hand and a thick cudgel in the other and walked to his grove. He squatted amid the bamboo grove near the grove's gate. Remembering that posture, now he laughed, for it reminded him of the defecating posture. Luckily Lakkoo did not wake up. There was a distance of two furlongs between the village and the grove, and one had to cross the water of the first sluice of the village tank. Everywhere, there was dense darkness and there were twinkling stars in the sky. When Kanchi started thieving coconut bunches, it is said, he used to bring his dog with him. But the dog would bark looking at frogs, hare and other small animals. So he started coming alone and the whole village knew this. Manjayya thought, if there would be a dog today, surely it would bark when it smelled him. If Kanchi was really a man and had understood my words, certainly he would come to my grove today. If he could not understand, his wife would have explained my message. Would she explain the meaning to her husband or keep it to herself? If so, it would still be a better deal. Manjayya felt a sort of tit-for-tat satisfaction by thinking so; just like that bastard trespassed into my grove and lowered the bunches, he too would trespass, enter into that bastard's wife and plant seeds. If that idiot had understood, he would come today. If not, he would never step into my grove. He decided to wait for Lakkoo somewhere and talk to her.

He felt so self-confident that it was not possible even for the gods not to believe his logic, and was so delighted that he felt like smoking a cigarette. But he became cautious that if he lit a cigarette, this slut lying next to him would wake up and his memories would scatter away. Manjayya was delighted to remember how he had killed Kanchi who had entered his grove and decided to give up the pleasure of smoking to enjoy that memory.

After a while, Manjayya thought that it was not a good idea to be sitting there. Kanchi would be carrying bunches of eighty to hundred coconuts and he would go out only through the grove gate. Though Manjayya doubted it would be difficult to squeeze through the newly laid thorn hedge, he came to the conclusion that it was not difficult to make a hole in the bamboo thorn fence for a man like Kanchi with the body like that of a hound. Manjayya decided that Kanchi would not enter from the grove gate side, and stood behind the thorny babul tree, so that it would be convenient for him to survey the top of the coconut trees. Everyone in the village knew Kanchi had a long powerful torch, the beam of which would not spread and light would be focused only on the bunch. Manjayya was sure that Kanchi would not come without that torch. He waited and waited for more than three hours. There was no sign of Kanchi. Not only Manjayya's wrist-watch, but even the stars of the sky showed it was past midnight. Kanchi had not come yet. He thought, perhaps that bastard did not have the courage to trespass into the land of Manjayya. But Manjayya wanted to wait a little more. For there was no reason to doubt his logic that if at all he came, he had to come that day only. After an hour or so, he saw a coconut tree which seemed to be bathed in light from bottom to top and then the light vanished. Yes, his guess was right. Excitement, not fear, caused his hands and feet to tremble slightly. This Manjayya was never afraid and under any circumstance, he did not lose heart. Manjayya is a *man*, fearless. Yes, this bastard had understood Manjayya's words. Thinking so, he came to the grove gate from the thorny babul tree and entered into another bamboo grove. Nothing was seen. Kanchi didn't need to switch on his torch a second time. His eyesight was so sharp that he would see everything very minutely in a flash. Thinking so, Manjayya touched the sickle in his waist and felt comforted. Then he grasped the cudgel firmly. Manjayya thought, how much time he might take to climb such a tall tree, cut the bunches, lower them down, tie them up and sling them on to his shoulder? Could he get coconuts required for him from one tree? Or would he climb up two trees? When Manjayya was staring, another coconut tree was bathed in light just like the first. Manjayya understood that Kanchi had already finished his work with the first tree. That was the one next to the jackfruit tree. There were at least fifty coconuts in each bunch. It was not possible for any man to carry more than hundred coconuts. So, Manjayya calculated that this was to be the last tree he would climb and guessed there were only ten to fifteen minutes left. He did not light the torch and looked at his watch. When he was counting time, he heard the panting and gasping of the man who had climbed down two trees and was carrying on his shoulder the weight of hundred coconuts, though he treaded as silently as a cat. Manjayya knew this and stood still without breathing. Kanchi had carried the bunches on his left shoulder front to back, and was dragging himself to the grove gate. Manjayya had kept the gate half open, deliberately. Before Kanchi crossed the gate, Manjayya followed him. Listening to the sound of Manjayya's steps, Kanchi realised there was someone behind and turned around. But as the weight was pulling him down, he was slow. In the meantime Manjayya raised his cudgel, brought it down on Kanchi's head and Kanchi fell down. Immediately Manjayya switched on his torch. Blood was flowing out from the top of Kanchi's head, which was broken in the middle. Bunches of coconut slipped from the shoulder and fell out in a heap. He was moaning and struggling to turn his hands and legs. Manjayya again switched on his torch and gazed continuously for a minute at Kanchi. Blood was gushing from the blow. The moaning had decreased but the thrashing of hands and feet persisted. Manjayya decided not to waste any time, hoisted Kanchi on his shoulders and walked towards the hut in the grove. Kanchi despite his lean appearance, weighed a ton.

Manjayya wondered, why this son of a bitch had to be so adamant to enter his grove that very same day! By the time Manjayya brought Kanchi and put him under a tree in the centre of the grove, Kanchi was dead. Then Manjayya went near the hut, searched for a stone used as foundation stones, brought it, buried it a little in the earth, so that it was four inches above the level of the ground. Then he put the corpse's head on it, lifted up the head and smashed it again on the stone. Then he returned to the grove's gate, took the rope that Kanchi had brought to climb the tree and came near a tree. Manjayya took off his shirt and dhoti, put the rope on to his legs and climbed the tree. Luckily there were two ripe bunches. He cut the bunches and caused the coconuts to fall down. While getting down, it occurred to him that coconuts should not fall on the dead body. Luckily, they had not done so. Then he took away the rope from his legs, threw it near the root of the tree, started from there, came to the grove gate, brought Kanchi's torch, long rope and sickle, put it on the ridge near the corpse, hoisted the tied up bunches on his shoulder, half closed the grove gate and came straight away to his house. Puttellayya who was waiting opened the door. With his help, Manjayya put the coconuts on the copra loft. He looked at his clothes. They were blood-stained. Quickly he changed his clothes and put those clothes into a bag. He held Puttellayya's hands and said, 'You see Puttellayya, you've grown up in our house eating our food. You must never tell anybody about these coconuts I brought now. Tomorrow morning peel off the husks and take them away somewhere. Whoever may ask you, you must tell them that I left this place two days ago. Don't say a word about what happened tonight.' Manjayya made the servant swear on his mother. He left the village in darkness.

Manjayya recalled and re-enacted this scene in his mind – not once or twice but thrice from the beginning till the end; why did he finish him off? Instead of hitting him on his head, he could have struck his legs and broken them, and then he could have gone to the police, caused Kanchi to be arrested or he could have held a council of village elders. If the knees were broken, let alone climbing trees, Kanchi would have been unable to even carry coconut bunches with his lame legs. Yet, why did Manjayya want to finish off Kanchi? What would happen to his reputation and prestige in the village if a thief like Kanchi had trespassed into Manjayya's grove? He justified himself that what he did was the wisest and most reasonable deed, for now, all the fifty six villages around knew that no bastard would be alive if he dared to enter Manjayya's grove. Suddenly Lakkoo stopped snoring. She poked Manjayya's shoulder, trying to wake him up and blabbered, 'Wake up, the moon is set. It's already dark, get up.' Manjayya did not understand. He asked, 'Why, what's the problem?' Lakkoo said, 'You said you were going to Rangashetty's grove today. Get up, or you will be late,' saying so she suddenly sat up. Only after half a minute, she realised this new situation, chuckled once, yawned and slept again. Manjayya smiled to himself. He remembered how he had decided to see Lakkoo the same night when he was talking to Parameshwarayya, for he had thought that if only he could win over Lakkoo to give evidence in his favour, certainly he would be acquitted. He was not sure of winning Parameshwarayya to his side. Even if he succeeded in his effort, Parameshwarayya, however, was his father-in-law. Manjayya felt proud of his 'valiant deed' of subjugating Kanchi's wife by cajoling, coaxing and making her feel his sexual prowess. This was a point which did not occur to advocate Ventakatramayya, even in his dream. When he recounted his adventure to the advocate of getting the widow of the murdered man to his side, the advocate guffawed and snapped his fingers and said, 'Let us ask the judge to discipline the police.' Now Manjayya began ruminating more about how he subjugated Lakkoo and made her give evidence in his favour, than saying that he killed Kanchi. It was Thursday, the fifth night after Manjayya had finished off Kanchi. It was eight in the night, the dark night of a new moon. Lakkoo's elder sister and her two children had come to her house from Hassan. Her daughter who was studying in Hassan had also come. Grieved by her father's murder, she wanted to console her mother. The girl was sixteen. Lakkoo's brother-in-law worked as a coolie in a saw-mill in Hassan, and her sister worked in a coffee-curing factory. It was eight in the night. Lakkoo was milking buffaloes in the cowshed in the backyard and was alone when Manjayya entered the cowshed. The light of the lantern cast a shadow on the wall and she turned back. As soon as she saw him, her face turned as white as a sheet and she trembled with fear. But before she could open her mouth to shout, Manjayya went near her, grabbed her and put his hand on her mouth and whispered in her ears, 'Listen Lakkoo, I know you're angry with me. You abuse me however much you want. Thrash me with your chappals. I came here because I wanted to speak with you. Your sister and daughter are at home and we cannot talk there and I cannot ask you to come to my house for everyone will know about it. I swear touching the feet of Goddess Maaramma, hands on my heart, that I did not kill Kanchi. He slipped, fell off from the tree and died. Police are spying on me and waiting to catch me, for they hate me. I came here to talk about that only. You don't tell about this to anybody. Believe me Lakkoo. After you take the milk inside, come out pretending that you have to go to the toilet, to the cactus lane that is near the Indian beech tree. After you have listened to me, you may do whatever you want. You know this: Manjayya will never break his promise. I have not done anything wrong. Look at my face, you will know.' After saying this he held Lakkoo's shoulders. She was staring at him. Anxiety, fear and unexpectedness had filled her eyes. Manjayya gazed into her eyes, and this caused confusion in her mind. He had cast his spell over her. Then he held her hands and pleaded, 'You must come Lakkoo, hold my hands and say 'yes'.' He squeezed her hands and said, 'I can't stay here longer. Whatever I possess is yours. That's why God has done this to both of us. He has separated my wife from me and has taken away your husband. I came here to talk these things.' He squeezed her hands again, walked out of the cowshed, went to the backyard, and noiselessly slipped off the wall so lightly and silently that even the dogs did not hear. Climbing down the fort pit, when Manjayya was waiting in the cactus lane behind the tree, his mind said that Lakkoo would certainly come. When had his mind miscalculated or misunderstood in such matters? Which woman had failed to be there when he had asked her to come at such time and such place, to date? Did his expectation go wrong that Kanchi would certainly come to his grove and Lakkoo would surely send him? Yet when Lakkoo did not arrive, he felt uneasy. In such a situation which son of a bitch would have had Manjayya's courage. He sat there waiting. Lakkoo, however, had to finish milking the buffaloes, finish her meals if ragi-balls were ready and only then could she come out on the pretext of toilet. Besides, if her elder sister wanted to come with her, for it was dark, Lakkoo had to avoid that too. Manjayya thought, it would take time, switched on the torch, looked at his wrist watch, waited alone in the darkness even without lighting a cigarette, cautious that it would spread the smell. A sudden suspicion gripped him. Knowing I would be waiting here, this bitch might have informed the police who have camped in this village and plotted to get me caught. Manjayya waited, felt like touching the sickle in his waist. Then, yes there was the sound of chappals. A woman's footstep. He stood up. He could know from the distance, it was Lakkoo. He went near her and said, 'Come, Lakkoo, let's go to that beech tree. Here someone may come for toilet and find us.' At once she raged, 'You adulterous bastard, you killed my husband, now have you come to kill me too?' saying so she lifted her right hand. If he had been a little careless for a fraction of a second, he would have been dead then and there, caught by her sickle. He turned swiftly, held her hand, plucked away the sickle and Lakkoo began screaming 'Ayyo, ayyo,' but Manjayya put his hand on her mouth and said, 'Come, let's not talk here. I have come to tell you something. Come near that beech tree. If I had come to kill you, I could've killed you in the cowshed itself. Truth never comes out when we speak in anger. Come Lakkoo,' he said and walked forward hugging her. Manjayya thought, it was never a lie that if bodies came into contact, the mind and heart change as if an electric current passed through them. When Manjayya led Lakkoo slowly pressing her to his side, she did not try to escape from him. She was weeping, sobbing, but walked with him. When they were beneath the beech tree, he pressed her shoulder and asked her to sit. Lakkoo was still obstinate and said, 'No, I won't sit. Why should I? What have I to talk with you? Give me my sickle. I'll cut your neck, make your blood flow and offer it to my husband's ghost.'

Manjayya said coolly, 'Wait, I'll bring it to you. It fell off somewhere near a field, a furlong away. You wait here. I'll bring it. I bow my head before you and stand like a kid goat before Goddess Maaramma to be sacrificed. Yes, you may cut off my head. What will you do afterwards?' Lakkoo smashed the water-jug she held on Manjayya's head, but it fell on his shoulder and tumbled down to the ground. Water flowed away. Then she started beating him with her hands continuously and said: 'Let your lineage be destroyed. You bastard. I am not Lakkoo, if I will not make you swing from the gallows.' Manjayya remembered now, what a wise thing it was, being beaten by her so peacefully! They were sharp blows from hands hardened by manual labour. His sides began to ache, but he managed to hold himself. Lakkoo became still more enraged, bent down, took off her hard leather chappal from her left foot and began to beat him persistently on his head, back and sides and shoulders. Unable to bear the pain, when he moaned, she beat him still more. When that chappal slipped from her hand, not knowing what to do, she began to sob. When only her sobs were being heard in the darkness, Manjayya said, 'The chappal fell off from your hand in this darkness. You have another on your right foot. Take it and beat me with that also. I'll not raise my hand on you however much you may beat me. No, my hands can never rise to hit you, never ever, understand this.' When Manjayya spoke these words, Lakkoo was in a hazy state of mind and could not understand anything. Manjayya knew there were tears in her eyes. After a little while he said, 'I'll switch on the torch, look for the sickle and bring it. I had already told you. I bow down my head like a kid-goat before you, and you cut off my head. I will never get angry with you, even if you kill me. But before I die, I want to talk to you about something, so I have come. First you sit here and answer my question, then I'll bring you the sickle.' Manjayya after saying this, pressed her arms and made her sit on the furrowed ground. Mud was wet from the water flown from the jug she had smashed on Manjayya's head. After she sat there, he took out a handkerchief from his pocket and wiped her eyes and asked, 'Do you know why I wiped your eyes? So that you may see my face clearly. Look at me, you may know what is in my mind.' He stretched his hand to hold her hand, but she tried to withdraw. But Manjayya did not leave it at that. He held her hand tightly and squeezed and asked her after a while. 'Why did you send Kanchi on that same night, I had come to your house?'

Lakkoo did not answer. He could see her eyes were glaring at him. He asked again, 'Tell me, why did you send him. I know for sure he did not come on his own.' Still she did not speak. He said, 'Only to know this, I asked you to come here. Come on, tell me, why did you send him?'

'How dare you speak such taunting words that cut through me?'

'Kanchi did not understand what I said but you are smart and clever, you understood. I knew he was stupid. You should have kept quiet if you had understood. Afterwards both of us could have met somewhere like this and could have talked.'

'What was there for me to talk with you?'

'We could have talked about what was not there. However, it was wrong on your part to send him. Okay ... It seems you have informed the police that I have murdered Kanchi. Did you see me killing him? Doesn't anybody become weak, slip down from the tree in the darkness and die? Is it right that you cover your wrong and put the blame on me and accuse me?'

'What wrong have I done?'

'Okay, you have not committed any wrong, but neither have I. I'll tell you something. Do you want to listen?'

'Be quick. My sister would be waiting. My daughter will also be worrying why am I so late.'

'Put your hand on mine and swear,' he said and moved closer to her. He sat so close that his thigh should touch hers, held her hand, squeezed it and said, 'People say this Manjayya is a lecher and he is wicked. Do you believe it?' Lakkoo did not answer. Manjayya said, 'Whether you believe it or not, I'll tell the truth. Why do people say I am a bad man? Because I abandoned my wife. Do you know why I gave her up? I am a landowner and an agriculturist. The woman who came as a wife did not take care of buffaloes and did not milk them. She did not carry food to the grove for her husband. Does the house prosper if the housewife is like a celluloid doll sold in fairs? When I told her to work, she said she would go to her father's house. I said, *go*. Really, it is true that I saw you with desire. Now also I look at you and in future also I'll look at you with desire. I wish to have a wife like you. How many buffaloes you do rear, how much of milk you draw? How much butter do you sell? If a landowner like me has a wife like you, how much I could have prospered! I am fed up with these things. Now I'll tell you one thing, will you listen to it?' When Manjayya said this and stopped speaking, it did not occur to Lakkoo to say, 'yes'. Manjayya himself said. 'If you say yes', I'll tell you.' Then Lakkoo said 'Yes'. By then Manjayya had understood that her heart had already melted towards him. He moved still nearer, sat rubbing his thigh against hers and said, 'I am going to be acquitted in court. Police won't be able to do anything. You need not worry for anything. After I come out of prison, let us live together. You're my wife and I'm your husband. Your daughter is my daughter also. She will be the elder sister to all the children we will bear together in the future. But for the time being, don't tell this to anybody, not even to your sister. Let it be a secret. I don't care about caste taboos. I will announce to the whole village that Lakkoo is my wife. Look here, this beech tree that gives oil to the lamp, is a witness. You must accept this.'

She pulled away her hand with a jerk and said, 'What are you saying? How could you dare to?'

'Why? what's wrong? If it's wrong, say so. Is it wrong to say that I like to live with you? If you don't like it, let's have a proper marriage with pipers and drummers. I'll bring you gold chokers, chain, earrings, bangles, bracelet and jewels for your hair. Anyway you look like a bride. Now, look at my face.' Manjayya, switched on the torch, raised her face so as their faces should be seen and said, 'Look at my face properly. If we marry, you will get a son like me.' When he said these words, Lakkoo was completely won over and Manjayya knew it. Lakkoo's eyes looked at the earth. Manjayya took out a packet containing a gold chain of three strings, shone the torch on it, showed it to her and said, 'Look here, I'd ordered this to give to Parameshwarayya's daughter, my wife Savitri. She left me saying she would not do agriculture work of my house. So

I had kept it. Consider this as a "*taali*" tied in marriage. I swear on this beech tree, on the village Goddess Maaramma, on you and on me,' Manjayya said and put the chain around Lakkoo's neck, drew her close and embraced her tightly. When in a confused state of mind, she was breathing heavily, he said, 'Lakkoo, today you became my wife and I your husband.' Even before she could realise what was happening, without giving her a chance to realise, Manjayya hugged her, rolled her over, mounted on her, directly entered deeply inside her, without allowing her to say anything or to protest. 'No, no, don't do it. I am still in defilement caused by my husband's death.' But Manjayya had closed her mouth with his mouth. When Manjayya remembered this, he turned to his left and looked at Lakkoo still sleeping on his left arm and snoring and said to himself, If you finish this business with a woman, she will never bargain or try to escape from you. This is the only medicine to keep them obedient. He swelled with pride as if it was his great discovery. Manjayya's mind continued to remember the details. Initially it was not easy for him to control the struggle of Lakkoo, beneath him. She was trying to escape from him. But slowly she had given up her struggle, loosened herself, relaxed and had given herself. He sensed this change, found her pulses, applied his skills and when she too got excited and began to moan, he put his lips into her ears and said, 'I swear on you Lakkoo, really Kanchi slipped, fell off from the tree and died. Police have brought charge against me because I did not bribe them. You are my wife, don't you know the truth?' Manjayya again and again whispered it into her ear and drove it home while she was in her peak. Now he was certain that Lakkoo's witness would be in his favour only. He knew, that prosecution of police inspector B.S. Narayana Murthy, who was supposed to be a very strict officer would utterly fail and he would have to eat humble pie in court. Along with it, Manjayya remembered the verdict of the court,

'Police have not performed their duty properly. Prosecution has failed to produce conclusive evidence and it is not possible to decide precisely whether the dead person Kanchi fell from the tree in the dark night while stealing coconuts or was murdered. Even if we accept that he was murdered, bearing in mind the testimony of the dead man's widow, the argument that Manjayya committed this murder cannot be accepted. Even without the witness of this dead man's widow, this charge of murder on the accused cannot be proved beyond reasonable doubt. The police themselves have admitted that Kanchi, the dead man, was stealing coconuts from everybody's grove. The police should have investigated the possibility of someone murdering Kanchi and putting the corpse in Manjayya's grove.' When Manjayya recalled to his mind this verdict of the court, he had a victorious laugh. Lakkoo woke up at this sound. As if startled, she sat up, and looked around not realising where she was. Manjayya asked, 'Why, hey Lakkoo, do you daily wake up at midnight?'

'Yes, I still wake up at midnight,' and now she realised where she was. She could not get sleep. She knew, at least for another two hours she would not get sleep. Looking at her sitting there, Manjayya's lust was provoked. But he felt cautious and thought that he should not show too much of desire. He closed his eyes as if he was sleepy. Actually he felt like sleeping, but she sat awake and was bored. That was the first time they were together after Manjayya's release. This was the first opportunity they got to talk comfortably with each other. She decided to raise an important matter and settle it now and said, 'I am going to Hassan to tell my girl and my elder sister about us.'

'What are you going to say?'

'We are going to get married or we might live together.'

Manjayya turned towards her and asked, 'Why? What's the urgency?'

'Isn't it true that we married under that beech tree? Haven't you put this chain around my neck? Then, why should you be afraid and sneak into my house, why should I hesitate to come to your house? Husband and wife should be like this in one bed. I should cook and serve you, take care of you. Is this the way to live? Coming to Tiptur, engaging a room in a hotel, staying there stealthily, being scared of people?'

Manjayya replied, 'Yes I too am thinking along the same lines. But do you know what people are saying? I heard them talking that both you and I wanted to live together, so we have finished off Kanchi. Now if we begin to live together, that is, if we marry at once, it would be tantamount to accepting that it was true. Moreover it is said, until the annual ceremony of Kanchi is over, it is not right to marry. I have checked up the shastras. However, if you do not believe in, or do not want to observe *shastra* or custom, I am ready.'

Lakkoo's heart began to beat slowly. She was scared of what people would say, but the real source of her fear was this: a *preta* would know everything, they say, if the *preta* of Kanchi knows this, what may happen ... She asked, 'For how long does this *preta* exist after death?'

Manjayya said, 'It will depart after the annual community meal and rites are performed.'

'Does it know everything?'

'What do you mean by everything?'

Lakkoo stared at him and hinted with her eyes. 'Aha, you stupid woman, how can it know all this after death? What I said was only custom, *shastra*, that is until the annual ceremony of the dead is over, we should not get married – that is you being the wife of the dead man. All these talk about *preta* is nonsense. You know this,' Manjayya said. But Lakkoo's mind got confused. If the existence of *preta* is false, then how can it stay to eat meal at annual ceremony? If it is a man, he may marry within one month after the death of his wife. She had not seen women who began to live together or get married in such a short time after the death of their husbands. So, she thought not to rush into this thing. Then Manjayya spoke, 'If we are going to marry or begin to live together at once, what would your daughter Latha think of us? You have just admitted her to high school. Already some people are talking that Manjayya and Lakkoo have together finished off Kanchi. Yes, these are all rumours. But nobody speaks it openly. But Latha should not believe these rumours. We must take care of that. You do one thing Lakkoo, you must say this to your daughter in a convincing way. 'Manjayya and your father were close friends since a long time. Your father entered Manjayya's grove by mistake that night. He slipped, fell off from the tree and died. But that inspector Narayana Murthy out of his hatred towards Manjayya, filed a case against him. The court acquitted Manjayya because he was honest and truthful. And now, after your father's death, Manjayya has agreed to help me earn my living. You tell her these things and mould her mind to be kindly disposed towards me and be friendly with me. Let us wait for some time and marry. If we are hasty and tie the knot, your daughter may turn against you. I don't want you to lose your daughter's love, would you like that?'

Lakkoo felt that what Manjayya said was quite reasonable. She had already told Latha that her father slipped, fell off the tree and died and he was not murdered. Yet, Lakkoo thought of driving this home to Latha, when she visited her daughter in Hassan. She decided to make her daughter believe that Manjayya would be like her father and would take care of her. Before that, Lakkoo had to speak with him about the means of her livelihood. Except half acre of dry land behind the fort, a grove of ten coconut trees in front of the village, Kanchi did not have any other lands. But nobody knew how much of copra he used to sell per year with those ten coconut trees. Even Kanchi himself did not know. What he knew was, to go out from his house in the dark night, bring home bunches containing sixty to eighty or sometimes even hundred ripe coconuts. Hoisting them on to the loft, calculating, peeling husks after they had dried, taking copra bags in the cart to Tiptur, selling them to the warehouses, bringing money and investing it in lending and jewels etc. – everything was Lakkoo's responsibility. Kanchi, without a second word, had accepted the fact that his wife was more intelligent than him and left all business to her. As he owned a very small area of land, he never worked on the field, nor did he own oxen and cart. Lakkoo herself used to take care of the buffaloes. As such, he did not do any other work except to climb on coconut trees and steal coconuts in the dark of the night. He could have earned money by climbing trees, pluck coconuts and get one coconut per tree. But he did not want to tire himself by climbing forty to fifty trees during day time. He would do no work in daytime except to eat, sleep or swim in the tank. Nobody in the village had the power or mental courage to stop him, catch him or beat him when he went for theft. He had the strength and built of body that he could escape and run away even when four people held him together. Majority of them would plead with a helpless familiarity as if it was an unwritten agreement: 'Oh brother Kanchanna, we knew that you had stepped into our grove yesterday. Please do not come again for six more months. We are poor people.' Manjayya had not only smashed and finished off Kanchi once and for all but had hoodwinked the strict police inspector B.S. Narayana Murthy also and had come out of court. Manjayya knew that he had become a hero in the eyes of his villagers as well as in fifty-six surrounding villages. After B.S. Narayana Murthy took over charge as inspector in Channarayapattana, he had earned the nickname 'Tiger.' He would never stretch his hand for bribes. Whenever he had to visit any village on government work, he would make his servant draw water from the well and drink it but wouldn't accept even a tender coconut from anybody's house. He would pursue any case he was entrusted to its logical and rightful end. If Manjayya's case was entrusted to any other dafedar or inspector, he would have totally turned, twisted and closed the case at the *mahajar* level itself. Now, the case was in Narayana Murthy's charge. So the villagers were sure that Manjayya would either be hanged or would get life sentence. But, a person like Narayana Murthy himself had to get a remark from the judge that he had not investigated carefully. What could one say about the power of Manjayya and the advocate Malali Venkataramayya, who held a brief for Manjayya! Along with these, people felt curious – what was the secret behind twisting and turning of evidence in court by the widow of Kanchi? Some people who were romantically inclined, concocted a story: the moment Lakkoo saw Manjayya's face in the witness box, she had lost her heart to him. She thought, anyway my man is dead. If I can help this fellow to be acquitted, today or tomorrow he will look after me. With this intention or desire, Lakkoo twisted the evidence. This story spread in the village. This rumour reached the ears of many women who had contact with Manjayya, and these women felt proud as well as jealous. Even some chaste women who had thought Manjayya to be a rake and a mean fellow, noticed him with curious eyes after they heard this story. His enemies too had to concede that Manjayya was handsome and attractive. But difference of opinion would arise when describing and analysing the features of a male. It is not that nobody had the physique, complexion or facial features. But who else had that strength and purpose to concentrate his body build, facial feature, his stance and looks to hit the precise target? Public opinion generated out of achievement, success and repute account for more than half of a person's personality, over and above his physical attributes. Fame and infamy are nothing but two viewpoints, two sides of the coin called public opinion.

After winning the court case, Manjayya desired to visit Lakkoo's house openly and wanted to enhance his value in the eyes of the villagers, especially in the eyes of youngsters. But he did not want to be bound by any shackles like living together or marriage. Lakkoo was a courageous and determined woman. So Manjayya had carefully thought that if he gave her the status of a wife socially, she would take away all his freedom and keep it in her fist. But, people must know she has fallen for him, is under his thumb and his strength and power should get publicity, but she should not get any kind of power or authority. This was the subtlety of his calculation. Balance of power should always swing in his favour. He had thought in advance, what aspects Lakkoo would raise, what answers he had to give, as that was the first day they would be meeting after his release.

Lakkoo asked, 'What shall I do for livelihood hereafter?'

Manjayya said, 'There is half acre of dry field and ten coconut trees. How many buffaloes are milching?'

Lakkoo said, 'If it was only me, I would not have worried. My daughter is studying in school. She wants to continue her education at any cost. I've left her in my sister's house. My sister too is not well off. We used to send coconut, chilly, pulses, ragi, etc. to her. I used to send her twenty rupees every month for fees, books, soap and other things. She says she will not discontinue her studies.'

Manjayya had already thought out this aspect and asked, 'How much have you saved so far? How much have you lent out on interest?'

'Hey, what do you say? Where have I saved money to give it for interest?' Though he could not see her face turning pale, in the darkness, he noticed the crack in her voice.

Manjayya said: 'You see, don't lie to me. You tell me precisely how much you have. If it is not enough, I'll give you more and instruct you how to invest it wisely.'

Lakkoo pretended to be recalling and thought that she should not give away the actual state of her finances to Manjayya then itself and said, 'I think, about two to three thousand, maybe. That's all.'

Manjayya said, 'Well, Lakkoo, Do one thing. Give me that gold chain. I'll either sell it or pawn it and bring you the money. You may get three thousand rupees. With this capital, you can open a small grocery shop in the weekly marketplace in front of the village. I will get you provisions at a cheap rate from Channarayapattana or Hassan. If you tell me what is out of stock, I'll get those supplies. I will keep visiting there often. You may earn money sitting comfortably. Besides, if you buy ripe coconuts, that too from the growers who need advance, you will get more profit. If you sell them at wholesale rate in Tiptur warehouse, there will be a lot of profit.'

Lakkoo was excited at the idea of starting a grocery shop. She too found it profitable to buy coconuts from those who needed money. But, she felt angry with Manjayya for asking for the gold chain in her neck for the capital. She expressed her dissatisfaction in her voice and said, 'Should I take out this *taali* and pawn it while you're still alive?'

'Who says it's a *taali*? It is only piece of jewellery. I told you that night to treat it as *taali*, because at that moment, how or where could I go looking for a goldsmith? After an year, I'll order a true *taali* and tie the knot. Now, because you said you didn't have enough money for capital, I suggested that.' Manjayya mixed neglect, comfort and persuasion and yawned.

By the time Lakkoo spoke the words 'If capital is needed,' he was already breathing heavily and had fallen asleep. She kept quiet.

Although the thumb-sized *preta* of Parameshwarayya was not in the presence of Yamadharma, the Yama-conscience was always awake in it. It was reporting its every observation to the *Niyantru*, through that conscience. 'Oh *Niyantru*, it is true that the mind that withdraws itself inside, fails to know anything. I knew the news of Manjayya's release cursorily, but did not want to know the minute details of the verdict. Either Ramakrishna or any other person, I think, did not come near me to explain the details, looking at my face. Perhaps, Manjayya was planning to meet and win over Lakkoo the same night he was talking to me that evening in the grove. How could I know that this murder was not committed with vengeance or enmity? Within the span of thirty years, he has become an expert. Now I am able to see so many thoughts that are hovering in Manjayya's mind, regarding the relation between him and Lakkoo. I feel sad and sorry, for they cause a terrible injustice in the future. But, you have put a restraint, a limit on me as I am a *saakshi*. I do not have the power to avert, stop anything or to warn anybody. To participate is not the quality of a pure *saakshi*. Yet, I have become curious. Insatiable curiosity of observing what will happen further has enveloped me. Your Chitraguptas may be free from even this sort of curiosity. But this life story relates to me. Therefore, I think, I have not been able to be a pure and detached witness.'

A large number of people, both invited and uninvited, had come to attend the *Vaikunta Samaaraadhana* ceremony of Parameshwarayya on the fourteenth day, somehow having got to know the news or reading about his suicide in the newspapers. Committing suicide for uttering a single lie was an interesting news for the newspapers and naturally it was published and publicised. Wayfarers and travellers, whoever had taken food in Parameshwarayya's house, had come from different districts and villages, after they heard this news. Parameshwarayya did not distinguish between caste and creed in his daily *annadaana*, nor did he restrict his hospitality. Jains, Lingayats and others who did not take food in his house were given rice, lentils, vessels to cook and a pot and rope to draw water from the well and he would see that they had their food. Such people too gathered and there was a huge community meal on the occasion of *Vaikunta Samaaraadhana*. Ramakrishna had a firm belief that his family's greatness and distinction existed in *annadaana*. He took loan from Chalapathi Shetty of Channarayapattana and arranged for meals and cooking on a large scale for the people of all castes and creeds in the compound of the Shivaalaya. It was on the branch of the banyan tree opposite the Shivaalaya that Parameshwarayya had hung himself. Everyone saw that branch and folded their hands in respect. His eldest son-in-law Satyanarayana of Mattikere, and his *sambandhi* Nagappa, the copra warehouse owner in Tiptur had come on the ninth day itself. They offered *dharmodaka* and stayed there until the *Vaikunta-Samaaraadhana* was over. Satyanarayana was coming to Bilikere after a very long time. After his wife died giving birth to a child, what connection was there with the house of his father-in-law, when his mother-in-law too was dead? Moreover the taluks they belonged to were different and the centres of their business too were different. As such there was not much communication though there was much mutual affection. Satyanarayana respected his father-in-law and brother-in-law. Parameshwarayya also respected this eldest son-in-law. Relationship with this house was caused because of their mutual respect. Satyappa (Satyanarayana), from his student days, was a staunch follower of Gandhiji. He had participated in the freedom movement of the country and had experienced life in prison. He used to spin charkha, and wore khadi only. Even today, except khadi, he would not use bed sheet manufactured in mills. Wearing khadi dhoti and jubba and leather chappals of cattle hide made in the village, he was spreading the principles and teachings of Gandhiji in villages. In his youth, he had to come three times to Bilikere in connection with his work. He had got his meals in Parameshwarayya's house. Satyappa had heard from others that this man performed *annadaana* even after his wife was dead and he never uttered a single lie. Parameshwarayya's face expressed such an honesty and righteousness that Satyappa found him similar to Mahatma Gandhi of Sabarmati ashram. When he came the third time to Parameshwarayya's house, Satyappa, by chance, saw Seetha, Parameshwarayya's eldest daughter. By that time he too had desired to be a *gruhastha*, a householder. He thought, if at all he was going to marry, he must marry this girl of Parameshwarayya's house. He started from his village and came through Neelakunda state forest, Melenahally toddy palm groves, climbed Ranganabetta and reached Bilikere of Channarayapattana taluk which was fourteen miles away from Mattikere. Satyanarayana thought that the daughter of a house which had the tradition of cooking and serving any number of guests with devotion as if it was their dharma, would have more patience and less selfishness; it would not be difficult to make her follow Gandhian principles with such refinement of culture. Besides the tall body build, complexion and features of the girl had cast a spell on his mind. When Satyanarayana came to Parameshwarayya's house, there were already four other guests for lunch. As he had been there thrice before, Parameshwarayya easily recognised him, and said, 'Please be seated' and showed the mat, where other guests used to sit. Satyanarayana sat there for ten minutes and heard sounds from the kitchen and sensed delicious aroma coming from there. His mind thought it was Seetha cooking and she was a good cook. He got up, went into the bathroom, washed his hands and feet, wiped with his khadi towel, came into the hall and said to Parameshwarayya, 'I would like to speak with you privately. That is why I have come.' Parameshwarayya told the other guests to wait a little and took Satyanarayana near the tulasi plant in the backyard and asked him to be seated on the stone bench beneath the canopy of jasmine creepers. Satyanarayana bent, touched the feet of Parameshwarayya, prostrated and then sat on the bench at a little distance from Parameshwarayya and said.

'Daily four to five guests come and have lunch in your house and depart. Perhaps you may remember only my face. Even if I had told you any details about myself, you might have forgotten. I am from Mattikere of Tiptur taluk. I lost my parents when I was quite young. Talakere Subramanya is our distant relative. In fact, it was through him that I was attracted towards Gandhiji and his satyagraha movement. For some time, I studied at gurukula in

Kengeri. I was a disciple of writer Goruru Ramaswamy Iyengar there. But I could not study there for long. My lands were being neglected in the village if I was away. So I came back, began to look after my lands. But my mind could not be withdrawn from satyagraha and freedom movement of Gandhiji. I used to read books about Gandhiji and his teachings and *Swarajya* newspaper. Meanwhile I went twice to Sabarmati ashram, once to Wardha, stayed there for a couple of months, learnt about the pattern of work there and returned. Now I am going round the villages teaching and implementing those with faithful intention so that our rural areas may be improved and saved. I have tried to popularise these new ideas in my village and the surrounding ones. Everyone cannot become a Mahatma Gandhi, I know. But I believe, after being born a man, if he does not work for the upliftment of society his life is futile. And now I have decided to settle down and be a family man. I have got three hundred trees giving good yield of twenty five thousand to thirty thousand coconuts per year along with this four and a quarter acres of dry lands. Though I have two acres of wet land, we get paddy when the tank is full. If not, we get black gram, green gram and horse gram. Come to my village, look for yourself, enquire there and confirm about these. I am twenty-six now, you may enquire about my character in my village or you may ask Talakere Subramanya, Goruru Ramaswamy Iyengar or anybody at Kengeri Gurukula. I saw your daughter when I came here last time. Since then, I have been thinking that a girl from your family which is practising the tradition of hospitality and daily *annadaana* will be suitable to be my wife. So, I myself have come requesting you to give her to me in marriage. There is no falsehood in my words. Please think about this, enquire everything and if it is acceptable to you and your daughter, please accept my proposal.'

So, this is how Satyanarayana became the eldest son-in-law of this house. As he had wished, Seetha was an ideal wife and followed the footsteps of her husband. As Mattikere was not located close to the road, there would not be daily guests in Satyappa's house. Still a lot of people around who were concerned with Satyappa's programmes and activities of upliftment of villages, would come there. Many groups of village councils would be gathered on the platform in front of his house. So, people from other places who came for the village council would have their food at his house. Compared to the daily *annadaana* in her father's house, this hospitality was not difficult for Seetha to manage. Though at first she was confused at her husband's behaviour of neglecting his own lands in his ideal of working for improving the surrounding villages, she quickly understood her husband. After she started reading books on Gandhiji and his teachings written in Kannada or translated into Kannada, she began to like and appreciate more and more her husband's ideals, purpose and his point of view. Although Satyappa wore khadi, he had not compelled his wife to wear the same. But once or twice he had explained to her the ethical stand behind that. After starting to read the books of Gandhiji, Seetha too began to spin on the charkha. Satyappa asked her 'What, you too have started to spin?' She had said, 'Oh it is a good time-pass' and laughed. After she had spun ten balls of thread, she said to her husband, 'Please give it to the weaver and bring me a khadi sari. Let me see how it feels.' Her eyes shone bright while she said this. Seetha, who did not know how to speak fluently before her marriage, gradually began to mock and tease her husband. Ridiculing his coarse clothes that were hard to wash, she too began to wear the same kind of coarse khadi saris, by spinning the thread for it herself. But she did not burn all her mill saris and other clothes. She put them in a box with some moth-balls. As communication with people was essential for his work, Satyappa became an eloquent speaker. Whatever may be the topic, he would speak seriously about the dimension of social upliftment, laced with enough humour and wit also. Looking at Seetha who became so articulate and witty, Satyappa understood that given the right opportunity, his wife had wit and oratory power more than he did. Such a wife, after two and a half years of married life gave birth to a male child and died at childbirth in Tiptur hospital. The child survived. When Seetha left for her husband's house after her marriage, she had expressed her desire to her husband to take her younger sister Savitri with them. Satyappa requested his father-in-law to send Savitri with them, more enthusiastically than Seetha. After the elder sister left for her husband's house, there was no female caretaker for the seven year old girl in Parameshwarayya's house. Ramakrishna had to leave the house early morning to attend to work in the fields and Parameshwarayya would go to the grove. Even after lunch, they had to attend work at the fields and grove. Even though she attended school, the girl would be alone rest of the time. So, Parameshwarayya and Ramakrishna agreed to send Savitri with her sister. Moreover, Savitri was more attached to her sister after their mother's death. Now she got adjusted to her brother-in-law more than her father and brother. Her father was of a serious nature and would talk very little. It was better when her mother was alive, he used to talk with his little daughter and would cut jokes too with her. But after her mother's death, Savitri had not seen her father laughing. Even her brother Ramakrishna was a silent person. However, he would bathe her, wash her clothes as she was his little sister. Whenever he cut fruits, he would make her eat from his share also. Sometimes he would call her 'Amma', but he spoke very little. But this brother-in-law was not like that. In his marriage itself, he would sneak behind her, pull his little sister-in-law's plait, squeeze her ears, pinch her arms and withdraw his hand swiftly before she turned around to check. He would tell her wonderful fairy tales. He would start the story as if this little girl sat on the horse grazing in the field. And so suddenly two wings would sprout on its side. Oh, it would fly and fly to the sky crossing hills, forests, rivers and seas and reach the twinkling stars and go beyond them. Finally, the horse would come down in front of their house. By that time, the elder sister would be waiting for the little girl with sweets and fried snacks. After Savitri came to her brother-in-law's house, sometimes Satyappa would give her piggybacks, make her eat from his plate. Her sister and brother-in-law allowed Savitri to sleep in their room, as she was a little girl and it was a new place for her. Savitri even now remembered this. By the time Seetha died, Ramakrishna was married and a sister-in-law had come. Parameshwarayya told them that he would ask his daughter-in-law to bring up Ramachandra, Seetha's motherless child. But Satyappa did not agree to this proposal. With the help of a maidservant he brought up his son. Savitri, now a girl of nine and a half years, returned to her father's house. Her sister-in-law Sukanya was not a bad woman, but she never allowed Savitri to sleep in her room like Seetha did.

As soon as he knew about his father's suicide, Ramakrishna felt that he was the root cause for it and his mind sank into despair. From the very beginning, he had realised that if he had not forcefully suggested to his father to commit perjury, he would not be ready to do so. Ramakrishna's conscience felt the terrible agony and torment his father was bearing inside. But he did not know how to console his father. Ramakrishna's faith in truth got sharper and more profound; his mind was caught in surprise and shock looking at the naked form of lie when the widow of Kanchi, Lakkoo, herself had given evidence in favour of Manjayya. How would his tongue utter any word of comfort to his father while his mind weighed and rejected whatever word of comfort he would say as being mean? By nature he was reticent. Now, in such a situation it seemed as though his tongue had suffered a paralytic stroke. Was it not he who had vehemently protested against the marriage of Savitri with Manjayya. Parameshwarayya had made it clear in one word that it was impossible for him to accept Manjayya as a son-in-law. Finally it was Ramakrishna who agreed to the marriage, thinking it was her fate and he was not able to cope with her stubbornness. When he recalled this, he was haunted by the feeling that he was morally responsible for his father's suicide. If it was known to him earlier that his father would commit suicide, could he have averted it? What reason or argument could he have given? No, nothing would have struck him. He thought like this; if I had held his feet firmly, directly going near him and said, if you do such a thing, whole of my life, right until my death, will be a burning hell. You see I too am suffering. Please, do not give me a more severe punishment than this. You must live here and be with us, and bear agony, however acute it is. Until you promise to do so, I am not going to leave your feet. If saying so, I had prostrated, perhaps it could have been possible for him to change his decision! Ramakrishna turned still more reticent and introvertish in the grief that he could not get any clue of his father's thought. His face was taut and drawn by the silence in which nothing flashed.

Savitri's head and heart were aflame. Her father had given false evidence for her sake and committed suicide. She came to Bilikere as soon as she got the news. Looking at the police who had come there for *mahajar* and the corpse of her father hanging down from the branch of the banyan tree, she had decided to commit suicide by hanging herself with the same rope and on the same branch. When her brother came near her and stood there holding her arm, she felt a little comforted. She wondered whether Ramakrishna was standing there holding her arm for her support or for his own support? But if he had not supported her like that, her wish of committing suicide by hanging would not have diminished! The whole night her sister-in-law kept herself awake, slept near Savitri, guarded her and tried to console her. Her brother and Ganesha had busied themselves with the arrangements for cremation on that night itself after *mahajar* was over and the body was released. Savitri began reminiscing, the root cause of her father's grief and then suicide was not only lying in courts but it was her stubbornness in marrying that wretched fellow. Her father, who had never beaten anybody, who had not even lifted his hand at a stray cattle, had mercilessly beaten and kicked her. Even then, why was she so stubborn? What had possessed her? Was it the power of mere infatuation, blind passion, malefic planets or mere obstinacy? That night, while she was suffering severe grief she realised, obstinacy or stubbornness was a form of ego. She remembered, after a little while that it was what her father had explained, when he had advised her not to marry Manjayya and now she felt that was true. Stubborn, she had gone ahead, married Manjayya. After seeing with her own eyes his conduct, escapades and night adventures, she had left his house with the same sort of stubbornness and was seething with insult and injury. Yet, neither her father nor her brother, ever blamed her or suggested that she had brought this upon herself because of her obstinacy. Yes, her sister-in-law had blamed her. Though her father and brother had objected, she went alone to Channarayapattana looking for a job, as a means of vengeance not only on herself but on her father and brother with whom she had been so stubborn. But now after her father committed suicide, she felt that the very foundation of taking revenge, let alone on them but even on herself was sunk and she felt completely lost, directionless. She felt like sobbing convulsively, putting her head on the shoulder some very intimate person, her mother maybe. Her mother *should* have been alive. Even though she would be drowned in grief bearing the loss of her god-like husband, she would have consoled her daughter and caused her daughter's grief to subside. Or only if Seethakka were there! Savitri remembered her childhood. Yes Seethakka was dead, but what about her brother-in-law? Why hadn't he come? Did he think that there was nothing important in his father-in-law's house after the death of his wife and mother-in-law? Was his affection towards me generated only through his wife? Couldn't he have continued his affection? She felt so angry that she wanted to leave for Mattikere at once and question him.

On the ninth day, Satyappa came to Bilikere to attend the ceremonies of his father-in-law, but Savitri did not speak to him, even though she saw him. He had come to that house after the lapse of twenty-five years and was feeling a little ill at ease. He sat alone in the hall leaning on the pillar. He wore a white khadi dhoti, white khadi shirt; his thick white hair was combed back. There were no other men at home. Ramakrishna had gone to the cremation ground where rituals of the ninth day had to be performed with the *jois* Subbannayya and Hiriyannayya of the same street. Ganesha had gone to Channarayapattana to bring provisions and necessary things for the ceremony. Sukanya came out, spoke to Satyappa, and went inside. A cook had come into the hall twice and went to the kitchen. He did not enquire of Satyappa, who he was or where he was from. Satyappa knew that his father-in-law had committed suicide either as repentance for perjury or as giving false witness became intolerable to him. On his way to this house, Lakkappa Gowda who belonged to the same village recognised him and spoke to him, 'You have become a stranger to our village,' and described the truthfulness of Parameshwarayya. He said, 'From now onwards, we won't get good and timely rains and crop yields.'

Though Gowda explained about the wrath of God, the rule of dharma that punishes, Satyappa, who had struggled in the villages for so many years teaching the principles of Gandhiji and working for the upliftment of the village, could not believe it. He knew by personal experience about the honesty and truthfulness of his father-in-law. He had seen Gandhiji. So, he was not surprised at his father-in-law's decision and self-punishment. But, he would feel disdain, if Lakkappa Gowda or any other person spoke about divine wrath or not getting good rains and yields hereafter. He was confident that after this country got freedom the age of superstitious belief was past. Now, when he was pondering over this, leaning on the pillar, Savitri came swiftly and said, 'Please come to the cowshed. I want to talk to you.' Satyappa got up and followed her. She took him into the tiled bathroom in the backyard, where there was a well, a big copper pot and heaps of firewood, sufficient for a year. She asked him to sit on the stone bench made to keep coils of ropes, pots etc. She stood facing him and said, 'You have proved the saying that after the death of the wife, no relation remains with the father-in-law's house.' Satyappa looked at her face. He had known that Savitri's face would glow whether in grief, anger or neglect. When she saw the feeling of guilt manifesting itself on his face, she asked, 'Do you know that it was I who killed father?' He simply kept looking at her face. Her eyes filled with tears as if they could no longer bear the lone responsibility of the whole injustice that had happened to date. Even as Satyappa was watching, her eyes started streaming. He remembered the seven-year-old Savitri, whom he used to caress, carry on his shoulder and pamper. He got up, put his right hand on the top of her head and stood silently. He could not say anything to console her. She began to sob uncontrollably. He stood still, aware that now she was a grown up woman of thirty-five. He remembered those days when she was a little girl and had sobbed like this. Many a times, he had hugged her, kissed her and whispered something in her ear causing her to laugh. Then the cause of her sorrow, she thought, was her elder sister coming in her way and correcting her in everything – speech, behaviour, etc. Whenever the little girl complained against her sister to the brother-in-law, he would whisper in the ears of this little girl. 'Don't you worry let's teach her a lesson, the two of us.' That was enough for her. Afterwards her brother-in-law too would say the same thing that her sister had said and gently correct her. She would never get angry or feel like crying when her brother-in-law corrected her. Satyappa did reminisce and felt these incidents should not have happened to such a girl. He thought, Savitri was deprived of family happiness by falling in love with a rake like Manjayya and now she should not suffer with the sense of guilt that she was the cause of her father's suicide. But he did not know how to remove that. However, assuming that some means would flash by thinking about it, he said to her, 'After these ceremonies are over, come with me to Mattikere and stay there for some days. Let us talk over all these matters.' She was silent and continued to sob. Satyappa held her hand, made her sit beside him on the stone bench, bent her head, laid it on his shoulder and caressed her softly. She wept for a while and lifted her face. Satyappa said, 'Have you forgotten that if you drench this white khadi shirt with your tears, it would get stained?' Those were the words of her elder sister. Whenever she would cry, her brother-in-law used to wipe off the tears with the edge of his shirt and Seethakka used to say this. Challenging her sister, little Savitri would make her brother-in-law take off the shirt, go and wash it in fresh water and would say, 'See where is the stain now.' This memory seemed to have lessened a little the weight of sorrow on her face.

Satyappa decided to lessen the grief of Savitri at any cost. But how? Her thought that she was indirectly the cause of her father's suicide was quite reasonable. But it was not possible to negate or to undo what had happened. Satyappa found some hope and comfort in thinking so. Somehow, if he could change Manjayya's mind and make him realise the error of his ways, if he could be made to understand the difference between truth and falsehood at least marginally, he would accept his wife and lead a family life. After Savitri got out of the cowshed and came inside, he went back into the hall and sat there. When he began thinking about this, Satyappa felt that by his effort, he was not only giving Savitri a companion and direction to her life but he would get a good name for reforming a person like Manjayya. He remembered what Mahatma had said about satyagraha 'Even in a cruel wretch and sinner, deep down there lives the soul, the *antaraatma* and there dwells god, the *paramaatma*. To awaken him is our fundamental duty. This is what is meant by satyagraha.' Even a person like Manjayya would melt, at least a little, when confronted with the context in which Parameshwarayya had committed suicide. Satyappa felt confident that if Manjayya was caught now and pressed with love and friendship, he would surely mend his ways. Satyappa's reformer-mind, which had become passive since ten or fifteen years, got excited and he became enthused, looking at the opportunity of this new motivation. He decided to know all details from Ramakrishna after he came home finishing the rituals and then he would meet Manjayya. He thought, in fact he knew Manjayya better than Ramakrishna and Parameshwarayya knew. Satyappa was well aware of the fact that Manjayya was a liar and philanderer. Though deceit was not his chief tendency as falsehood and adultery, if needed he deceived too, easily and without any qualms. But comparatively his tendency to cheat was on a lesser scale. Satyappa's mind pondered a while in analysing whether these three, that is, lying, adultery and deceit, were different faces of a single tendency. Adultery does not happen without lies. But all liars are not adulterers. Even adulterers can do it with honesty and without deceit. A person without having a modicum of knowledge of adultery may be a deceiver. It is not necessary that the close relation that exists between lies and deceit, should exist in the other case also. When Satyappa analysed in this way, he remembered some examples of liars who did not have the purpose of deceit. So, when he decided it was deceit which was more fundamental and not lie, his mind tried to categorise to which class Manjayya belonged. Satyappa thought that it was easy to speak to Manjayya; perhaps he was a liar, but he spoke copiously. He was an orator full of practical experiences, anecdotes and stories, was entertaining and with humour and seriousness, he captivated his listeners. So, if he comes, there would be no boredom. Manjayya has not come since a long time. He used to visit our village also and of late, he has not come. After Ramachandra's marriage, he has not visited us. If he had come, I would have had to hint to Susheela, not to come out when Manjayya was there. While remembering these one thing suddenly came to Satyappa's mind. He did not stop coming to Bilikere, because his wife was dead, and there was no bond now with his father-in-law's house. Haunted by Seetha's memory he had come to Bilikere three times. But there was nobody in that house to speak with. His father-in-law was always serious and introvertish. Ramakrishna too was generally silent. Certainly they, who performed daily *annadaana*, had to be courteous. But unless that cordiality was expressed through speech, how could one know it? 'Did you arrive just now? Please be seated!' – was this kind of friendliness and intimacy sufficient between brothers-in-law? Then after an hour, there would be another question. 'How is the farming at your place?' Satyappa felt, why should he visit such silent people. If at all he had to speak, it was with Savitri. She was a schoolgoing girl. How much and what could he have talked with her. He remembered, how his contact with Bilikere had become infrequent and then rare. Along with this, he remembered how this Manjayya who would always be visiting places, would come to Satyappa's house also, go into the kitchen, cook delicious food, serve Satyappa and he too would have lunch and entertain with his talks. Even before Satyappa became his brother-in-law by Savitri's marriage, Manjayya used to call him Annayya. He would always win over people with his talk. Moreover, the scope of his work also was very vast and not limited only to Channarayapattana taluk. Satyappa remembered an incident he had heard about the scam Manjayya had pulled off ten years back, in Beeragunda of Arsikere taluk. It was Gandasi Gurunanjayya who told this. There was a stupid shanbhog called Manjunathayya, in Beeragunda of Arsikere taluk. Satyappa also had known him. Anybody would have known that the shanbhog was a stupid one. He committed some mistake, and perhaps because of that stupidity was suspended. Though he was suspended only for two months, he did not meet the higher officials, or bribe them in the office, did not present his case properly. Suspension continued for more than six months. This idiot Manjunathayya sat at home, whiling away his time tending his oxen. Our Bilikere Manjayya, however, knew this situation. He straightaway went to Hassan district office, did some trick, deceived the officials there, went to Beeragunda, took charge as the shanbhog there and established himself as shanbhog of Beeragunda. Like everywhere here too there were some people who opposed this. They took that stupid Manjunathayya to the District Commissioner, presented an appeal by him. The D.C. ordered his subordinates to enquire. Finally the Revenue Inspector, it seems, had written the report like this: 'It is true that Manjunathayya was suspended because of dereliction of duty. After that he was warned properly, and the same Manjunathayya has been given charge and now he is the present shanbhog. Another person named Manjunathayya has appealed to D.C. Sahib, now playing some deceit. When enquiry was conducted it has come to light this petitioner was insane. Often he claims that he is the Maharaja of Mysore State, he is God Manjunatha of Dharmasthala.' Bilikere Manjayya had bribed the Revenue Inspector and proved himself as the original Manjunathayya, established himself as the shanbhog of Beeragunda. Manjayya had lured with his show of prowess the wife of the real Manjunathayya and won her. After living with her for three months he felt bored. Then he bribed the same Revenue Inspector, handed over the charge as shanbhog to the original Manjunathayya, left that village and returned to his place. During that period of his administration as shanbhog, it is said, he had created quarrels, parties, disputes and divisions and had caused perplexity and distress in that village. After two months Satyappa came to know about this. Once Manjayya had come to Satyappa's village. When asked about this, Manjayya had proudly hinted with his eyes 'Yes'. Satyappa still remembered. Drinking tender coconut water in his grove, he asked Manjayya, 'Look here Manjayya, you're lucky. There's no dearth of food or any amenities of life. You've lots of lands. Let's forget about deceiving and cheating that stupid fellow. But was it fair to ruin the chastity of his wife?' What should Manjayya's answer be to that question? He said, 'Annayya, if he was too stupid, I would not have done that to him. I wanted to deceive the whole government, the Revenue Inspector, Shirastedar, Amaldar, Assistant Commissioner, District Commissioner, including this khadi government of independent India which your Gandhiji brought. Is it not thrilling to cause these people to dance like monkeys? And as for that poor man's wife's chastity, I did not do anything to her chastity. People like you assume a woman to be a paragon of chastity. But you understand one thing, women too have desires. When they see a handsome man, they too feel desire from inside. Many men do not understand this, but I understand it well. You know one thing. I've never forced a woman. That wife of Manjunathayya begged and beseeched me not to leave her and that village.' Manjayya was such a bewitching conversationalist that whatever he spoke, any listener would believe it to be true. Satyappa also felt it was not easy to drive home the subtlety of truth and lie to a person like Manjayya. Yet he felt hopeful that now he had got an opportunity. If he tried to awaken Manjayya's conscience even a little, passivity of his own life of so many years would find new direction.

Ramakrishna returned by 3:30 in the afternoon from the grove where the rites were performed. Subbannayya, Hiriyannayya and Naga *jois* were with him. Satyappa was acquainted with them. Ramakrishna enquired about Ramachandra, his wife and children. That was all. There was no other word. Ramakrishna was reticent earlier also. Now along with that, the seriousness of carrying the weight of death on his conscience was clearly visible on his face. He looked as if he had taken on him the experience of all dead persons. Looking at him, Satyappa thought of comprehending the state of mind of his father-in-law who sought salvation in suicide. Subbannayya and Hiriyannayya were the only two who were having conversation at lunch. They said, there would at least be hundred people coming to *dharmodaka* rite. Naga *Jois* talked about what was needed for the next day. Satyappa remembered that this was the same Naga *Jois*, who had married him with Seetha, in this very house, in this very village. After lunch, Satyappa went to Subbannayya's house with him and Hiriyannayya too accompanied them. Both of them explained with compassion and cordiality, the background of Parameshwarayya's suicide, as far as they knew. Subbannayya's wife Vishalamma, who was of the age of Parameshwarayya's wife, too joined in this conversation and said, 'The root cause of all this is Savitri marrying that Manjayya, so stubbornly, even though her father and brother tried to prevent her. She married him knowing fully well what kind of reputation he had. Well at least she should have stayed quiet with him, thinking let him do whatever he wants outside, but if he is good and right at home, it is enough. But she could not turn a blind eye to her husband's affairs and came back to her father's house. She felt bad and a little embarrassed to live in her father's house, insisted on getting a job, went to Channarayapattana got a school teacher's job. That was over. And now, if she was firm, thinking she did not have any relation with Manjayya and did not bother even if he was hanged, why would this man have gone to give false evidence? Why should this have happened? Couldn't she realise that her father would not bear to live after telling a single lie?' Vishalamma put the burden of mistake solely on Savitri. Satyappa had come to Bilikere to attend Savitri's marriage. After that, he had not come here. He had heard about Savitri leaving her husband's home, returning to her father's and joining as a teacher in Channarayapattana, only as distant news, but he had not known the details. So Satyappa decided to know all these details before meeting Manjayya and talking with him.

By the time Satyappa returned home, Ramakrishna's father-in-law, Nagappa, copra warehouse owner from Tiptur had arrived. He wore a white mill dhoti, a collarless, long-sleeved white shirt with three pockets inside and outside. He was sitting on the mat. Beside him there was a black cap and a handbag of carpet cloth. Satyappa had known him when he used to sell coconuts and copra at the warehouse or to the market-yard in Tiptur. He had now stopped taking them to Tiptur. But from the very beginning his business was with Channaveerappa's warehouse. So, though relatives, there was not much harmonious relation between him and Nagappa. Difference of nature was another reason. Nagappa too had come to offer *dharmodaka*. If the self-earned good deeds of deceased Parameshwarayya would not be enough to cross the Vaitharani river in the netherworlds, the good deeds of this man too would be credited to the dead man and his *preta* would reach the next stage! Satyappa remembered, what he just now heard in Subbannayya's house. Nagappa was one of the chief witnesses, who had told that Manjayya was with him in Tiptur on the night of the murder. Nagappa had received one thousand rupees from Manjayya as reward for this, even before giving false witness in the court. And now this man would offer the fruit earned by his good deeds to Parameshwarayya! Satyappa felt disgusted. Yet he sat on that mat silently. Nagappa himself broke the silence. He asked Satyappa, 'How much does an acre of wet-land, dry-land or grove cost at your place?' Satyappa tried to silence him and said, 'Sorry I do not know. My son is looking after the business affairs.' But Nagappa was not a person to be silenced so easily. Luckily there was the sound of a bullock cart. Ramakrishna went out. His son Ganesha had brought provisions and all that was needed for the ceremony loaded in the bullock cart from Channarayapattana. Ramakrishna, Ganesha, and the servant of the cart were carrying the bags into the house. Satyappa too got up, helped them in carrying the bags, though Ramakrishna objected. Nagappa got up and went out. When he walked, Satyappa noticed a white bandage round his right calf. He thought it must be some small cut or wound.

Savitri was washing clothes on the stone slab near the well in the backyard. She did not see her brother-in-law come in and stand behind her. When he called 'Saatee', she turned back with surprise. Nobody used to call her 'Saatee'. While she stayed in this brother-in-law's house for two and half years and she was a little girl, Satyappa used to call her so. For a minute, she stood confused, but she was cheered by that memory and her face brightened.

Satyappa said, 'I have a lot to talk with you. I want to know everything, so, have come. Just the two of us, when are you free?'

Savitri replied, 'Let everybody finish dinner. The maidservants come to clean rice and pulses brought now. They work the whole night, we may talk without any disturbance.' After a minute, she said, 'But what is there to talk about bhaava? All has ended in silence.'

'I want to know all. You yourself must tell me. I do not like to hear about you from some third person.'

She did not answer. She began wringing the clothes. Satyappa still stood there. Savitri asked, 'Are not Ramachandra and his wife coming?'

'It's the second delivery for his wife. The baby is only two months old. He will come by bicycle for *Vaikunta* ceremony and return in the evening. His mother-in-law stays there, yet she feels lonely and worried without a male in the house with the little baby and a nursing mother.'

Nagappa who had gone out, returned late and dinner was delayed. As he was a diabetic, he ate only ragi-ball rolling it in sambar and drank butter milk. The rest of them had rice for dinner. Nagappa, while eating ragi-balls, narrated the story of the philosopher king, Rajarshi Krishnaraja Wodeyar IV of Mysore. This king used to eat ragi-balls and that is why ragi-ball was nicknamed Krishnaraja Wodeyaru. Anybody who eats ragi-balls without fail would have the same sort of balanced mind. Nagappa described the great quality of ragi which was known to everybody. However, the story lightened the atmosphere. Satyappa guessed that Ganesha did not feel either love or respect towards this grandfather. He knew that Ganesha had stayed at his maternal grandfather's house while attending high school and now he left there and was studying in Hassan. As for Ramakrishna, he stayed unbearably silent.

Three maids came in just as they were all about to retire for the night. In the dining hall opposite the kitchen, they started opening bags and packets of coriander, rice, pulses and all other things needed for *Vaikunta-samaaraadhana* and began cleaning. Satyappa who had slept in the hall got up after Savitri called, went to the shed, sat on the stone bench on which he had sat in the afternoon. A smoke-stained electric bulb burned dimly. Savitri sat on a mat made of coconut leaf near Satyappa's feet and said, 'Bhaava, I know what you want to ask me. Till today, I have not opened up to anybody. I have not told the details to anyone, of how and why things happened the way they did. Why should I? People who listen to you, do so only out of curiosity. Do they have a heart to stomach all that and understand? If my mother was alive, I would have told her. If Seethakka was alive, I would have told her. And you, you did not turn up here at all. Only today you came and called 'Saatee'.'

Satyappa remembered how he used to call little Savitri 'Saatee the proud one'. Now, he realised that self-respect was an intrinsic personality trait. He felt that he could have a straightforward talk with her, as she too had suggested the familiarity of earlier days. He asked, 'The whole village knew about Manjayya's reputation, everybody knew he was a rake. You too were a woman of strong will. Even so, why were you so stubborn as to insist on marrying him?'

As if she had the answer ready, she said, 'Why did I?' The self-deprecating sad smile on her face disappeared and she continued, 'I have been pondering over this question about a hundred thousand times; no, no, not *have been*, I *was* pondering. *Not now*, now I have stopped doing so. If I say *praarabdha* or karma, it is trying to evade responsibility for my action. So, let us not take that line. Let us say pure passion, simple infatuation. I was caught in that vile grip and to cap it, *pride*, the ego that arises in girls of seventeen fuelled it. Let me tell you how it happened. You can imagine, you will understand. You have imbibed Gandhiji's teachings, studied Vedanta and have practised these. You remember, don't you, that rock, like a camel's hump, in the tank of our village, that high one. Around that rock, the waters run deep, there is a whirlpool too.

The rock is slippery and its formation is such that you cannot get a foothold to climb back, if you slipped. It meant sure death for anyone who lost his footing. None of the village women go there for washing clothes. Do you remember, mother had gone there to wash clothes and had slipped and drowned?'

Satyappa agreed, 'Yes, yes. I remember. Once I dived from that rock and began swimming. Seetha who was washing clothes on the steps of the tank nearby, saw me. At once she came running towards that side crying and shouting loudly. I turned back, to see why she was screaming and said, "Don't worry, I'm a good swimmer. A swimmer gets more happiness in deeper waters." But she did not listen to my words, and said, "Promise me, promise you'll never go near that rock; swear upon God, please, it's a wicked rock," and extracted a promise from me.'

'Yes, the very same rock. I didn't know swimming. Yet I used to go to that rock to wash clothes. Why? I don't know, did not understand. But thinking back, I feel perhaps that rock was drawing me because it was the place where my mother died!

'After Seethakka died and I came back to the village, it was hurting me inside that I was a motherless orphan. I felt the death of my mother so intensely that my heart and mind would be drawn to anything connected to her. The attraction of that rock which killed my mother was also the same or perhaps there might have been the unconscious desire to slip and follow my mother's fate. When I sat alone on that rock and lathered the clothes, how forceful were the winds, how violent were the waves! Rising from the bank of distant Aralihalli grove lines, the whole tank would be filled with thousands and thousands, no lakhs of huge waves that rolled in one after the other, dashed urgently on the rock, drenched not only the clothes I had lathered but even me, right up to my knees. Oh, my mind yearned to extend my eyesight, to fix my eyes across the entire length and breadth of that tank which created such perplexity inside me. And such a thrill swelled up inside me that I felt the rapture of reaching the sky. When the wind blows from that side, waves rise in our tank as the afternoon nears. I always longed to see that, especially, I had an irresistible desire to see the waves whipping the water, standing on that dangerous camel rock. I could not resist this desire. One day when I was washing clothes, Manjayya swam up to the rock. But he did not come near the rock and climb up on it. He came swimming in that whirlpool of deep water. He swam away through that path nearing the rock. I saw his physique inside the water. I feel shy, bhaava, to share this,' Savitri stopped.

'Why should you feel shy or embarrassed? Tell me.'

There was the continuous sound of cleaning rice and pulses in sifters and sieves. Savitri sat looking at the smoke stained bulb. Satyappa waited silently. After a couple of minutes, she resumed, 'The Savitri of those days was different. The one sitting before you and narrating this is altogether different. That Savitri was set fire to and burnt to cinders long back. And after Appa's death, all is destroyed and mere traces of that old Savitri remain. So, why should I feel embarrassed?' When Savitri uttered those words, her voice had the detached tone of a pure *saakshi*. She said, 'Yes, Manjayya was handsome, very attractive. His skin had a pinkish texture and tone, a blend of red and white. Since he was often outdoors in the hot sun, his face, neck and elbows had tanned and were darker. But the body under the transparent sheet of clear water was extremely attractive. That day I experienced it. The waves had not built up, were not yet strong and swift that particular day. Had the waves been fast-rolling and rapid, as usual, the swimmer's profile could not have been seen so clearly. But the soft and slow rhythm of the waves created new forms, making the figure appear and disappear, and a magic was born. When I saw Manjayya that day, the vivid picture of him was imprinted in my mind. There was a girl called Rangamani who lived in the street next to ours. She was of my age. A young man had come to their house with the intention of marrying her. The preliminaries were over, he liked the girl and the marriage was fixed. That girl had told me four or five times, 'All sorts of young men come to see me and they are interested. But why doesn't a man like Manjayya come?' Another girl named Subbi had also showered praises on Manjayya, about his charming and handsome features. Many girls were attracted to him, in fact were secretly in love with him. That day, standing on the rocks, I too felt the stirrings of love. I fell for him, who swam away in the deep water, or to be precise, fell for his body. After that he did not come back to the rock for seven or eight days. I don't know whether he did not come to swim at all or did not come that side, or he had not come when I was there. But, now I am almost sure, he purposely stayed away. I used to stand there on the rock and look at the water. 'Why didn't he come? Why didn't he come?' My mind started worrying. Then one day he came, the next day, and the day after. He came on four consecutive days and swam away near my rock, just on his own, without noticing me. The fifth day, there were violent winds, the waters were rough and choppy and the waves were plenty. I thought he would not come that day. Though you can swim even in those rough waves, what happiness will there be in it? But when I was wringing clothes with the disappointment that I would have to go home without seeing his swimming, I heard his voice calling me 'Savitri'. It was the voice coming out of the deep waters of the tank. I turned back. Yes, it was him! He swam over towards the rock. I had told you it was very difficult to have a foothold from the deep waters on to that camel rock. He too was losing his hold and the waves were pushing. Somehow he managed to find a hold and hoisted himself half way up the rock. His striped shorts were seen inside the water. I was frightened. Not because of any other thing. Just the unexpectedness of it. He was also breathing hard, but in a minute he controlled it and amidst the sound of waves dashing on to the rock, he said: 'Since long I was wanting to speak to you. I've seen quite a lot of girls of marriageable age. They showed me girls from very well-off families as well. But your picture stays right before my eyes, wherever I go. If there were no waves in this tank, I would have shown you, how your image looks in these deep waters. Tell me, will you marry me?' saying this, when he looked at my face, I felt shy and lowered my eyes. I felt as if I was being washed away, caught in the rapid waves. He was silent for a minute and said, 'People may say all sorts of things about me. Your father may say, Manjayya is a rake, don't marry him. Well, to be honest, I haven't remained as pure as gold, nor am I an angel. But neither am I as wicked as people make me out to be. Don't I know how I should behave after I marry and become a family man? If you come to my house as my wife, you will be the queen of my home. See, I swear on this goddess of water Ganga,' and cupped his palms, filled them with water and poured it down as oblation. The waves were rising and dashing on to the rock. But I was not in a state to hear anything. Even in that state of mind, I heard him say. 'You think it over. I'll act according to your decision.' Then he dived swiftly head first into the water. Though I knew he was swimming under-water, when he did not come up for a long time, I became a little anxious. Then I saw him surfacing in the distance and swimming away towards the centre. I had stood there not being aware of anything. My mind had flown inwards to the base, away from external things. I was not aware of the tank in front of me or the wind and waves. Though I was drenched up to my knees, I was sweating. Again I gazed at the middle of the tank. The waves were rising higher and higher and were rolling. He was not seen anywhere. Finally a tiny black spot was seen like a head. I was furious. Why did he have to go swimming so far while such fierce waves were rising.'

She paused. Satyappa sat there trying to comprehend the details and the background against the backdrop of the sound of winnowing and sieving being heard from the dining hall. Savitri said, 'I have told you how the infatuation started. Anybody can explain how it starts. But Brahma alone knows why it does. Isn't it so?'

Satyappa asked, 'Didn't Manjayya try to meet you afterwards? Did he not speak with you? Did he ask your father for your hand or did you yourself ask your father to marry you off to Manjayya?'

'Three days after this incident, he met me. Yes in the same place, in the deep waters of that camel rock. He came swimming near the rock. "If you consent to marry me, ask your brother to give you in marriage to me. I know your people won't approve easily. They say Manjayya is a wicked fellow. They will advise you against marrying me. They will be adamant. But if you stand firm and are equally stubborn, our marriage will take place. You have to manage it. I am not going to marry any other girl except you in this life" he said, leapt into the water and swam away.'

'So, there was no protest from the family.'

'Protest! There was terrible opposition. Had Appa ever raised his voice or scolded me? Or raised his hand? He tried patiently to drive home the right and wrong of the matter into my head. But when I did not budge, he gave me a severe, merciless beating. His anger did not abate. He then kicked me nonstop landing kicks on my waist and back. In the ensuing pain, I lost count of the times he kicked me. Manjayya must have known that my father would never agree to this marriage. He was well aware of human nature. He understood what kind of people value certain ideals and who would never agree to some things. Perhaps that is why he told me to ask my brother. In the end, it was my brother who managed it all for me. Appa had remained detached since long. After my marriage he became even more detached. He knew it was impossible to change a person like Manjayya and thought, if she was stubborn enough to marry him, pain and sorrow were foretold in her stars, were her destiny. Protesting or worrying was pointless. Detachment alone was the answer to the foolishness of this girl. Even when I left Manjayya's house and came back, Appa did not express grief. He had achieved complete detachment.'

Satyappa remembered his father-in-law. As far as he could recall, his father-in-law was always detached and disinterested. Suddenly he felt a sort of complacency and fulfilment. Like Manjayya, Satyappa too was the son-in-law of this house. Satyappa himself had asked for Parameshwarayya's daughter's hand in marriage. Parameshwarayya had readily agreed after enquiring about Satyappa. His eyes had filled with tears when he sent his daughter to her husband's house. After marriage, Satyappa never hurt Seetha. She was happy and when she went to her father's house, she made him happy by telling him how contented she was. This little girl Savitri also stayed with them. Recalling all these, Satyappa felt ashamed for comparing himself with Manjayya and feeling superior. As if to escape from this internal comparison, he asked, 'Well, so you married him. Did he make you happy at least in the beginning of married life? Did he treat you nicely? How and why did you leave that place?'

Savitri did not answer at once, sitting quiet, head downcast. Satyappa too did not press. After a while, as if she had come to a decision, she spoke. But she did not raise her head or meet his eyes. She spoke in a low voice, looking at the huge soot covered cauldron, 'I have already told you that I speak now like a *saakshi*. If that Savitri was alive, it would not have been possible for her to say what I am sharing now. What I am revealing is very important to understand what sort of a person Manjayya is. He made me feel, when I went to his house, that no woman was as fortunate as me. He opened up and showed me layers and layers of happiness I had never heard or known. He won over my heart on the first night of our wedding in the bedroom. I am talkative, unlike my father and brother. Within half an hour, he made me lose the shyness and embarrassment of a new bride. He described how he fell for me. He praised my beauty, complexion, height, contour of face, adjusted my hair, appreciated the fragrance of flowers I wore in my hair and said what a lovely body I had. He did not show any haste. He removed my anxiety, held my hand and said, "Only if you consent ..." Thus he rested the responsibility of the next step on my shoulders. He made me feel, if I disappoint such a husband on the first night itself, what sort of wife am I, and won me over. The third day we moved into his house. There was no one else in his large house. It was totally ours! How romantic it seemed! There were two big mirrors next to the bed. Three months back, I could never have imagined this would be so exciting and joyful and that I would do these sort of things without feeling shy or embarrassed. Nor could I guess, my figure, complexion and my body could give so much pleasure. I swelled with happiness, feeling I was really fortunate. I was proud of my handsome husband with such a build. Moreover, I did not have to do any household chores like washing clothes, fetching water from the well or the like. It was a brick and mortar house. We didn't have too many visitors. The servants were obedient. They never spoke unless spoken to.'

Savitri paused for a while and after she subdued the shame and disgust that welled up inside her, she raised her face and looking at her brother-in-law's eyes said, 'Six months passed. I was quite unaware of what was happening outside, for, I was totally immersed in happiness that was not found by any new bride. Have you seen Doddammatte of Middle Street? That short lady with a round nice face, who always used to smear turmeric copiously on her cheeks?' Savitri looked at his face. He could not remember. She continued, 'Doesn't matter. She is talkative. She had come to our house one evening for *arisina-kumkuma*. I was alone. She enquired about my welfare and asked why wasn't I pregnant yet. You know it was the sort of question that old ladies ask young, newly married girls. What could I answer? I too had thought about this. But there was another strain of thought also. If I got pregnant, this wonderful pleasure I was sharing with my husband would stop, at least until delivery and the period of nursing the child. Doddammatte did not stop at that. She raked up the matter and questioned. "Tell me dear girl, does your husband sleep with you or not?" Remembering my husband's vigour and virility in bed I smiled. Doddammatte again insisted, "Hey, come on, why are you so shy? Don't I know what sort of a person Manjayya is?"'

'What do you mean, Doddammatte?'

'"You liked him intensely, insisted and married him though many people were against it. But even after marrying you, it seems, Manjayya has not given up his old habits. Daily he enjoys different women in the evenings at the hut in his grove. That's why I asked you whether he sleeps with you or not. Besides, you have not yet become pregnant. Oh, you are so beautiful, my dear girl, that one feels like washing hands before touching you. Having such a wife at home, why does he chase those whores and bitches?"'

'Doddammatte planted the seed of suspicion and went away. Should I believe her? He, who immersed me in romantic pleasure every night, how was it possible for him to go with other women every evening? There are some women who sow seeds of discord between husband and wife. This Doddammatte too belonged to that category. I knew she had caused discord and quarrel in many people's lives. When my husband came home at eight in the evening I observed him minutely. Even after dinner, I kept a close watch. But I could detect nothing. He yearned for lovemaking with me with such intensity as though except me there was no woman in the world for him. It was better than ever. I felt guilty for having suspected such a husband and thought I should slap myself. In that penitent mood, I confessed to my husband whatever Doddammatte had reported. Do you know what he said? 'Oh that Narasappa's old wife Puttani? Even at this age she needs at least four men like me.' He thus tarnished and scandalised the character of Doddammatte. But Doddammatte was not a woman of that sort and I knew it. 'After our love-making was over and we were about to go to sleep, he suddenly got up, wore his clothes told me to keep the door closed for a minute, till he went out and came back. Going straight to Middle Street, he knocked at the door of Doddammatte's house, woke up her husband and all the neighbours, shouted before the gathered crowd and narrated what Doddammatte had told his wife. And then began to pour insults, using all sorts of obscene words. "Yes it is true. Every evening I take to bed a different woman in my grove. So? What's it to you? Is she your daughter or your granddaughter? If you are raking it up and taunting, you old hag, you too must have been itching inside, must be in rut, dancing. Narasappayya, your husband, has grown old, and has started to sleep outside on the platform. So, that itching is causing your insides to jump about." People gathered there bowed down their heads listening to these incessant abuses. It seems then Narasappayya too started shouting and accusing his wife. After scaring the ghost out of Doddammatte with his obscene abuses, Manjayya came home and went off to sleep. He had rightly surmised – this incident would be round the village the next morning and no woman would dare raise this topic with his wife. And nobody raised this matter with me afterwards. In fact nobody even came for *arisina-kumkuma*. Are you listening bhaava?'

Satyappa said 'Yes. Of course, I'm listening.' Even as he said this, his mind was thinking about the behaviour of present day politicians who employed hooliganism to threaten or intimidate people. But he was also paying attention to what Savitri was saying. And he asked her, 'But didn't you have any suspicion? Didn't you feel like finding out the truth?'

'Won't I? I began to guess that he has in his blood this tendency of seeking pleasure outside the marital bed. Another suspicion started gnawing me. Why wasn't I pregnant yet? Was there any connection with his womanising and my pregnancy? He was thirty-four when we married and I was only seventeen. But he did not look so. Nobody could guess his age. He looked as young as a man of twenty-three or twenty-four. Even today he is the same. I don't know, if you have seen him recently. Anyway, I became curious to know what he had done before we got married and what mischief he had played. But whom could I ask about all these details? Again and again suspicion would raise its ugly head, however much I tried to console myself. Moreover, he would go to Channarayapattana and Hassan frequently to attend somebody's court work or business. This was another reason for my doubt.'

'Once he was away from the village for four days on some business. Is it not when we are alone that suspicions and doubts grow like devils? I decided to find out the truth at any cost. By that time, I knew how Manjayya had abused Doddammatte. Our maidservant Kempamma had informed me. Kempamma was a loyal servant. We gave her fifty rupees per year and free lodging and boarding along with saris and other clothes. She had to stay at our home and do all domestic chores. She was friendly with me and was affectionate also. It seems she was boiling inside seeing that her master did not give up his old habits even after marrying such a beautiful, intelligent daughter of a pious person. At the same time, she was careful that what happened to Puttanamma should not happen to her as well. She reported that her master had taught a lesson to Puttanamma who brought discord within families and talked in Manjayya's favour. But the unsaid implied something totally different. I keyed into that and professed intimacy. "You see Kempamma, when I look at you, I remember my dead mother. Who else is there to care for me except you?" I went near her, held her hand and said as if to a close friend. "Look here Kempamma, I swear on you I won't breathe about this to anybody. And I swear on God, under any circumstance I shall not tell Manjayya. I want to know the truth. It is rumoured my husband had many affairs before he married me and even now he continues with them. Not only Doddammatte, many people say so many things about him. Is it true? Please tell me."

'Kempamma did not open her mouth, except to say, "Why do you worry about what people say, Amma?" But I could not leave it at that. Again I insisted that we were like mother and daughter and there was heartfelt pain in my voice. To tell you the truth, who was there intimate to me, save Kempamma? Finally she said: "Yes, Amma, it is all true. My master had affairs not only in Bilikere, but in Channarayapattana and Hassan also. Even now he has those affairs. Whenever my master sees or meets a woman, the very first thought that comes to his mind is 'How can I net her? How should I possess her?' He is adept in this matter. Looking at the face of a woman, he knows what sort of a woman she is, as if he got hold of her pulse." Kempamma substantiated the incident at the hut in the grove. Further, she continued, "But this man, my master, never wastes money. If somebody asks for money, he gives it. But it is rumoured that women who sleep with him once and enjoy his skill and prowess in bed, come on their own and invite him without asking for any favour, let alone money. They say he has such cleverness of winning over minds." When Kempamma said so, my suspicion got stronger and I thought, did I offer my mind to him only bewitched by this art of his? I felt as if I had been stabbed in the back. I was overwhelmed with grief. My self-respect prevented me from sobbing.

'This information reached my insides and invaded my being. But I found it hard to digest. The whole night I could not get a wink of sleep. That bed on which both of us slept and were dreaming, caused disgust in my mind. I became so angry looking at those two long mirrors next to the bed that I felt like smashing them into pieces, for I thought they showed only deceit. I got up, went out of that room, spread a bed on the ground and slept there. Kempamma saw this and pitied me. The next morning, I called Kempamma and said, "You see, this time when your master returns home and goes to that hut in the grove, you must keep an eye on him and give me information. But she was alarmed and said, "You have sworn that you would never breathe about this to anyone."

"Well, again I'll place my hand in yours and swear. My name is Savitri. I am the daughter of Parameshwarayya. I'll catch my husband red-handed when he is with some other woman. Then the thief ought to hang down his head, caught while thieving. And then such a thief will give up thieving. Anyway, what has happened cannot be changed. At least in future, I want my husband for myself only. Is this wish wrong? Look Kempamma, you are a mother, you have a daughter like me. Once a year you go to visit her family. Tell me, is it wrong of me wanting to keep my husband to myself?" I said this, held her hand and once again told her, "I won't tell anybody. If you want, I'll take an oath," and said, "You must understand one thing, husbands with this habit are always afraid of their wives."

'The same evening he returned from Hassan. He brought me strong scented champak flowers, big red and yellow oranges, sweet smelling delicious Mysore pak, ribbon, powder box and gold-dotted glass bangles. His face had turned red and sweat was pouring down his face because of the bus travel, yet, as soon as he saw me, he smiled. He washed, freshened up and had his dinner. All the time, he was hinting with eyes and words. Then he held my hands, slipped the bangles on to my wrists, set champak flowers in my braid, smeared powder on my face, took me to the bedroom and showed my face to me in that big mirror. I too behaved as if I knew nothing. He urged me to give Kempamma her dinner and finish mine soon and come to the room. And then, really bhaava, I am telling you without any embarrassment or shyness, looking in the bright shining light of the bulb on the mirror, the pair of our bodies so near, to those whispers of love enveloping my whole body, I forgot myself. What Kempamma told me must be a lie. I thought he talks a little loosely and that is why people concoct all sorts of stories. I am not a girl of seventeen now. I have become a *preta*, a ghost who has crossed all ages and differences of male and female. He observed that my mind now and then wandered and asked 'Why?' I smiled and said, 'Won't I be bored if you leave me and go away for four days?' But afterwards when he went to sleep, I did not get sleep at all. The whole night I rolled about without getting a wink of sleep, and was confused in deciding the difference between truth and falsehood.

'The next day it was five in the evening. It was Friday, I remember it clearly. He had gone out to the fields. Kempamma who had gone to graze the cattle, rushed alone into the house. She stood in front of me and whispered, "Now you go into the grove, don't make a noise but stand near the hut and listen. The gate will be locked. Take this key. Put your hand in the wicket gate. Without making a sound, open the lock, enter, close the gate, lock it and go inside the grove. Whatever happens, you should not take my name. Swear on your mother," she said, held my hand, made me promise and went away swiftly. Do you understand bhaava? Now I come to the main part.' Savitri looked at his face.

Satyappa was taking in everything and prompted her, 'Yes I'm listening. You went into the grove.'

'My heart began to race. There was anxiety, excitement and a sort of rapture that I was going to catch the thief red-handed. I decided in a minute. I locked the door of my house, walked briskly, crossed the small wet field and waded through the sluice canal and reached the gate of the grove. I didn't wear chappals, I opened the lock with the key Kempamma had given me, noiselessly and with the same noiselessness, I closed the gate, locked it and went inside. I had just washed my face before Kempamma came to the house. But I did not put any cream or powder. I had not set the champaka flowers that he had brought yesterday, on my braid. So, I was confident, he would not get suspicions, by the scent of flowers or powder. I crossed the ridge and stood beside the hut. The door of the hut was closed. Cajoling and caressing seemed to be going on. The scent of champak flowers, he had brought from Hassan yesterday, was coming out of the hut. I felt, someone was stabbing my insides. A female voice from the hut wafted out, "Mysore pak of Hassan will be tastier than the Mysore pak prepared by Gandasi Banajiga Shetty in the fair of our village goddess. Oh you didn't taste it at all." 'This man was telling, "While you are here, why do I need Mysore-pak? You eat it. I was walking down the street in Hassan. I saw this sweet shop. Immediately I remembered my Malli. I thought, it does not matter even if I miss the bus, I must buy the sweet for her. The whole night I was dreaming of feeding you this sweet." She replied coyly, "Oh, if you say such things, I feel I don't know, how and what all …" "Oh, what all?" I heard the rustling sound of the reed mat. "Oh my god, don't hold so tight, I am breathless. Don't suffocate me, oh, please …!" I stood outside listening. The same sort of conjuring, casting a spell through clever words … perhaps there was the spell of body also. The power of conjuring a woman by praising her and winning her over. At home, he used cultured and refined language with me, but here, a coarse and rustic language. But the meaning and the method were the same. Now the male voice: "Hey, give it properly." And now female voice, "I'll give it whichever way you want. But will you promise me one thing?"' "What's it you slut, tell me what is it. Yes it is in such moments women extort promises" "You please hold my hand." "Ok, tell me" "You must not take any other women except me into this hut." "Hey, what do you mean? I have a wife at home." "When did I ask you not to be with your wife?" she continued. "That house is your wedded wife's. This hut is mine. No other woman must enter it." "What's it to you if any other woman comes?" There was silence for a while. Again, he asked, "Tell me, if any other woman comes here, what do you lose? Your mother's money?" "Look here Ayyanore, you will believe whether I tell you the truth or a lie. After I enjoyed it with you that day, I don't want to have any other man. Having tasted a sweet and juicy mango once, shall I hanker after sour mangoes?" "Wah, what a clever girl!" "Hey, I am not telling this for fun. Really, I swear on my mother. If you take any other woman, I feel someone rubbed chilly paste all over me."

'I felt giddy, just sat on the ground. A sob pressed my insides threatening to break out. I stuffed the edge of my sari into my mouth. I had come to catch the thief red-handed. I must not weep. Within two minutes I recovered from giddiness. I just sat there. Heads of coconut trees had turned flame-coloured in that twilight, but darkness was spreading on the ground. The dialogue within the hut. The period without any speech.' While Savitri was narrating this, she had completely forgotten the existence of her brother-in-law, sitting on the stone bench opposite her. She was just talking to herself, as if turning over the memories and the tongue was automatically uttering, "Oh my god, stop it, I can't, I can't bear," moaning of Malli, rustling of reed mat. Oh this is endless lewd game, the same he was playing with me, on the big cot. If it continues like this, perhaps it would get dark. If he goes towards the fields, he returns after seven thirty or eight in the evening. I thought of getting up and silently going back home. I may go out, lock the gate, without leaving any clues. I could visualise what would happen if I went back. He would come back about eight. There would be smiles, dinner, asking me oh so nicely to have my dinner too. Then he would enjoy the betel leaves that I give him and in the same way as here, he would continue the cajolery, foreplays and the game, until midnight, with the electric light on, on the cot, before the reflective mirrors. He creates in that mirror the drama of pure offering, without a slight hint of pollution, as if it was not contacted with ort. I felt a sort of retiring mood; although it was the creation in the mirror, it was there daily. There would be no quarrel, no battle. Anyway this hut is separate. And that house is separate. Nobody would enter into the house. He will not bring any woman into the house. It was only for a minute. Yes, only one minute. I remembered my decision of coming there. If the thief is caught red-handed, his boldness in thieving will disappear. Yes I must subdue this. Not only that, this hut too must be destroyed, burnt to ashes. Meanwhile again bits of dialogue was heard. "Oh Ayyanore, leave me, it is already dark leave me, I must go." "Well, go, have I tied you? You may go" "If I was tied with a long rope, I would have untied and gone away. But, when you have held me, even if I want to, can I loosen myself? If you want, I will come tomorrow afternoon itself and you may hold me until evening. Now, please, let me go." I pondered, if only I had brought a match-box with me, I could have set the hut ablaze along with the two of them inside and got up. In a little while, both of them will come out. The moment of catching them is nearing. Oh! my heart began thumping. Again giddiness, no, no, I should not allow it. Though the top of the coconut trees seemed burning like fire in the setting sun, all around and underneath was darkness. Silence. Silence all around. But inside the hut? Fie, I should not hear that sound. I felt disgusted. Nausea gripped me. I felt like retching. How could I catch the thief and the stolen thing in my state? But I didn't lose heart. The thief in this matter was more experienced, but to the family man it was the first. Yet I stood with determination, as if I was also a coconut tree, so that I must make them know that I had seen with my own eyes and I had known the truth. I felt they would just come out. I became bolder. I walked towards that hut and stood straight at the door of the hut just five steps away. Within two minutes the door was opened. Malli first came out. In the darkness, her features were not clearly seen. She was straightening her sari, saw me and asked. "Who is there?" He came out shouting arrogantly, "Who is it?" He recognised me and stood stunned for a moment. But only a moment, not more. Then he turned towards Malli who stood confused and said, "Why are you standing like a dumb idiot? Get out." She swiftly moved towards the fence near the water pit. Then he closed the door of the hut, came near me, as if nothing had happened and said, "Come on, let's go," and stood before me. I did not move. He waited for a minute and said, "If you feel like standing here, it's okay. I'm just asking you to come with me, because it is getting dark. Let's talk about this at home." Saying this he walked away, his manner clearly proclaiming, Come if you want, if not go to hell ... Darkness was spreading fast, so I followed him. He went near the grove gate, saw it was locked, waited till I reached there and said, "Open the lock with the key you have." I silently unlocked and slanted the door. He came out, closed the gate, took the key from me, locked and walked forward. While crossing the canal and walking on the ridge of the wet fields, he kept me in front, walking behind me as a guard and then walked along with me. If anybody had seen us walking like that on the road, they would have thought, the couple after finishing a happy stroll in the park were returning home.

'By the time we reached home, Kempamma had already milked the cows, and was putting the pot of milk at the door of the kitchen. I came inside and stood still in the hall. He called authoritatively. "Ai, Kempamma, come here." When she came he held her right shoulder in his left fist and slapped her cheeks, left and right. Grinding his teeth, he said, "Since I took you in as a servant, you have had no shortage of food or clothes. I've given you more money than was agreed. Whenever you visited your daughter, I have given you copra, jaggery, chillies, old clothes and what not. I have kept quiet, though I knew you were selling coconuts that had fallen off from the trees in my grove to Channabasappa's shop. And today you ingrate, you have committed this unforgivable crime. Get out of this village, this instant, bag and baggage and all or I'll finish you off!" He slapped her repeatedly. Giddy, Kempamma sank to the ground.

'He went away to the bedroom that had mirrors.

'For a little while silence enveloped the house. It was like that for about half an hour. Then suddenly I heard Kempamma loudly cursing me and crying. "You swore that you wouldn't whisper it to anybody. But what did you do? You went and told everything to your husband. You ungrateful slut. You will come to ruin. Your future life will be the proof of this deed. I am going out of your house in the darkness after evening lights have been lit. Very soon, you too will leave your house. Just like this." Saying so, she stomped out of the house. Though I wanted to tell her that I did not tell anything to my husband, I've not broken the promise I gave you, though I wanted to call her and desired to pacify her pain, my words got stuck in my throat. I don't know why it happened, whether it was the result of what I had witnessed or of his cruelty while beating Kempamma who was old enough to be his mother. I cannot understand even now, though I remember it.'

Savitri became silent, as if there was nothing more and as if she had said whatever she had to say. The sound of cleaning rice inside the house was intensifying the silence. Satyappa too, who was pondering over the problem, that is, how to ask Savitri to live with Manjayya after all this, did not want to probe further. Meanwhile Nagappa woke up and came there. He had come to urinate, and went towards the haystack in the backyard. He came back, went to the bathroom, washed his hands and feet and went to bed, leaving wet footprints behind. Looking at him, Savitri's mind that was till now in the detached state of an impartial witness came down to the normal state. Satyappa sat, thinking about the wound, bandaged in white cloth on the calf of Nagappa's right leg. As if to escape from the topic they were reflecting upon till now, Savitri said,

'You know, this Nagappa had gone out in the evening, don't you? He had gone to Manjayya's house, and spent two to three hours there, talking with him. He is the other chief witness who took oath in the court and said, Manjayya was with him in Tiptur on the night of Kanchi's murder. He agreed to give false evidence only after getting one thousand rupees from Manjayya.'

Satyappa said, 'I knew that, but I was not aware that Nagappa had gone to Manjayya's place this evening,' and picking up the threads of the previous topic asked, 'Yes, Kempamma left your place on that day itself. Did you not speak with him about this matter afterwards? Didn't you take him to task?'

'Oh, taking to task!?' Savitri withdrew her mind as if to recall and then said, 'I went into another room and threw myself on the mattress. He was alone in his bedroom. He did not demand dinner nor did I cook and serve. The whole night I was suffering pain. Courage to confront and question him disappeared. Oh, his cruelty in beating Kempamma! Born and brought up in this village, it was not rare for me to see people beating each other.

But, gripping Kempamma's right shoulder tightly, hitting her, who was, perhaps of his mother's age, that too repeatedly, that cruelty, no, it was not mere anger, it was the cruelty of a wild beast and that had caused horror in my mind. You see, I felt as if I was imprisoned as a prey of lust by a brutal king, as it is shown in the wizard's stories in films. Yes, only a man with such violence and cruelty is capable of committing murder. My mind began to feel guilty thinking that because of my mistake, Kempamma had to suffer beatings and leave our house. But actually I had not told him anything. Then how could he know, as unerringly as an arrow hitting bull's eye, that Kempamma had given me the hint? The grove gate had only one key. Did Kempamma have the other key? And did he know that? He asked me straight away, "Open the gate with the key you have." Perhaps he wanted to make sure it was Kempamma I had got the key from. Whom should I ask? Kempamma had left the place misunderstanding me. She thought I had broken my promise. This intensified my grief.

'And the next day Kempamma was not there. I had to attend to domestic chores like milking, sweeping, washing the front of house, drawing rangoli, cooking, etc. First I thought of not doing any of these tasks. He did not speak to me. As if towards fields, he left home. However, as I thought, I should not be at fault, I did every work. He came and had his breakfast. Stayed at home, finished lunch, put a towel on his shoulder, went away as if to work in the wet fields. Yes, that Malli had told him, she would come there afternoon itself and he could hold her till evening! I understood that he had gone to do so. I felt like going to the grove and checking after a little while, but I could not. I was disgusted and also thoroughly scared. Moreover, even when I did see them face to face, what did I do? And even today, suppose I go there, push open the door of the hut, rush inside and see that; fie, fie. What could I have done after seeing? I didn't know what to do, and just lay down, felt a little drowsy. But even before I could fall asleep, I woke up, startled. He came back by evening when it was time to light the lamps. I knew for certain he had gone there. I did not raise my head or look at his face. He washed his face and went into his bedroom. He came out at dinner time, ate what I served and again went to the room. I felt like crying, thinking, that room is his, there is no relation between me and that room. When I thought of sleeping in the separate room like the previous night, I felt like deciding this matter once and for all. I convinced myself that I am not a weak or feeble woman and entered his room. The door was not closed. A little hope arose thinking he has kept the door open for me. I gained courage to speak. I entered and just stood near the door. The big electric bulb was burning. I saw my image in the mirror, by the side of that bed. I could see his reflection also, as he lay on his bed. I began to boil with rage deep within. But somehow I controlled myself. When I stood like that for five minutes, he got up suddenly, took me by the hand, led me to the bed, made me sit down on it.

"How could you do what you did?" I asked. "What did I do?" He countered, like a lawyer without a trace of guilt. "What do you mean? Didn't you lie to me?" "About what have I lied to you? Tell me, what have I lied about? What is the lie I told you?"

'After fumbling for words, I said, "Having a wife at home to go with another, not only one other, with hundreds of women." "Suppose I go with a hundred women. Yet, how would it be a lie?"

"Don't you tell me every day, showing in this same mirror, there is no one so beautiful as you, this and that?"

"Well, that is true. Where is the lie in that? Yes, even now, I swear, there is no woman as beautiful as you in the whole world." Saying so he tried to take me in his arms and kiss me.'

'But I pushed him aside and asked. "Is it not a lie to say that there is no beauty like you and then carry on with other women?"

"No It is not like that. It only means that I went with a woman who was not as beautiful."

"Don't argue like a lawyer, cast off your lawyer coat. Why did you lie to me? Answer me."

"Look here, you remember correctly, think carefully and answer: had I ever told you, I would never look at any other woman except you?"

"Every day you were telling so."

"Oh, really!? In the very same words!?"

"It means the same when you say there is no woman like you."

"You see, you cannot and should not assume words of people, as you wish or like. Now, let's not beat around the bush. You know, on that day Puttanamma said something. When I was away from the village, that Kempi carried tales against me. Yesterday she gave the keys and sent you to the grove. Tomorrow another woman comes and tells another story. Today, you see, the matter should be finally decided. Since the day I have married you and brought you home, have I made you feel the lack of pleasure in bed? If any day you have felt so, tell me. It is my duty to satisfy you, not once or twice a day, even four times if you like. But once your stomach is fully satisfied, you have no right to prevent me feeding any other woman."'

'Only then I understood his words clearly. I felt disgusted to know, to what level, to what sort of calculation he has pulled down conjugal relationship. I asked, "Why did someone like you bother to get married?"

"Yes, I regret that. I made a mistake in getting married. If you want you may go back to your father's house. If not, or if you prefer, I'll build or engage a separate house and send you rice, pulses and anything you need. Or be happy in being my wife. I've already told you, I'll feed you as much as you want. But if you talk about or prevent me from carrying on with other woman, just remember what happened to Kempamma. Now, go and sleep in that other room. I'm not going to cajole you. If you come to this bed of your own free will, it is a pleasure for me. I want to sleep now." He said so, turned towards the wall with the mirror, covered himself and put off the bed light. I did not know what to speak or what to argue.

'Bhaava, I went to the other room and slept. What did I suffer then? Was it just pain? No, it was the pain of the whole foundation of my belief melting and sinking. Appa, Annayya, Attige, Doddammatte and many others had told me, warned me not to marry Manjayya. But I had created answers to all their objections and stubbornly married him. And now it was painful when I realised that my decision itself was an illusion. I stopped speaking with him, but I cooked and served him food and slept in another room. No change occurred in him. He neither regretted nor came to me and said sorry nor did he promise that he would not do such things again. I ruminated; if only he had promised so, I think I would have kept quiet! But why didn't he do that? Didn't he have a liking for family life? Or was it not in his nature to be faithful to one woman? Do this type of men naturally get that smile, facial features and speech which can win over any woman they come into contact with? I was ashamed to go back to my father's house in the same village. After all, I was the one who had praised Manjayya and said, I would lead him by the hand and reform him, I would build up my family. Not just that, I had fasted, not taking even a drop of water and had married him with such stubbornness. One day my annayya came to visit me. He asked me, "Why have you become so thin and dried up as a T.B. patient." Then I could not hold myself. I sobbed and sobbed. How was it possible not to share my sorrow? To get some consolation, I came to my father's house with my brother. After that my mind protested against my returning to that house. One day Annayya went to Manjayya's house, talked about these matters and asked him the reason for the discord between husband and wife. But, oh! how easily did that rascal tell such a lie! He said to my brother: "You see your younger sister is too proud of her beauty; she thinks she is the most beautiful woman in all the three worlds. Moreover you have pampered her like anything. She must have thought that she is beautiful and her husband should be like a slave, always begging and beseeching her saying, 'oh save me, protect me.' What man would suffer such insult? Moreover she always suspects me. Where or how can I get only male workers to work in the fields and grove? How is it possible if she insists that I should not have female workers and I should never talk with them?" he said. Then my brother said, "Look Manjayya I know everything. The whole village knows what you are. Is it not true that you sleep with Siddamma's daughter Malli and Naagi of the Other Street, and her sister, and still many more women in that hut in your grove? Tell me!" When my brother asked, it seems Manjayya unashamedly said, "I am ready to wear a garland of red oleanders and swear before the village goddess that it is a lie. But would you swear that it is true, before the same goddess, wearing the same red oleander garland?" How can my brother talk with such a fellow? My brother came back thinking that Manjayya is a rascal.'

By then Nagappa woke up once more and went past Satyappa and Savitri, reached the haystack in the backyard to relieve himself, came back to the bathroom, washed his hands and feet and went back to bed. Savitri and Satyappa sat there for a long time in the sort of silence that fills the mind when talk is ended or it has reached a certain stage. The sound of cleaning rice was also slowing down.

After a long while, Satyappa broke the silence and said, 'You see, my mind is thinking about an idea after Nagappa came out from his bed the first time. I am acquainted with Manjayya quite well. And I am well aware that it is difficult to know the truth by talking with him. Now, even a heinous fellow like him must have melted inside, looking at his father-in-law giving up his life for truth. Perhaps he must have realised his error. My first question is, will you go back to Manjayya and live with him, if he confesses his guilt to you and asks you to go back to him? And the second question is,' ... even before Satyappa could finish, Savitri, cut him short.

'If only my appa had not given up his life and if Manjayya had genuinely repented, perhaps, I might have agreed! But now, when Appa has punished himself by committing suicide for telling just one lie, even if this Manjayya happens to be the original Harishchandra himself, there is no relation between him and me. Please leave it. You said there was a second question, what is it?'

Satyappa asked, 'You said you were disgusted and felt sick of the cruelty of Manjayya when he hit Kempamma so wildly. Kanchi might be the worst thief, still, is murdering him a lesser cruelty? Manjayya might have beseeched your father and stated that now he was a changed man. But how did you consent to live again with him who had committed such a cruel deed? If you had not agreed, why would your father have stood in the witness box to commit perjury?'

Savitri felt trapped. Her face turned white, then crimson. Her eyes looked down, as if it was difficult to meet her brother-in-law's eye. Satyappa did not repeat his question. After a while, she said, 'It is not that I do not know the answer. I do know the real answer. But I have talked too much today. I feel ashamed to answer this. Please do not force me.' Saying thus, she kept quiet.

Some more time passed. Satyappa began to yawn. He looked at his watch. It was already half past one. He had walked fourteen miles in the morning, had started at dawn, so that he could reach Bilikere during the cool hours of the day. Savitri said, 'It is better you get some sleep bhaava,' and got up.

Nagappa was pondering why he was not getting proper sleep, two times he had to get up for relieving himself and there was no change in food. He thought, perhaps it was due to the sound of cleaning rice and pulses in the dining hall, but he felt that alone could not be the reason. Some business offer of Manjayya's haunted his mind. He was in a dilemma whether to accept Manjayya's offer or not. As per Nagappa's experience, so far, Manjayya had been an honest man. He spoke openly about any matter. On the night when he came to ask Nagappa to give evidence in his favour, Nagappa at once agreed and Manjayya had given him one thousand rupees, ten hundred rupee notes. However careful you are, some fake notes would be mixed, these days. That evening when Nagappa took two notes of hundred, gave it to Manjayya and said, 'Look here, I am not satisfied with these two. Will you replace them?' the very moment he took them inside, brought two new notes and gave Nagappa. There was no word of complaint, no second word. Yet Nagappa brooded whether he should agree to this deal or not. Of course, this was not a new proposal by Manjayya. He had proposed it when he came secretly in the dark midnight, to call Nagappa to give evidence. Nagappa thought Manjayya was a courageous fellow. If he was not confident of being acquitted in court, how could he have thought about this deal and proposed to me? Manjayya asked, 'How is it, copra from our place usually are sold to different wholesale warehouses. Why not to yours?'

Nagappa answered, 'You see people who sell to the wholesale warehouse have the territory marking tendency of dogs. They go to the places where they are used to. If people like you come forward and change their minds, they would sell to my warehouse also.'

'Brokerage is a bit difficult and risky.'

Nagappa said, 'You see, I'll never cut in the percentage to be given to the broker. Nagappa never goes back on his word, you know.'

'No. No, that is not the point I wanted to make. You tell me, is it not below my status, if I am a middleman? Let us do one thing. Let us make a deed of agreement that I am also a partner in your wholesale warehouse. Of course, all the legitimate management of business, signing the cheques and all such things will be purely in your authority. I'll look to it that the copra of all the surrounding villages will come to your warehouse only. If you agree to this deed, you see, I'll have a point to say that this warehouse belongs to me also. However, it is my responsibility to get you ten lakhs of copra from my side. There is no urgency, think over the matter.'

He made the same proposal this evening also. Nagappa brooded over the matter. If Manjayya manages to supply ten lakhs of goods, it would not be a great loss if a partnership of one anna is given. Yet, even if it is only a partnership of one anna, it is just breaking ownership and putting a portion in another's hand. As the saying goes, agricultural work should be in many hands while business should always be with one man. Why should there be written deeds or the like? Nagappa hit upon an idea. Let us tell the customers of these villages that Manjayya has equal partnership in business. Nagappa decided that he would make Manjayya agree to this. So, this point was decided. Manjayya said he would take Nagappa on the bicycle to see some prospective sellers in some villages. But Nagappa thought, it would be a good idea to let the customers come to his warehouse instead of he himself going to their doors. That would impress them. Anyway he decided to visit some of these customers who were trading with him from the beginning. In any case, there was nothing to do here, after *dharmodaka* and until the *Vaikunta*. So, he thought he could go alone hiring a bullock cart for three days. Only then, his mind found some rest.

After his business matters were decided, Nagappa began to think about the disorder of his son-in-law's house. He had firmly believed that after marrying off his daughter, it was not proper to poke his nose in the activities of her in-laws house. As such he had kept himself aloof. Was it not sheer foolishness to invite all the wayfarers and travellers and feed them daily in the name of *annadaana*? He thought, weren't there hotels for them and subtly hinted about this to his daughter. Nagappa had not done anything more than that. He believed in the common rule of 'you always reap what you sow'. He felt in his mind that to commit suicide by hanging for perjury in court was the incident, which was the height of stupidity not seen or heard anywhere in the world. But till now he had not mouthed this to anybody. His line of thought was: courts are there to demand for witness and evidence. We give witness to help our clients. As such there is no question of right or wrong in this. Nagappa wondered how it was possible that his daughter's family be set on track and he be called Dharmaraaya? Didn't Dharmaraaya too utter lies? It was not simply he said 'hatah kunjarah'. He went to king Viraata's court and said his name was Kankabhatta and he was a brahmin. Was it not a lie? He should have hidden in a cave and lived incognito. Thinking so, Nagappa remembered his *sambandhi's* madness and pitied him. He tried to find out flaws in Manjayya also. When you are married and have a wife, and are maintaining her, giving food and clothes, you should satisfy your body requirement there alone. If you go with this woman and that and spend money on her, how can you save? Moreover semen too is to be protected, saved as carefully as money. What wisdom is there in mere spending? After the death of his wife, Nagappa had not looked at any other woman, nor did he think of second marriage. He did not lose semen even by ejaculation in his dream. If he did not possess such a firm mind, how could he have earned so much of property and hoarded money? He thought of advising Manjayya regarding these matters. If he did not advise him being his wellwisher, what was the use? He decided to advise him this morning.

By the time Nagappa came home after *dharmodaka* ceremony and lunch was over, it was already four in the afternoon. More than seventy people had attended the ceremony and all of them left for their places. Nagappa hired a bullock cart, told his daughter that he would be back by eight or nine and went to visit Thimmappa Gowda of Kalenahalli, who was the customer of his warehouse from early days.

Satyappa, as he had decided earlier, went to visit Manjayya. Manjayya knew who had come and who else would come to attend the ceremony of his father-in-law. However, he had thought, this Mattikere Satyanarayana perhaps would not come on his own to visit him at home. Now, looking at this brother-in-law, Manjayya felt a sort of assurance as well as delight. Manjayya felt a rare pleasure in boasting about his exploits to his brother-in-law Satyappa and to create more logical and reasonable answers to moral and ethical objections that Satyappa would raise.

Manjayya welcomed Satyappa cheerfully. 'Oh! Annayya, please come in. It must be sixteen or seventeen years since you came to this village. Isn't it?'

Satyappa looked at the coat rack and asked, 'Oh what is it? You always used to wear black coats. And now there is a khakhi one too on the peg, how is it?'

Manjayya dusted the wooden chair in the shape of a sofa, as if to show his respect to Satyappa and said, 'Didn't you know, now I have become a contractor of the forest department?' Manjayya was a sort of dandy. He always wore a black serge coat, which was tailored only by Ghous Mohiuddin in Hassan. When he attended courts or offices on business, he would always wear a black cap. Otherwise his hair would be neatly combed. He wore broad collared, snow-white shirts with a set of shiny gold buttons. Three years ago, when one day, he entered this village in a khakhi coat, khakhi pants and heavy boots, people were surprised. They were anxious and scared, thinking whether the police department gave Manjayya any new power of authority or supervision. Manjayya would never try to ward off the anxiety people felt about him, though it was without reason. In fact he seemed to enjoy the sense of fear and mystery he had created. Who else would know the secret more clearly than him that, "no one offers even bael leaf to the deity that does not hiss." People began to be more scared and respectful towards Manjayya. Finally it was known that Manjayya's job did not have anything to do with the police department, but was concerned with the sandalwood department, that is, the department of forest conservation. People of Channarayapattana knew what was meant by a forest only by looking at its picture. How then can they be expected to understand about forests and conservation? So, everybody would call it something connected with sandalwood. In the capital city of this state which is hailed as sandalwood state, the government had established sandal oil factory. Sandalwood should be available to the factory at a cheap rate. So, all sandalwood plants wherever they grow – private lands, gardens, kitchen gardens in houses, garbage hills – they were considered government property. As per the order of the government, the owners of those particular lands were responsible to protect the plants. When the core of the tree ripens, when the oil can be extracted, the department officials cut the tree and take it away. They give only nominal price to the farmers. Even if a small branch is broken, the department officials may file a case against the owner of the land. It is well known to everybody what the officials with such authority can do. So every farmer tries to ward off this menace in the bud itself, by uprooting every plant of sandalwood in his land. People were earlier scared of the sandalwood department. But after Manjayya became the contractor, they were terrified. According to the rule, the Forester or the Range Officer's work was this – he had to decide whether the core of the tree was ripe and if it was suitable for cutting. And then he had to uproot the tree, take out the bark before the farmer and burn it there itself. He had to inform the weight of the wood to the farmer and then it would be stored in the district depot for sandalwood. The government would offer commission according to the weight of sandalwood. It is irrelevant here to know about the method of calculation and the money given by the government. But, what happened in the department of this taluk after the entry of Manjayya is relevant. This person without having any legal qualifications, becomes a lawyer, judge, even a high court justice, merely by wearing a black coat. What all would he become after wearing the khakhi coat of this sandalwood department? It was not known even to the district level officers of this department, whether khakhi dress was compulsory for the contractor. Should it be? Is there such a rule? Watchmen, guards, Forester, Range Officer, Assistant Conservator, Deputy Conservator, Conservator and other employees of the department wear their own brand of khakhi. If the contractor too wears khakhi, will it not be helpful for the growth of identity with the department? If Manjayya wore a black coat and moved closer to famous lawyers near the court, clients would get more and more scared of him and feel more respect for him. So, now Manjayya had started to keep with him two sets of dresses, a khakhi coat and a black coat whether he was going to Hassan or Channarayapattana, and would wear one of them as the situation demanded. The other one would be folded neatly, kept in the leather bag. He bought a new Raleigh cycle of khakhi colour and rode on it. The Range Officer of the department Appajappa, Forester Prabhuswamy, Guard Vishakantayya, Watchman Usmani and Manjayya would enter the villages on their bicycles in this order. First Watchman Usmani, Manjayya behind him, then Forester Prabhuswamy, the Guard Vishakantayya bringing up the rear.

Satyappa guessed what might be Manjayya's business as soon as he mentioned that it was the contract of the forest department. Satyappa knew that Manjayya would always choose new fields for his adventures and push himself into it. He expected to hear some new interesting matters related to this department and sat in the chair. But Manjayya did not broach upon that matter. He asked, 'Did *dharmodaka* ceremony go off well?'

Satyappa answered, 'Yes', and felt he had an opening for what he wanted to say.

But Manjayya continued, 'You see Annayya, I too had half a mind to come and if at all I had a little bit of merit of my good deeds, offer it to my dead father-in-law, so that it would facilitate his *preta* to track the trail of *paapa* and *punya* in the court of Yamadharma. But you would now be well aware that all people gathered there believe that he committed suicide as an atonement for the sin of lying to save that murderer Manjayya from being punished. I did not come there, for they may create a ruckus if this murderer Manjayya went there. They may think that the *dharmodaka* they offer will be polluted and become *paapodaka*, the water of sin. So, I did not come. It was not difficult for me to prove that I was innocent, what they thought was wrong. You see, Annayya, a man who tells the truth may stand alone. And there may be hundreds of people who have filled their minds with their speculations without having the knowledge of truth. If you unravel correctly and explain, only truth wins in the end. Is it not so Annayya? How many were the imperialist Englishmen? How did just one Gandhi make them open their eyes and realise their mistake? Was it not with the strength of truth? Really, I have been fed up with the talks about this. Let people think whatever they want. I am least bothered. Moreover, I was about to leave for Channarayapattana. If you had come half an hour later, you would have missed me.'

Satyappa remembered that this was Manjayya's style of speaking. But he had never in the past spoken about the philosophy of truth and falsehood with Satyappa. Such a situation had not come till now. He understood that the context itself was such that Manjayya talked in such a manner. Anyway Satyappa felt a little relieved, for he had an opening to broach the topic he wanted to speak about, and said, 'Well come on, sit down. Why are you standing? Now tell me what really happened.'

'Oh, I feel so relieved; you have come to me to learn the truth. You are my brother. But do not accept what I say because of the affection and regard you have towards me as your younger brother. If you really think that there is truth or a facet of truth in what I have done, only then accept what I say. If not, let us argue, discuss. Truth comes floating up while discussing, just like butter floats up while churning curds. Have not our forefathers realised the truth thus and preached it to the world?' Having said his piece, Manjayya went to the back door shouting loudly 'Puradamma'. When he heard the voice of the maidservant, he asked Satyappa, 'Annayya, would you prefer coffee or lime juice, we have lemons too.' And then told Puradamma to bring two cups of strong coffee, and sat in the chair near Satyappa and narrated in a soft voice.

'You see Annayya, there is nothing special or unusual about what happened. All the villagers would toil from morning till evening, raise saplings and cultivate coconut groves. But, then a thief who decides to live comfortably without working, breaks into someone or the other's grove each day and makes off with hundreds of ripe coconuts in each round. It had been going on since fifteen years. In the village there was not a man born who had the guts to catch him and break his legs so that he might never be able to climb trees and pluck coconuts. He started stealing from my grove as well. One night I lay waiting for him in my grove. I wanted to break his legs with my cudgel. But he had a sickle with him and threw it at me. You know that people who go about stealing or robbing would be prepared to kill if the situation demands it. Fortunately, I ducked. I had with me only a cudgel, no sword, no sickle not even a knife. When I had no intention at all of killing him, why should I carry all those weapons with me?

'I promise you, I had gone there with an intention of maiming one of his legs so that he is not able to climb trees hereafter. I mean to tell the truth only to you. Because you are the only one person who though wears khadi, do not wear a khadi cap after the death of Gandhi. All the others are khadi-cap-liars and cheats. As far as I know, Gandhi too did not wear a cap. Let me come to what happened in the grove. I think you have heard what a strong man that Kanchi was. When he began to brandish his sickle, I too started swinging my cudgel in self defence. You know, it was dense darkness. The cudgel hit his skull. He fell down. Thinking, why he fell down, I pulled his torch, switched it on, looked at what had happened, ran, brought cold water and sprinkled on him. Yet it was of no use. He died. Did I want all this? Murdering a man in my grove, where I spend time, moving there day and night and being haunted by his ghost? Oh! who needed all this? This is one part of the incident. Yes, the first chapter.

'Now begins the second chapter. If I had to be acquitted in the court, without being prosecuted, I had to weave a story and does that story flash in my head? I borrowed thousands and thousands, paid to my advocate and was saved from being convicted, yes only for my mistake of guarding my grove. And that's how, you see Annayya, I am fortunate enough to be sitting and talking with you today. To help me to win in court, my father-in-law, yours too, agreed to give evidence in my favour and he came. But what did he say in the witness box? He stood there and blabbered something that caused me more harm, created problem in my release. If the first witness in favour of the accused lets you down like this, what would be the fate of the case. However, by the grace of god, I won. But I don't know what thoughts churned in his mind. He hanged himself ten days before. People with angst or enmity towards me say that Parameshwarayya hanged himself because of Manjayya. Anyway, thank god, they have not concocted a story, it was Manjayya who hanged his father-in-law. If they had done so, I would have again had to run around the court.

'You see Annayya, I did not force maava to come to the court or insist he ought to give evidence in favour of me. You do know what sort of relation he had with me. Anyway it is true, I did ask him to come and give evidence in court. It is also true that if he would give evidence in favour of me, I would bring back his daughter to my home and live with her, although it would be inconvenient for me and I do not like it. But I did never compel him that he ought to come. Coming to court, giving evidence that created opposite feelings towards me in the mind of the judge and then blame me that I did not fall at his daughter's feet and beg her forgiveness? Do you think it is proper or just? Let us leave it. Why did he hang himself ? Really it is to me a great mystery that cannot be unravelled. He had nurtured a delusion that he was a chunk of truth or truth incarnate. Four or five persons have questioned him. "Oh what sir, could a person like you tell lies?" I have received reports that it is true. Two persons, who had asked him this question, have told me. According to my analysis, unable to bear this shattering of delusion, he has committed suicide. They who do not keep contact with the world, do not talk to people, are not open to criticism and are great idealists, such people would have a violent delusion about themselves. If it is pricked ever so slightly, they feel as if the universe has ended and thus create another delusion for themselves. You see, Annayya, please correct me if I am wrong. Oh Puradamma, is the coffee ready?' Manjayya loudly demanded.

Puradamma, about fifty, brought two large glasses of coffee on a platter, held before those two. After they took the glasses she went in silently. While drinking coffee, Manjayya said, 'Come on, let us go to the grove. I'll show you from where the thief entered and what I did and all other things.'

Satyappa got excited, as he was keen on knowing what actually had happened. Manjayya stuck a sickle into his waistband. Satyappa understood that it was to pluck tender coconuts, that too for that special 'Gangaapaani' variety. While walking along with Manjayya on the street, Satyappa felt an embarrassment and seemed to shrink within himself. Only very old people in this village could identify Satyappa, that too in the Brahmin Street. He was not known to any other people. Yet this fear was squeezing him inside: what might people think if they saw Parameshwarayya's eldest son-in-law walking very intimately with his brother-in-law, who was the cause of Parameshwarayya's death and that too when Satyappa had come to attend ceremonies of his dead father-in-law! What if either Ramakrishna or Ganesha saw him walking with Manjayya! Though once this thought occurred to him, Satyappa remembered he had said to Savitri, the previous night, that he would meet Manjayya and try to reform him. Yes he had come to meet Manjayya, he was firm and determined. And he knew that he had to pass the Shiva temple and the banyan tree to go to Manjayya's grove. When Manjayya came near the banyan tree opposite Shiva temple, he paused and said, 'See, look at that first branch, he hanged himself from it. He climbed up, tied the rope to the branch and to his neck and jumped down. That too in a public place where the whole village passes through in the morning. He has selected the best place. It is right in front of the temple and there is good publicity to his act.' Manjayya explained and stood there until Satyappa stared at the tree and the branch. Only after Satyappa started, Manjayya stepped forward. Holding their chappals in their hands, they waded through the canal of sluice of the tank, walked on the ridge of wet fields and came to the grove gate. Then Manjayya walked explaining what happened on that night; where did he stand, how did Kanchi enter into the grove, the dense darkness where it seemed as if the eyes were tied with a cloth, and how the light of Kanchi's long torch climbed coconut trees, showed the bunch and vanished. Satyappa's mind was attentive. Yesterday night Savitri had described how she had slanted this same grove gate, locked it and in the same hour she went near the hut and had known about her husband's extra-marital affair and had heard the erotic speech of the pair. This was being concretised in Satyappa's mind. Manjayya went on describing that his intention was only to break the leg of the thief so that he would never be able to climb trees, but he did not let on his real intention – that he actually wanted to remove Kanchi forever. After they came near the hut, Manjayya went to the third gangaapaani tree. This was not the first time Satyappa had come to this grove. He precisely remembered which were the gangaapaani trees here and he could identify them also. Moreover Manjayya himself had described to Satyappa what were his exploits in the hut. Satyappa knew that too. When Manjayya walked towards the coconut trees, Satyappa came to the hut, opened the door, went inside and looked around. Yes, there was that soft reed mat. If you stepped on it, there would be a rustling sound. Dry flowers, pieces of broken bangles, hairpins and other things were scattered there. What Savitri told was the story that had happened seventeen years before. Does Manjayya still use this hut? Or what about his house? Or doesn't he give anybody lenience of getting into the house? When Satyappa was brooding upon this, he heard the sound of tender coconuts falling from the tree. One, two, three, four, five, six. Then Satyappa came out of the hut, fixed the wire hook to the door and came to the place where he had stood. Manjayya was always like that. He would persuade you to drink three or four tender coconuts. Even monkeys do not know the ripeness of coconuts as Manjayya. They sat talking in the grove till seven in the evening. While returning, when they reached the banyan tree opposite the Shiva temple, Satyappa told Manjayya that he would come again tomorrow and turned towards the street of his brother-in-law's house. Actually he had no work to do in the ceremony. He too knew that himself and all other relatives had come only to console and comfort the grieving kith and kin of the deceased.

Satyappa went to bed and slept well for some time. But by eleven in the night, he was awake. Today also the maidservants were cleaning rice and pulses. He felt that it was not merely because of that noise he woke up. Though there was silence outside, sleep had abruptly stopped and he was awake, perhaps it was due to his habit of getting up and going for a nightly round of his coconut grove.

Nagappa had slept on his bed. Satyappa got up and went to relieve himself, either because he could not get sleep or because he had drunk the water of three tender-coconuts in the evening. Savitri had not asked him to talk with her today. Perhaps she must be sleeping. But her face showed that she spent a sleepless night or she had no other work to do and as there was no other way to ward off physical tiredness, she must be lying down. Thinking thus, Satyappa too went to bed. In a short while, he was aware of a change inside him. By the same time yesterday night, when he heard Savitri's narration in the cowshed, Satyappa's mind was immensely filled with the idea of moral-ethical fall of Manjayya. He was not deceiving only his wife Savitri. It had been seventeen years since Savitri left him, even after that he continued his exploits. He himself had told about them to Satyappa. After listening to these, Satyappa had advised him and preached some moral standards also. But Manjayya had never frowned and had never got angry. Once or twice he said, at a ripe old age, when my strength fails me, I swear I would accept not just celibacy but sanyasa itself. Satyappa now decided not to let Manjayya get away with his clever talks and somehow drive home his own point to Manjayya by words that could bind him to a moral life. Manjayya should be made to realise that it was not mere sensual pleasure in his limitless, wayward, lecherous life that he was living but it was the life of falsehood that completely enveloped his conscience, the *saakshi* within. Such was the light of conscience that was in the act of maava's suicide. If it would be possible for him to make that light flash even for a moment in Manjayya's mind, Satyappa felt that he would have achieved something. While listening to Savitri the previous night, these thoughts were clear in his mind. With that very intention, he visited Manjayya this evening. But when he met Manjayya and listened to what he said, Satyappa felt he had lost his power to think and act independently and wanted to accept whatever Manjayya said. Satyappa could not know if what Manjayya told was either true or false. Only god and Manjayya knew if Manjayya had gone into his grove to kill the thief or to cripple him. For the time being, except Manjayya, there was no one else to inform us about that incident. Whoever may be the thief, is it not natural that the owner sets out to break the thief's leg? So, Manjayya's words should be believed. Moreover, Kanchi was a deep rooted menace of a thief and he had got night-ownership of all the groves of this village since many years. Subbanna and Hiriyannayya also said this. Everybody agrees. If so, what was wrong in Manjayya's deciding to cripple Kanchi? Yes, he was perfectly within his rights to stop Kanchi. When Satyappa thought 'what was wrong?' he remembered his coconut grove in his village. Here in this village there was only one thief, Kanchi by name. But in his village it was not precisely known how many thieves were there who would push into the groves on dark nights. Even from the banjaara settlement, at a distance of three miles, thieves would enter the groves. Satyappa, who slept on the platform in front of his house, would wake up at least twice in a night and patrol his grove and was able to save eighty percent of the coconut yields. If we did not accept that the remaining twenty percent did not belong to us, there was no peace of mind. Whenever the theft of coconuts was known, Satyappa had wished many a times to break the leg of those bastards, if he could catch them. They should not be able either to climb the tree or to carry off the bunches. But he felt sad that he could not make use of the cudgel, the companion in guarding the grove even on a single day to cripple the thief! He would simply hit the ground with the cudgel, make a noise, switch on his torch, wave it around the grove and thus warn and frighten the thief away who was at some distance. Satyappa felt that this was the result of his cowardice. If only he was as courageous as Manjayya! He would have hidden silently so that not even the sound of his breathing could be heard. The thief would certainly have his sickle and would be ready to kill, if necessary ... if creeping from behind, he could hit the thief on his legs and on his skull. No, Manjayya was courageous, Satyappa was not. Not a single person was brave in his village. He felt everyone was like the owners of groves in this Bilikere. Even today he was feeling so. Satyappa was in a dilemma. If this was the situation, should Manjayya be prosecuted and punished by the court or should he be acquitted? Without committing perjury and without false arguments, how can he be released? Now Satyappa began to feel that there was no meaning in Parameshwarayya's suicide. People who came to offer *dharmodaka* at noon, appreciated the indomitable truthfulness of the deceased, but at the same time they praised Manjayya's courage also. If only he had some control over his lechery, such a valiant person is not found in our taluk. People who pointed out this also appreciated Manjayya.

The whole episode seemed strange and paradoxical to Satyappa. Oh! what a dream of ideal society he had visualised, when he jumped into Gandhian ways of life and freedom struggle thirty three years back! Though young, he was not unaware of the disorders and ills of society. Mahatma Gandhi had thought out solutions for all that. He had met the Mahatma and talked with him three times. Only after reading his books, articles, the *Harijan* magazine, he had requested the Mahatma for permission to meet him. When he heard directly from the Mahatma whatever he had written and preached and lectured, those ideas would reach the heart as complete truth. Satyappa would never feel like asking any sub-questions. Instead, he would get the impetus to spread and propagate it in his village and in his whole province and to try to make people practise that truth in their lives. He would return from Sabarmati ashram and engage in his social service. Even then Satyappa did not directly enter into politics. He had firmly believed that, unless upliftment of villages was achieved, success of independence would never be complete; and how much he had struggled with firm faith that independence had to be achieved starting from the upliftment of villages? From village to village he had gone round, to spread ideas and principles of the Mahatma. He said, villagers do not get justice from the foreign pattern of courts. Courts in distant towns needed documents, deeds, letters, witnesses, statements, cross examinations, lawyers and judges and what justice may villagers get from this system? Satyappa worked hard to establish these village courts. Most of the rules prevalent in government were the relics of foreign rule. Instead of confusion to the villagers of getting documents and stamp-papers, which are not easily available to them, not to forget the bundles of currency notes to be given to the lawyers in instalments, which was difficult for them to provide. Instead, both the concerned parties should sit together to settle their dispute in the presence of the village jury and consent to their verdict. There are chances of facts being concealed or twisted in courts. But it is not possible to conceal facts from villagers. It is enough if the jury is loyal to law and justice. This system ran successfully for two or three years in seven or eight villages. But as soon as our country became independent, all these experiments were completely lost. 'Gandhi-yuga' was ended and the age of people's representatives started. Then started the difference of opinion between Satyappa and the representatives. Naturally people favoured the representatives. Caste politics spread in all villages. Because of party politics, village courts started to twist and trample down justice with insolence. Then Satyappa himself told the victims of injustice to go to courts in Tiptur, Tumkur and Bangalore. Satyappa's mind began to ruminate the details of how the age of downfall started and grew in his region, and how his village courts, khadi cloth, 'Ramayana and Mahabharata' in Yakshagaana form, fell down, bent their knees before town markets, lawyer's points, hotel snacks, Binny and Khatau shirts, Finley dhoti and tent cinemas. Nevertheless, Satyappa sent his son to school, cooked, looked after domestic chores and his fields, and was working for the upliftment and self- administration of villages. He brooded – when did my zest and enthusiasm finally sink? He clearly remembered, it was not when the Mahatma died. Satyappa was under the delusion that Mahatma's spirit would be immortal in this country. He had built an optimistic world that the great spirit confined in the small frame of the body while living, would cast off its limitations and permeate on its own through the length and breadth of the country, and had spoken with emotion in the condolence meetings he had arranged. When he was collecting shares to open the coir factory with the cooperation of villagers, his intention was not limited to collecting shares, but, to develop faith in people about how the upliftment of villages was possible with mutual cooperation, by practically showing them through demonstration. When a people's representative favoured a Marwadi to start some kind of factory, Satyappa publicly explained economical damages and disasters this would cause to villages. The people's representative warned Satyappa not to come in his way. Satyappa was not scared and continued his work of bringing awareness of the dangers involved in such factories owned by businessmen. When the representative slapped Satyappa in front of the public, not a single person supported him. The representative asked, 'Oh, you were saying, there should be no police, is it not? Now, to complain against me, would you go to the police station or will you call for that village court?' Satyappa tried to gather the village court, but none came forward. He then went to the police station and got this answer, 'Oh, Satyappa sir, somehow you have to forget it. What action can we take against representatives of people?' It was then that Satyappa's enthusiasm waned. His mind got a severe shock when he was beaten publicly. He believed that a person following the doctrine of non-violence should not react violently to such violence. Now he thought, if he had slapped me four times, I could have at least slapped him once. But that was not the reason for Satyappa's dejection. The reason for his grief was that the social attitude which needed to follow the path of non-violence had vanished so early. He thought of starting satyagraha, of fasting before the house of that representative. But he felt, fasts that were successful in that age when the British ruled, and when the Mahatma was alive, would not be successful now. Meanwhile, Satyappa's son Ramachandra joined a hostel in Tiptur to study in high school and he insisted on getting only terylene and nylon clothes. Satyappa could not argue with or convince his son and failed to mend him.

When Satyappa went out to relieve himself the second time the maidservants were filling the rice into bags. He felt he would get sleep. He remembered this was the time, he would go to bed after going round the grove once and began to yawn. At the same time a question arose in his mind, 'What punishment could have been given to a person like Kanchi, if he was brought before village courts? If he had asked, "provide me also fifty coconut saplings and one and a quarter acre of land, sir, I will never step into another's grove." what could the courts have done? There was no place at all in the village and they who have acres and acres of land won't give up even an inch of land. That *bhoodanayagna* of Vinobhaji was totally defeated and deceased. The village court did not have any enforcing power to punish Kanchi. So, as nothing else flashed, he began to yawn incessantly. Another question arose in his mind – If the Mahatma was there when the representative beat me, or if he had beaten the Mahatma himself, what would have been the reaction of the Mahatma? No answer followed, instead he fell asleep.

Satyappa woke up again. It was already two thirty, early in the morning. It was the time of starting the second round of watching the grove. Now there was no noise of cleaning rice. The whole house was silent. He did not feel like relieving himself. Lying on his back in the darkness, when he remembered the thoughts that flashed in his mind during the first period of sleep, suddenly an idea formed in his mind. If the light that originates in the inner being of an individual permeates into the outer world also, that may be considered the truth. That light instantly realises what should be done in any critical context. The Mahatma was such a one. Parameshwarayya also had achieved that maturity. But to people like us it would be mere darkness, when such a critical or unfamiliar situation occurs. Satyappa felt this was the suitable description of reality, but his mind became restless and he could not get back to sleep again.

Ramachandra who had told that he would be able to come only on the day of *Vaikunta*, came the previous day itself on his green Raleigh bicycle to attend *maasika* ritual by eleven in the morning. He left on his bicycle immediately after lunch, for his wife, children and mother-in-law who had come to take care of her nursing daughter were alone. Moreover, after Satyappa left for Bilikere, daily three to four bunches of coconuts were stolen. Satyappa had told that he would return after the *Vaikunta* and the next day's ritual. But it seemed Ramachandra had come only to command or warn his father to return immediately. Moreover Satyappa's staying in Bilikere would give another chance to the thieves. Ramachandra felt he had attended the ceremony of grandfather one day and got the prasaada, and he did not think it necessary to stay for another day. Besides, his uncle Ramakrishna was always a silent man. For aunt Sukanya, he had only respect. He was a little friendly with his mother's sister Savitri. She insisted four times to leave after *Vaikunta*. But he exhibited his anxiety each time, 'No there is nobody at home Savitri Chikkamma, there are only those two women.' As anyone who came to attend such ceremony should not take leave or say goodbye, Ramachandra left immediately after lunch.

Satyappa felt agitated to hear about so much of theft in his grove. The idea of catching the thieves and breaking their legs recurred. But this time he felt ashamed at his thought. Nevertheless, all who stole did not do it because they had to starve having no other means for livelihood. Satyappa remembered there were people who took to stealing for many purposes such as cinemas, to taste hotel snacks of towns, for cycles and wrist watches and to have a comfortable life without labouring as also the jealousy that hinders them to see and be happy at the sweat and toil of people that had blossomed as coconuts. Satyappa thought, in a village where there was unity among people such thefts did not happen, because thieves were afraid of their legs being broken. He felt a little comforted by thinking that the unity of the village was also a form of village court. But he was really displeased with his son Ramachandra, Ramachandra's wife and her mother. This Ramachandra was a young man of twenty-six, a father of two children. Couldn't he go to the grove, holding a torch and cudgel, at least once in the night? Thieves knew that Satyappa was not in the village and they also knew that this Ramachandra was a coward. That is why they had entered the grove every night. Ramachandra had another excuse. That the two women in the house would be scared if he left them alone and went to the grove in the night. Satyappa thought, theft would happen if he stayed in his village also. As such, why shouldn't he have stayed on this night? It is his grandfather's ceremony, that too such a great and noble being. Ramachandra has become a slave to his mother-in-law's affection and wife's endearment. He dances to their tunes. Thinking so, Satyappa became uneasy, yet he decided to leave Bilikere as soon as the *Vaikunta-samaaraadhana* was over.

It was four in the afternoon when the *Vaikunta-samaaraadhana* lunch got over. It was not possible to walk fourteen miles home, that too in the dark night, on the road full of hillocks and bushes. As it was a road not so frequently used, not only in darkness, even in the moonlight, there was the possibility of missing the road. So, Subbannayya suggested, 'It is better to go to Channarayapattana by bus, even if it is a roundabout way. From there, there is one bus to Tiptur. If you get down at Mattikere Gate, you can walk five miles straight on even if it is dark, and reach your village. I think that would be a wise thing to do. Satyappa held his bag, rushed to the bus-stand and got into the bus to Channarayapattana but the bus broke down on the way. By the time he reached Channarayapattana, the last bus to Tiptur had already left. So he was forced to stay there.

Channarayapattana was not his taluk, nor was it the place he used to come for business. When he made enquiries in the bus stand, he was told to go to the Travellers Bungalow, where he could hire a room for a night's stay. The charges were also reasonable. He moved towards the Traveller's Bungalow.

When he reached the bungalow, Manjayya stood right in front of it. Satyappa had not seen him for two days in Bilikere. Of course, he did not have anything to talk with him, for, in the previous meeting of two days, Satyappa had spoken whatever he wanted to. Now Manjayya had a jeep with a government number plate, one officer and two ordinary officers under him. Behind them were some lower class workers, who wore khaki uniforms. Looking at the style and colour of the uniform, Satyappa understood that they belonged to the Forest Department. Higher officers spoke English with their subordinates. Manjayya stood there, radiating an aura of obedience clearly establishing that he belonged completely to that circle, at the same time exuding the feeling of freedom, a freedom a servant would not have or exhibit. After a little while, when the higher officer turned towards him, Manjayya said, 'Yes sir, I'll surely come and see you sir, I've understood everything sir, I have understood sir.' The higher officer sat in the front seat of the jeep. The other two got into the back and the driver started the jeep. When the jeep began moving, Manjayya again went near the jeep, folded his hands as if combining acquaintance, familiarity and obedience.

Then he came to Satyappa and asked, 'Oh, how is it Annayya that you are here? I was not in the village yesterday and the day before. I was wondering whether you would come to visit me. I had some work and started urgently. I think you left that place after *Vaikunta*.'

'Yes, I came here to catch the bus to Tiptur but it had already left. I was told that I could go to the Traveller's Bungalow for a night's stay. Would it be possible for you to get me a room?'

'Oh, by all means, let us get you a room. If you cannot get a room, what's the use of this government building, this Traveller's Bungalow?'

The remaining four persons of the department came near Manjayya and said that it was already late for the bus and they would leave. Manjayya gave a ten rupee note to the person who was standing in front and said, 'Go, have some coffee. I shall meet you in Hassan.' They left. Meanwhile the caretaker of the Traveller's Bungalow came and asked Manjayya, 'Are you vacating the room sir?' Manjayya said, 'No. Look here, give him a room,' pointing towards Satyappa. The caretaker said, 'Not possible sir, there is the minister's programme. All rooms are reserved in advance.'

Manjayya said, 'Don't say no. He is my brother.'

The caretaker was unmoved. 'If he happens to be your brother, you may accommodate him in your room itself. Anyway there are two cots there aren't they?' By then Manjayya signalled with his eyes. The caretaker, catching the cue, said, 'What can I do sir? If the minister or any other officer comes at midnight, I'll be in trouble. You too will have to move into the room in the old building. There is only that one room vacant.'

Satyappa said,: 'Don't bother, I don't mind sleeping outside on the platform or in the veranda.' Manjayya felt a little embarrassed.

'Don't worry Annayya, we can adjust. Come with me,' he picked up Satyappa's bag. The caretaker took them to the room in the old building. There were two beds there. Manjayya told the caretaker to bring some food by seven.

Lying down on the bed, Satyappa asked, 'How is it, there are so many officers of the Department of Forest here?' Manjayya answered, 'You see, there is a corrupt Range Officer. Shouldn't there be a limit to taking bribe and sucking the blood of people? Hundreds of farmers, especially sandalwood growers from the whole taluk who were not able to bear his harassment, wrote a petition against him. So, the Assistant Conservator personally came, conducted an enquiry and suspended him until further enquiry. So, I had to start suddenly from Bilikere, day before yesterday evening.'

Satyappa reflected – if hundred farmers have complained against a corrupt officer, what sort of scoundrel must he be? He was pleased to know about the awareness that had sprung up among the peasants. Again his mind was engaged in the idea of Gandhi's village upliftment. Taking bribe is the same as thieving. Perhaps the farmers who oppose this sort of theft might be the people who do not give opportunity for thieving in their villages. While Satyappa was brooding over this question, the caretaker brought two plates full of meals. Satyappa said he did not want food and he only needed sleep. Manjayya insisted, 'No, no, we should not waste food, I forgot that you had *Vaikunta-samaaraadhana* lunch and ordered two meals. Well, I'll share some rice from your plate. Come on, have some food.'

After meals, Manjayya asked, 'Annayya, there is a good film "Lust and Love," running in the theatre close-by. Are you interested?'

'Oh no, I stopped seeing films long back.'

'Annayya, you must watch this movie. It doesn't matter even if you're tired, I'll get you a ticket.' Manjayya insisted. Satyappa flatly refused. After bargaining for some time, Manjayya came to the point, 'Annayya, why should I hide things from you? I thought of getting you a separate room. That damned minister fixes his programme today itself. If the minister comes with his retinue, not a single room will be available. What I want to say is, I have arranged for a girl-friend to come and meet me here. She will not stay the whole night. Even if I keep her for the whole night, you see, it is not my age to make use of her. By the time you come back from the film, I'll send her back, or if you want you too can enjoy her. I'll tell her so, leave for the film and stay out for a couple of hours.'

Satyappa felt disgusted. He was caught in a quandary! He thought of moving to a hotel and spending the night there, whatever kind of a hotel it might be, even if it was infested with bedbugs it would do. By then the caretaker came and took away the plates. Manjayya looked twice at his wrist watch. Silence permeated everywhere. But, despite the net of darkness spread outside, his auditory zone alerted his ears to the sound of footsteps outside. Manjayya got up and opened the door. After half a minute, he said, 'Come in' and a woman came in. She wore a silk sari with shining lace and a blouse of puffed sleeves. She had liberally applied cosmetics, wore earrings and eardrops of white stone. The build of her body exuded strength and youth. Manjayya asked her to sit down. Feigning coyness, she sat in the chair. Manjayya said, 'Please look at her Annayya, if you want, you may enjoy her first or you may watch the film and come back. I won't send her back until you return. Moreover, I myself will have to escort her, as it would be dark. Your name is Chandrika, isn't it?' The girl smiled. Satyappa was embarrassed, he picked up his bag and started out. But Manjayya came forward, snatched the bag from Satyappa's hand and said, 'No, you must watch the film and come back here. If you take your bag and walk away, I don't know what sort of sin I have to suffer, for sending you away, for not providing a place for a virtuous person like you to rest the night. The film is really good Annayya, watch it and come back.' Manjayya pressed a five rupee note into the pocket of Satyappa, though he strongly protested.

Satyappa had given up the habit of watching films thirty years back. While studying in high school, he used to watch films. After that, till now, perhaps he might have watched some ten or fifteen films. Today it was the worst. He felt tired, sleepy and began yawning. He chose a back seat leaned on to it, and watched the film in a state of drowsiness. The film was replete with scenes where a young girl was provoking the hero. Her dress, swaying large hips, swell of breasts, dancing, all were intoxicating. Satyappa thought perhaps, for Manjayya this must be 'very good, really good'. By the time the interval was over, the film continued in the same manner. Now it was the scene of that girl taking bath. Again the provoking build of body. There was not much difference in detail. However, when the film ended it was past midnight, 1:30 am to be precise. The question was, should he go to the Traveller's Bungalow? If not, where could he sleep? Satyappa's bag containing his dhoti and shawl was with Manjayya. So he walked towards the Bungalow. Everywhere silence reigned. There were many trees and small plants near the rooms in the back of the old building. Manjayya's room was also dark. Hearing Satyappa's footsteps, the light was switched on. Before Satyappa knocked, the door was opened. The girl sat on the cot. The same silk sari of lace border and blouse of puffed sleeves. She had set right her clothes as if ready to leave after everything was over. She smiled looking at Satyappa. She sent a message to him through her eyes. Manjayya asked, 'How was the film Annayya?' Satyappa answered listlessly, 'Oh, it was so-so.'

Manjayya said, 'Well know something Annayya, what's so special about these sluts who emote? I've seen them all. It's all make-up. Why see all those actresses when our Chandrika is here? You see, she too is a drama artist. Raise your eyes, look at her once and say who is more beautiful. This Chandrika or those girls who were shown in the bathing scene?'

Looking at Satyappa's khadi clothes, Chandrika asked Manjayya, 'Is your friend an M.L.A?'

Manjayya said mischievously, 'Oh, What? Are you already in love with him? Annayya, you stay with her comfortably in this room. The minister did not come. I'll move to another room and sleep.' When Manjayya hinted this, Satyappa was shocked and asked angrily, 'What do you take me for?'

'Hey, why are you getting so angry ? If you don't want, say no. If not today, some other day. We have to wait for the right time for everything,' said Manjayya, waited for five minutes, wore his chappals and said, 'OK. Please stay here. I will see her home and be back!'

Chandrika stood up, turned towards Satyappa and asked as if they were acquaintances, 'Shall I take leave of you then?' and on the pretext of taking her chappals from under the cot on which Satyappa sat, brushed her shoulder slightly against him. Manjayya, as if for the last time, said, 'Annayya, please don't hesitate, don't feel shy. Don't be embarrassed if you don't have any money on you. You are my guest. You decide. Even now you may have her the whole night.' He persisted. 'Don't you understand that it is as good as insulting the woman if you refuse even after my beseeching you in such a manner?' He then went out. The girl too flashed an alluring look towards Satyappa, wore her chappals and went out. The sound of their chappals gradually became fainter and fainter in the dark silence outside.

Satyappa went to the cot, took out the shawl from his bag, lay down and wrapped the shawl around himself. The light was still on. The door was not bolted from inside. Manjayya, however, would come back within ten or fifteen minutes. Why should he again get up to open the door? Thinking so, he lay down but could not sleep as he had already had a snooze while watching the film. A question rose in his mind, 'Why does Manjayya indulge in such a thing having a wife like Savitri? Then his thoughts turned towards his own life. His wife Seetha was really a beautiful woman. That was also one of the reasons for Satyappa's remaining unmarried the second time, after her death. He thought, after losing such a wife, what sort of marriage would that be? Manjayya's wife Savitri was more beautiful than her elder sister Seetha, Satyappa reflected after seeing her for four days now in Bilikere. As she is

Parameshwarayya's daughter, you need not bother about her conduct. Even if there were some faults, Manjayya had the power to rectify them. Yet, this malaise was in his blood. Satyappa felt disgust, he was wearied. He decided to talk with Manjayya without any obligation or mincing matters, when Manjayya came back. He felt something strange. Once he took a deep breath he became aware of the smell of cigarette pervading the room.

Within fifteen minutes, Manjayya came back. He lit another cigarette, put out the light and lay down. He asked Satyappa, 'Can't you sleep?' Satyappa answered, 'No, I'm not feeling sleepy.' And then Manjayya spoke as if to justify something to himself. 'Oh, well, how can you get sleep after refusing such a beautiful girl like Chandrika and sending her away? You see, Annayya, these desires and temptations should be satisfied as and when they occur. You should learn to give in to them. If not they create turbulence when they remain suppressed. You see, it's like this: when you suffer from cold and your nose is blocked, what would you do? You simply blow out the mucus. Do you let the mucus remain inside?'

'Well, Manjayya, is this the only habit you have or are there others? I mean, do you take drinks?'

When Manjayya pulled in the smoke in the dark room, the burning tip of his cigarette started glowing. The thick smell of cigarette reached Satyappa's nostrils. 'No, Annayya, I have only this bad habit of smoking. I'm thinking of giving it up. This Manjayya, you know, doesn't have any other bad habit. Alcohol is the destroyer of all pleasure. Once after tasting it, getting the experience, I gave it up the very same day and have never touched it hence. Oh, What sort of experience that was!

'There was a house in Hassan, which kept four or five girls who were lovely and beautiful. Especially one among them, I've never seen that build of body in my whole life, Annayya. There was a separate room and everything was very clean. There was a mosquito net too. Yes I chose her, she was maybe nineteen or twenty. You know, Annayya, how smart a talker she was? Even a script-writer for films will not be able to write such interesting conversations. After talking a while, she asked me, 'Do you take drinks?' I countered: 'Do you?' She said, 'If you like, I can accompany you, if not, even I don't want.' Really Annayya she talked very entertainingly. We both had a few drinks. I don't remember what I did or didn't. When I woke up it was daybreak and she had left. The whole day I thought about it and came to the conclusion: alcohol is really bad. It destroys control over your mind. When you take it, you cannot enjoy any other pleasure. Some people say you get stimulation by taking it in small quantities. But only people who lack power say so. I can argue with illustration before any doctor or any lawyer that alcohol diminishes vigour. That was the last. I won't touch alcohol in this life. I've not met again with such a girl. Because of that damned drink, I could not enjoy her.'

Manjayya was not joking. His voice and expression had sincere regret and a truthful visage. Satyappa felt that though the topic was trivial, the openness and concern in Manjayya's words developed a trust towards him. Though Satyappa could not help smiling at the example Manjayya cited to prove drinking was bad, he suppressed it. Satyappa's decision to raise Savitri's issue and bind Manjayya had awakened. But he did not know how to start the subject. He knew well that Manjayya was an expert in twisting words and somehow he would wriggle out of the subject. So Satyappa questioned him in a roundabout manner, very casually. 'You see, Manjayya, you sleep with so many women. Won't they get pregnant?'

'They may. It is their responsibility.'

'Okay, that's alright. Suppose a women gets pregnant and gives birth to a child. What happens to that child? It grows up according to the status of the profession of those people, scabies, boils, lice, mucus and no education at all. No future for the child.

Wouldn't you feel sad to look at such a child? Have you ever thought about it?'

As though Manjayya had kept his answer ready, he said immediately, 'You see, Annayya, if we start to think along the lines you are talking, nobody can ever enjoy happiness. As your Gandhi said, one has to tie the loin cloth tightly. If not, you will start preaching Dharmashastras like aashramadharma, family man's life, etc. Do you know what happened once? Once I went to Hubli ... you know that Kattepura that is near your place? I went to buy a big iron safe for that Boregowda. In the centre of Hubli city, there was a big red light area. Just like you described now. Children were playing outside. I went into a house. I paid money to the woman there. She told me to give money to the boy playing outside. I asked, "Why should I give money to him?" She said. "Is he not your son?" She was just twenty or twenty-two. I said. "How could he be my son?" and she countered, "Why not? You yourself might have come to me before. Why couldn't he have been born to you?" Oh, a clever woman. But I said, "Look here, this is the first time I have come to Hubli. Suppose he was born to me, then too he would never have been my son. Because when we mated, I have given you money and you have taken it, so the business is over." That woman was struck dumb. I threw a one-rupee coin at that boy. He brought it to his mother gave it to her and went out to play. Those people would have trained their children in that manner. After that she closed the door and came near me.'

Satyappa felt it was not possible to convince Manjayya with any argument. Moreover he knew very well that it was impossible to change anybody by argument alone. Such people may change only when a person like Gandhiji or a Mahatma who has achieved spiritual heights would influence them. But where can we find such mahatmas now? Thinking thus, Satyappa shook himself, not knowing how to start talking to Manjayya. He felt Manjayya was a mean scoundrel and cruel. But in spite of all this, Satyappa's mind had not hardened towards him. It was not possible for his mind to completely reject and throw away Manjayya. He twice changed sides, wondering why he could not understand Manjayya's ways. He questioned himself whether it was for this reason that Manjayya had killed a coconut-thief like Kanchi?

Manjayya asked, 'Are you unable to sleep?'

Satyappa spoke half heartedly, 'Yes and no.'

Manjayya said, 'Me too, I am not able to sleep. I shouldn't have sent away Chandrika. I should have kept her for the whole night. Even now I can go and bring her back. But when I went to send her away, we walked like two people coming out of the film. Now, if I go alone, dogs bark, and people who are sleeping on the platforms outside their houses will be woken up. Okay Annayya let us leave it at that. I'll ask you a question. Will you answer me honestly? Your wife died when you were still young. You say since that day you have not touched any woman and you have not slept with any. I believe your words. But what did you achieve by this? You have got your son married off. That could have been done even if you had slept with any other woman. What relation does it have with your son's marriage? What else did you achieve except being called by some people that Satyanarayanappa is a true follower of Mahatma Gandhi? By the way, don't you feel that urge or desire even once? What nonsense are all this, controlling food like sanyasis, drying the body so that no desire should be born, oh what are all these Annayya? Please listen to me. This Manjayya has never betrayed friendship. I won't tell anybody. I swear, my hand on yours, solemnly. Whether it is tomorrow or any other day, you come to me. It may be anywhere, Bilikere, Channarayapattana, Hassan or in any other town. I'll call for you a woman of your choice, secretly, unknown to any other person. You enjoy her and if you don't like it, it is okay. You weigh yourself before that night and again you weigh yourself after that night. Really your weight will not have decreased. Actually it would increase. You simply live in a world of illusion, imagining what is not there. It is just like taking food without salt, isn't?' Manjayya said and kept quiet. Satyappa was listening. In a short while Satyappa slipped off into sleep and began to snore softly. It was his habit to get up twice during nights and make rounds in his grove, come back, sleep again and rise at daybreak. Here also he woke up early in the morning, thought of going directly to the bus station and catching the first bus in the direction of Tiptur. He thought, as the night was spent here, there was no point in reaching the village early at day time, for the duty of watching the grove would begin at night only. So, Satyappa decided to talk openly with Manjayya and tell him what he had to say. Manjayya was still sleeping. Satyappa did not want to wake him up for in the state of disturbed sleep, Manjayya might not listen calmly to what he had to say. So, he opened the door silently, walked two miles on Holenarasipura road and came back. Manjayya was still sleeping. Satyappa went into the bathroom, bathed in cold water, washed his undergarments and wrung them tightly. By the time he came out of the bathroom, Manjayya was awake. Meanwhile the watchman brought two cups of coffee. Manjayya told him to bring breakfast and went into the bathroom, finished shaving his face and bathing urgently and came out. Two big plates with kesari bhat, masala dosa, uppittu and uddina vada along with milk were brought. While they were having their breakfast, Satyappa said, 'Look here Manjayya, it is seventeen years since you left Savitri, from then ...'

Manjayya intervened sharply, 'Wait, I did not leave her. She walked out on me.'

'Okay. Let's put it that way. You see Manjayya, nothing is decided by mere arguments. You had told me once, long ago that she was vain and proud of her beauty; it was not possible to live with her. But nobody forsakes his wife only for that reason and no wife leaves her husband for that reason alone. What I want to say to you is, the suicide of our father-in-law must cause each one of us to introspect. It has really perturbed me. At least in this context, if you call back Savitri, stop your habit of sleeping with other women and become a worthy householder, the suicide of maava will not have gone waste. Really, Manjayya, I would like to plead with you on this matter. That is why I broached this subject with Savitri. Nobody's mind would continue in the same way after utter loneliness of seventeen years, boredom and anger. My intention was to know her mind and then talk with you. She said, "Perhaps, I would have accepted this proposal if Appa had not committed suicide! Now, Appa's suicide has revealed the clear truth. The very thought of living with him is abhorrent. Leave it bhaava, let it be, please."

'Well, let's not talk about that at present. Moreover man need not achieve everything only by being a family man. In several matters, family is really a hindrance to higher achievement. Anyway, you must start to introspect at least a little because of maava's suicide. It is enough if awareness of what is permanent and what is transient is awakened, then change occurs on its own. Yesterday it was only the fourteenth day since maava died, yet you slept with Chandrika here. If so .....'

'No, no. The second day after maava died, as also the day you visited me. When I climbed on the coconut tree to pluck tender coconuts and you opened the door of the hut in my grove and examined it, on that day I had enjoyed a woman called Siddi in my hut in the grove. Do you know, what a tight build of body she had? Oh this Chandrika was only showy with those glittering clothes. Siddi did not wear that sort of clothes, true. But as the clothes are removed, while being united, I tell you, Chandrika is no match for Siddi.' Manjayya interjected.

'I know that while I climbed the tree to pluck tender coconuts, you opened the door, went inside the hut and scrutinised it.' Hearing his words, Satyappa felt his moral fortitude sinking from within. It was true that he had entered the hut and had examined without the knowledge of Manjayya. Which meant it was a stealthy act. How could he know it so accurately? He was climbing a tree which was far off, how could he know about my scrutiny? Has he the power of Chitraguptas within him? When Satyappa thought so, he began to sweat inside. His shorts and banian were clinging to him.

Manjayya continued, 'If only Parameshwarayya had introspected, he would not have committed suicide. After the death of his wife, he completely turned his mind inwards, to what you people say, to that *aatma* that is within. And then he was only forty. However, if he was ashamed to search for new sort of pleasures like me, at least if he had married again, you see, this disease of always turning and looking inside could have been averted. You see Annayya, what solution other than suicide is there to those who have supported their life on strict celibacy? It is the same with you also. When your wife died, you were exactly twenty-eight and a half years of age. You opted for celibacy because your Gandhi recommended it. Okay, you need not have married, but what an amount of grass you could have got if you went on grazing! You did not do anything. What did you achieve? Only selfishness. You got your son married off, gave away everything to him and are working like an unpaid servant in his house. What else did you do? There is neither fulfilment of vows nor enjoyment of pleasure. Though there may be vows if you unravel it, you will see that it is all false. Listen to me, Annayya, any man who enjoys this pleasure abundantly will be generous. A man who practises celibacy and sticks to it will become hard inside. That is why I am telling you. You return to your village and think about it calmly. You come in search of me any day you feel this desire within you. You have seen Chandrika yesterday night. I'll fix you a girl more youthful, more beautiful than her, by looking at whom your youth of twenty-two will return. And that girl will offer herself to you with supreme faith. I'll not tell this to anybody. I swear on you. Manjayya has never broken his promise with anybody regarding this matter. And you understand another matter. Friends who share this will never betray one another. Well, kesari bhat won't be tasty once it gets cold. Eat it while it is hot.' he concluded, erupting into founts of laughter.

When Satyappa started, Manjayya packed his bag also. He took out from the peg, the khaki coat of the Forest Department, folded it and put it in his leather bag. He took out the lawyer's black coat from the bag and wore it. He called the caretaker, gave tips of ten rupees along with the room rent and the cost for food and snacks. He then went to the bus station holding his leather bag. Though Satyappa refused, Manjayya got a ticket for Mattikere Gate and forcefully gave it to Satyappa and said, 'Please keep visiting my place. What will you do sitting at one place only.' And then, brought his face near Satyappa's ear and whispered, 'I told you all this because I care for you. There is no compulsion that you must do it. You see, I consider my brother-in-law as my own elder brother. So I've spoken to you openly.'

Kalenahalli Thimmappa Gowda was the only person who could be compared with Parameshwarayya. He was of Parameshwarayya's age and was as pious as him, but not silent like Parameshwarayya. Thimmappa Gowda liked good conversation, but he never talked either flippantly or rashly. While conversing with people of his own age or with youngsters, he would crack jokes.

Parameshwarayya did not have any addiction, but Thimmappa Gowda always had to have betel leaves and tobacco with him. He did not approve of cutting the bunches wholly from coconut trees. He believed that if tender coconuts were plucked, the tree would wither, and if you use ripe coconuts fallen from the tree it would not hurt the tree. But after the thefts had increased, he had agreed to pluck ripe fruits directly from the tree, saying that it is kaliyuga. Though the accounts of the warehouse were in his name, he had handed over agricultural business to his sons.

Not that he had not committed any mistakes in life for which he had to regret. But he consoled himself that they were not done intentionally. As he did it believing it to be the truth, those deeds could not be considered sins. It was Thimmappa Gowda who proposed the alliance of Sukanya and Ramakrishna. Parameshwarayya always had respected the opinion of Thimmappa Gowda and consented to this marriage. Even after the marriage,

Parameshwarayya had consoled Thimmappa Gowda, 'You see, Thimmappa. You did not lie to us intentionally, after knowing the facts or truth. You suggested this alliance with the intention that we must get a good daughter-in-law and that Ramakrishna gets a good wife. Moreover, what has happened now? It is enough if a virtuous girl comes to our house as daughter-in-law. Why should we bother about her father's nature?' Thimmappa Gowda always sold his copra to the warehouse of S. Nagappa and Co., since the day the coconut trees in his grove began to yield fruit on a large scale. His business had run with only Nagappa from the beginning to date for Nagappa maintained accounts scrupulously, his wholesale weighing scales were never faulty and the rate of interest for loans was also fair. Looking at Nagappa's clothes and style of living, Thimmappa Gowda had thought it was his simplicity. Nagappa's wife was dead and he had only one daughter. Thimmappa Gowda strongly recommended Nagappa's daughter to Parameshwarayya's son, with the good intention that the whole property of Nagappa would pass on subsequently to these people, if this alliance came through. Even now, after going to Tiptur once in a year with cartloads of copra, he would come to Parameshwarayya's house, have a talk with Sukanya for a while and would report about the health of her father.

After the funeral rituals, the *Vaikunta* and the *kaimande* of Parameshwarayya were over, Savitri also returned to Channarayapattana. Ganesha went back to Hassan, for he did not want to miss his classes. Ramakrishna, who had gone to Holenarasipura to immerse the ashes of his father, brought a big bundle of Vedanta books from 'Adhyatma Prakashana'. After his work in the fields and the grove, he would be engaged in reading them, sitting in the grove. Earlier, he used to stay at home after lunch, until evening. Now after his father's death, the duty of guarding the grove had also fallen on Ramakrishna. One afternoon, around four, Thimmappa Gowda came to Ramakrishna's house. He had come immediately, once he got to know about the suicide of Parameshwarayya and had his lunch on the day of *Vaikunta*. But on both these occasions, he could not talk to Sukanya. Today, she was alone at home and was happy to see Thimmappa Gowda. She spread a mat for him. Looking at Thimmappa Gowda, Sukanya would feel as if someone from her father's town, Tiptur, had come on a visit. Thimmappa Gowda praised Parameshwarayya wholeheartedly and said,

'You see Sukanyavva, Parameshwarayya is a god-like man. Such a person will not take birth in our region hereafter.' He added, 'Look here Sukanyavva, I came here to tell you something. But, I don't know the nuances of dharma and I am not sure if I should share it with you or not. You tell me what I should do,' he said, pulling a long face.

'How can I tell you, when you yourself are not sure, Gowdare. Anyway, you have come walking so far, why do you hesitate? Please feel free to tell me whatever it is,' Sukanya said and sat down facing him, leaning on the pillar a few feet away.

'Your appaji is getting old. His mind too is a bit so, so.'

Sukanya zeroed in. 'Did he say something about us?'

'I thought I should not tell you. But I cannot keep it to myself either.'

'Please tell me Gowdare. Why should you hide matters from me?'

'Well you know how his mind works. He came to attend the funeral ceremony of your father-in-law and you are aware that he stayed here for four or five days. During his stay, he has gone round the surrounding villages with an intention of buying coconut groves, if a good bargain was available. Let him purchase, it is his money and if he buys anything with it, what is wrong? But that is not what I wanted to tell you about. He had visited our house also. You know, he is very calculative and meticulous in keeping accounts. Didn't you leave your son there to study for three years? It seems your appaji has written in a log book the account of how much has been spent on your son. How much of rice, how much of pulses, on which days vegetable like brinjal was bought, how much oil for seasoning, soaps for bathing and washing clothes, how many books, etc. Your son had to borrow books for studies and your appaji would let him borrow only two books at a time. Only after he finished and returned those, could he borrow two more. To return them on time, your son would have to read them even after midnight. And the lights would be on. The rise in electricity bill because of this was noted. Everything, a pie to pie account has been maintained by him. From the day you sent your son, to date, he has kept accounts of every rupee, anna and paisa along with interest. He mentioned some amount Sukanyavva. Listening to this, I felt bile rising up and could not concentrate on what he was telling. If not, I would have remembered and told you the exact amount. He said it was 2300 and something or 2400 or so. Isn't this madness?' Thimmappa Gowda laughed.

But Sukanya did not feel like laughing. She knew that her father maintained accounts, when she left her son for three years in her father's house. She thought that it was as per his habit of writing and keeping account of everything. But when she knew that her father had told this even to the clients of the warehouse, she felt sad and angry. She asked, 'Gowdare, did Appaji, merely tell you this or did he ask you to tell us as well?'

Thimmappa Gowda couldn't grasp the subtle difference immediately. Did Nagappa just tell him or did he send a message across through him? He thought for a moment and said, 'Well, you know, he did not specifically mention, "you go and tell them this." But if he has told me all this in such detail, is it not his wish or at least his idea that I should convey it to you?' He paused for a while. 'This began to prick inside me, really, Sukanyavva. This house and this family has been providing daily *annadaana* since the period of the great ancestors of Parameshwarayya. Now Ramakrishnayya too is continuing the same. I felt angry, for now he has to feel indebted to somebody because he left his son in their house for three years, eat their food.' After sometime Thimmappa Gowda said, 'I don't know why he wants to acquire more property. Your appaji asked me, "Thimmappa is there any coconut grove for sale in your place? If you know of any, please let me know. I want to purchase it." Then I said, "Look, Nagappa what is the use of investing in property at my place? You buy lands in Bilikere. At least, your daughter will enjoy it. When I said so, your appaji did not speak about it again." Thimmappa Gowda opened his pouch of betel leaves, tobacco and lime. He held a betel nut between his still strong teeth and started smearing lime on the betel leaves.

'Wait a minute, have some coffee first before you start chewing betel leaves,' Sukanya said and went inside. She was burning all over with humiliation and rage. It was not only because of her father's words and attitude, but also because it was she who had insisted on sending Ganesha to study at his grandfather's place. Though there was a high school in Bilikere, it was she who had started saying that it was a village school, classes would not be held regularly, etc. Ramakrishna had said, if so, let us send Ganesha to Channarayapattana. Savitri is there and she will take care of him. But Sukanya could not voice out her principal objection and said instead, 'I feel it will be difficult for a woman to control a boy. Moreover he is bound to take more liberties with his aunt. If we leave him in Tiptur at his grandfather's house, he will get strict care and the school will also be good.' When Ramakrishna said, 'If your father has not asked us to send the boy to study there, why should we leave our son in his house?' Sukanya struggled to find the right answer. She remembered that after their marriage,

Ramakrishna had not visited his father-in-law's house, not even once. When Sukanya went to her father's house, uninvited, Ramakrishna had not accompanied her. Nagappa too had never invited his son-in-law. But to date, Ramakrishna had never spoken sarcastically about her father. When she remembered this, she felt scared of her proposal, but she could not leave that matter and the next day she again broached the subject. 'Don't we have any right to leave him in his grandfather's house? Ganesha has passed his examination. If my father had known that the high school of this village is not good, he would have certainly written to send Ganesha there. You see, some people speak openly and some keep their opinion inside. Like you, he is also silent by nature. But I know he loves his grandson very much.'

Ramakrishna did not speak. Sukanya thought he had agreed to the proposal. But even before she spoke, he said, 'Let him be in Channarayapattana. Ganesha is an adolescent. By leaving him there, if he acquires his grandfather's nature, our son may become a stranger to the tradition of our family. Let him study in Channarayapattana itself.'

It took her a couple of minutes to understand his words. Once digested, she felt tongue-tied. She felt angry, for her husband, who had never spoken a word about her father's nature, had hinted at it today. The whole day she was silent. By evening she realised that Ramakrishna did not mean to disparage or slander her father. Yes, by leaving our son with him, what if he too cultivates his grandfather's qualities? She too felt scared, but found consolation after thinking over the whole night. Ganesha resembles his paternal grandfather in his looks. His nature would not change wherever we keep him. Anyway, if the boy learns to be a little thrifty and to cut his coat according to the cloth, what is the harm? Moreover what bad habit did her father have? Beedi, cigarette, gambling, drinking, women – no, he had no such habits. Then, why should he be disparaged? The next morning, again she opened the topic with her husband, shed tears, cried loudly and spoke scathing words, 'Yes, I did not give birth to him, did not suckle him, I did not bring him up. He is completely your son. I need not say anything concerning his education. If you alienate him from his grandfather, you will feel happy.' It was the first time, since her marriage, she had argued and protested with tears, before her husband. Ramakrishna said, 'If that is what you think and feel, I have nothing more to say. Please do as you wish.' Then he called Ganesha, asked him in front of her. 'Look here son, your mother says the High School in this place is not good. You know your aunt studied in this school only and she studied well. Now, it is true this school's standards have gone down. I want to know, whether you would wish to stay with your atte in Channarayapattana and attend to your studies or would you prefer to stay with your grandfather in Tiptur and study. Tell me.' Sukanya had planned to first get her husband to agree and then tackle her son. But she had been thwarted by Ramakrishna's asking Ganesha before Sukanya had got him around to her viewpoint. Her son at once blurted out, 'I'll stay with Atte in Channarayapattana!' Her husband said, 'Did you hear what he said,' and went towards the fields. As a last recourse, she became obstinate, shed tears and said angrily, 'You, father and son, have ganged up together to make me look a fool, a useless woman.' Giving in to her tantrums, Ganesha agreed to study in Tiptur.

After getting the school certificate and other documents from the school, Sukanya left with Ganesha in a bullock cart along with Honna and his wife Boravva to Tiptur, as there was no direct bus service then from Bilikere to Tiptur. Ramakrishna did not go with them. She had prepared sufficient quantity of rice flakes, parched ragi flour, kodubale and tambittu for their journey and for her father's house. It was a journey of twenty miles. When she went into the house, there was neither a piece of jaggery nor a spoon of sugar. Not even a fist of rice was there. In a tin, there was half seer of dal and a basket plastered with cowdung contained five to six seers of ragi flour. Her father was a diabetic. The doctor had advised him not to eat rice, potato, jaggery, banana, mango, melon and any other thing which had sugar content. He had to eat wheat or ragi. Wheat was not grown here. It was grown in the regions of North India and was expensive as it had to be transported from there. But ragi was grown locally and was cheap. So, her father used to eat ragi roti and ragi-balls only.

Sukanya took her father inside and told him, 'You see Appa, you are alone here. At our place, teaching standards are low in that school. Ganesha will never be a burden to you. But somehow, he does not like ragi. From the very beginning he is like that. Not that he is proud or anything. But he can cook ragi-balls as soft as ripe bananas. He prepares rotis very well. He knows how to make soft-swelling rotis. You leave the responsibility of cooking to him. He will wash your clothes and do the shopping too. He is honest, never steals or lies even for a single pie. He will do his work quietly and will be company for you.'

She thus decided to leave Ganesha there. Next day, she prepared some sambar and rasam powder. The following day, early in the morning she started back in the same bullock cart. Before she left she called Ganesha to the backyard, held his hand and took an oath from him. 'Look here son, you must serve your *thatha* with devotion and take good care of him. You should never argue with him. Don't go roaming with useless rakes. You must study well and get a first class.'

The coconut leaf that Sukanya had lighted and held to boil water for coffee, was blazing and the steam from the water was slowly rising. Her memory was bringing up all past incidents before her mind more speedily than that blazing fire.

Ganesha stayed in his grandfather's house for just three years till he completed his schooling. When he was to be admitted to college, he was adamant and insisted: 'Look here Amma, if you force me to stay at *thatha's* house, I'll run away from home,' and joined a college in Hassan.

When he had come home for Navaratri holidays, after a four-month stay at his *thatha's* house in Tiptur, he was silent and morose as if he was angry with her. When she asked him, 'Why are you so quiet?' he retorted, 'What is there to speak about?' When she had insisted, he changed the topic and said, 'That school is very good.' When she enquired about his *thatha* his answer was cryptic, 'He's fine.' Sukanya asked, 'Doesn't he love you? Except you, his grandson, who else is there for him?' Ganesha said, 'Don't you know it all?' and went out on the pretext of drawing water from the well. When he was to leave for Tiptur after holidays, he put rice flakes, parched ragi flour and sambar powder in the bullock cart, then came near her and said, 'Amma, we have to buy rice from the market. If you have paddy from our wet-land, put four quintals of paddy in the cart. Carrying it is not a problem.' Sukanya thought her son was acting too big for his boots. She scolded him, 'Look, Ganesha it is okay if you take parched flour, rice flakes and such things. If you take rice along, what would your *thatha* think?' Ganesha got into the cart without another word.

When he came home next during summer holidays, he said, 'You see Amma, when I had come here for Navaratri holidays I had asked you to send four quintals of paddy with me and you made a surly face. You did not understand why I asked you.'

She looked at her son's face. She felt he had grown mature, had become very subtle for his age. She did not ask him the reason immediately. Naturally, the meaning flashed to her, that perhaps the grandfather must be taunting the grandson, for serving him rice. It was not surprising if he had said so. She need not have tested his nature afresh. But if there was something like that, this boy should ignore it and keep quiet, as if he knew nothing. If he could have such subtlety of understanding his *thatha's* words, why doesn't he have the same subtlety to know his mother's intentions? Sukanya felt like asking her son. 'What did your *thatha* say? Tell me frankly.' She was afraid that if she gave her son an opportunity to speak, she would have to agree to his leaving Tiptur. So, she kept quiet. Ganesha waited for his mother to start speaking. Seeing her silent he could not contain himself and blurted out, 'You see Amma, I cannot touch rice at all. *Thatha* says he has to buy rice only for my sake, same with sugar and jaggery. He says, 'You don't like to clean your teeth with charcoal powder. So I have to buy toothpowder for your sake. Do you know how much I have to spend for you in a month? You see Amma, he keeps saying this again and again. What else could I do, except asking you to send paddy?'

Sukanya did not speak. It is difficult for water to gush out when the sluice of the tank is closed. But once the floodgates are opened water gushes out into the canal. Likewise, Ganesha spoke out everything he had kept locked in his mind. Thatha would ask him to buy only two kilos of rice at a time; that is, he would throw one rupee before the boy and ask him to buy rice for it or he would say. 'Look here, come with me to the warehouse. I will buy it for you.' The boy had to go with a bag in hand behind his *thatha*. His *thatha* would examine four or five varieties of rice in Panchaksharappa's shop and select the cheapest variety and tell him to put it inside the bag. Only two kilos at a time. Once that rice was over, again the boy had to tell his grandfather, with utter mortification. The boy felt disgusted to eat the cheapest rice. But the grandfather did not make any distinction. He used to select ragi which he ate in the same manner, two kilos of the cheapest variety of ragi at a time. His two kilos of ragi would be enough for six to seven days. But Ganesha's rice would finish within four days. He would die a thousand deaths inside before saying, 'We need to buy rice.' Then grandfather would comment, 'Oh, what did you do? Did you waste that rice? Did you allow the rats to eat it? Had you closed the lid of the tin properly?' It was the same with pulses too. He did not use soap while bathing. He used to rub his body with a smooth quartz stone and remove dirt from his body. Ganesha used soap while bathing. His grandfather constantly advised him about economy. Ganesha said, 'Amma, the expenses of rice, pulses and soap should at least be equal to the work I do for him – sweeping and mopping his house, washing his clothes and cooking for him, but still this advice of economy. What happens in the end to the bundles of notes he saves? Amma, it is really a torture to live in that house. It is such a torture that I feel like running away. Oh! why have you imprisoned me there?' Ganesha repeated what his *thatha* used to say, 'Look here Ganesha, even if you throw stones into a river, you must count them before throwing. If not, will a man prosper? You are my grandson. I don't object to what you eat. But, you write the accounts, then you will know how much I have to spend per month because you are staying here.' It was not a casual comment or one made in anger. Now and then he would ask his grandson to bring the account-book. He would often question whether the boy was writing accounts or not. He could never get sleep until he wrote the day's expenses in his thick diary kept in the locked wooden almirah fixed on the wall. Sukanya remembered, not only now, it was so when she was a little girl. If one coconut was broken for preparing curry, the other half was to be kept for the next day. Grandfather would ask 'How much did the salt cost?' He would say 'Four annas.' 'Where is the remaining money.' 'I've kept it inside the niche, fifty paise, because I also brought a matchbox for twenty five paise.' 'Oh a match box? Wait, let me check!' He would search in his diary and say, 'Look here Ganesha, you had bought a matchbox on the fifth, that is ten days back, it contained forty sticks, why do you simply waste matchsticks? You may use one matchstick to light the stove in the bathroom and may bring fire from it to the kitchen stove to prepare breakfast and lunch. Then one matchstick for evening. That means, one box should last for twenty days shouldn't it?' If Ganesha did not reply, he would remark, 'Are you deaf?' Then Ganesha would try to pass the blame and say, 'No, thatha, there won't be forty sticks in some boxes. Some sticks would go out as soon as you light them. What can I do? If I put a drop of kerosene oil, it would be lit at once. But you say don't waste kerosene oil to light stoves.' Then his grandpa said, 'You will realise the difficulty of earning only after you gain experience.' Ganesha asked his mother, 'Tell me Amma, why should I be tolerating all such troubles?' But how could Sukanya unravel before her son the hidden agenda? Not that he should not be aware of that. Who else, except he should know about it? Yet she felt embarrassed to spell it out and restricted herself to saying, 'You see, Ganesha, it is his nature. You must bear all this, my son. He should develop a love for you as his grandson. Except you, who else is there for him? He has only a daughter and you are her son. Should we stay away from him just because he behaves like that?' By the time she uttered these words, Sukanya felt ashamed, but how could a boy of that age understand? Yet, he was adamant and left his grandfather's place soon after he finished high school.

Sukanya brought a cup of coffee and placed it before Thimmappa Gowda. After he took a sip or two, she beseeched him in a cringing voice, 'Gowdare, you should not tell my husband what you have told me now. You know well what my father's nature is. If these words reach my husband's ears, he will be really upset. Please don't tell him anything.'

Thimmappa Gowda assured her, 'Well, I won't tell him Sukanyavva.'

After two weeks, one afternoon, Ramakrishnayya came home, washed his hands and feet, did his *sandhyavandana*. While Sukanya was serving him lunch, Ramakrishnayya told her, 'You see, Ganesha stayed in Tiptur. It seems your father had to bear the expenses of two thousand three hundred and eighty five rupees to keep our son in his house. I have decided to add some more to that amount, make it two thousand five hundred rupees and return it to him, so that I discharge this debt and am free of it.'

Immediately she blurted out, 'Oh, has Thimmappa Gowdaru already carried tales?'

He asked. 'Which Thimmappa Gowdaru?' But she did not reply. Within a minute, he understood. 'So, he told Thimmappa Gowdaru also and Gowdaru told you. And you did not think it fit to tell me. Well, it was Govinahalli Hanumanthappa, Chikkenahalli Marappa and Byaladakere Chenne Gowdaru who told me this. When he had come to attend father's ceremony, your father had gone round these villages and told them this. I came to know about this some ten or twelve days back. I owe two and a half thousand rupees to this Chalapati Shetty and have to give two and a half thousand to the Tiptur man. Terinamane Siddayya says he will purchase our wetland for eight thousand rupees. Let us sell it and pay up these two amounts. We shall arrange to send money once a month to Ganesha from the remaining three thousand rupees. It would be difficult for the boy studying outside home if he does not get money every month. Having said so, Ramakrishnayya started doing *parishechana*, '*chitraaya namah, chitraguptaaya namah, yamaaya namah, yamadharmaaya namah, sarvabhooteb-hyo namah.*' After chanting this, he took an *aapooshana*.

Sukanya realised that her father had told this not only to Thimmappa Gowda, but also to the clients in the surrounding areas, who went to his warehouse. However, she was angry at the decision of her husband to pay back that money. But she did not dare express her anger. Was there anything new in her father's nature? If he said so, why should her husband go and give back that money all at once? He had spent it for his grandson only and he had just said what he did. These words should be forgotten then and there. This person, my husband, has too much of arrogance, too much pride and he is too stubborn. Thinking so, Sukanya began to boil inside. But she did not have the courage to speak. Anyway, since she felt that if she did not speak it would be as good as agreeing to whatever he said, she taunted, 'If you sell the wet lands, what should we do for food?'

Ramakrishnayya was always slow in his speech. It had almost become his habit that there would be a gap of silence of about two to three minutes between the question asked and the answer he gave, whether it was an ordinary answer or a seriously reflected topic. However, this time around, he answered without a pause as if he had already thought about it. 'Ragi that we get from our dry fields is enough for our daily meals. Whatever rice we need, we can buy it.'

Sukanya's wrath did not cool down. Her mind was trying to grasp that even if her father had said so, why should her husband pay back? Somehow she could not muster up her courage. At last the words flashed and she thought it was the perfect needle to prick her husband with. 'This house has performed *annadaana* as a *vrata* since time immemorial for so many people. You have the ego not to be indebted even to your father-in-law.'

Ramakrishnayya did not reply. He did not speak, not for just two, three or five minutes, but even after ten minutes. Sukanya assured herself by looking at her husband's face that now he would not talk of giving back the money. As usual, Ramakrishnayya ate silently, but she felt that there was a weight in his silence that was pulling him down. She became aware that she too had not spoken so sharply till now and felt repentant. But what was said was said.

The stone that was thrown had reached its target. It could not be taken back. Yet she felt she was not completely wrong. Let him answer this too. I will pose another argument, 'Let us send for Ganesha and ask him whether it is right to pay back the money to his *thatha*. It is the grandfather who spoke those words and the grandson who had taken the food. As such, the decision should be made by Ganesha.' Sukanya thought this argument was a wise one and it boosted her self-confidence. She wanted to see what her husband would say to this. After lunch, her husband lied down for a while. Not that he felt sleepy. Sukanya knew that after his father committed perjury in the court, the son lost his sleep and the sleep completely vanished after the suicide of the father. Finishing household chores in the kitchen, she too lied down, had some sleep too. By the time she woke up, her husband had gone out. She thought he must have gone to the grove taking with him the Vedanta books he had brought from Holenarasipura. When she was alone at home a thought flashed in her mind. 'If her father-in-law, Parameshwarayya, was alive, would he have paid back the money? It was seventeen years since Savitri's marriage. Since then, he had not interfered in any household responsibility. He did not express his opinion about sending Ganesha to Tiptur. When Ramakrishnayya asked his father, he had said, 'It is for the two of you to decide.' Now, if her husband wanted to pay back the money, what would her father-in-law have said? It was difficult for her to guess. But, if her father-in-law was alive, she would never have dared to say to her husband that he was arrogant and proud because his family had continued *annadaana* since generations. Sukanya was surprised to discover that she had lost all fear after the death of her father-in-law. Not only that, there was a sense of imbalance in the whole house. The form and quality of these were not comprehended by her fully but they crossed her mind as vague, abstract feelings.

Four days passed. Her husband did not speak a single word. But it could not be construed as a sign of anger. Such was his nature. More so after the death of his father. he used to remain reticent. On the fifth day, he woke up, asked her to prepare breakfast early, finished his bath, ate roti and chutney and went out. It was already evening when he returned. He announced, 'I went to Channarayapattana to register the sale of the paddy field. Tomorrow morning let us both go by bus to Channarayapattana and to Tiptur, pay back the money and reach Channarayapattana by the evening bus.'

She felt cheated, so she asked, 'Did you complete the sale without even asking me?'

Ramakrishnayya answered promptly but calmly, 'I had told you that day. I knew what you would have said, even if I had asked you.'

Sukanya raised a legal point, 'When there is a son, who is an adult, without his signature, how can the sale deed be valid?'

'Yes, I know, I asked him to come down to Channarayapattana,' he said and went into the bathroom to wash his hands and feet.

She was doubtful whether Ganesha too had agreed to pay back the money to his grandfather and she felt alienated. When her husband returned from the bathroom and was wiping his face, she asked, 'Did Ganesha agree to pay back the money to his *thatha*?' His mind seemed somewhere far away, as if her question did not reach his ears. He wiped his face and neck, sat for a while looking at the beams in the roof and then said, 'This is not a question to ask Ganesha.'

Sukanya could not think of anything more. She went into the cowshed and freely let out the pressing sorrow through her eyes. But she cried with controlled sobs, for if her husband knew about her crying bout, she would feel humiliated further. She then washed her face and came inside. She thought of telling her husband, 'I won't come to Tiptur. It is you who want to pay back. If you want to, go alone and pay the money.' But another thought struck her. If she said so, her husband would surely go alone and her father would certainly take that money. At least, if she was with Ramakrishnayya, her father would refuse the money either because of affection for his daughter or feeling ashamed to take it in front of her. When this possibility flashed across, she decided that it was right to go with her husband. While she was lighting the lamps in the pooja room, she found another helping hand. She decided to make a vow to Lord Rangaswamy of the Hill temple and prostrate before him on the way before reaching Tiptur. She thought of praying to Him to give her father the good sense to refuse that money. If her father rejected, her husband would be taught a lesson. Sukanya drew some hope from this decision, came out and told her husband, 'Though the bus route is round about, it is comfortable. Were we not going by bullock cart before the buses plied on this route? Even now, don't people go by cart to sell copra? You tell Honna to harness the cart. I want to climb the hill and light a lamp to god Rangaswamy. He is our family deity.'

Ramakrishnayya went to Honna's house.

Sukanya woke up before the cock crew, had her bath, scraped coconut, made chutney and prepared ragi rotis. Ramakrishnayya finished his *sandhyaavandana*. Honna harnessed the cart with arched cover and came by daybreak. They requested Subbannayya to take care of their house and cattle during the night, gave him the key and both of them got into the cart. Sukanya was very familiar with the route. After they passed the tank-bund, she said, 'Let us go by the base of the Rangaswamy hill.'

Honna said, 'No, it is not suitable avva, let us go from the right side. In the steep and uneven hilly road, we have to climb the shoulder of the hill and then descend on the other side. The bullocks will be too tired.'

But Sukanya insisted, 'I've brought coconut to offer to the God.' Ramakrishnayya intervened, 'It doesn't matter even if there is a delay, Honna, drive the cart from that side. After all, it is for offering worship to God.' So, Honna turned the cart to the left. Three or four times both of them had to climb down from the cart and Ramakrishnayya had to raise and push the wheels from the ruts. It was really a road that would exhaust the bullocks. Near the foot of the hill, Honna removed the harness, untied the bullocks and stayed there. Ramakrishnayya climbed the hill with Sukanya. She was panting while she climbed. Although he too was tired, he allowed her to walk and followed her closely. He prostrated before the door of the shrine on the hill and stood silently looking around in the strong wind that could push you down. She broke the coconut she had brought, put the flower on the threshold of the door, circumambulated the shrine, closed her eyes and sat. By that time, the priest had come on the hill and finished his worship. So Sukanya sat, closed her eyes with intense supplication and pleaded, 'Oh Lord Ranganatha, if you will, you can change anybody's mind. Please grant my father the wisdom to refuse this money. I make vow to you, vow to you, vow to you.' She prayed, closed her eyes and sat there, continuing her prayer. After a long time, when she opened her eyes she saw the flowers the priest had put on the god. Then she closed her eyes and prayed, 'Oh god, if you have accepted my vow give me the prasaada of flower from your right side'. She opened her eyes and sat staring at the god. Outside, there was a strong wind, roaring away. Inside that small shrine, there was such stillness that not even the tip of the burning wick in the lamp was shaking. She did not get up at all. She was well aware of her husband's nature. However long she might spend here and however restless Honna might become, her husband would never intrude in the middle and ask her to get up. At last from the right shoulder of the god, an oleander flower fell down. Sukanya's eyes filled with tears of devotion and assurance. 'Oh, Lord Ranganatha, you are the one who takes hold of the mind of everyone and cause them to act. Now I have nothing to worry, for you have decided.' She said this loudly, so that he too could hear and got up, again went round the shrine, prostrated and started back.

When she was about to climb down the steps, Ramakrishnayya told her to stop for a minute. As the wind blew strongly with a roar and all the leaves of the banyan tree were shaking violently, words could not be heard correctly. He came near his wife, stood before her and said, 'On the other day, you would remember you said, "with the pride and arrogance that yours is a family which has performed *annadaana*, you have decided to pay back the money to my father." Look here, from that day onwards, with an impartial mind, I am scrutinising it. Even now in this height of the hill, I was thinking about the same matter. Sukanya, you please understand this, I have not done this because of that pride or arrogance. Your father has experienced the loss of money. Consequently he has lost his peace of mind. That is why, he has gone around telling this to so many people. I am doing this, so that his mind may be calmed and his peace of mind restored.'

His words did not reach her mind which was immersed in devotion. 'Ranganathaswami is the greatest of all. He moves the minds of all,' saying so she began climbing down. Ramakrishnayya followed her.

Ramakrishnayya could imagine what Sukanya might have been praying for in the shrine on the hill, closing her eyes. He thought it was natural to understand what goes on in the mind of the other, as they had been running the family together as husband and wife for so many years. He brooded, just as her thoughts were understood by him, did she also understand his thoughts? If she knew his thoughts, why didn't she respond? The question arose in his mind. He recalled to mind the thought he had framed, that family, that is, *samsaara* was also a karma, an action, which was the means to develop detachment. Sukanya was climbing down swiftly with enthusiasm. Ramakrishnayya's gait was slow. Again and again he tested his words that he was not going to return the money to his father-in-law with the arrogance or pride that he was the eldest son and now the master of the house which had the reputation of performing *annadaana* for generations. He tried to remember whether from the day he decided to pay the money, until today, if such thoughts of pride or ego had taken birth, taken root in his mind. He felt no. Never. And he remembered to have read in the Vedanta book that it was difficult to fathom in which imperceptible forms ego works. Even pain does not generate without the support of ego. Contempt does not arise without the feeling of superiority. He knew that he had a contemptuous feeling towards Mandi Nagappa, but he had not spoken about this to anybody, not even to his wife. Again he questioned himself. Was he justified in wanting to pay back the money to Mandi Nagappa. The thought gave rise to laughter. If we go on analysing actions and discussing self-perfection, no work is possible. Not even saving one's self-respect. What were the aspects that decided the differences between self-respect and egoism and between self-respect and effort to protect self-respect? By the time he could find an answer to his question, the bullock cart reached his father-in-law's house. He was certain of one thing. That he would take out the money from his coat pocket and hand it over to his father-in-law. Ramakrishnayya understood his mind.

Within two miles, there was a bus-route. Honna untied the bullocks near the well beside the road, made them drink water and the three of them ate the packed rotis and chutney, drank water and Honna harnessed the cart again. Sukanya leaned on the frame of the cart and fell asleep in the shade of the arched cover to the sound of the moving cart. Though he knew he would not get sleep, Ramakrishnayya too closed his eyes. However, he thought, if he could achieve control over his mind, he could sleep and if control over the mind was achieved, there was no need for Vedanta. He looked out from behind the cart. Where was this cart going to? How many miles were there still to reach Tiptur? He became curious.

He guessed that perhaps one third of the total distance must have been covered. Along with this he remembered that it had been twenty-two years since he had come on this road. He had come to his marriage by cart; totally there were eight cartloads of people. After that, he did not set foot in that direction. A question arose in his mind: was it anger, disdain, neglect or detachment? This marriage proposal had come from Kalenahalli Thimmappa Gowda. Appa had consented to this alliance. He had come and seen the girl. That was all. Oh what sort of a marriage it was! He celebrated his daughter's marriage like an utterly poor person! How miserly! There was not enough food for people who came with us. Appa had the provisions bought and had instructed to make uppittu and coffee in the bridegroom's camp. One student of sixteen years was taking his breakfast and lunch in the marriage choultry. This Mandi Nagappa asked him, 'Who are you?' The boy said he belonged to the bridegroom's side. Nagappa verified facts keeping his face in mind, came back and said, 'You said you were from the bridegroom's side. Come on, prove to me to whom and how you are related. Do you think it is a choultry to have free meals.' Saying so, he seized the boy, pulled him out from the row of diners and threw him out. By then, the afternoon ceremony of the *kanyaadaana* was over and it was time for the new couple to have their first meals together from the same plantain leaf. Parameshwarayya said, 'If I had known that this Nagappa was such a miser, I would never have agreed to bring his daughter to my home.' I too saw what happened, called father who was near and said, 'You see, Appa, I don't want this relationship. Let us harness our carts and return to our village. You please inform our people.' Sukanya who sat next to him during the ritual of eating from a twin plantain-leaf, overheard his words. Then the father said, 'No son, we must not be rash. The relation of marriage is not to be repudiated after tying the *maangalya*, even if you say 'I don't want'. First complete this ritual. Afterwards let us talk it over.' Thus he calmed me then. Later he took me and Sukanya into a room privately and told her, 'You see dear child, we did not demand a single paise of dowry or any usual article given for the bridegroom. As the middleman said that it was a good family and the girl was virtuous, I agreed to take you as my daughter-in-law. Now I came to know the nature of your father. Even now, if we say that we don't want this girl and refuse to take you to our home, nobody can stop us.' Listening to Appa's words Sukanya started to cry. Then Appa said, 'Look here, don't cry. It does not necessarily follow that the daughter should have the qualities of her father. You see, we will have daily four or five guests for lunch in our house. This is *gruhasthadharma*. If you are ready to promise me on the name of god that you will always uphold this dharma, faithfully continue the tradition and never even in your mind think against this, tell me, and we will accept you as our daughter-in-law and take you to our house. If not, you may stay back at your father's house.' Then Sukanya said, 'Yes father, I promise.' Appa said, 'If so, you start with us tomorrow itself.' Ramakrishnayya remembered: all these years Sukanya had cooked in his house and served all the guests who came there. She had been obedient. He wondered whether she had developed generosity. He pondered – when there were no similar qualities to unite the minds of husband and wife, were these characteristics hereditary or were they born of association? Could he have asked his father about such things? After his mother's death, his father became silent. It was true that he felt great grief for the death of such a good wife like my mother. Yet he brought himself to a stage of not speaking with anybody at all. Once when Ramakrishnayya asked about this, he said these words and closed the topic, 'You see my son, you must practise detachment. You are still young. Yet, if you practise detachment seriously, you will never face distress.' Ramakrishnayya brooded: was there a precise meaning to words like detachment in life or family? Was it detachment to stay passive, thinking – let the wife and the children do whatever they want, it is not my concern? Or to hold on tightly to what you thought was right and to live according to it? Ramakrishnayya determined in his mind, 'Yes, I must hold on firmly to what I think is right, I must not take to mind other's emotions.' A sort of consolation was born in his mind for Sukanya was suitably punished now for her trickery of leaving Ganesha in her father's house. But to give it words was against his self-control practised for so many years. He recalled that he had never ridiculed or taunted her about his father-in-law and he decided not to speak so in the future too. Now, he realised even though he wanted to taunt, it would not be agreeable to his mind. After Nagappa married off his daughter and sent her to her husband's house, he had not once invited his daughter of his own accord. He had not taken his daughter to his home, not even for the delivery, nursing of baby and the mother, that too when Sukanya had only one child. Ramakrishnayya kept quiet when Sukanya explained though he did not ask: 'You see, mother is not there in that home, father doesn't know how to manage all these subtleties.' Truth be said, Nagappa did not love anybody. All his love was centred around money. Yet, when Sukanya would go to her father's house once in two years on her own, Ramakrishnayya agreed to send her without a second word. Sukanya well knew what her father's nature was. Once when she returned from Tiptur, she cried and shared her feelings with her husband: 'Why does my father not have the wisdom that his daughter should be happy, eating well and wearing good clothes, jewels and the like when he is living? After his death, what does it matter to him whether his money belongs to her or not? I doubt whether he desires that the property should belong to his daughter. When it is impossible for him to donate voluntarily to charity or religious causes, unless to his daughter to who else would the property go? If such a father dies early instead of living long, at least the children would get the pleasure and be happy, while they are young enough to enjoy.' Then Ramakrishnayya had said, 'You are wrong in expecting money and property from him. Why do you desire to enjoy what your father has earned? You understand, only what we have here is ours. Wicked thoughts enter one's mind only because of one's desire.' When Ramakrishnayya consoled her, how angry she had become against her husband! He recalled all this. His mind suddenly wanted to halt this memory-train. He took the Vedanta book which he had put beside him, opened the page which he had marked and began reading.

By the time the cart reached Tiptur, it was evening and streetlights were already lit. Nagappa was in his house. Sukanya went inside. Nagappa was surprised to see his son-in-law who had never come to the father-in-law's house. He enquired about the well-being of his son-in-law, spread a mat and asked him to sit down. Sukanya stood restless near the inner door, to call her father inside and to beseech him not to take back the money that her husband had brought. Her father had stood near the mat on which his son-in-law sat as if he was conversing with his son-in-law. Nagappa asked, 'Did you have enough rains in your place after I left there?' 'Yes with your blessings we had a few showers.' Saying so, Ramakrishnayya got up, bowed down, touched the feet of his father-in-law and said. 'I've come here for some work.' Nagappa was scared, for the son-in-law had touched his feet while speaking. Meanwhile the son-in-law took out the bundle of notes, held them before his father-in-law and said, 'I had left Ganesha in your house for three years. I didn't give money either for soap or tooth powder nor for food. As I had sent him as per Sukanya's wish, I did not enquire about those things. I had paid money only for books and school fees. Please accept this money in connection with those other expenses and free me from the debt.' Nagappa stood still for half a minute. Sukanya held her breath and was chanting in her mind, 'Oh Lord Ranganatha, Ranganatha.' Then Nagappa stretched his hand, took the bundle of notes, counted with the speed of a teller in the bank and said, 'It is two thousand five hundred.'

Ramakrishnayya said, 'Yes. I thought in your account of two thousand three hundred and eighty five rupees, you might have forgotten some items. So I felt it was better to pay back a round figure. If you accept and say the debt is fully discharged, I will be grateful.'

'Yes of course, it is over, what else is there to say?' Nagappa said and as if he had hit the target, zeroed in on a note from the bundle, showed it to Ramakrishnayya and said, 'You see, this note, it does not look genuine to me. Will you please exchange this?'

'I have not brought any extra cash with me,' Ramakrishnayya said.

'Well I'll send it to the bank. You see, hereafter, when you take a hundred rupee note, you have to be careful. Fake notes are increasing these days. I can catch them while counting itself. See, this one. Okay, it is not fake. Yet you must be careful. Times are not good.' Saying so, Nagappa folded the notes and squeezed them into the hidden pocket of his inner shirt.

Sukanya who was thinking of Lord Ranganatha of the Hill, felt ashamed to let it be known that she was witnessing this repayment standing near the door. She rushed into the kitchen and began searching the shelves to cook something. But except for three or four handfuls of ragi flour which had turned musty and was emitting a foul smell, there was nothing else in the kitchen. No rice, no sugar or jaggery, no milk or curds. Not even a coconut.

Meanwhile her father came into the kitchen and asked her, 'How did you manage to get two thousand and five hundred rupees?'

'He sold the wet land. He didn't tell me. Neither did he ask me.'

'At what rate per acre?'

'Lands were a little less than three acres. He sold it for eight thousand.'

'That means, three thousand per acre. While you sell, shouldn't you raise rates, create competition and then sell? If I had known that it was so cheap, I myself would have bought it. If you know about any property for sale at your place, write to me. I'll purchase it. It doesn't matter how much it costs. Well, he paid me two and half thousand. What did he do with the remaining amount?'

'He repaid some of the loan he had taken. He has kept the balance for Ganesha's education.'

'If you run the family without wisdom and spend unwisely, you are sure to have loans. Wait I will advise him.'

'Appa I beg of you, please don't do so,' speaking so, Sukanya's eyes filled with tears and a sob broke out.

Her father started counselling her. 'Don't cry child. If you are a little strict and exercise your control, he will get wise. I hope he doesn't have any other habit, does he?'

Ramakrishnayya who was standing on the mat came out. The bullocks needed water. Then they were to be given fodder. He told Honna, 'Honna, our work here is over. It is cooler now. Let us head back right away. Honna replied, 'But, the bullocks are exhausted, ayya.'

'Yes they are,' Ramakrishnayya thought for a moment and said, 'See Honna, you do one thing. You harness the cart again. Let the three of us have our meals in a hotel. You drive the cart slowly, encouraging the bullocks. Three miles near this town, didn't we come across a village? Somewhere the road deviated from the village called Yedagarahalli. There beside the road, there is a stone pavilion with a canopy. You stop the cart there, give fodder and water to the bullocks. You can sleep in the cart and we will sleep in the stone pavilion. It is near the village, so we need not be scared.'

Though Honna did not know the precise purpose of Ramakrishnayya and Sukanya's coming here, he had known the real state of this relationship. So, he immediately agreed to what Ramakrishnayya suggested. Ramakrishnayya came inside, stood near the kitchen door and said to his wife, 'You see, Honna said, he has to attend a marriage of his relative tomorrow. He is urging me to start immediately. So come on, let us start.'

'What, immediately?' she asked.

'Yes, it is not a problem for him. If you want to stay, you may. But I am leaving right now.'

Sukanya looked at her father. He said, 'Oh what sort of a cart man is he? He has come just now and already says he has to move. Why couldn't you get anyone who could sleep here at night and start in the morning?' Sukanya prostrated before her father and said, 'No Appa, why should we cause him trouble.' And taking leave of her father, got ready to leave.

Her father said, 'There is kumkum in the casket near the niche of god. Apply kumkum and then leave.' It was an old wooden casket given to Sukanya's mother by Sukanya's grandmother. She knew that her father kept kumkum in it, to apply on top of the vibhuthi, after he lit incense sticks to the gods. She opened the lid, took a pinch of kumkum, put it on her forehead and smeared what remained in her fingers on the *maangalya*, came out, got into the cart and sat. Honna harnessed the cart. Nagappa who came out said, 'Oh yes, there is moonlight outside. Yet it is a night journey. Take care!'

On the night of Parameshwarayya's *Vaikunta* in Bilikere, six bunches, which contained nearly 200-250 coconuts were stolen from Satyappa's grove in Mattikere. Satyappa had started from Channarayapattana and when he reached home in Mattikere, it was already one in the afternoon. Ramachandra was raging and abusing the coconut thieves. When he saw his father, his anger turned towards him, for, if father had not stayed back the previous night, this theft would not have taken place. Ramachandra questioned his father in the same tone in which he was abusing the thieves. 'Look here, Appa, I had come cycling so far to Bilikere one day earlier only to tell you that you should come as soon as *Vaikunta* ceremony was over. But you didn't come at all. After you left the village, nearly seven hundred to eight hundred coconuts were stolen. Who is responsible for this?' He put the blame entirely on his father and went away into the room, where his wife, the nursing mother of three and a half month old baby was sleeping and the room spilled a sweet fragrance of betel leaves, areca nuts, copra, cardamom, cloves, a kind of camphor used in foods and the aromatic *lehya* for the nursing mother. As he was sweating, Satyappa took a cold bath, ate a two course meal of rice and sambar as well as rice and buttermilk. Ramachandra's mother-in-law served him. He went to the grove and examined the trees. It was clear to him from which trees coconuts were stolen and he was accurate about the number stolen too. But how to catch the scent of the thief ? Was it Siddura or the Alam Sabi gang or of banjara settlement? If six bunches are plucked in one night, it was impossible for one man. At least two persons must have come twice. When they were certain that I was not in the village, there was no fear or hindrance for them to come twice. Satyappa felt that at least if he could catch one thief and break his leg, all the thieves in the village would be silenced. He remembered what the people of Bilikere talked about when he had gone there for Parameshwarayya's *dharmodaka*. They were saying that after Manjayya had removed Kanchi, not even a coconut frond or tender coconut was stolen from any of the groves in Bilikere. A thought entered his mind – what if any one thief was removed in that manner in this village too? But at the same time, he felt ashamed. Oh how mean and wicked was this thought of removing the life of a man to abolish thefts in the groves. All his anger then turned towards the politicians who fought to become the people's representative and he thought, if the villages were developed according to his concept of rural upliftment, for which he had worked hard, there would not have been such problems. He felt, this country would not progress and be saved unless these politicians were destroyed en masse. They use the name of Mahatma Gandhi, show his photo in election meetings, wear khadi and exhibit a peculiar ethical character. Until these people are lined up and shot down, it is not possible to offer even first aid to the malady this country suffers from. This blanket solution crossed his mind. He felt sleepy. If he had not heard of the theft of coconuts in the night, when he came home, he could have slept for a while at home and then gone to the grove. He yawned thrice. He had not slept properly the previous night. That Manjayya had sent him to that film. Remembering that, he thought of lying down in the shade of the suragi tree with fragrant flowers and was crossing the ridge. Then the cow named Kaali, which was grazing there, lowed loudly. Satyappa went near the cow and softly scratched its neck. He felt that even cattle felt neglected, for he was not there since six days. He crossed the ridge, spread his towel beneath the suragi tree and lay down. The heat of the sun was hurting his eyes. He shielded them with his right arm and slept for a while. Because of the stinging rays, he dared not remove his arm from the eyes. He thought, if there was a small hut in the grove, it would offer protection from this severe heat and from rains too. As he was deciding to build a small hut, he slid into sound sleep.

When the shade moved and the sun directly shone and scorched his body, he woke up again. He felt his body, face and eyes were all sticky. Immediately he got up, sat and moved into the shade. After a while, when he recovered from his drowsiness, he got up, went towards the well, splashed water on his face, washed away the sweat from his neck, came back and sat in the shade of the suragi tree. Then he recalled what Ramachandra had said. Now a young man of twenty-five years, how well he had brought him up as he was a motherless child! Satyappa fed his little son with milk, curds, fruit, grapes, almonds and the son had grown up as tall as the front door and was a strong and sturdy youth. But he is such a coward he can't do a round of the grove during the nights. He would make the excuse that his wife would be alone. But what was the excuse now? His mother-in-law was there! He remembered the false respect his *sambandhi* displayed. How dare Ramachandra turn his anger against the thief towards his father, in front of his mother-in-law? Was watching the grove the sole responsibility of Satyappa? Satyappa was fuming inside. However, after a while, he consoled himself – Ramachandra was still immature, a mere boy. He got up, went around the fence and checked. He decided to tighten the fence. After sunset, while going home, he decided to stay in the grove and keep watch the whole night, with a torch and a cudgel for company. Though he thought of carrying a sickle too, he decided against it. He came home, spoke of the urgency of mending the fence, took his grandson of three and a half months with little cap, socks and finger rings, hugged and kissed him. He forgot his son was angry with him. He held the hand of his granddaughter Aashaa and played with her and his mind was fully consoled. After dinner he announced that he would be staying in the grove the whole night and took a blanket and gunny sack, rolled them up, tucked them under his arm and went back to the grove.

As the night turned darker, Satyappa felt a bit scared. Every night he used to visit the grove twice. He would come flashing his torch, thumping his cudgel on the ground, so that if there were thieves, they would be alerted and run away. He knew he adopted this trick to avoid direct confrontation with the thieves. But it was not to be so from now on. He would wait silently and if there was a hint of a thief, he would move silently and stealthily, not making a sound, even that of a dry leaf that moves with the wind, until he breaks the knees of the thief. After all, what harm can the thief do? Worst come, he might brandish his sickle and end my life. Satyappa mustered up courage thinking, even if I lose my life, it is worth it. It is better than this stupid life of being scared, bolting the door and lying down inside the blanket, allowing daily thefts in the grove. After half an hour, he got rid of the fear. When the twinkling started clearly in the dark sky, he felt this was rather pleasant, much better than the platform of the house. He sat on the stone slab of the step of the well and looked at his watch. It was just ten. He could not sit on the slab the whole night. It would be better beneath the suragi tree if he could spread the gunny bag, cover himself with the blanket and lie down. Anyway, he decided to sleep after midnight, and then he remembered how Manjayya had forcibly pushed him to see the film. Oh! that damned

Manjayya! After some time, Satyappa thought, although he was utterly corrupt, he was stupendous. If you argue with him, the line between right and wrong blurs and vanishes altogether. Not only that, the colours switch places and change sides. He could make white seem black and black seem white. Though we know well that he does not stop at anything, nor does he abide by any rule, we completely lose our power of refuting his argument or clarifying his mistakes. Despite all that, it is not possible to hate him. Everyone in the village, for one covert reason or the other, likes him. At the same time, Satyappa felt that liking or admiration of someone was not a benchmark to assess their character. He sat for a while, got up and went round on the ridges, came back near the well and sat down. Presently, he felt drowsy. He decided that the suragi tree shade was suitable only during daytime. It would not do for the night under the star-studded sky. He spread the gunny bag on the stone slab near the bank of the well, put the blanket over his legs and lied down looking at the sky. There was a sort of contentment and a shining peace. He recalled how he used to sleep outside during summer, looking at the sky, when he was in Sabarmati ashram. He mused, oh those were the days! Of dreams, of achievements, of ideals! Where did that time vanish? He fell asleep with the awareness that should a thief come by, he was sure to wake up.

When he opened his eyes next, it was half past three. He felt disgusted with the vivid memory of the thoughts and scenes running across his mind while asleep. The film he saw yesterday, yes what was its name? The provocative scenes of half naked woman; then that girl who had come to the Traveller's Bungalow, what was her name? She thought Satyappa was an M.L.A and had called him so; who knows whether she was a girl, a young woman or a grown up woman. Her physique and figure concealed her age. Oh, what was her name? She too had come half naked and was bathing half naked in the pond of the grove, that too during midday. Oh, her excellent physique! She was provoking him through her eyes invading his head and heart. Fie on such dreams! It is said dreams would not sustain throughout sleep. It was just like encapsulating the gist of an year's events in the span of a minute, as is done in films and creating the illusion of an year gone by. Dreams too were such. That is how Satyappa felt that he was looking at that girl the whole night. Yet she and by the way, what was her name? Even in the dream, when he asked her name, Manjayya said laughingly, 'Why do you ask me? Asking, "what is your name?" is a nice way of starting conversation with such women.' Satyappa got up. He was confident that no thief had entered the grove. Yet he thought it proper to go for a round. Flashing his torch in the darkness, he walked with the eye of a detective, to check whether there were any signs on the ground of coconuts that fell from the tree. He kept a watchful eye for snakes and other reptiles. Nothing was amiss. He thought his intuition that though there was no sound or movement, somehow the thieves would have the inkling that someone is watching was right. Or, possibly, they might have learnt of his return. So, naturally, they did not set foot here. He had a mind to go back to sleep again, came to the stone slab in front of the well and sat down. The memory of that dream haunted him again. Oh, yes, I now remember, her name was Chandrika. She was bathing half naked in this well, as in that film scene. Dreams are really strange; they connect things from some far off places to the now and here thought Satyappa as he lied down.

He slept until the rays of the sun pierced him and the flies were buzzing. He did not have any distorting dreams. He went around the grove once more, looked up, checked the coconut bunches and went home.

When he mentioned his idea of erecting a hut in the grove, Ramachandra felt relieved and agreed immediately. For, if there would be a hut, his father would almost always stay there and no thief would dare step into the grove. The same evening, he went to Voddarahalli and placed an order for two stone pillars. He did not ask his father about the details. Within eight days, instead of just a simple structure, a small hut, its roof thatched with palm-leaves and spliced bamboo strips was ready. The surrounding wall was waist high. Coconut tree trunks were used as crossbeams on the two pillars A door fashioned out of a plank of wood was affixed. Inside the house, there was a thick mattress and a block of wood to serve as a pillow. All these were brought by Ramachandra. Looking at the hut and the arrangements, there arose in Satyappa's mind a picture of *vaanaprastha* and a bower made of leaves and grass. He felt, as soon as he got his son married he should have built such a hut and started to live there.

He went home only for lunch. From dawn to dusk, Satyappa began living in the hut. A feeling of contentment and a sense of detachment seemed to grow within! He was a bit scared to be alone in the grove. Until midnight, he would sit near the well and look at the darkness of the sky or the stars, the moonlight and the moon. And then he would enter the hut and sleep. As he was sleeping inside the hut, there was no possibility of getting cold or being drenched in the dew. Somehow he felt, it was as if the place naturally belonged to him and this feeling strengthened his contentment. The feeling he had experienced in Sabarmati, that memory, nurtured his peace.

The thefts stopped completely. There was not a sign of any other footstep. A sense of fulfilment strengthened. He felt happy that he stopped the thefts without maiming or killing someone. He thought his achievement was better than that of Manjayya. But he pushed away that comparison from his mind, for he thought, it was too mean to compare himself with the likes of Manjayya.

However, this euphoria lasted for only eight to ten days. After the anxiety over the thefts had ceased and he got rid of the fear of being alone, sleepless nights began to grip him. Sometimes, the question would torment him: After all what did he achieve by this guard duty? To top it, as soon as he entered the hut, his mind would be flooded with memories of what Manjayya might be doing in his hut, the exploits Manjayya had described, the lewdness that Savitri had talked about, Manjayya's boasts and bragging. Again and again pictures of Chandrika bathing half naked in the midday sun or stepping into the water fully naked would occupy his mind. However much he tried to push them out of his mind or trample on them, it would not be possible for him and the same thoughts, same images would fill his mind. He began to find a sort of pleasure in this imagination as a youth or an adolescent suffering the pangs of puberty. Sometimes he would get scared and sometimes a feeling of disgust would envelop him. He felt like going out of the hut. Some nights, he wouldn't get a wink of sleep and while turning sides on that thick mattress, he could hear a rustling sound. The hut would change in all manners into the hut in Manjayya's grove and Satyappa would walk out of the hut wearied with the urge. If he came near the well, the scene of Chandrika nakedly stepping into the dark water would be seen even in the night. He would start searching the history of this distortion when his mind was calm and try to find out since how long was it there in his mind. Not that he had not been haunted with such thoughts in the past. For a year after his wife's death, his mind was immersed in grief. After that, his mind would fly towards such imaginations. There was an urge either to get married again or to talk to women working in his fields. Gradually, engaging his mind in various activities had helped him control the urge and make it bearable. After that period passed, if such thoughts did occur they would appear very rarely, in a dream or as a dream. Immediately he would wake up and feel guilty. He had become completely successful in keeping a complete check on it, in waking hours. And now after the birth of his first grandson, the feeling he had become a grandfather occupied his mind and even that rare negative stream in the dream had almost ceased. Satyappa thought: why had it suddenly resurfaced? It had never before haunted him so violently, so lewdly, so continuously. Why was it so? Was it Manjayya's influence? But his mind refused to accept it. That could not be the sole reason. Before this, how many times had he spoken with Manjayya, how many times had Manjayya come here? He was always sharing the intimacies of his adventures, exploits and conquests. He had indirectly made fun of Satyappa's celibacy earlier too. Why had it affected so deeply this time around? Satyappa could not find an answer and more than the pressure to know the answer, his mind began to struggle, not able to bear this distortion. Till now, during the course of a normal conversation his mind did not dwell on the fact that the person talking to him was a man or a woman. But now, as soon as he spotted a woman, his mind would begin to guess her age. Imagination of her limbs and other features and body parts would begin and finally to stop that, the same mind would, with great effort, feel disgust. Yet, his roaming imagination would not stop getting stuck in the mire of filth. Many a times he thought of speaking with a woman working in his field or farm. But he was afraid his eyes might give away his dirty thoughts and someone might notice that. Why was he undergoing this? His mind did not agree to put the blame on Manjayya alone.

It is true that the fault was created by association. Even then, let him say and do whatever he wants to, my mind is mine only. If it starts dancing madly, this hopping or dancing must have been lurking in its original nature itself. He understood, perhaps the self-control he practised was the artificial weight he put on himself when he decided to bear all the responsibilities by himself.

Satyappa spent nearly two months in this new arrangement. Then he remembered what Manjayya had told him about Parameshwarayya: If Parameshwarayya had ever introspected, he would never have committed suicide. What other outlet except suicide existed for people who practised strict celibacy? What else have you achieved? Only selfishness. You brought up your son, married him off, handed over the charge of everything to him and became an unpaid servant in his house. What else did you do? Even if you had lived together or made contact with women, you could have brought up your son. What is the connection between one and the other? What else did you achieve, except to gain the respect of a man or two, except for someone praising Satyappa is a true follower, a carbon copy of Mahatma Gandhi?

Satyappa thought perhaps Manjayya's words were true. A feeling that his ideals and goals were a total failure haunted him. He had rejected the responsibility of family and opted for *vaanaprastha*, to fulfil his dream of village upliftment, but that too had rejected him. Though he had voluntarily handed over the charge of property to his son, his son started treating him as a dependent. Though he did not show it openly, while deciding business matters, he would never consult his father and would decide on his own. A sense of sadness began to haunt Satyappa: perhaps reaching this hut in the grove was his natural end from all points of view. Along with this feeling, his physical desire was intensified like a flaming torch.

Satyappa felt weary – why did he have to live? Not that intense physical urge haunted him. Even if it didn't haunt, it was simply living in this hut. His son and daughter-in-law had their own family. He might play with the grandchildren and caress them. Inevitably, nothing more. He might live for fifty years more, but what pleasure, happiness or what attraction was there in life? Sometimes Satyappa would feel that perhaps in a way Manjayya was correct. He had no illusion of any sort of idealism. He had precisely understood the source of his pleasure. But within one or two days Satyappa's mind would think in a totally different direction and begin to re-evaluate. Manjayya's was a basic animal like existence. Should he think of it as the true source of life.

One day, he left the hut, leaving behind the well and the suragi flower tree, which was causing in him these sensual images, went far away from there, and sat beneath the *jamun* tree, the purple berry tree and began to unravel and scrutinise his mind layer by layer. It might be Chandrika or Siddi who was more taut and strong as Manjayya had described, or it might be any woman roaming either in the grove or on the village road, everyone would be culminated in this grove in the newly built hut, on this soft mattress. A similarity had developed between this hut and Manjayya's hut. This hut recalled to mind that one and this was built from the memory of that hut. Perhaps in erecting this hut, the purpose of watching coconut thieves and the inner purpose of living inside it and indulging in psychological lewdness were equal motives. Even without this hut he could have watched the thieves. So, so ... the stream of thought ceased there. He tightened his mind like a fist. He got up, walked towards the hut, opened the door, entered and observed it with a firm resolve. The same soft mat, if you step on it, lie down and roll on it, the same rustling sound. There was a folded blanket on it. Beside it, there was a torch and a cudgel. Satyappa stood staring at them. As if he had decided on something, he came out, walked rapidly to the main gate of the grove and walked towards the village. He met someone on the way, but he was not of that village and not a person of any nearby village. 'From where are you Gowdare?' Satyappa asked. He answered, 'Kundooru'. 'Will you please spare me a match?' Satyappa asked. It is a well known fact that in village roads, people addicted to beedi ask for matches and the people who have the same addiction, generously spare them, though they may be utter misers in other matters. That traveller took out the match box and pulled out his beedi also to light it from the same stick. But Satyappa opened the match box, took out a stick, and tore a part of strip that was smeared with gun powder, and returned the match-box. The traveller asked, 'Why, don't you have beedis? Please take one, if you like.' But Satyappa did not notice the stretched hand, turned back and went in rapid strides towards the grove. As soon as he reached the grove, he identified the direction from which the wind was blowing, stood in that part, struck the match stick on the strip, cupped it with his hands so that it should not be put out and lit the dry leaf on the roof of the hut. Within two minutes the roof caught fire, though there was only a mild breeze. It spread, scattered, blazed and in five minutes the entire roof caught fire. Crackling yellow and red flames rose to the height of two men and smoke spread in the sky. Satyappa stood there, without even blinking his eyes as if that blaze was filling and creating images in the space of his eyes. All the coconut leaves were burnt out. The bamboo strips then caught fire. The roof made of palm leaves, began to sink. The mattress caught fire when a strip of burning leaf fell on it and the blanket too started to burn. The cudgel turned into soot. The door and the door frame caught fire. Satyappa stood watching while the blaze in the shape of a tower was being reflected in those blankly staring eyes. His mind ruminated, 'Oh what was achieved by burning this hut, borrowing a matchstick. What was the use? It should have been burnt with the Third Eye, the one on the forehead! How wonderful if he had that power! he laughed deridingly and meaningfully at his own weakness. His mind was engaged in the imagination of the Third Eye. Shiva was really great, worthy of worship. With these thoughts, he walked back a little and sat on the ridge. But his look was directed towards the beam and the door that were falling down consumed by the fire and the walls that had charred. His mind acquired a feeling of contentment akin to the peaceful surface of water after the storm has abated. When he sat there with a feeling of suspended animation, someone came running opening the main gate of the grove. He knew it was Ramachandra. He was panting and asked, 'Oh Appa, somebody told me that there was a big smoke and fire in our grove. That's why I came running. The hut has caught fire and is completely burnt down and you are calmly sitting there, watching.'

'Yes, I myself set fire to it,' Satyappa said.

'What? Why did you do that?'

'You see, Ramachandra, since the day it was erected, a snake had entered inside. Whatever you did, it could not be driven away. I set fire to the hut, so that the snake might die inside. I am not sure whether it died or escaped.'

'Did you have to set fire to the hut for that? We could have brought in a snake catcher,' Ramachandra said accusingly,

Satyappa didn't answer. He sat silent, unaffected by his son's words. Ramachandra went near the hut, looked inside from the place where there was a door earlier and shouted, 'That blanket cost thirty rupees, the mattress too is burnt. There was a cudgel and a torch as well.'

Satyappa sat still. The father's act seemed strange to the son.

From that day onwards, Satyappa began sleeping on the platform in front of his house. As earlier, he would go round the grove, but the thieves did not step in. His mind too felt contented but only for five days. Again, that physical urge gripped him on the sixth night, when he lied down on the platform. The burnt out hut would take its original form in his mind, and there, a softer, rustling mattress would be created. It did not stop there. When he came out, all the plants, trees and stone pillars began to take female forms. Either day or night, waking or dreaming, it was the same. He began to spot gender distinction even in cattle, sheep and goat. Clouds in the sky, aerial roots of banyan trees, bulges and depressions on a stone boulder began to attack him as forms of female organs. Satyappa felt if this continued, he certainly would go mad. He was haunted by fear that without his knowledge his tongue might reveal his lewd thoughts. He felt it was a torture, a hellish pain, why did it happen so to me, this inner ache which did not appear when I was a young man of eighteen, oh why did it appear now? He could neither find an answer however much he thought nor could he get any comfort. Yes, what Manjayya says is correct. If your nose is filled with mucus, it would be heavy and painful. Once you blow it out, it is over, then you would not remember it. Satyappa determined this was also the same.

He began to feel that by setting fire to the hut, he simply committed a mistake. He thought he was a stupid fellow who did not know that if you strike on the ant hill, the snake inside would only slither away. At least if that hut was there, he could have invited a professional. Oh where is such a one? Such women are everywhere. Yengati of the Outer Street, but of course she is aged, her daughter Puttalakshmi, Eeravva who comes to carry coconuts, Cheluvamma of the shop, there are eight to ten women in this village alone. But how to approach them? Satyappa found this a big obstacle. He walked in front of Cheluvamma's shop twice. He saw she was alone. His eyes caught her body build. But how could he turn towards the shop, enter inside and then, then, how could he talk and what would he ask? Scared, he returned.

Again, Manjayya's words flashed the solution; he had said, 'Now you return to your village Annayya. You think leisurely and when you feel the desire, come to me. You saw in the night that Chandrika, I'll fix you up a girl who would give herself up to you without a second word, a girl more youthful than Chandrika.

As soon as you see her, you will feel you are twenty-two. I'll not tell anybody. You may trust me. Manjayya has never broken his promise in this matter. Moreover partners in such matters never betray each other.' So, Satyappa decided, yes he is the answer. Except him, there is no other refuge. Yes it was just like blowing out mucus. It is the nature of sex, if you let it out, when swelled, the ache would stop. It is like cutting the swell of the wound and squeezing out the pus from it. After all what else would be there at my declining age! It is a craving that has appeared lately. The more I repress it, the more it throbs and comes to the surface. Satyappa defended his craving and when he decided to go to Bilikere the next morning, his mind became calm.

In the early morning, he knocked on the door, woke up Ramachandra and said, 'I had forgotten that I should go to Bilikere. I had said that I would come and attend the third month's ceremony of your grandfather!'

'If you leave the village, what if the thieves strike again in the grove?' Ramachandra asked.

'No, no, I'll return early,' Satyappa said, put a pair of khadi clothes in a khadi bag and set out. While walking rapidly he became aware of two things simultaneously. Till now, he had never uttered a lie and now he had told a lie to his own son. The second one was the objection his son made. 'If you leave the village, what if there is a theft.' Satyappa tried not to worry about both, and began to walk. He thought somebody in Bilikere would identify him, and there would be all sorts of speculations if he goes to Manjayya's house instead of Ramakrishna's. So he decided not to go from the front of the village but to go to Manjayya's house through the potter's lane. There nobody would know him. He thus circumvented this problem as well.

He climbed and got down the rising ground of the hill of Lord Rangaswamy, crossed the gorges, walked on the tank bund of Bilikere and reached the place by eleven in the forenoon. Fortunately, Manjayya was at home. Looking at Satyappa, Manjayya smiled. But Satyappa felt embarrassed. Manjayya told Satyappa who sat on the mat and was wiping the sweat on his face, 'You don't have to spell it out. I know why you've come.'

Satyappa controlled his smile and said, 'What do you know?'

'You see, Annayya, an expert doctor, even before feeling the pulse of a patient, diagnoses what the sickness is. Shall I tell you?'

'No, you need not . Give me some water to drink. I am hungry too. Please arrange for some snacks.'

'Puradamma is cooking. Meanwhile you finish your bath,' Manjayya said and moved near Satyappa, lowered his voice and asked, 'That Chandrika you had seen in Channarayapattana has gone to Mysore, for she could have a better business in the big city. Would a nice one from here do instead?'

'Oh I don't know. I leave it all to you.' While uttering this, Satyappa cringed with shame.

While he washed his clothes and bathed, Manjayya went out, came back within half an hour. Puradamma served them. After their lunch, she removed the plantain leaves on which they ate, cleaned the place and went out. When there were only the two of them, Manjayya told in an intimate tone, 'Look here, Annayya, I'll give you some rice flakes, jaggery powder and scraped coconut and a vessel. You put them into your bag. Now you go off into my grove. Open the lock on the gate, lock it from inside and wait in the hut. She will come by one o'clock. Her name is Naagi. She will stay till evening and if you want she will be with you up to midnight. If you feel hungry, soak this parched rice and eat. Take the sickle with you. You can then pluck and drink tender coconuts from young trees. She herself would pull down tender coconuts, splice them open, make you drink it, scrape the kernel of tender flesh and feed you. I have told her not to take a single pie from you.

It is my account. She will not ask you. Yet you tip her a rupee or two. She will feel elated and touch your feet and say, "Please come tomorrow also sir." By the by, do you have some money with you? If not please take this.' Manjayya then took out from his pocket two one rupee coins and placed it before Satyappa. Then he said, 'You must start within fifteen minutes. Wait a minute, I'll instruct Puradamma to powder some jaggery and scrape coconut and I'll give you rice flakes.' Then as if he remembered another matter he said, 'I've given her a new toilet soap and told her that my relative is very clean – I have asked her to apply it twice while bathing and clean herself rubbing well with coconut coir. She is always clean and you will never get bored. You see, by evening she will swell your youth four times. After coming back, you will tell me, 'Yes, Manjayya you cannot find such a woman in this world.'

Holding in one hand the bag containing rice flakes, coconut scrapings, jaggery powder and a vessel, in another an umbrella, when Satyappa walked in the afternoon sun, there was no one on the road. On his way to Manjayya's grove, he had to pass the Shiva temple in front of the village. When he reached that spot his eyes turned to the big banyan tree before the temple. His eyes were fixed on the branch, on which his father-in-law had hanged and was seen dangling. This imagination caught his mind – generally the persons who hang themselves would first tie the rope to the supporting branch above and then pull the noose around their neck and jump down. Satyappa stood staring at that branch. Manjayya may say, 'There is no way out except suicide for people who choose strict celibacy,' but Satyappa felt, it was not possible for him to remember his father-in-law with that sort of levity. Satyappa's head automatically bent backwards like the handle of the umbrella he held in his left hand and was gazing at that branch in which was his father-in-laws's final step of life. The reason that he had committed suicide for telling only one lie, elevated his memory into the level of devotion. Satyappa became aware that if he stood looking, someone from the village would recognise him and remembered that it was the main road to enter the village from the village tank, wet field and groves. He strode rapidly and crossed the first canal. Now he began brooding: Is not adultery also a lie? For this, I told two lies as soon as I woke up and started. A thought crossed his mind: he should go back to Manjayya's house and tell him 'I don't want this. It is true that desire gripped my mind. But looking at the banyan tree on which father-in-law committed suicide, that desire melted away.' Without knowing either to step forward or backward, he stood there for a while. He closed his eyes, began to comprehend his inner emotion. It is a fact that adultery is a step of falsehood, a false relation and it is true that this banyan tree brings to mind the punishment that falsehood should get. But he felt that it was also not a lie that this desire which was crushing him inside was to find satisfaction. He was going there not to commit adultery, but to a prostitute, to a woman who took it as her profession to sleep with men like him and calm down their passions. Comforted clearly from this line of thought, Satyappa walked on rapidly. As Manjayya had told him, he closed the grove gate from within, locked it and reached the hut. Now all the lecherous images that were encircling and haunting his mind in the hut of his grove in Mattikere at once replayed in his mind. He opened the door of the hut and stepped inside. Oh, lo, she was already there. As he had walked in the hot sun, he felt it was dark inside and could not see her form or figure clearly. He stood there. She rose immediately. He did not go inside. He felt lost. His eyes were gradually adjusting to the difference of light. Her form and figure took shape. Satyappa thought, her figure was at once the manifested embodiment in one woman, whose organs and figure he imagined in trees, plants, clouds and rocks and got excited. He stood there gazing at her. His pulse raced, and the eager pain started throbbing to come out through the face and body. He was feeling a state of intense excitement which was pushing him into an unconscious state and he could see nothing else. Even from that state, he was vaguely aware that he was losing consciousness and a rope of jute was tightening around his neck. By that time, she herself came forward and closed the door of the hut. She hugged him, took him on to that rustling mat, and just like a wrestler in the wrestling match abruptly pulls down the adversary on the floor and defeats him, she threw him down on the mat and seized him. He gave himself over to her passively, thinking that all the powers that were maddeningly active in his mind had become positively active in her form.

Then there was absolute nothingness. It was mere madness. It was not getting rid of the source of madness. A feeling that the flood of madness flushed away his inner power and created a state of disgusted satiety rose in him. Sadness, sorrow and despair encircled him: the sort of shame that occurs when he who has enough strength, instead of fighting, surrenders everything he had to the robber who attacked him and saves his life, enveloped Satyappa's mind and body. Now the interior portion of the hut seemed to him, as if it was an enclosure smeared with his downfall all around and the place he should not have come to. He recalled, on that day when Manjayya went to the other side of the grove to pull down tender coconuts, he had stealthily entered this hut. At that moment itself, this contagious devil had struck him! Gradually it did sow its seed and developed crores of poisonous atoms, and had dragged him to the same place and caused his downfall today. Satyappa created a metaphor of his fall in this way. He turned to a side and lay down like a corpse without movement, wondering – why did I not understand in the beginning itself that this was likely to happen? Why didn't I even imagine it? She tried to turn him towards her, putting her hands on his chest. He felt disgusted. He burnt with anger for a moment and felt like turning to that side and slapping her. At the same time he felt doubly ashamed. He thought he was an unworthy person who wanted to slide his mistake on to that woman who did her profession honestly. He did not speak a single word. He sat up, rose swiftly, opened the door of the hut and came out. The sun was scorching and it seemed as if it was causing the heads of coconut trees to let out steam. Far off the grove gate appeared. It was there that Manjayya had struck the thief, killed him and had dragged the corpse under that tree beyond the ridge and had put the body so that the head should fall on the sharp stone. Oh, Satyappa remembered and felt it was cruelty. He did not feel like staying in that grove. He walked barefoot to the grove gate, took the key from his pocket, opened the gate, forgot to lock it again and strode rapidly towards the village. He crossed the canal and when he came near the Shiva temple in front of the village, he had a mind to stand beneath that banyan tree and stare at that branch. He stood thus for a while, saluted the branch in his mind and came back directly to Manjayya's house.

Seeing him, Manjayya looked at his watch and said, 'Oh, what happened, it is not even two yet.' Satyappa kept quiet. He stood as if his lips were sewn together!

'Why so early? Did she create any scene or play any mischief?'

'No, it was not her fault. I felt I did not want it again.' Satyappa said.

'You should have stayed for some more time and you would have wanted it again.'

'No, I was not aware of my temperament. Now I am feeling sorry. Did I suffer for three full months just for this?' Having said so, Satyappa sat on the mat in the hall. Manjayya put on his pump shoes and went out swiftly. He did not tell Satyappa where he was going and it did not occur to Satyappa to ask him. He just lied down. Tiredness of walking fourteen miles in the morning, now going to the grove and coming back in the hot sun and that excited, mad disgust about life. Though he was yawning, he could not get sleep. As if he had just recovered from some severe sickness and did not have strength to turn sides, he stretched his legs in the same posture he had lied down.

Manjayya returned in the evening. He brought with him Satyappa's chappals, umbrella and the sickle he had taken with him, along with the bag that contained rice flakes, jaggery and such, empty now. Manjayya looked at Satyappa, who was still lying down and smiled at him with derision, pity and scorn. Satyappa understood what Manjayya was thinking. But he did not speak; rather he did not know what to talk. A sort of emptiness had filled from within. Satyappa felt, even if he stayed there that night, he would not have anything to speak with Manjayya. Until now he was participating as an intimate listener to whatever Manjayya would say, by making some notes and comments on those matters. But now to speak on such matters was meaningless. Satyappa felt it would never be possible for him to speak with Manjayya hereafter. He finished his dinner and went to bed silently. He decided to wake up early in the morning and leave for his village. He had told his son, he would go to Bilikere to attend Parameshwarayya's ceremony of the third month. It would seem unnatural to his son and daughter-in-law, if he returned the next day and that too if he went without prasaada, it would be more unnatural. Satyappa had to create some lie for that and had to say Ramakrishna and his wife had gone to the sacred places on the bank of river like Paschimavahini, Narsipura or Ramanathapura. His mind became uneasy thinking he had to tell yet another lie.

He reached his village by ten in the morning. Ramachandra's mother-in-law had returned to her place and his daughter-in-law was cooking. Ramachandra took care of the child. Before

Ramachandra asked, Satyappa lied about having gone to Paschimavaahini. Ramachandra said in a complaining tone filled with weariness, 'Yesterday night two bunches of coconuts were stolen.' Satyappa knew that his daughter-in-law did not have the concern to make roti and chutney for her father-in-law, who had walked the distance of fourteen miles. Satyappa knew that his son had given such prominence that she considered it an act of kindness and a favour bestowed if she worked in the kitchen and cooked something. If she had to enter the kitchen, the husband had to take care of the child. Satyappa knew that if his son did not take charge of the child, the kitchen stove would not be lit. So, Satyappa went to the grove thinking, he could drink two tender coconuts. The hut he had set fire to was erected as before. Though black with soot, there were the same walls and the two stone pillars. There were new beams, bamboo strips and coconut leaves and a new door frame and door. It could not be done in only one day. He understood that Ramachandra had instructed the carpenter earlier, who had prepared and fitted them yesterday and spread palm leaves for the roof. He understood that it was his son's intention that the father was to spend his time there even during the day. However he had to spend the night in that hut only. When he entered, the walls and pillars turned sooty and black. It seemed to suggest his previous state of mind. But now he was a completely different man and the suggestion of the hut was also different. He felt the walls were showing disgust at his fall. Satyappa felt like lying down and resting for a while in that hut. He was tired. There was no mat inside. He spread his towel, lied down on his back and for a while, he slept. When he woke up, he was aware of one aspect. He was not feeling such turmoil only for his breach of celibacy yesterday. The turmoil was for the final stage of his whole life which suddenly lost direction. He ruminated: if he had married again, or kept a woman, or had slept with numerous women, couldn't he have brought up his son? There was probability of his son being spoilt or taking to the wrong path following his father's example. But it was only a probability. Is Ramachandra now not spoilt? Is he good? Is it being good, listening to whatever his wife says and being obedient to her in matters of money and physical desire? He felt totally empty inside.

That night, he slept in the hut. But he was now free from the desires and erotic feelings he had felt earlier. He was sure that he would not get such desires again. But there was an utter nothingness inside him. Loss of celibacy, of all the principles he believed till now turning topsy-turvy, topped with the feeling that he was reduced to the status of a servant whose job was to watch this grove. This sense of worthlessness occupied his mind. He fell asleep after a long time. By the time he woke up in the morning, he felt an itching sensation. He came out, took a peek and found some blisters, that too when minutely observed. He thought, they might be owing to prickly heat or ... He was scared. Manjayya had said that she was clean. She might be externally clean, but a woman of such profession ... His fears increased. He consoled himself thinking, he need not panic. By afternoon, the itching was lessened. When he went to bed, he wanted to scratch. He could not get sleep for a long time with the suspicion '*it had to be that.*' By the time it was past midnight, he got up, switched on the torch and inspected. Yes, the blisters were spread densely, and there was a bit of swelling also. Now there was no doubt at all. At once he had to consult a doctor and take treatment. If he allowed it to develop, if he allowed it to develop ... The very idea made him shudder. It was only half past twelve in the night; he lied down. He had a feeling that the fitting punishment for his sin had already begun. After a little while, he remembered his thoughts of earlier days that it was not correct to apply the ideas of meritorious deed or sin to each and every act. Whatever he had thought about replayed in his mind: right-wrong, justice-injustice, were enough to identify the vicissitudes of rise and fall of man and his mind turned to those thoughts and the present danger vanished.

He woke up early in the morning, went home, told his daughter-in-law in a commanding voice, 'Prepare some breakfast for me soon,' and took his bath. Then he asked his son, 'I need money. I must go to Tiptur to attend to some business.'

'What business do you have in Tiptur now?' Ramachandra questioned him.

Satyappa got angry. More than being angry, he was pained. He felt that his son spoke to him like a strict father who admonishes his little son who doesn't know to manage responsibility or money. He said curtly, 'That's not your concern; just give me twenty five rupees.'

Though Ramachandra said, 'It is the last month to remit the final instalment of land tax, how am I going to manage,' he went in, took the key from his wife and gave his father the money. The daughter-in-law took forty-five more minutes to prepare roti and put pickles with it.

Tiptur was ten miles from Mattikere and it was their taluk-centre also. Moreover it was the place Satyappa used to visit, to deposit copra in the wholesale warehouse and buy clothes and other things needed for household use. After he had handed over all the responsibility to his son, he had not come to this place. It was five miles to Mattikere Gate by walk. From there eight miles by bus. But many times the bus would be overcrowded and would not stop there at all. So, to avoid this he decided to walk. When he was walking holding his umbrella, he felt a burning sensation when the cloth touched the spot. Which doctor should he consult? If they were seniors, he would be known to them, as he was participating in the freedom struggle and other movements. At least they would have heard his name. So it would be better if it was some new doctor. Many new doctors from far off places had come and opened clinics, and he decided to consult a new doctor. He reached Tiptur at three in the afternoon and took his meals in a hotel. While walking on the market street, he spotted a board Dr Prakash, MBBS, and thought he must be a new doctor and went inside. Yes, he was a new one, nearly thirty or thirty-five years of age. Satyappa's mind was cringing with shame. There was no other patient. The doctor was reading a film magazine full of pictures. He said 'Please be seated.' Satyappa took his seat. The doctor looked at his face. Satyappa did not know what to say and how to start. He could not speak. His voice refused to come out. When the doctor asked, 'Yes, tell me' in an ordering tone, it flashed to him how to convey his problem and he said, 'I have to talk to you in private.'

'There is no private room, please come behind this screen,' the doctor said. Without making any test, not enquiring the character of the illness, he asked, 'Well, who were you with?'

'Some evil thought caught me, doctor. Please cure me,' said Satyappa.

The doctor tested him with his eyes, looked at Satyappa's face and said, 'Look here, this is a matter to be kept secret. You have to take injections. There should be no delay. I must get those special injections from Bangalore. Sometimes it will not be available in Bangalore too. It has to be procured from Bombay. There are only two tubes with me, which I have reserved for another patient. It is my responsibility to get the tubes by ordering through telegram by day after tomorrow. You have to take twelve injections in all.'

'How much would be the fees, doctor?'

'You see, curing you completely is my responsibility and it is also my responsibility to keep it a secret and guard your reputation. If you go to other doctors, your cure would be only temporary and the root of this illness will not be destroyed. Do you understand what I said?'

Satyappa simply nodded. And the doctor continued: 'It is very important to guard your reputation in such matters. I do not write your name either in the book or the prescription slips. You must stay in this place for twelve days. One injection per day. I do not cause pain like other doctors, who use a thick and long needle to administer this injection. I have with me a very delicate special American needle.'

Satyappa looked at the doctor as if he was reassured. The doctor said in a decisive tone raising his index finger, 'Give me one thousand rupees in all; I do not ask you extra for the ointment and tablets. Everything is included.'

By then Satyappa had become a bit confident and had developed trust in the doctor. So he spoke without faltering. 'You see doctor, in my condition one thousand means ... Please, I will never forget your kindness. But in my condition ...'

'Look here, you did not remember your condition when you slept with such women. But you remember conveniently that condition when you have to pay money to the doctor who cures you. Anyway, let it be. You have to engage a room and stay at a hotel and manage your expenses of food, lodging, etc. I do not ask you about your name. I told you it is important to guard your reputation. You give me eight hundred rupees and arrange for your food and stay in a hotel for twelve days. An injection, a tablet and an ointment are the only remedies for this infection and there is no restriction of diet. I leave it to you to decide.' By then another patient came in.

Satyappa did not say anything further, but just said, 'Yes I'll come again, how long will your clinic be open?'

'Until seven.'

Satyappa came out. Even though other patients had not come to the shop, Satyappa did not feel like bargaining. It was enough going to this doctor alone, shrinking his six foot frame to the size of a fist. He did not want to consult any other doctor or enquire about fees and face the same humiliation. However, he had to arrange for one thousand rupees. With this intention, while he walked towards the railway station, he remembered Channaveerapa, the wholesale copra dealer. It was the copra warehouse to which he carried his copra. Now Ramachandra often comes here, gets a loan of one or two thousand when needed, and clears the loan during the copra season. Satyappa remembered, before he handed over the responsibility of managing the property to his son, he was also doing business in the same shop. He turned to the left, went directly to 'Ravaani Channaveerappa and Sons.' He could not find the senior proprietor. The servant who was at the door of the shop told that the master had gone on a tour of North India with an intention of visiting Kashi, Gaya, Badri, Kedara, Agra and Delhi, along with 'Yatra Travels' company and he would return only after a month. The elder son Shekarappa sat near the cash till. Satyappa got inside, introduced himself, and Shekarappa greeted him with respect. After mutual enquiry of welfare, Satyappa asked him for a loan of one thousand rupees against his copra account.

But Shekarappa, with the typical false modesty of the businessman begged to be excused and said, 'The accounts are in your son's name. If he comes and signs, I can give you the amount.'

Satyappa argued, 'Look here, it is only six years since I handed over the property to my son. Before that, for twenty-five long years, that is after the demise of my father, I was the one who conducted business with your warehouse. If you want, please check the old account books.'

Shekarappa replied, 'Don't I know sir, that you are the owner? But, if accounts are to be tallied, the signature of the account holder is needed. If my father were here and if he had agreed, I could have given you a loan. If you please, bring your son here, or bring a signed letter from him, I'll surely give you the money. After all, your place is not all that far.'

Satyappa said, 'If there was time to bring such a letter, would I be wasting time arguing with you? I am asking you because I need the money urgently. I myself will write so and sign in the account book.'

The young owner remained stubbornly silent. After ten minutes Satyappa repeated his request. Shekarappa, feigning humility yet again, folded his hands and said, 'Excuse me, if Appaji was in town, I could've done something. He has still not given me the permission or freedom to decide on such matters.'

Coming out of the warehouse, Satyappa felt helpless. He felt angry, not against that young boy in the shop, but against himself, who had given away everything to his son, without keeping back a single pie, not even for contingencies, for himself. When he walked the cloth brushed against the skin, and the burning sensation aggravated. It was now more severe than it was in the morning. It might further intensify by the morrow. He thought if I have the first injection today, I might get some relief. But he could not find out how he could do that. He walked slowly, avoiding contact with cloth, reached the railway station and sat on a bench. More than his present situation, his inner emptiness surfaced. He began to feel the burning sensation though there was no contact with cloth. He brooded upon his condition: 'Oh what a state have I reduced myself to. Even that man in the copra shop does not value my signature.' Though Satyappa wanted to inspect the present condition of the blisters, he dropped the idea. After some time, he thought of another way. There was a bus service from Tiptur to Channarayapattana. He could go to Bilikere from there and ask Manjayya for money. It would not be difficult for Manjayya to manage one thousand rupees. Satyappa could pay it back after he got cured. Moreover, Manjayya was the root cause of this ugly desire being born inside him and it was only just and fair that Manjayya should help in its treatment and cure. He did not think it necessary that he could ask Manjayya to engage a doctor for him who would charge lesser fees. He walked to the bus stand. Somehow he spent the night and took the morning eight o'clock bus to Channarayapattana. With the jerks and jolts of the bus the blisters got itchier and the burning sensation too increased. Not only that, it was difficult for him to hide the expression of pain from his face. Looking at the face distorted with pain, the co-passengers were bound to ask the cause of the pain. By chance, if they knew the nature of the disease, they might ask him to get down from the bus. He felt it was easy to face death than to bear this pain. Tolerating this strenuous journey for more than two hours, when he got down at the Channarayapattana bus stand, he saw Manjayya. Yes, it was Manjayya, who had put on the khakhi coat of the Sandalwood Department. Satyappa began to walk rapidly. The contact with cloth intensified the pain and burning. He shouted, 'Manjayya, Manjayya,' as if afraid Manjayya would escape from there. Manjayya came near and Satyappa said, 'You see, Manjayya, I came in search of you.'

Manjayya said, 'Today, the Hassan bus is a bit late. Otherwise, you would not have met me. I have some work in the forest office. What's the matter?' Satyappa pulled Manjayya by his arm and walking towards a desolate spot, allowed his face to contort with the pain he felt as the cloth rubbed against the rashes.

He pleaded with Manjayya. 'Look here Manjayya, please don't go now. Whatever important work you have, come here. Let me explain my problem.'

Manjayya said, 'Oh is that all? I know it. You have got this disease from Naagi. But you know, she is clean.'

'Do you know what has happened to me? A continuous sensation of burning and more burning. Those rashes have spread densely.'

'Do you know Annayya, women who are used to cooking can hold any hot vessel with their bare hands and put it down. Their hands won't burn nor do they get blisters. Do you know why? Practice. Look at me, I don't get that sort of thing, whichever women I sleep with. But, you don't have the practice. That's why it has happened. Once you get used to it, just like me you too will have no such problem. Don't be scared,' saying so Manjayya laughed loudly and patted Satyappa's back.

Satyappa asked Manjayya to sit on the platform of the veterinary hospital and narrated his going to Tiptur, and the obstacles in getting money. Manjayya said, 'Look Annayya that doctor of Tiptur is a greedy bastard. Looking at your face, he surmised that you were scared and demanded one thousand rupees and then had come down to eight hundred. Here, in Channarayapattana, there is a doctor by the name Hasheem in Market Street. He is very pious and decent. His fixed rate is three hundred rupees. He treats all such diseases. You tell him my name, if you like.'

'Then I need at least three hundred rupees, Manjayya. And to stay in this place and for food and other things, don't I need an extra hundred? You must give it to me. I will somehow pay it back,' Satyappa said and held Manjayya's hand.

Manjayya sat for two minutes as if he was thinking seriously and said, 'You see Annayya, it is not a problem for me to arrange four or five hundred for you. But you being the owner of lands and property, have returned empty-handed from the copra wholesale dealer who said there was no value for your signature? How then do you propose to pay me back? Now what I suggest is this. You must return to your village, call your son and tell him, "You bastard, I need one thousand rupees. Today, immediately. Come on, bring it here. Right now." And if he asks you, "Why do you need so much money all of a sudden?" tell him, "I need it because I slept with a woman and contracted venereal disease. I need money for its treatment." What is there to be ashamed of? Is it a disease no one in this world has ever had? You see Annayya you considered yourself Mahatma Gandhi and handed over all the property to your son. Because of that, you are undergoing all this shame and turmoil. Just understand this: on the very day the desire to sleep with a woman arose in you and you came to Bilikere, that day itself it was all over. Now return to your place, take back the management of your business from your son. Nothing serious happens in this disease, if there is a delay of one or two days in taking injections. I know more than that Tiptur doctor. Why do you struggle to hide your disease from your son? You know, you need courage to tell the truth. Take a lesson from me. This Manjayya will never bother to conceal any of his diseases. He never tells a lie. Oh, look, that Hassan bus ....' Manjayya stopped speaking mid-sentence and ran towards the bus.

Satyappa was bewildered. It was not possible for him either to walk or run to keep pace with Manjayya. Manjayya stretched out his hand, stopped the bus, squeezed himself inside and the bus went away raising dust.

Satyappa's last hope was sunk. He could not understand whether Manjayya had meant all he said or he had said it with the purpose of putting an end to the path that Satyappa had chosen. But Satyappa was stuck with the problem of managing this situation, solving this issue. He did not have the time or patience to analyse the workings of Manjayya's mind. He felt he did not have the strength to stand. He sat on the platform of the veterinary hospital. When he sat, because of the contact with the ground, he felt the burning sensation increase. Stumbling in the dark recesses for half an hour, his mind dwelt on the question, 'What was he to do now?' If it was Dr Hasheem of Channarayapattana, it would be five hundred rupees, if it was the doctor of Tiptur, it would be one thousand. He brooded: Didn't he have the means? Didn't he have any friends at all? When he stirred his memory, the names of Olagerahalli Ningappa, Chikkegowdaru of Basavampura, Halage Gowda of his own village came to mind. All these were close friends of his while he was engaged in public service. If he would go to any one of them and request that he needed a loan of one thousand rupees and that he would repay it within six months but the fact that he took this loan should be kept a secret, would they refuse? Or if he would go to all of them and ask for a loan of three hundred rupees each? So, it was not such a big problem to arrange for money, Satyappa felt. Within ten minutes, he got up decided to go and have his meals in a hotel in town, get into a bus bound for Tiptur, get down at Mattikere Gate and walk straight to Olagerahalli. He proceeded towards Market Street. There was a hotel to the left. When he stood before the hotel, he saw a big provision store next to it. Inside the shop, coils of jute rope of varying thickness were hung. As soon as he saw the rope coils, Satyappa was drawn to them and stood gazing, for more than half an hour. The shopkeeper, who was watching him from inside asked, 'What do you want, sir? Please come in.' Satyappa, as if awakened from a dream, muttered, 'Oh nothing,' and quickly stepped inside the hotel. While he was having his lunch, a clear solution flashed across. Whoever it was Ningappa, Chikkegowda or Halagegowda, he would have to lie to them.

He was fed up with telling lies since the last four days, from the time he went in search of a woman in Bilikere. And now again telling lies, taking loans, later paying back through false means, oh, it is better to buy a rope for eight annas, go directly to Bilikere, hang himself from the branch of the banyan tree his father-in-law had chosen, the one in front of the Shivaalaya. This thought took root in the depth of his mind and as a result, there was contentment. Moreover, there was a bus service from Channarayapattana to Bilikere. All he had to do was to enquire about the evening bus timings, travel by it, lie down on the platform of Shivaalaya as a visitor from another place and get up around midnight. Thus a clear plan took shape in his mind and he decided it was the most appropriate thing to do. By then he had eaten a little rice and felt he could not eat any more. He felt an aversion to food. What he had eaten now was enough to walk up to the bus stand and travel by bus. He got up, washed his hands, paid up and came out. He went to the shop, bought eight cubits of soft jute rope that could easily slide into a noose. He wound it into a coil, put it in his bag and walked to the bus stand. He came to know that the last bus to Bilikere was at five in the evening. It suited him perfectly. But it was still only 1:00 pm. Where should he while away the time? He thought for a while and walked towards the Traveller's Bungalow. He was not feeling the pain even when his dhoti touched the skin, now, after he decided to end his life. He said to himself as he walked towards the Travellers' Bungalow, 'While the body itself is ready to cease to be, what matters if there is some pain in a small part?' He sat on the platform outside the room where he stayed with Manjayya on the night of Parameshwarayya's *Vaikunta*, the day he saw Chandrika. There were two big trees in front of him and there was no one else. He spread his towel on the stone slab and lied down on his back. He began to recall that his fall had started from that same room. Suddenly a thought entered his mind. Saati was staying in this town. It was not such a difficult thing to search her house. If he went there and asked her, 'Saati, I have a problem, I need some money. Can you somehow arrange one thousand rupees. If not, can you at least give me your gold chain, please. I will pawn it and get the money. Within six months I'll redeem the chain. Without asking for the reason, she will oblige. Then I can cure myself. At once Satyappa got up. But within two minutes, his enthusiasm died down. He thought: if I do not tell her that I am suffering from such a disease and I want money for treatment, and simply ask for the money, it would tantamount to telling a lie. He could have got the money from Ningappa, Chikkegowda or Halagegowda by uttering lies. But to tell lies to Saati seemed utterly mean. Another brave idea took root. 'Why not tell her the truth?' Though he reflected for a long time, he failed to decide, and felt a sinking feeling closing in on him. Again, he lied down and looked at his watch. It was three. It was enough if he started at half past four. If it was twelve o'clock midnight only nine hours of his life remained. This knowledge caused grief and gnawed at his insides. He felt his throat choke, but his eyes remained dry. After a little while, there was sorrow and a sadness. Sorrow means losing the fondness and love of life. But what was left to lose? The question arose, but he neither understood the question nor did the answer occur to him. He ruminated, why was he going to Bilikere, in search of the same banyan tree on which his father-in-law hanged himself as if there was no other place in this world. Was it his intention to follow the path of his father-in-law? Did he want to prove that he was also as truthful as Parameshwarayya? Or did he feel that his final punishment too should take place in the same village where his downfall took place? No suitable answer flashed across. Parameshwarayya was a person worthy of reverence. Morally, he stood tall. But he? He had opted to surrender to the noose, for committing a wretched deed and not knowing any other means of coming out of it. So, he should not pollute that tree by climbing on it and hanging himself from its branch. Immediately he felt that this was right. If he had to hang himself, it should be either in the hut of Manjayya's grove or in his own grove. He saw the propriety in his decision that the venue of his death should be different. Within five minutes he decided it should be his own grove. Why should Manjayya be unnecessarily involved. He decided to catch the Tiptur bus and get down at Mattikere Gate, got up, slung the towel across his shoulder, took the handbag which contained the coil of rope, held his umbrella and walked to the bus stand.

At five, he boarded the Tiptur bus. While the bus moved, with every bump, he suffered the burning sensation and pain. It did not matter in whatever posture he sat. His mind wondered, How was it? Even when he had decided to commit suicide, this bodily pain refused to be alleviated. His mind began exploring the relationship between pain and life, death and cessation of pain. It was a journey of one and a half hours. He got down at Mattikere Gate, when the evening light had dimmed and darkness was thickening. By the time he reached Mattikere, it would be totally dark. Why should he go home? If he went straight to the grove, at that hour, there would not be anybody moving. Thieves were the only ones who might enter the grove knowing that he was not in the village, but they wouldn't start their work before midnight. So, he thought of going to the grove directly, climbing the *jamun* tree that he already had identified in his mind, sit on the fork of the first branch that had stretched and tie the rope. He could finish the job by eight forty five. His mind too approved it. When his mind made note that there was only a span of two hours left for the end, it felt a sort of lightness. But suddenly, he perspired profusely. The whole body was drenched, the inner garments became sticky. His pace decreased. He thought of sitting somewhere for a while and resting. But with a stubbornness, 'Why should I rest?' he increased his pace, though the pain and burning sensation aggravated because of the brisk walking as the cloth brushed continuously against the blisters. After he had walked for two miles, there was a stone bench at the turn to Olagerahalli. When he sat on it, a cool breeze blew and there was a clarity in his mind. For half an hour, he sat there and then the chain of thoughts started: Why did he decide to end his life? Was it because he could not arrange money for the treatment? If he determined, it would not be a problem to adjust money. Where was the need to tell the reason for taking loan when he reached Basavampura and had gone to Olagerahalli or to Mattikere Halagegowda. It was enough if he said there was an emergency and he needed money. Not a problem at all. Was suicide the only punishment for the loss of the celibacy he had willingly undergone? Oh how many crores of men and women in this world have such relations! That means, if you marry and proclaim it before society and then have physical relationship it is legal and if not it is illicit. If that is so, should the final punishment be suicide? When his thoughts moved in this direction he did not find any reason to end his life. Would he not have taken treatment if he suffered from any other kind of scabies, boils or ulcer? Don't the doctors themselves say that three fourths of diseases are contagious diseases? Such and other reasons formed in his mind. He thought of throwing away the jute rope and resuming his walk. But he did not do so. He did not feel like turning towards Olagerahalli. He got up and proceeded towards his village. He thought it was better to put an end to his life. Even after getting treatment by somehow arranging for money, what did he have to live for? He did not find any difference between living or not living another twenty or thirty years more. It was half past nine when he neared his village. By then he had defended once more that it was wise and reasonable to end his life. When he came in front of the village, he stood for five minutes oscillating between the two roads, whether to take the one that directly turns towards the grove or to take the other to go home and then to the grove. Ramachandra had got the hut repaired and Satyappa had to go there to watch the grove. Finally he walked homewards.

The children were asleep. Ramachandra and his wife were preparing to go to bed. Ramachandra opened the door and asked, 'Where were you? Since yesterday, we waited, and waited and ...' he did not continue after looking at his father's face. Enough food had remained from what had been cooked in the afternoon. The daughter-in-law went into the kitchen placed a plate before her father-in-law and served him. Satyappa washed his feet and hands and swallowed quickly. Ramachandra asked him, 'Are you going to sleep on the platform or are you going to the grove?' He answered that he would go to the grove. Immediately the son said, 'I have put a new mat there and a wooden block for a pillow and everything else. I did not let out the secret that you were not in the village. So, no bunches were stolen.' When Satyappa took his blanket, torch and cudgel, he took out the coil of rope from his bag, put it in the blanket and folded it. He asked his son, 'I want a sheet of paper and a pen.' 'Why do you need them now?' He answered, 'I have to write some accounts,' Ramachandra gave his father two sheets of paper and a pen. Satyappa folded them and put them into his pocket, wore his chappals and went to the grove. He put down the torch, cudgel, blanket and the rope and then folded the paper, placed it on his lap and wanted to write two or three lines rapidly. He switched on the torch, adjusted it and placed it in such a way that the light would fall on the paper. Now, what should he write? Nothing struck him. 'Nobody is responsible for my death. I have committed suicide of my own free will.' This was the sentence, that was written by all who committed suicide. But Satyappa felt that he was different. That means, he should write the true reason, not the standard lines. It seemed insignificant to him whether to tell lies to get money for his treatment or to tell truth for any other thing. But he felt that a man while dying, at least when he had decided his own death and was going to implement it, must tell the truth, why he had decided to die. He should not lie for any other reason, good or bad. He should not write a death note that could harm another person. But he decided to tell the truth precisely by which nobody would be harmed. Then he began thinking: why was he committing suicide? The torchlight started dimming. He switched it off thinking the battery might be exhausted by the time he finished his death note. Sitting in the darkness, he began to analyse things one by one. There was still the smell of burnt walls inside the hut. But however much he pondered, a suitable reason did not occur to him. The words 'of my own free will' had only meant that police should not suspect any other person and it did not have any other meaning. Disappointment, frustration, diseases, loans, defeats – these will never be the chief reasons for suicide. He thought, just as it was difficult to find precise reasons for man to live, so was it impossible to find precise reasons to commit suicide. However, he felt, that the only sufficient reason might be that one doesn't want to live. His thoughts thus wandered and lost direction. At last he looked at his watch. It was fifteen minutes to two. He thought if he continued to brood so, the night would be over and switched on the torch and wrote: 'I have committed suicide of my own free will. Nobody is responsible for this. Nobody had any hint or idea about this.' He signed, put the date, week and time, folded the letter, kept it in his pocket, held the rope and came out. Except the sparkling stars in the sky, there was dense darkness below on the earth. It is said that persons who commit suicide would want their final wish to be satisfied before dying, like their wish of seeing their near and dear ones or eating delicious sweets they most liked. That's why even the courts had the system of asking the final wish of the criminal before sending him to the gallows. For a minute, Satyappa thought whether he too had such a final wish. Nothing came to mind. Again he stopped for ten minutes, yet nothing flashed. He convinced himself that was the most suitable condition of mind for hanging and walked towards the tree he had earlier identified.

He tucked up the dhoti at the waist so that the knee movement was unhampered, put the coil of rope around his neck and switched on the torch. He looked for a hollow in the tree and for small branches and curves that would be convenient to climb. He put the torch in the side pocket and began to climb slowly. When the sore spot touched the hard trunk of the tree, a severe burning sensation started and he felt as if he was dying then and there. It was a huge trunk and he could not climb it without it coming into contact with his skin. He determined that it might burn for two minutes but he had to pursue. He switched on the torch twice and climbed on to the first branch. When he sat on the branch that was nearly eighteen feet high from the ground, another new aspect occurred to him: whatever was written in the suicide note, the police would conduct post-mortem. The doctor would certainly come to the decision that Mattikere Satyanarayanappa slept with a diseased woman and contacted the disease and not able to bear it, he committed suicide. The same decision would be spread in the surrounding villages. By chance, if it was published in a newspaper, the news would spread everywhere. People working for newspapers hanker after such news. And his reputation would be torn to shreds. Satyappa broke out in cold sweat as soon this thought crossed his mind. So, he felt it was better to live and get himself cured. For more than ten minutes, he was absorbed in his thought and almost throwing down the rope was in the process of getting down the tree when, oh! another thought crossed his mind. He did not buy the rope, and climb on that branch, for fear of his reputation or because he was ashamed of his deed being known to people. If he had that fear, he would have taken a loan from some of his old friends and could have taken treatment. If he himself did not exist, what was this concern he had about his reputation or infamy. He justified that all those concerns were only while living. He remembered the aspect of his strength: that he was never caught in the illusion that even after his death, his name and fame should remain the same, people should think of him in the same manner and his name should last as long as the sun and the moon exist. Again ten to fifteen minutes were lost. He switched on the torch, looked at the watch. It was already three, getting closer to dawn. Somewhere from the distance, the chirping of birds was heard. He thought it wise not to delay anymore, uncoiled the rope, measured it – four cubits were enough to hang the rope. He left out the rest of the rope empty and tied the central part firmly to the branch. He put a knot tightly to one end of the rope, made a noose like the one used to wrap the rope around the neck of pots, while drawing water from the well. He put it around his neck, letting it loose so that it could easily slide. He decided, there was no need for unnecessary delay now, put his hand into his pocket, ascertained that the death note was there, closed his eyes and imagined, 'Yes one, two, three, thumping sound, noose would get tightened, breathing gets choked, hands and feet struggle. Hands stretch to untie the knot, meanwhile the noose would tighten, consciousness would dim, the hands fail to know what to do and the body would start sweating. Further, there would only be the writhing of the body. In the end, that too would stop and there would only be the motionlessness of a hanging corpse. Satyappa had sat still on the fork of the branch along with the rope around his neck. He was sweating. He could not know the depth of the ground beneath the branch in that darkness. He turned his neck. Here and there behind the leaves, he saw stars. Suddenly he took off the noose from his neck and threw it away. He switched on the torch he had still kept in his pocket, began to descend from the branch to the trunk, from the trunk to the ground. He was no longer aware of the pain or the burning though the skin contacted the tree trunk while descent and the cloth after touching the ground. He rushed towards the hut. He took the cudgel he had left there, forgot even to switch on the torch and ran towards the grove gate and from there to his house in rapid strides despite the darkness. When he came near the village, alerted by the sound of his running feet, the dogs began to bark. Hearing the barking of these dogs, all the dogs of the village returned the bark. Some dogs rushed to attack him. People who slept on the platforms got up and some followed him. But Satyappa, blissfully unaware of all this, went directly to his house, thumped the door with his cudgel ... *khat, khat, khat,* and shouted, 'Hey Ramachandra open the door, get up and open the door! Will you open it quickly or should I break it open? You bastard!' By the time he recognised his father's voice and opened the door, people from ten neighbouring houses woke up and came. Ramachandra switched on the lights inside and outside. People crowded in the street, on the platform and near the door of the hall. The dogs were still barking.

Satyappa shouted loudly, 'Listen De Ramachandra, after your mother died, I did not marry again, because I wanted to bring you up decently and comfortably. Since then I had not looked at a woman. Five or six days ago, I made contact with a woman. Disease has caught me and it is swelling up. When I went to that Channaveerappa's shop and asked for money to pay the doctors fees, that bastard Shekara of your age said, "You don't own the accounts, without the signature of your son, I won't give you a single pie." Not finding any other way I thought of hanging myself. Even now there is that rope on the *jamun* tree in the grove. Now, here and now, you write on this paper, "My accounts actually belong to my father. From today I am not the owner of this property or any business. You do all your transactions with my father only and don't call me for any transactions." You rascal – will you write it and put your signature to it or not?' shouting so, Satyappa began thrashing Ramachandra with his cudgel, raining repeated blows on him.

Two men who thought Satyappa had gone mad, held him from behind. But Satyappa escaped from their hold and used his cudgel on the fellows who tried to catch him. The rest got scared and started running. But running was not easy, for so many people stood so very close to each other. Some stumbled and fell down. As if his throat had stretched and spread to the surrounding one lakh villages, Satyappa shouted so that the whole village should hear, 'Yes listen all of you. I slept with a woman and contracted a disease. I need money to cure this. Having my money in the warehouse, why should I ask from someone else?' He turned to Ramachandra and said, 'You stupid bastard, why are you standing like a dumb fool? What are you gazing at?' When Satyappa raised his cudgel again, Ramachandra sank to the ground. Satyappa threw before his son the sheet of paper and pen his son had given him earlier. Ramachandra began writing rapidly. His wife was scared and stood near the inner door. Satyappa took what his son had written and read loudly in the light. He then folded the paper, put it in his pocket and walked swiftly outside the village into the darkness. Nobody dared follow him. Even the dogs were barking against one another, but did not follow him. Everybody looked at Ramachandra's face. Ramachandra, numb with fear earlier, now felt the pain of the blows which were swelling up and turning to bruises.

The unexpected meeting with Satyappa at the Travellers' Bungalow in Channarayapattana, actually helped Manjayya to push the turmoil in his mind to a corner. How could he expect that Satyappa would come to Channarayapattana, that too to the Travellers' Bungalow and meet him. Not that he would not have invited Chandrika there. Winning transactions with the higher officials of sandalwood department was enough to satisfy his ego. But his method was to satiate his ego by enjoying a girl who dressed like a film star, the same night. It was easy for him to push his inner emptiness after Chandrika left, because Satyappa was there and Manjayya could share his thoughts with him. But after he seated Satyappa in the Mattikere bus, bid goodbye and got into the Hassan bus, while travelling to Hassan, Sarojakshi occupied his mind. That man, her husband, got nervous while giving statement when there were complaints from so many people. Surely he will be suspended. Let the suspension order reach him. Then she will understand what this Manjayya is. Let her face the state of starvation not having salary for two months and spending whatever little she has saved. Then the slut would come in search of him, wherever he would be. He would tell that slut: 'First sleep with me, any further talks only after that.' Thinking so, he imagined the picture of Sarojakshi surrendering to him in bed. In such affairs, Manjayya was not successful in getting every woman he targeted. Though he was extremely confident of his aim, when he was not able to get the fruit, he remembered, he had never taken it so seriously as this time around. Were it not so, he thought, why did he wander from village to village, caused so many farmers to write complaints and created a case, so that her husband would be suspended? Was she such a ravishing beauty? Mother of two – a boy of ten and a girl of five. What did she have? Complexion? Build? Tightness of body? What tightness would a woman have, after giving birth to two children? Was he not uncontrollably attracted to her soon after he saw her and talked with her? She too had behaved as if he was someone special. Yes, he was attracted and she had consistently encouraged that attraction. But when he was making that final move, she had humiliated him by slapping his cheek. Remembering that even now, travelling in the bus, he suddenly felt a burning sensation in that cheek. It was not merely the red burning sensation, but the burning caused by the humiliation of being slapped by a woman and slapping her back. He had left her house then and when he went on his own and asked her help, she should have told her husband to save him from punishment, if she really loved him. But how cleverly the slut evaded! Manjayya still burnt with anger. Why does she still haunt his mind? He began to remember all the details about his relation with her, to understand the workings of his mind clearly. If beauty can be decided only by complexion, colour, height and size, we have to call the mannequins, standing in the glass cases draped neatly in varieties of saris … beautiful women! That's not a woman's beauty. Sarojakshi's complexion was dark. But her eyes, bright like torchlight, reflected an inner power and intelligence. The row of beautifully shaped, gleaming white teeth and shining earrings of white studs in the ears were attractive. Manjayya wondered whether the brightness of the three – eyes, teeth and earrings – joined together to create the power of a magical spell. From the very first day he saw her, he had felt that in keeping her house neat and aesthetically pleasing, in embroidery, in the manner of bringing up her children, in the method of cooking and serving, she was a cut above the rest. He remembered how she had served the uppittu she prepared, in the lovely shape of a plate, matching spoon, glass and water pot on the first day of his visit. When her husband introduced Manjayya, she said 'Namaskaara' stylishly. He recalled, 'Did he not then have a feeling of inferiority?' Even the dresses she put on her children were stitched by her. Manjayya said to himself. 'Oh which bastard professional tailor knows that kind of stitching?' Sarojakshi cast such a spell over him. Was it a new thing for Manjayya to be attracted to a woman? But he felt a sort of fear, which he himself could not define, towards Sarojakshi. He was very careful, scared, whether he would speak or behave like a country bumpkin before her. Not that he was unused to educated urban people. Many a times he stayed in the houses of Hassan lawyers and took food with them. He had spoken with the wife of the famous lawyer Venkataramayya, once in a way he even took flowers and fruits for her. But while talking to her, he had never felt that he was a villager or a country bumpkin. He did not feel, he should be careful in the use of language. Didn't he know the difference of language to be used in courts, offices, mutts, temples and mantras? While that was the case, when he spoke with this Sarojakshi, why did he want to think and be sure of the meaning before speaking? Again, he wondered, what sort of fear or respect was it, which he had not shown to any D.C. She too behaved so, cooked with special attention. He did not know whether she cooked dishes so deliciously because they were for him or whether whatever she prepared was naturally tasty. Manjayya wondered, how could she know he took meat at Santosh Non-veg Restaurant only, though he never ate meat at his place? If he asked Puttellayya and Puradamma to prepare non-veg, they would gladly prepare it for him and they too would happily eat it. But, he was a pure vegetarian in his village, not letting out even a hint about his meat eating. That 'Gangadikar Military Hotel' used too much chillies and in that Rahamania there was the overpowering smell of nutmeg, clove and mace. Either in Mysore, Bangalore, Davanagere or Hubli, you could not find the perfection of Santosh Non-vegetarian Restaurant, was his firm belief. But once, when Sarojakshi served him mutton biryani, he felt it was tastier than that served by Santosh Restaurant. Even today it is so, her recipe is not mastered or bettered even in Santosh Restaurant! Anyway, Manjayya still wondered, how did she come to know about his meat eating? He had never visited Santosh Restaurant, either with her husband, or with any other known people. These village bastards who come here to attend courts, offices, Tuesday markets and fairs and car-festivals in January, do not know its place or name. They are simple boors who would have a heart attack looking at the bill. When this was the case, how did she know of his meat eating? Or was she confident that if she prepared and served, he would certainly eat. But what authority did she have to think that, think he would certainly eat? For weeks together, he searched for an answer, but could not find any. When he became familiar with her, one day when she was alone, he asked her: 'How did you know, I eat meat?' Then, how she laughed … as if she switched on the combined brightness of her eyes, teeth and earrings to dazzle his eyes and said, 'Don't I know the mind of my god?' What did she mean? It was thus with whatever she spoke. But he couldn't muster the courage to continue further. Why and how did she have such power, such a hold over him?

Not just that, after he became the sandalwood contractor, somehow, his craze for women decreased. Was it because the sandalwood business demanded a larger portion of his time and attention or was it tiredness, caused by frequent travel, much more than he used to earlier? But then, was it not on the day he took charge of the contract, that Appajappa had taken him to his house and Sarojakshi had served him uppittu? But it was not strictly true, that this disinterest happened after he saw her. Even after that, he remembered, how many women he had ensnared and slept with in Channarayapattana, Hassan, Bilikere and in various villages. And how he had seized Lakkoo, that night, tripped her beneath that beech tree, ensured her subjection to him, after enjoying her just once. And even after he was acquitted, he was managing to keep her involved to ensure she believed him. Manjayya reflected, why was his craving for women not as intense as it used to be? Why did that mad desire of his not rise so forcefully? Sarojakshi never provoked him either in dream or in fantasy. She did not have that beauty or build. He had not imagined even for a single day, lying down on his bed and seeing her naked in the big mirror beside the bed. Yet it had happened so. Was age catching up with him? After all, fifty-two. Was that so old? Was it not like the tamarind tree, the older one got, the tangier the taste. He berated himself, that he was a stupid man who was destroying the basic happiness of life by taking this contract and travelling in the hot sun. He did not need this contract or its income to earn a living, did not have expenses to be met out of this. What he got from that contract was just about enough to distribute to his superiors and subordinates, what remained a paltry sum. He thought, then, why shouldn't he give it up?

Yes, why should he not let it go? This question had risen in his mind not just once but several times, on the day she slapped him. Because of this contract his influence in the whole district had increased. Rajegowda, who contested the election had requested his help. He took Manjayya in his car to many towns. Why should he lose such a powerful position, for no rhyme or reason? But, though there was power and authority, what use were these if they were obstacles to pleasure? The same thought that Manjayya had reflected on earlier, resurfaced. Again the question sprang to mind – was she the reason for his mind being averse to that pleasure? Desire for mutton biryani, mutton soup and the chicken she prepared was alright, but the desire for her had not particularly surfaced. Then, it was not correct that his aversion was because of her. How does a woman haunt, when not appearing in mind as a nude figure even while he was alone and had desired her? But whenever he went to Channarayapattana, he felt he ought to go to her house, eat food prepared by her and talk with her. He should not go empty-handed to her house but should take fruits, flowers and biscuits for the children. What sort of a craving was this? When Appajappa was not at home, the children too had gone to school and there was nobody in the house, that desire had not surfaced. If he had decided, should somebody have taught him the turn of phrase to convey his desire? Did she need to be taught the sharp wit to comprehend? Yet he did not feel inclined towards it. It seemed strange, even now he found it strange. The incident that happened one day came to mind and even now it seemed strange and surprising. On that day when there was no one else in the house, he was speaking with her and suddenly his desire raised its hood. Yes, it was his basic nature. He was scared, in case this clever woman would understand, what was going through his mind. In such a condition, he had to find a woman and finish the job. That was his instinct and he knew that. He suddenly got up and said, 'Sarojakshamma, you please cook something. I have some business. I'll return within an hour.' As if she had a natural claim over him, very sweetly, with authority, she protested. 'How can I let you go out in this hot sun? No, no, I won't.' Manjayya insisted, 'No please, I've some urgent business, I'll be back soon. Just make rice and sambar, that's enough,' and rushed to Kanthamani's house. She was alone and feigning anger said, 'Ages since *Saahukar* stepped this side!' Without indulging in any repartee, he made her close the door and pulled her close. Oh, shouldn't the urge be ready and rising! For the first time in life his virility let him down, made fun of him. Kanthamani was furious. 'Hey, did you come to Kanthamani, to mock and tease her?' He did not know how to pacify her. He remembered, it was he who named her Kanthamani, instead of the drab Doddapaapamma of Belagola. She accused, 'I know you have slept with another woman before you came here. That's why you can't do anything.' Manjayya was in a dilemma. If he admitted, it would amount to insulting her. If he denied, it would be insulting himself. It was a tight situation. He averred: 'I have too many things in my mind; some urgent work in the Taluk Office. After finishing my work, I'll come here in the evening, I promise, swear on you.' He touched her hand, as a confirmation of the promise, freed himself from her, put on his clothes and walked to Sarojakshi's house. She served him on the teapoy in the silver platter, rice and rasam seasoned with curry leaves, coriander leaves and cumin. He felt ashamed to face her, embarrassed that he had lied to her. Was she a wife who had been tied a *maangalya* by him to have the claim, that I should not lie to her? Savitri, who wore his *maangalya* left him, because he did not give her the authority of questioning him. If so, how can this Sarojakshi have the authority to know whether I tell a lie or the truth? However she did not ask anything. Perhaps he had imagined it all. She cooks well, talks cordially and serves me food. Perhaps she does all this for the reason that I am helping her husband earn extra money, money that he never managed to earn earlier. If not, why would this smart woman have done so much for me? When Manjayya was consoling himself thus, she asked in a soft voice, 'Could you finish the work you went out for?' Alarm bells started ringing inside. He broke out in a sweat, drops of perspiration profusely covered his forehead. He was afraid to raise his face, afraid Sarojakshi might read his mind. He bowed his head down further and began gulping down his food rapidly. The shirt collar was completely drenched with sweat. He was yet preparing the answer, 'When it is Taluk Office, could the work be finished so easily?' when he felt a cool breeze. He raised his head and saw Sarojakshi standing close and fanning him with a bamboo fan! He was embarrassed. He rose from the chair shouting *ayyayyo*. 'Why?! Can't I fan you?' she asked him, her face bright. The thought crossed his mind yet again: When Sarojakshi speaks, words follow one after the other as continuous as waves. But by the time we try to see them in totality, like receding waves, they have vanished.

Sarojakshi pulled another chair near him, sat down and began to fan slowly. He thought, she was like a new wife in a film ... and remembered that Sarojakshi too now and then would see films. Embarrassment had him in its grip as long as she sat there fanning. She served rice and curds. He immediately said, 'Curds is cool, you need not fan, please.' Then she went into the kitchen and Manjayya pondered whether he should go to Kanthamani's house in the evening. Suppose he went there and again the same thing happened. What an insult it would be! Why did it happen so? He thought for a long time but couldn't find any answer. Even now no answer flashed. This Sarojakshi kept him ensnared, kept alive his infatuation, as he was helping her husband earn extra money. Was she cunning enough to not pay back the principal amount? Perhaps. Let the salary be stopped for two months. The slut would come crawling to him and then he would teach her a lesson. He decided so but the very next moment he developed a sort of disdain, with a lot of effort, thinking, after all she is not such a great beauty, is she!

By then the bus was moving beside Sankenahalli State Forest. All along the road, there was the plantation of eucalyptus trees in hundred and twenty acres of area. It belonged principally to the Forest Department and Watchman Usmani was responsible for its security. It was his job to plant, grow and guard the government forest near the handpost of Karadevu and Sankenahalli. He had to plant the saplings supplied by the government, water them for some time and when he obtained government approval, he could hire some coolies to water the saplings and repair the fence. He had to guard, so that cattle would not creep from nearby villages and to see that nobody cut the branches for firewood. Forest Guard Vishakantayya was Usmani's senior officer, Forester Prabhuswamy was Vishakantayya's senior and Ranger Appajappa was Prabhuswamy's senior. Usmani did not get any extra income, except ten or twenty per head which he got for allowing some villagers to graze their cattle and take away some firewood that was available in the two eucalyptus plantations that were in his authority. That amounted to three to four hundred rupees per year. After Manjayya was appointed as the sandalwood contractor for the taluk, Usmani too began to get some power and a good amount of extra money. Eucalyptus trees would be there of course. It was enough, if either Usmani's wife or his sixteen-year-old son Buden could come once a week and go round the plantation. Manjayya recognised Usmani's power and began to hand over jobs of greater responsibility. Whatever responsibility was entrusted to him, Usmani would prove that he was more strong and powerful than the work assigned and would achieve more than expected. He became very close to Manjayya. Usmani had the courage, skill and efficiency in gathering information about these matters – how many sandalwood trees were there in the groves, fields, wet-lands and dry-lands, of which taluk and hobli (cluster of adjoining villages administered together for tax and land tenure purposes in Karnataka and Andhra), what was the age of the trees, were they ripe, by frightening which person, or bringing the situation of booking a case against him, how much money could he be made to cough out. Along with this, he could go anywhere during nights and build up a case and return. Three months after Manjayya got his contract Usmani could buy a Raleigh bicycle. For him, Manjayya was greater than the Chief Conservator. Though it was the Ranger Appajappa who authorised his salary every month, Usmani respected Manjayya more.

When the bus stopped at Sankenahalli handpost, Usmani who was waiting there, came running near the window where Manjayya sat. He stood outside the window and said 'Salaam Conservator sahib.'

Manjayya asked, 'What's it? Why are you waiting here?'

Usmani said, 'I guessed that you would come by this bus. Any news about the order?'

Manjayya replied, 'The enquiry was completed only yesterday evening. How can the orders be issued so early?'

'Oh, sahib, if you are at the helm, surely that Appajappa would get his marching orders.' While Usmani was guffawing, the bus started. He saluted again, 'Salaam sahib'. When the bus moved forward and the government forest area ended, Manjayya recalled how he got to know the history of Sarojakshi from this Usmani.

One day, in the hot afternoon, Manjayya had gone to Usmani's house near the same handpost to the government forests. Yes, he had gone there on his bicycle. Under a terribly hot sun, the aroma of spices coming out from inside, spread and wafted over the eucalyptus trees. Usmani put the wooden chair on the platform, requested Manjayya to sit down and asked, 'We are cooking chicken sambar, would you please have hot ragi-balls and rice, sahib?'

Manjayya said, 'No, you use too much cinnamon and clove in your cooking. I don't want it. Just give me water to drink, that's enough.' Oh, how subtly and meaningfully did Usmani wink. 'That's right, sahib. After tasting her cooking once, how could you like any other taste?' Manjayya pretended he did not notice the wink, for, he did not feel it proper to have such a degree of informality with his subordinates. Usmani brought a brass pot full of water and a glass. After Manjayya drank water and began sweating, Usmani asked, 'Did you come from Channarayapattana sahib? It's too hot.'

Manjayya said, 'Yes.' After a while, as if something suddenly struck him, he asked Usmani, 'What were you saying, by the way?'

'About what sahib?'

'You said something about the taste of cooking.'

Usmani felt emboldened. 'Only he who has eaten knows the taste. How can we, who have only heard stories, know about it, sahib?'

Proffering intimacy, Manjayya asked Usmani to tell him the juicy details.

Usmani replied mischievously, professing familiarity, 'You see sahib, It is like hakim sahib asking medicine from a jatka-saabi.'

Manjayya countered, 'Honestly, I do not know anything Usmani, tell me.'

Usmani lowered his voice, so that his wife cooking in the kitchen would not hear and said, 'What, should I tell you sahib? The very moment you look at the face of a woman, you understand to which group she belongs, you aim at her and cast your net.'

'Well, let that be, tell me about this. I kept quiet. Working in the same department I should not ruffle feathers. You are a veteran there. You know everything. Come on, tell me!'

Usmani displaying intimacy and closeness winked and said: 'You know sahib, Appajappa has two children. The eyes of that boy and that girl sparkle like those of their mother, and they are clever too. But they don't resemble their father at all. Now you can understand the rest!'

Manjayya recalled, yes, he had seen them but he had never noticed it. It had not struck him. Yes, not only did the children not resemble the father in features, but even in the colour and complexion they bore no resemblance.

Manjayya said, 'Come on saabi! Just because the children do not resemble the father, can we say all this? Perhaps they resemble their grandfather or maternal uncle.'

Usmani elaborated, 'What sahib, do you think I talk without knowing facts? It is common knowledge in the department. After all, what sort of an intelligent man this Appajappa is to get promotion so early? It is all the favour of higher officers, sahib, promotion too and children too. If not, what kind of a husband would be so obedient to his wife?'

'Who told you all these details?'

Usmani said, 'Earlier this man was a Forester in Kunigal. My brother-in-law was a Watchman there. He said that the Conservator sahib used to come to Appajappa's house whenever he visited Kunigal.'

Didn't Manjayya understand that this saabi divulged all this to get closer to him? But, who might have told this fellow of my meat eating, that too in Sarojakshi's house? Did she herself tell him? But, seeing the reserve and self-respect she displays, it is not likely that she will indulge in loose talk with a Watchman. Perhaps Appajappa? No he too would not have been that free with this Usmani. Appajappa might have told Vishakanta and through him, this fellow must have got to know. Manjayya decided, let him know, I have no reason to be afraid. In any case, Usmani was his man. If he did not help Usmani to get the extra money he does, this Usmani would have to manage within his meagre salary. Further, Manjayya thought, however trustworthy this Usmani might be, he should have all information about Usmani's roots, origin and other things.

After Manjayya heard this gossip about Sarojakshi, he felt a great boulder lifted from his heart. Why so? It was not that he had never had a woman who had not transgressed family binding. Yet, now he knew Sarojakshi was an easy woman, he felt reassured. She could be easily and surely got! The turmoil inside his mind for the past six months, since Appajappa's coming there and Sarojakshi's acquaintance, now quietened. He regained his peace of mind. Why did it happen so? Whether it was from the surety of getting her or from the knowledge that she was not a novice and belonged to his own category? Sitting in the bus, even now he thought about it, but could not get an answer. His memory travelled back. Within two days he decided what should be done. Her complexion may be dark, but doesn't he know that beauty did not depend on colour alone? She may not have that perfect build of body, but again that was not the only criterion. His mind filled with the conviction that she was far superior to all the women he had slept with. He should not be indifferent regarding her and should plan to go ahead only if she was okay with it; and if not, he should drop the idea. At any cost, somehow or the other, he had to have her. What Usmani said was correct. Incapable husband, higher officer is paramour, who else was the Superior Officer in the Forest Department of this taluk except himself? Would that Assistant Conservator help Appajappa earn extra money? Manjayya thought along these lines. He remembered her features: ten year old son and five year old daughter. When Manjayya looked at his figure in the mirror, he thought – wouldn't she desire a son like him? Without such desire, would she show so much coquetry? Manjayya scolded his image in the mirror: 'Fie Manjayya, you are a fool, an utter fool. For six months you stayed so passive. Did not make any move. There is really no one more stupid than you!'

He knew that Appajappa would leave for Hassan that morning. He woke up in the morning, finished shaving, had breakfast, reached Channarayapattana by cycle, bought flowers and fruits, then checked into a hotel, washed his sweating face with Mysore sandal soap, combed, put on the khakhi coat of the

Forest Department and went directly to Sarojakshi's house. He knew that the children would be at school. She welcomed him: 'Oh it's so long since you visited us!' Yes, it was already five or six days. He sat in the chair and placed the fruits and flowers on the teapoy. She said: 'What's all this formality? Why have you made it a habit to bring something or the other whenever you come? I am angry, really angry.'

Manjayya smiled. 'No, no, no formality. What else can I get for you, save flowers? What can I do, whenever I look at flowers you come to mind.' He felt satisfied that the prelude was correct. Sarojakshi's eyes were towards the door.

'Look, your bicycle is there in the hot sun. Usually you never leave it out. Your mind is elsewhere today, I think.'

While Manjayya was trying to sort out whether she was hinting that she understood his words or was suggesting that she was cleverer than him and he could not fool her, she said, 'Look, it is not possible for me to lift that big bicycle of twenty six inches and leave it in the shade.'

He thought Sarojakshi was hinting about further programme and felt he would be surely successful. He got up, brought the cycle in and left it behind the door. With a lot of desire burning inside him, he sat in the chair and asked, 'When is Appajappa expected? In the evening or tomorrow?'

She answered: 'It depends, if his work is completed, he will return by the evening bus.'

The meaning of her answer was not clear. Again he asked, 'Children will return from school only in the evening. Isn't it?' Then Sarojakshi turned towards him, fixed her eyes on his face and said, 'You have come just now. There is brinjal curry prepared in the morning. I'll prepare some rotis quickly. Please wait,' she went in, brought the newspaper, put it before him and went inside. Manjayya could not understand what she meant. Did she mean that she would prepare food for him and more than that, she would not offer anything else? He felt hot and restless. Then, what Usmani told was a lie, probably. However, Manjayya decided, whether what Usmani told was false or true and at the worst this contract might be cancelled, but he didn't care. He got up, took off his coat, closed the front door and went into the kitchen. Sarojakshi was kneading rice flour for rotis. Manjayya stood before her and asked, 'Why haven't you worn the flowers I brought?' She turned and stared at him. He could not understand whether she was absorbed in her work or just pretended to be so. Manjayya continued, 'I thought I myself should put those flowers in your hair. If you don't want, it is okay.' Sarojakshi was silent. What was he to make out? He felt morose. Oh that dimness! He looked around. He could not find where she had kept the flowers. He could not get any clue even from the fragrance. He did not know what to say. His body began to tremble. He felt that if he spoke, his voice too would break. Since thirty years, Manjayya had never experienced such fear or uneasy feeling. Whoever might be the woman, he would courageously rush towards her, hold her, have her.

Why did it happen so with this one, he wondered. She put the dough on the pan, spread and patted it with her hand, washed her hands, struck a match and lit the kerosene stove. Then he felt that dimness was over. But the smoke of kerosene filled the space. She put the pan on the stove, covered it with a lid, turned towards the stove and just sat down. It was the silence that caused him embarrassment. He thought of going back and sitting in the chair. But he was ashamed to return defeated. Well, he thought, in the beginning, a man has to be aggressive and make a move, a woman will never take the initiative in such matters. As soon as the idea struck him, he came forward, hugged her, pulled her to him, held her in a firm grip so that she could not move and whispered words of love. He thought no woman could resist that. But somehow Sarojakshi freed her right hand and slapped him! Oh what a stinging slap! She quickly pulled herself away, ran out and opened the front door. Manjayya panicked that she might go out and call the neighbours and followed her. Sarojakshi brought a smile to her face and said. 'Please sit on the chair, the roti will be burnt. I'll just bring it in,' and stood near the pillar. Manjayya, who was sweating, felt relieved. No, she would not create a scene, he felt assured. But even if she called anybody, what would happen? Would she complain to the police? If he said, 'She herself had called me,' what would this slut do? His cheek was still burning. She still stood near the pillar. Manjayya reflected: Why did I let her free her hand? Had he finished it off at once, she would have been obedient like a bitch. Thinking so Manjayya, felt sad, coupled with the humiliation of defeat. When he sat with his head bent, she went inside. He thought of taking the bicycle out and leaving. How many times had he not done so in the past? He knew, if the man leaves the place at once in such a situation, a woman keeps silent, out of fear of losing her reputation. Afterwards, even if she meets that person she behaves as if nothing happened. But Manjayya felt his legs were rooted to the spot and he could not get out of that place. Oh, she came with the roti on a silver plate, in the corner of the dish there was brinjal curry, cut evenly and spreading its aroma. It seemed she had added groundnut powder too and there was thick ghee beside it. She put the plate on the teapoy, went inside, brought water in the shining brass pot which she always brought for him. She put down the glass and said, 'Please eat, the roti tastes good only when it is hot,' and stood near the pillar, as if she did not have any trace of anger. Manjayya had a mind to refuse the roti, but felt a sort of fear. Why was he afraid? What timidity had gripped him? He stretched his hand towards the plate and began to eat without a word. She went inside, returned within two minutes, and even before he raised his head she served another roti. She pulled up a chair near him, and slowly began fanning him. He felt confusion, shame and anger because he thought she was bent upon humiliating him. She was silently fanning him until he ate half a roti. Continuing with the fanning she said, 'I'll ask you something. But you should not get angry. May I?'

Manjayya thought, if he kept quiet, it would be showing anger and said, 'Yes!'

'You see, you should not get angry, swear on me!' She laughed brightly.

Manjayya said, 'Why should I get angry. Trust and friendship are important.'

'You are speaking formally. But I am asking you very intimately, that too a personal question. Tell me please. Till now, how many women, I don't know how to ask, okay, do you at least remember, with how many you have...?'

He had gained courage to raise his head and speak, but he quickly bent it down. Why did it have to happen? If any other woman had asked these words, that too if it was in the context of lovemaking, he could have flattered her and made her happy by telling, 'There is no other woman except you in this world.' If she had forced or tried to dominate him, he would have shut her mouth bravely saying: 'So what? I have had a thousand.' But why could he not muster courage to even boast so before Sarojakshi? She rephrased the question in a honeyed voice, the way a seasoned lawyer would, 'You see, it is like hitting a century in the game of cricket. Perhaps it is so many years, you have crossed one hundred. You are, however, the tiger of this taluk. Tell me honestly, how many have there been totally?' Manjayya did not speak or lift his head. She kept quiet for two minutes, then poured water into the glass from the pot and persisted, 'I know you will have forgotten names. But think, the total number at least would be in your memory. Do you know? If you ask the hunters in Malenadu, they would proudly announce that they have hunted down this many tigers, hyenas, stags and yet how many they intend to. Like those hunters, till now how many have you had and how many more do you aim to. Won't you tell me? Come on, remember I have asked you to swear on me.'

Manjayya did not speak. He began eating slowly, for if he finished eating he had to raise his head and had to see her face. Again she insisted in that honey-smeared voice, 'Please, won't you tell me?'

How much more could he endure? Moreover who was she, that he had to hang down his head? Who was the bastard that gave her the authority to investigate, to interrogate in this manner? Manjayya was furious and rightly so. He made up his mind, raised his head, glared at her with a searing look and asked, 'Oh, so you want all details about me. Now, come on, tell me, how many men have you taken to your bed. Tell me who fathered your children. Let me make it very clear, I have never felt such desire rise in me for a really chaste woman. Only after I knew your history. I felt the desire rise.'

Sarojakshi was furious, she was looking at him as if she would pierce his eyes with the brightness of hers and retorted, 'You, Manjayyanavare, what do you mean? I did not know that you were so mean as to throw such a question at a woman.'

He raised his hand and swiftly slapped her hard on the cheek. A tight slap! A slap fit for that shrewd slut who dared to hit Manjayya.

Travelling in the bus, the mere memory of that incident pleased him immensely. The impact of the slap made Sarojakshi fall down from the chair. Manjayya was scared. Did that blow land near her ear, was she in danger of losing her life. He quickly poured water from the pot on to his palm, patted it on her head, sprinkled water on her face, took the fan that fell down from her hand and fanned her quickly. Within two minutes, she regained consciousness and sat up instantly. After a minute she pretended as if she was ready to break into a sob but was trying to control it. She said, 'You have misunderstood what I was trying to say.' But he thought, need anybody teach Manjayya, 'Woman means only pretence and drama?' He got up, put on his coat, went behind the door, took his bicycle and shouted, 'I have understood you correctly, you harlot … you slut!' Sarojakshi said, 'Look here, if you were able to understand, by now you should have understood. Please stay back. I'll explain everything.'

But he was adamant. 'I have understood you perfectly. I have known hundreds of women like you.' He took his bicycle out of the threshold, pedalled fast and rushed out.

By then the bus had reached Shantigrama and was halting for the passengers to get down or board the bus. Manjayya told himself, 'What sort of an *Express* is this bus?' and looked at his watch. He wanted to get the report of yesterday's enquiry about Appajappa, somehow in Hassan itself. That typist Nanjegowda usually entrusted such work to Stephen. If Manjayya requested, Stephen would surely leak out, if not full, at least some details. With this belief, Manjayya comprehended the meaning of the needles on the dial of his watch. If it was only that much, he would not have instigated the farmers' complaint against Appajappa. Manjayya had helped her family by making Appajappa earn extra money. Should she not be grateful, give shelter and protect Manjayya during difficult times? He was never ungrateful, he had never forgotten persons who helped him. In such a case …

While he was busy with his thoughts, the bus resumed its journey and began to move speedily. He continued with the train of his thoughts – how critical that time was! It was a situation of getting capital punishment or life sentence if he were not to be acquitted. Even though it was midnight, it was dangerous for him to walk on the streets in Channarayapattana. For, every constable was known to him and constables roam the streets for night beat. In such a situation, Manjayya had taken courage, went to Sarojakshi's house, knocked on her door at midnight. Nothing should be heard by the neighbours. For, if she asked, 'Who is it?' from inside and he said, 'Manjayya', it might be heard by the neighbours, they might inform the police. The whole taluk knew that Bilikere Manjayya had murdered the coconut thief. It was published in Bangalore newspapers also, that means the whole of Karnataka knew about this. Her eyes were very sensitive. Her ears were very sharp. She at once recognised the voice and opened the door. Her husband was snoring. However, even if he had spoken with her husband, he would not do anything without consulting his wife. Manjayya said hurriedly, 'Please close the door, switch off the light. I think you know the police are searching for me!' Sarojakshi at once closed the door, switched on the torch she held and led Manjayya to the kitchen, the same in which he had held her and she had slapped him. She poured oil in the lamp in the niche she kept the gods, lit it, and whispered, 'Shall I wake up Appajappa?' Manjayya told her directly, 'Look here, please, that day I was hasty and advanced without knowing your mind. I am sorry. It was right you slapped me. But I shouldn't have slapped you back. I came to beg your forgiveness: please tell me, will you forgive?'

'You should not ask me in that manner,' she had said and squeezed my hand gently. The warmth of that squeeze generated trust in me and I said, 'I am sure you would have heard that the police have booked a murder charge against me. Now I've no time to explain the details. It was only an accident. The wife of that thief has offered a bribe of ten thousand rupees to the police. She is determined to send me to the gallows. Besides, she has some grudge against Appajappa too. I had caused some howling about a sandalwood tree in her fields and made her give money to

Appajappa. So, what I need now is just this: "If Appajappa gives witness that, on the date of murder recorded in the police files, Appajappa had gone to a distant village on government duty and Manjayya was also with him and we stayed the whole night there." If he gives witness, the court will surely believe him, for he is a government official. If you tell Appajappa he will surely agree.'

Sarojakshi stared at my face. Even in the dim light of the lamp, her eyes were shining more brightly than a torch with a new battery. I thought: did she stare so, to test me or....? She spoke: 'Look here, mere witness will not suffice in court. There must be a programme record, diary and other documents. This should be recorded prior to inspection. Witness of the villagers of that village is essential for the rest.'

I said, 'It is not a big problem to create all such things.'

Sarojakshi simply squeezed my hands. What was the meaning of that? I could not fathom and said, 'Please tell me quickly. It is inviting danger if I stay here for long.' Then she said, 'See, whatever record is created, Appajappa would be cross-examined in court and within a minute, he would be caught. When your chief witness himself fails, what will happen to you? If the judge wrote a remark that being a government official he had come to commit perjury and as a result my husband loses his job, what will happen to my family?'

I had said: 'Saroja, I will take care of you and your children,' and held her hand and took her before god.

He remembered angrily that the slut did not believe him, simply squeezed his hand and said: 'You see, I do want you to be safe. But any promise given in such distressful situation is not right. Nobody should promise anything to anyone under compulsion or in dire situations, even though it is asked or given conscientiously. You see, Appajappa should not get into trouble because of this. Besides, he is not intelligent enough to give evidence so that you may win your case. Please find another method.' I had gone there in the midnight to her house fully trusting her without caring for the danger of being caught. But I was totally disappointed. When I stood so, she said, 'You win your case and come, I swear on God, let us talk over the matters. I'll make a vow to god that you should win. Now, you move, wait, I'll open the door without making any sound, and check if there is somebody outside and give you a hint.' I was furious but could do nothing except to curse Sarojakshi, using all my vocabulary. That harlot, not giving me a chance to stay a moment more had sent me away, what a soft speaking harlot she is, oh that bitch is going to make a vow to god in my name. She is going to suffer any amount of trouble, for my sake. But no trouble should come to her husband. I'll see, how she is going to save her husband's job. Anyway she ought to come and prostrate before me, then I will tell her, 'You bitch, your hypocrisy will never work with me, understand it,' thinking thus, Manjayya smiled with satisfaction.

Smoking a Charminar cigarette, letting out the smoke through his nostrils, Bochihalli Ningappa stood beneath the tree in the compound of Hassan court and was telling Tagadooru Dalegowda. 'You see, it is not a great thing to throw away a hundred and fifty rupees. But honour and reputation are important. Tell me, if a man like me begotten to my father were to remit the penalty, is he fit to live? Should he not die before that?'

Though Tagadooru Dalegowda was of the same age as that of Bochihalli Ningappa, he was yet a novice at court and offices, so he had not yet promoted himself from beedi to cigarette. He had raised himself from the level of hand-rolled beedi to branded beedi. Ningappa insisted and gave him a Charminar cigarette and said, 'Take it Annayya, let us talk afterwards.' Dalegowda lit the cigarette, but did not feel it was in anyway better than the beedi. Ningappanna knew why Dalegowda had stepped into court. All that Dalegowda knew was that Ningappanna's case had something to do with the sandalwood department, but he did not know any details. Dalegowda had the common sense that if he heard and knew about several cases, his knowledge to deal with his business in court would increase. He asked Ningappanna: 'Well Annayya, you are smart. There is no one as clever as you in Bochihalli. How come, then, that this case was booked against you?'

'If I begin, it will be a story as lengthy as the Ramayana,' Ningappa said and looked at his watch. After he was involved in the court business, he felt, it would not be possible to keep up the time of bus and court, without having a watch. So he bought a wrist watch three months ago. He had gained by experience, the knowledge to tell exactly, hour and minutes by looking for half a minute on which numbers the needles stood. It was nine o'clock in the morning. There was one and a half hour left for the court to start. Jayadevegowda, advocate of Ninganna told him in his office to wait near the court and he would come. So Ningappa directly came there. But he had to while away one and a half hours. So, he started narrating his experience, adventure and plight to Dalegowda: 'Listen, I'll tell you everything, from the beginning. If I tell you in bits and pieces, you cannot understand clearly. Do you know, what happened one day? It is already a year ago. Morning nine o'clock. I was having my breakfast of roti. A boy of our village came and said: 'Forest Officer has come. He is sitting on the platform of the peepal and is calling.' Anyway I ate my roti as slowly as possible thinking, who might this officer be? Let him wait. And then when I went to the peepal tree platform, there was no officer, but this Bilikere Manjayya was there wearing his khakhi coat. Do you know Manjayya?'

'Is there anyone who doesn't know him? He came to our village also with Rajegowdaru, to beg for vote. He is a lawyer of sandalwood contract.'

'There was some difference of opinion between us. There was no goodwill or trust. I asked him, 'Hey, who do you mean by "this officer"?' Then Manjayya said, 'Yes, the officer himself has sent word through me. There is a marriage in the family of the sandalwood officer. They need one hundred copras. Will you give them? I said, 'Yes, copra costs one thousand five hundred rupees for a thousand. It is the rate at the auction in Tiptur. It costs one hundred and fifty rupees for one hundred copras. I will give even two hundred copras if you want.' Tell me what was wrong in what I said. Manjayya said, 'If that is the case, he can as well purchase from the warehouse itself.' Then I said, "Did I send word that you are drooling to eat our copras only?' And then Manjayya shut his trap and was silent. I saw a dog standing there. I abused that dog, 'Tut-tut, you shit eating fellow,' and came home. Tell me Dalappa, was this rebuking right or wrong?'

Dalappa replied, 'Isn't it so? These people who demand votes come to eat farmer's shit.'

'Hey, Dalappa, listen. The story is totally different. I'm only telling you the sequence of how things happened. You see, that shit-eating-fellow happens to be a different one. Fifteen days after this incident, I was about to take my lunch. Lo, the whole army of sandalwood department landed at my house. Watchman, Guard, Forester, Contractor Manjayya, all in khakhi dress. All had bicycles. As soon as I saw Manjayya, I knew he had come to threaten me and collect copra. I decided in my mind, not to give even one piece of copra and stood quiet. There is a Watchman called Usmani in Sankenhalli forest. Have you seen him?'

'Yes, I have, he had come to our village also, to search all our groves.'

'He started to speak in the style of a court-bailiff. He asked: "Are you Ningappa, Puttayya's son?" I answered: "Yes, I am, why?" He said: "There is a complaint that you have cut the branch of a sandalwood tree and put it in the haystack. We must check it." Then I browbeat him. Who is it that has cut the branch? You see Dalappa, don't you get angry if you are falsely charged. Then that Usmani said: "We have come here to investigate that. Come, let us go to your haystacks." I was confident that there was no sandalwood branch in my haystacks. I said: 'Come if you want to', put down the pot of water I had brought to wash my hands, went out, took the key of the shed where there were haystacks and took them to the place in front of the village. There was a strong fence surrounding that place and the wicket gate of the fence was locked. I opened the wicket gate and allowed all those five people to go inside and stood at the door. I said: "Go and search for yourselves." But that Manjayya said: "No, without your presence we cannot enter. The Patel of this village should also be present at the *Mahajar*." He sent a boy, and asked Patel Chikkayya of our village to come there. All those people entered the field where the haystacks stood. They bent down and searched beneath two haystacks, searched in front and behind. Then read the complaint once more, put their hands into the centre of the big stack and pulled out a branch nearly eight cubit long and as thick as a person's thigh. Manjayya said: "Look here Patel Chikkayya, you smell it and say what wood it is." Chikkayya stood silently. Manjayya again insisted: "A Patel is a government official. He must do his duty!" As if he was waiting for these words, this Patel of our own village who belongs to our own caste and is our relative too, this fellow bent down, smelled and dumbly nodded his head like Basavanna, the decorated bull, trained by the trainer, nods on being questioned. Manjayya asked me, "See, Ningappa you too smell this." That Manjayya himself wrote the report and took the thumb impression of that Patel. This bloody fellow did not refuse to put his thumb impression, nor did he say, "Wait, let us decide," though he was of the same village and same caste.' There was another officer Prabhuswamy by name. He said, "Come on, let us go to your grove." All of us went. I followed them. I thought they would ask me to give them hundred coconuts. I decided to give them not hundred but two hundred and free myself from the devil. That Prabhuswamy read the complaint once again and asked, 'Well, come on take us round your grove.' I walked in front and opened the main gate of the grove. As soon as I entered, Prabhuswamy again looked at the complaint petition in his hand and said: "Towards the East, means to this side," and as the surveyors find the way by looking at the map, he walked on with his army. Within twenty four cubits distance from the fence near the ridge, there was a big sandalwood tree, and a branch on top of the tree had been chopped off. Anybody could tell that the sandalwood branch which was found in the haystack was cut from this tree. He asked the Patel: "Patel, look carefully at this branch – its circumference, width and its colour. Certify whether this branch is of this tree or not." He said and began to write the report swiftly. This stupid bastard pressed his thumb. All of them mounted their bicycles and rode away.' Ningappa inhaled deeply the cigarette in his hand as if it would blow into the inner part of his lungs and looked at Dalegowda's face.

'Then it's certainly Manjayya's mischief, no doubt about that,' Dalegowda said confidently.

Ningappa continued, 'That morning itself, I sent my brother-in-law, you know that Yengategowda of Bogachikere, to Bilikere. I sent word with him: "Listen, I am ready to offer you one thousand rupees. Please do not book a case against me. It was my great mistake. I refused to offer copras to you," 'Do you know what that Manjayya told Yengategowda? "Tell him, it is Ningappa fellow's dog that eats shit. I cannot stop this case." I too kept quiet, thinking – let what is to happen, happen. A case was booked in Tahshildar's court. Summons would come, I leave for Channarayapattana, wait there like a cur, by evening there would be a shout "Case is adjourned" – today tahshildar has left by jeep, another day he is busy. Yet another day, the case would be scheduled to take place in the afternoon, but he would go to a feast of non-veg, at last, after making me wait and wait for argument, here was an enquiry. Oh what sort of enquiry it was! That bastard Tahshildar was fathered by a farmer, son-in-law of Yelekere Sanjeevegowda. He exercised authority on me and said, "If it is the case, how did the branch of the tree within the fence go into the haystack of your hamlet? If, what you state is the truth, prove it in the court, if not remit the penalty," and he fixed one hundred and fifty rupees as the penalty. You see brother, what sort of justice this is!'

'Hey, I know that Tahshildar. He swallows one goat in one gulp.'

Ninganna boasted, 'Born a male, could I leave it at that? I put an appeal at Hassan court and fixed advocate Jayadevegowda.'

'You should have fixed Venkataramayya. Expert, really it is said he is an expert.'

Now Dalegowda began to enjoy the taste of that cigarette. Ningappa continued his narration: 'You see this one is the junior of Venkataramayya. Junior means a disciple, Venkataramayya has said to him, "You conduct the case, I'll come on the day of the argument." Now, there are two parties in our village. One is that of Patela and the other is mine. Could that Patela put his thumb impression on the report against me? Big fighting took place. One tooth of Patela was broken. It is a police case, but on that day I was not in the village at all.'

Now Dalegowda diverted the talk towards the main dispute and asked: 'Well, is it the same case that you wrote a complaint against Appajappa? You came to our village and took our signatures stating, this Appajappa, the Ranger of sandalwood department, demands bribe from us.'

'What else did you think? Did you think Manjayya was an ungrateful man? I too had thought so. But, before one month, Rajegowda came in search of me. He did not show pride or vanity. He sat on the mortar floor on the platform. Manjayya also had come with him. I came out, looking at Manjayya, I made a wry face. Rajegowda sat silently. I went in, brought a mat, spread it. Both of them sat on it. And then Manjayya said: "Look here Ningappa, it is natural that your face has a wry expression upon seeing me. I came here to inform you the real matter. I brought Rajegowda also with me, so that a person who knows the truth will be here and wherever I commit mistakes he might correct me. But don't think I am afraid to come alone. You may or may not believe. I do not have to gain anything by people believing my words. It is enough for me if God believes me. Moreover, we two belong to the same taluk and we must be mutually helping until our deaths. But what of these government officers – today at one place and tomorrow another. Do you understand? Tell me Ninganna whether there is any mistake in my words." When Manjayya was questioning me thus, I could not understand the head or tail of his words. Again he asked: "If there is a mistake say so, if not say yes," well say "Yes". I nodded thinking he would say what the truth was. He said: "It seems you are telling everybody in all villages that it was Manjayya, who booked the sandal-tree-case against me. I know, you are not wrong. It was true I asked you one hundred copras for the higher officer. That's why you feel so. But you understand one thing: the government officers always get their work done through other people. You know, I am after all only a contractor. If I am ordered that the tree in your grove is ripe and the officer orders it to be plucked, I will weigh the core of the tree, peel the bark, calculate and send it to sandalwood depot. This is all part of my duty. It is I who have to obey him. Does he obey what I say? Tell me Ninganna, who has the authority to book a case ? Is it the contractor or the officer? Anyway, you have gone to the Hassan court. In the records, whose name is there? Is it contractor Manjayya's or Range Forest Officer Appajappa's? Tell me, if you are begotten of your father, tell the truth." Ninganna continued and told Dalegowda: 'What will you say now? Really, it had not occurred to me at all'. Manjayya insisted: "If you don't tell the truth, I'll not say anything further," and so I said "Yes" and Manjayya began to speak : "Now you have understood, I hope, he has created a case against you, because you refused to give him copras. I have a coconut grove of my own, have my own loft. Twice a year I sell copra to Tiptur warehouse. If it is so, should I come begging to you for one hundred copras? Do you know why have I come today? You assemble the people of the taluk on the Saturday market of Channarayapattana. Let both of us have a fight. If you are stronger you will beat me, if not you will be beaten. But let me assure you of one thing. This Bilikere Manjayya is not a man to stretch his hands to the bribe shit of other's wives for the greed of those worthless copras. I am a man who raises his hand to give, not to receive. I will never be called a wicked man by creating trouble to people of my own taluk. I know, Ninganna, how many people you have complained about me. But do you know what those people say? 'Oh Manjayya sir, how many people's case you have won in the court. But why did you do so to Bochihalli Ningappa? You, somehow make him win the case.' That bastard Appajappa would get transferred and leave this place. You are a local man. Why do you earn a bad name?" What do you say to this, Ninganna? I don't want a bad name. I am a local man. You understand, we are like brothers. If I am against the officer, I lose my contract. Who cares? I decided if it was lost, it is equal to the loss of just a strand of my hair and have come to your place, so that, let everything be decided in the presence of Rajegowda." Manjayya said so, opened his cigarette pack, put one before me, gave another to Rajegowda and he himself held one. Rajegowda struck a match and lit the cigarettes. Manjayya rode away on his bicycle with the cigarette on his lips. Rajegowda and myself were left facing each other. He said: "You understand one thing Ningappanna. Manjayya is a straightforward person. He always fights for justice. It is not difficult for him to make you win your case. But Manjayya has to incur enmity of the officer. And that, fellow Appajappa will pose an objection to his contract." I assured Rajegowda that I would turn all our farmers to Manjayya's side and said, that officer is not more powerful than us.

'You see Dalegowda, that Rajegowda's brain is very sharp. He thought for some time and said: 'The Judge gives verdict according to the record prepared by the officer. On the day of judicial trial, Manjayya also should give evidence. Along with him, the Forester Prabhuswamy, the Guard Vishakantayya, Watchman Usmani too stand in the witness-box. If these people twist their statements, the case would collapse. Don't worry about Manjayya, he can cast off that contract as easily as a broken slipper. But Prabhuswamy, Vishakantayya and Usmani are solely dependent on their salary. Until Appajappa remains the officer, we cannot turn them to our side. Do you understand what I am saying? That Appajappa is a poisonous snake. So, you collect fifty people from your side and submit a petition to the Conservator, that is the senior officer of sandalwood department, saying that this Appajappa demands huge amounts of bribe and whoever refuses to give bribe, he frames false cases against them and builds records. Manjayya will instruct you how to write such a petition. In the same manner, you should send petition from your people in Kalkere, Shravanabelagola, Nuggehalli and Baguru. The present Conservator is very strict, a firebrand. He will surely get this fellow suspended, or even dismissed. If this fellow vacates the office and other one comes and strips away two stripes from the edges of the case, the roof sinks down." Thus he revealed the secret. Did you now understand who was the bastard?'

Dalegowda was amazed at the turn of the story and put his hand on his mouth. Ningappa said: 'Already the petition had been sent. Yesterday evening the Departmental Enquiry also got over. All of us have given our statements in Channarayapattana Travellers' Bungalow. Within four or five days suspension orders of that Appajappa will be issued. The new officer will take charge. Till then we have to bide our time. Our lawyer will beg adjournment for today's hearing. Manjayya also had said, he would come now. It is almost time. Saying so Ningappa looked at his watch, the two needles on the dial and the numbers and began to decide time by calculating in his mind.

Savitri lived in a small rented outhouse, behind the main building of Kote Nanjappa. The outhouse was originally annexed to the compound of that big house. Earlier when Nanjappa lived as a landlord, he had built the small house as a kitchen, so that there should be no smoke in the main house. Now, his daughters had been married off and were settled in their husband's houses. Sons could have stayed comfortably and happily in this country with their educational qualifications and opportunities. But they had gone to America and settled there. And now the old couple lived in the big house. They had rented out the outhouse to Savitri for two reasons. One, to have a person whenever they needed company or help. Another, Savitri was the daughter of Bilikere Parameshwarayya. The rent amount was not important to the couple. There was a separate path to the small house, from the right side of the main house, after entering the front gate.

Savitri had gone to school. Satyappa, lying down in her house, was ruminating about his life. The abyss he had sunk into, this disease, his decision to end his life, his walking up to the brink of death and return and the frenzy he felt when he returned from that precipice. When he would be chewing this cud, sometimes his further path would flash like lightning. But nothing was clear. There was no longer any need to be anxious about the illness. The rashes had already dried up. He could walk across to Dr Hasheem's clinic in Market Street, take the injection and tablets and return. Three days before he had come to Savitri's house. Before that, for five days, he had stayed in the room above the doctor's clinic, the room the doctor had reserved for the use of such patients. It was a convenient room. Coffee, snacks and lunch would be supplied and the room would be mopped and disinfected twice a day using phenyl. Dr Hasheem was not as greedy as Dr Prakash of Tiptur. After examining Satyappa he said, 'Your disease is not very severe. Twelve injections will do along with an ointment and tablets. You will need to pay a total of three hundred rupees. If you do not have the money right now, give me whatever you have. I'll still treat you. To treat the disease is my duty. You know this disease attacks all sorts of people sometime or the other. Being doctors we are aware of that. You must take nutritious food. Do you eat eggs? If not, take lots of fruit and milk,' the compassionate doctor comforted Satyappa. Even though Satyappa said that he had with him ₹2500/-, Dr Hasheem refused to take even an anna more than ₹300.

Satyappa wondered, though it was quite convenient in that clinic, why did he send word to Savitri and come to her house? He began analysing his psychological condition of those five days. There was the doctor who created complete trust. The treatment already showed improvement. A servant supplied food, fruit and milk and cleaned his clothes and his room. There was nobody who asked about his name, place, caste and whereabouts. Even so, he felt life was unbearable. He strongly felt the need of someone who cared for him, who loved him. But who could that be? Satyappa thought, shall I send word to my son? Then he regretted that though in a moment of frenzy, he had loudly proclaimed his condition. Can he hope to receive any emotional succour from a son who judges his father against a model concept of father he had in mind? Would such a son empathise and understand his psychological condition? Would he not weigh the father on scales of morality and quibble, even if there was a difference of one milligram. The memory of Saati began haunting his mind. She stayed in the same town. He felt like sending word to her and conveying his condition. Why did he feel such an urge? Did he need kindness? Lying down in Savitri's house, Satyappa tried to unravel his psychological condition of the preceding days. He felt it was not the desire for sympathy or consolation. There was a difference between sympathy and concern. Mere sympathy bereft of compassion, of the sense of belonging, was just pity. Anyway, Savitri came rushing as soon as he sent for her. Anxiety was writ large on her face along with affection for her bhaava. Though there had been no communication between them for nearly twenty-five years, affection towards her bhaava had rekindled after she met him during her father's funeral ceremonies. And this was clearly visible. She asked: 'Oh bhaava, why are you staying here? What happened, what's this illness? Didn't you remember, Saati lives here? Come on, let's go home. The doctor will come there and treat you,' Oh the genuine concern on her face!

Satyappa said tonelessly, 'Invite me to your house after knowing what is the disease I suffer from. Look, your bhaava, at his age, lost control and contracted a disease. It is now being treated by this doctor!'

Alas, the pain that appeared on her face! Besides there was a certain hardening too. It was a harsh decision which weighed him and threw him speedily into the abyss – madness of women, touching one and sleeping with her! All the disgust and disdain she felt for her husband Manjayya, would naturally extend to anyone who committed such a deed. Now it had extended to him as well. The very moment Satyappa felt it, he knew that it was quite natural for her to feel so. He remembered, that this aspect had not flashed across his mind before sending the message across. Even if it had struck him, wouldn't he have still sent for her? In the moment of frenzy of disentangling from the noose and being alive he had shouted before his son, before all the villagers accompanied by the cacophony of barking dogs, the truth about his disease. But after that he was debating within himself: would it tantamount to telling the truth if he broadcasted it to everybody? Without propriety and discrimination of who should be told and why, whatever is shouted publicly on the street could not rise to the level of truth. Still, Satyappa felt that it would be concealing the truth and telling lies, if he did not tell Saati the true facts. She looked at his face as if she was debating within and coming to a decision. He could understand that the softness she brought in her voice was with some effort. Then she said, 'You see bhaava, since we had lost touch completely, I had no memories of you. But when you came to Appa's funeral ceremony and I spoke with you, I felt so consoled that at least there is one person who has saved his honour, reputation and merit. But, if you too have done this ... it means...' Savitri stopped speaking, either not knowing what to say further or to limit the severity of reproach to one or two words. Abruptly she turned and went away. Satyappa could clearly hear the sound of her chappals and knew she was climbing down the steps. He now realised, 'We have to guard our character, not only for our own sakes, but for the sake of others who are related to us. It had not struck me till now that, if the power of our character is lost, power of those related to us also decreases. Saati shunned him and left. But he did not feel she would reject him completely. His conscience was prompting, 'Though her intellect is telling her that it is right to reject me, her heart will not allow it. But he was not prepared to accept pity or mercy, not even hers. He had decided to earn a strength that could surpass sympathy. His mind too attained that level of maturity. His gut feeling was proved right. After two hours Savitri returned. 'Bhaava, though you were suffering from illness, I became angry and went away. I remember you calling me 'Angry Saati' when I was a little girl. Even at this age, my anger refuses to leave me. Please get up, I'll get your clothes. Let's go to my house. Let the doctor come there daily and give you medicines.' She forced a smile on to her face. But the face betrayed that she had cried a lot, wiped her tears and come there. Satyappa said, 'Let me stay here. It's more convenient. If you come once a while and talk to me, that's enough. Moreover, this is a contagious disease. There's the possibility of others too contracting it when the disease is fresh. So, after I am fully cured, I'll come and stay with you for four days. I too feel like confessing everything to you.'

'I've spoken to the doctor and told him, the patient in the room upstairs is my brother-in-law. I'll take him home and look after him. He said, "He does not need to be here. You can take him home. Let him stay in a room or in a corner of the hall. Just be sure you wash the place daily with phenyl and keep his clothes separate. Even these restrictions are only for eight to ten days. By then it will be completely cured. He may come here on foot, take the injection and go home. He is alone here and feels bored. Moreover, hotel food will not do him much good." So, come on, get up, let's go home. Put your clothes in a bag. I'll ask the doctor for a bottle of phenyl.'

Savitri brought him home and took care of him. She gave him nutritious food, fruit and milk and was looking after him like a good nurse. But Satyappa felt that she had not completely forgiven him. She was not a person to lie that she had forgiven him. Though he had been in her house for the past three days, she had not asked a single question. Her not asking and his not talking about it seemed artificial and caused them both embarrassment. He felt that unless they fully discussed this filthy but sensitive issue threadbare, any open or natural conversation between them would not be possible. The previous night, after supper, she broached the topic. 'Bhaava, I know you're a very strong willed man. How could you go for such a thing? I think, it happened because of some bad company!'

Satyappa got the opportunity to open the sluice gates of his mind. 'No, Saati, my conscience does not allow me to call myself guilt-free and put the blame on another person passing it off as bad company. I am solely responsible for what has happened. I intended to kill the snake ... no, no ... not kill it, but remove the snake's poison bag by surgery and change it into a virtuous one. But I myself was bitten by it.'

'Well, what happened bhaava? Did you try for social upliftment or to solve the problem of prostitutes?'

'No, no, nothing like that. When I came to the funeral ceremony of your father, that night in the byre in the backyard, you told me about the mean acts of Manjayya. Listening to that my mind thought of reforming him at any cost and somehow to kindle his conscience. That morning I went to his house'... Satyappa described every step he took, every word he spoke and all the ups and downs that happened in his inner mind. He explained how all frustrations and failures he experienced in life rose up together and a fissure opened inside him. He told her how he voluntarily went to Manjayya and asked him for it, and how he fell in the same hut of Manjayya's grove. Then how he went to the Tiptur doctor, wandered to the warehouse of copra merchant, met Manjayya in Channarayapattana, what Manjayya said, his decision to commit suicide, with the illusion of following the path of his father-in-law. He explained how he had tried to hang himself from the branch of the same tree and then, stubbing out the idea of taking a loan from Savitri, returned to his village, climbed the branch, put the noose around his neck to end it all, but ultimately changed his mind and climbed down. He narrated how he ran home, called out to Ramachandra, shouted at him and made him write a letter to transfer the authority of property back to his father. While

Satyappa ended this lengthy narration, it was past midnight. Saati was just nodding but did not say whether his acts were wrong or right. After he finished his narration, she switched off the light and lied down. But he could not sleep. She too did not sleep until dawn. What were Saati's thoughts? Satyappa reflected, let her think whatever she wants. I have felt comforted sharing my sordid tale. And she was the only person who merited this confidence.

Savitri came early in the evening. She brought a bagful of apples, grapes and oranges. She freshened up, cut the fruits, put a big plateful before Satyappa and said, 'Now finish this up,' and sat leaning on the wall at a little distance. Satyappa too felt the air had been cleared and the unnatural and tense atmosphere of the past few days and the uneasy silence that existed between them had vanished. Savitri ordered, 'Come on, start eating. If you do not follow Dr Hasheem's advice, won't your recovery be slow.' After he had eaten some pieces of apple, she said, 'Remember, I told you everything that day. That was the last. I then wiped out the memory of that damned fellow from my mind. But after listening to what you told me yesterday night, his memory is haunting me again. If a person like you is victimised by that poison, what sort of a poisonous snake must he be? It is impossible for anybody to reform him. Till now, no one has removed him – killed him when he went to hunt, to seduce other people's women – just as he removed Kanchi for stealthily rushing into other people's groves and stealing coconuts. This thought has occupied my mind since yesterday. I heard Appa saying to Lagniappe of our village, when he was solving a dispute sitting on the platform, that however wicked a person might be, we should never wish for his death. It is the greatest sin. I was then a mere girl of nine or ten. But the thought had so firmly imprinted itself on my mind that in any context, I never wished that he should die or that someone kill him. That day itself I told you, that I became totally a different person after Appa committed suicide. And now after listening you too were about to commit suicide, I am certain in my mind that death penalty or capital punishment is the only sentence suitable for such sinners.'

Satyappa looked at her face. His face too reflected the same firm decision that was in her face. Savitri had expressed her affection for him. It pleased him and comforted him. He said, 'Look here Saati, the injustice Manjayya has done to you, the treachery he has done to maava are both unforgivable. But the complete responsibility for what he did to me rests on me alone. He only gave a hint. In an intimate tone he stimulated my licentiousness that was within me already and made the whole thing attractive and simple and touched my mind and heart. It was just like drunkards insisting with love, that others also drink and smokers urging others to take a puff for the sake of friendship. But if I was strong and adamant, why would I have been victimised? Instead, as if possessed by madness, waking up before daybreak, walking fourteen miles, I stood before him and said, 'Look here, I have come!' Manjayya did not tie a rope around me and drag me into his grove hut. Again, he did not bluntly refuse me five hundred rupees for my treatment. He only said, why do you conceal the deed? If you are courageous, go and tell your son. In a way there is no duality in his words. I think these words opened my eyes!'

Savitri could not understand this 'dharmaraya-hood' of her bhaava. But her respect towards him increased seeing his attitude of shouldering the whole responsibility of his mistake, even in such intense pain. How terrible the power of longing for physical pleasure was, was not an unknown experience to Savitri. Now when she knew that the desire was intensified in her bhaava, her anger almost completely vanished. But it was unbearable to her that the desire for pleasure was stimulated by that damned Manjayya and that her bhaava succumbed to it. Somehow her mind began to yearn that her bhaava should be great, greater than that vile fellow and should never ever be overpowered by him. She raised her neck, looked at Satyappa's face and she felt that it was the sign of victory that he had realised his mistake and shouldered the responsibility. She was certain that he would not be overpowered. She got up and went into the kitchen.

After supper, he retired to his room. The door was open. Savitri spread her bed outside the room. The smell of phenyl spread outside also. Satyappa understood that Savitri had spread her bed there so that she could talk with him until she felt sleepy. She switched off the light and said, 'I have applied for eight days leave from work, starting tomorrow.'

Satyappa protested, 'Why do you waste your leave? Now I am recovering. When I went to the doctor yesterday, he advised me not to keep lying down but to go for walks on the tank bund. Within four or five days, the treatment would be complete and I may return to my place.'

Savitri asked. 'What will you do after returning to your place?'

'Yes, what shall I do going back there? I am also thinking of that,' Satyappa said.

'Why should you leave here as soon as the doctor permits you? You ask the doctor today if I can wash your clothes, clean the plate and glass you take food from. I'll take care of you for some more days and I'll continue my leave. You see, bhaava, now after you return home, what will be Ramachandra's attitude? Will his wife have the same respect she had towards you earlier? Have you thought how the people of the village will behave?'

'Well Saati, the moot point is not whether they look after me respectfully or not, it is did they treat me with respect earlier. But you know, now I have taken complete authority of the lands and monetary business. So, respect ought to follow automatically.' Satyappa laughed loudly. But even in that darkness Savitri understood from the tone that it was laughter drenched in sadness.

None spoke for a while. Then Satyappa started speaking. 'See Saati, after I came to this town, Dr Hasheem started injections and controlled this disease and I felt I was better. All my thoughts began to flow towards the purpose of my life. I started to think, 'Where did I go wrong? Many reasons appear before me. You know Saati, if we speak with an open mind to someone close to us, our thoughts will become clearer to ourselves. So, I will tell you everything. Do you know what mistake I committed? Mahatma Gandhi tried to establish a different system, awareness and a sense of ethics in the whole society and the country. Perhaps it was possible for such a great man to achieve a huge expanse of programme. But now, when I look at the situation, I feel that the meanness of this country surpassed him. The mistake I did was, I wanted to implement all his ideas and programmes simultaneously and thought that I could do it alone. I could not bring even a little bit of change, even within one taluk; it was not possible to bring any change. A new type of government came into existence. Leadership that stimulates the baser tendencies of people and wins the elections dominated. As our people have a mean mentality, these leaders stimulate and nurture it. With their nourishment it grows still more widely. I thought people were honest and pure and the leaders were wrong, dishonest and tried to protest against the leaders publicly. I tried to show greater leadership than those political leaders. Do you know Saati, moral leadership also develops ego, more than what corrupt political leadership does. I completely failed in it. I should have had its practical knowledge. That is, our people also are corrupt, rascals. But they have the basic quality of becoming good, latent in them, if they are aware that unless they become good, they do not come up in life and do not prosper. We may educate them on what is meant by goodness, what is the meaning of coming up in life. Then they may be wide awake, think and know about the correct way. On the whole, no one can save or reform them unless they gain quality and power to love them abundantly, continuously, knowing fully well that nine hundred and ninety nine persons out of one thousand have the tendency to become corrupt. Do you understand what I say?' Satyappa stopped talking.

Savitri did not react instantly. Then she said, 'Well, bhaava, what do I know about politics and the condition of our country? You had participated in the freedom movement and had met Mahatma Gandhi and spoken with him. Moreover you have studied so much, yet I feel, I understand dimly what you are saying.'

'It does not matter, leave it. I told you that I am lying alone and pondering, yet nothing is clear to me. You see, let me take an example from actual life. I hope you know the Banjara settlement near our village. You have seen it when you were a little girl. I had taken you there one day. There, those who were children then are now young men. They do not have education nor any job. They do not own lands. There is no uncultivated land in our place. If there was some kind of industry or something to employ them, they would have worked and earned their living. But now, they steal coconuts during nights from the surrounding villages. They break into groves in groups of eight to ten. All the grove-owners are afraid of them. What did I do to solve this? Just like all other people I too was caught in affection for my son and my grandchildren and decided to guard my own grove. You see, Saati, instead of choosing a whole taluk to implement my programme, if I had chosen a small village, stayed there, developed their knowledge and cultivated trust and honesty needed for cooperation and had started the coir industry, it would have run well. We could have sold the product cheaper than that of the Marvadi or started any other industry for the boys. However, a government school is started in that village. That school is not developing good quality in the children. I could have stayed there with them and concentrated on building up their character. I did not do such work also. I simply sat guarding my grove. Is not lust the distilled form of what is called 'I'? What else will happen except succumbing?' Satyappa became silent. Savitri was reflecting on these words in the silence of darkness. She could understand these words more clearly than what he had spoken earlier: for half an hour neither of them spoke. But, they knew, neither of them was sleepy. Finally Satyappa said: 'You know, I did not bring up my own son Ramachandra properly. I was caught in the affection that he was a motherless child. Now this blind pampering turns affection into poison. His wife is everything to him. She has made him her bonded-slave. She knows he is the servant of physical pleasure. Besides, he is a timid fellow. He doesn't have the courage to go to the grove during the night, make a round, shout a warning and come back. Who is responsible for this cowardice in him? Is it not me?'

Satyappa turned silent again. Savitri too knew about Ramachandra. He and his wife were not bad. Yet how could virtues be cultivated? What were the methods? Savitri's mind dwelled on these thoughts as she had been working as a teacher since so many years. For another half an hour, their minds were travelling out in their own directions. Then Satyappa said, 'You see Saati, now I am thinking about what I should do. After I return to my place, I will divide the lands and give half of it to Ramachandra. If he works hard independently on the lands, he need not worry for food, clothes, etc. If his wife cares for the cattle and looks after the cows, there will be no scarcity of milk. If not, there would be nothing. I am not taking this decision with an intention of punishing them. If a man eats food that he has earned by his toil, three fourths of his selfishness vanishes. I will keep the remaining half for myself. I told you that there was a hut in my grove. When I stayed in that hut or lied down there, all the lewd thoughts and deeds of Manjayya's hut were haunting me. I will live there only, cooking my own food. I'll keep there only earthenware pots and pans so that there is no risk of theft. It is enough for me. I will see that the income from my portion of the land is saved. From that capital, I will have a small planning and start my work which would bring in difference in a small village, one street or only four families. It is only a motive of uplifting them. But the purpose is I should not fall down. I will explain all this to Ramachandra and his wife. I know, they won't understand. I am aware they think that I have left them in the lurch. But to tell them is my duty. I do not want to waste my time explaining to them and make them agree. Moreover I live in a different place.'

Savitri did not find this plan unusual. Even while she was a little girl, she had seen her father after his wife's death, along with looking after agricultural work, the burden of bringing up children, would daily go to Shivaalaya, bring home guests and serve them food. Her elder brother Ramakrishna too, was almost of the same nature. After her elder sister Seetha's marriage, Savitri stayed in this bhaava's house for two and a half years. Though she was a little girl, there were some vague ideas imprinted in her mind of her bhaava busying himself in public service. Along with this, she had her own experience of seventeen years, that too gained after just six months of marriage with Manjayya. Savitri tried to understand the thoughts of her bhaava in the background of all these. But neither the enthusiasm of her bhaava nor the confidence about its success developed in her. But, she was clearly aware of one thing. Her elder brother Ramakrishna was an utterly silent person. It was impossible to talk to him. She remembered what he had said one day. 'Ninety nine percent of what we speak is useless, unnecessary and waste of time.' She thought, no matter how much of goodness and generosity is there, if it is not expressed through speech and if other persons are not encouraged to express their minds and the turmoil within them, how can the hearts get closer? She felt, this bhaava was okay and whenever she felt like talking, she could go to Mattikere. With this thought in mind, she slept.

The scorching heat and burning sensation on Sarojakshi's cheek did not subside long after Manjayya left. She felt as though solid iron was moulded into the shape of human fingers, heated in fire and pressed on to her cheek. She had experienced the cruelty she had not imagined till now, at that moment when the blow fell and seared her cheek. After he rode away on the bicycle, its form began to appear, expanding itself in all dimensions as a poori swells when plunged into hot oil. Though strife, quarrels, blows were common in love, Sarojakshi felt this sort of cruelty was possible only in lewd persons of beastly level. Her mind filled with distress and reproach towards herself for being attracted to that animal Manjayya.

By the time the children came home in the evening, Sarojakshi applied more talcum powder on her face than she daily used, so that the swelling on her cheek was not noticed. In case her husband enquired, she could counter, 'Nothing. What are you looking at my cheeks for?' And if she showed some resentment, it was enough. Somehow there was a feeling of shame, though she had readied an answer for her husband. Oh what sort of a life was this! Terrible fascination towards that beast and a terrible aversion, pity and rejection for this cow called husband. Sarojakshi tossed and turned for a long time that night as sleep eluded her. Her mind began introspecting: whether she was the one who had started it all. When there was such friendship between a man and a woman and both of them were aware that there was something more than mere friendship, it was but natural that the man would desire for 'that'. It was really surprising that a man like Manjayya did not push things earlier. Now when he grabbed her, she had not only broken free but slapped him as well. If she had not hit him, he would have again held her and would have had his way, held her in such a way that she could not have freed herself and finished off everything; no, he would have satisfied the burning desire inside her too. Then, after four or five such experiences, he would have lost interest. So, what other device did she have to hold him at bay except to slap? Her mind was consoling itself with these thoughts. After she freed herself and slapped him, she herself began speaking. She wondered why she had to ask the number of women he hunted down? But she knew her purpose: she wanted to make it clear that she was well aware of his history. Yet she wanted to have his friendship. At that moment, she thought she could win him over through this method. But did she win? Within two days she began to feel, of course he did not win by slapping her cruelly. That caused a terrible sense of burning, but she was not defeated by being slapped. She had to wait. But she did not expect that he would come on his own to her house presently. Yet there was a little expectation that he may come one day all of a sudden and ask her, 'You said something about some meaning, what was that.'

After a week, her husband asked her, 'What happened. I haven't seen Manjayya? Hasn't he come?'

She retorted, 'Is he in your office or mine? How would I know?'

Appajappa kept quiet as though he had committed a crime.

Sarojakshi began brooding continuously. Why was her mind glued on to Manjayya. One phase of her mind that was stuck to this glue was always thinking, though she tried to discard the idea.

The very first day when she saw him at her house, she felt she was in the proximity of a real man. Her mind would descend to the last step of memory, light the lamp and scrutinise: was she caught in his web that day itself ? She was not inexperienced about relationships between man and woman, nor was she a novice. She was not a woman limited to a single experience, who did not touch any other man except her husband. But, till then she had not met such a man, whom the very moment she saw and spoke to she was gripped by the feeling that he was a man, a real man, who would engulf the mind. No, not Lakkappa, nor that Subbayya. She gave Manjayya coffee and snacks. And the attraction towards him increased just after speaking four or five sentences with him. Sarojakshi questioned herself, whether she was attracted towards him because he helped her husband to earn extra money and was actually managing the Forest Department of the whole taluk. Her mind introspected intensely on this aspect. Perhaps this was one reason for their friendship moving towards intimacy. But this seemed a very insignificant reason for the mind to flow towards him and be fixated on him. Every moment she would compare her husband with Manjayya and fume at the thought, why can't her husband be like Manjayya. She was aware that for no reason at all, she would get angry with her husband. Oh what a husband he was. Neither bad nor wicked, he was a weakling who could not rule or master anyone or anything. In the early days of the marriage, when a woman feels fear and anxiety about her husband, this obedience of consulting the wife for everything had given Sarojakshi some satisfaction. But this turned quickly into dissatisfaction. Very shortly, she realised that her husband had a personality which was not fit for either a good fight or quarrel, for love or for displaying anger. How many times had she thought, a husband must do anything, even if it be cheating his wife, with confidence. Even in the physical act, if she faked anger and said, her eyes reddened,

'Oh, why do you have to pester me, go away,' he would beg pardon with the meekness of a mere servant and become submissive. How can love be born for such a husband who never dares to commit the 'mistake' of pestering his wife? Only pity was possible there. Either in speech or deed or transactions, her husband did not have suggestiveness at all. He was a fool – a stupid animal that did not know there would be some suggestion, some meanings, some wave of feeling beyond denotations. She pressed him to read literature and thrust some books in his hands. But he would say, 'I won't understand all this,' and stand petrified like a stupid student before a teacher. His only merit was that he would always say, 'You see, I obey whatever you tell me, I never go against you.' How much did Sarojakshi try to get rid of that obedience and make him a competent, strong man! How intimately she had elucidated character and qualities in a male which a woman appreciates! He could only listen to all her talk with meek obedience. Sometimes she would lose patience and get enraged and provoke him, 'I know you want to thrash me, you won't be satisfied until you beat me. I promise I won't shout or create a scene. Beat me, come on thrash me,' saying so she would turn her back towards him and bow down. But that man of six feet, that man with a sturdy build of body that was most suitable for forest department, would not understand her action and stand baffled. And then he would try to prove his innocence and say, 'Well Saroja, when did I ever say so?' Sarojakshi would say, 'No, you did not say so. But I know what's in your mind.' But that dunce of a husband would again defend his non-violent nature.

Sarojakshi's cheek still burnt if touched, though it was five days since Manjayya had slapped her. She felt, perhaps the thin surface layer of skin would swell and drop off and a new layer would grow from within. But she thought, that beating by Manjayya was not an indication of self-confidence of controlling a woman. It was sheer cruelty. How could it be possible to beat so harshly and so crudely a woman he loves? Was his love real? She remembered she had read somewhere that if people in love are disappointed, they hurt themselves and punish themselves, but if it is merely their lust that is thwarted, they hurt and punish others. Was it only lust in Manjayya's case? Somehow her mind did not agree to this. She would clarify her feelings to herself that she too was not longing for Manjayya just because of sexual frustration. She was fed up with mere liaisons and sexcapades. While the affair was going on there would be the feeling that this really surpassed the level of mere physical relationship. But actually how could she have introspected so minutely in those delightful days? While her memory glided into those days, it would bring back to her mind the details of her relations with Lakkappa. Though he was not six feet tall or did not have the broad shoulders of Appajappa, he was a young man with supreme self-confidence. He had passed the competitive exam in the first attempt itself, completed the probationary period and was appointed as an Assistant Conservator, a superior officer. Was there a dearth for good hotels in Mysore? Yet, as Lakkappa was still unmarried, Sarojakshi sent her husband to invite him for lunch and when he was acquainted and familiarity developed, she said, 'You need not feel shy or embarrassed if my husband is not at home. You must have your meals here every night.' When Saroja insisted before her husband, he too had added, 'Yes sir, yes sir, you must come.' Thus Lakkappa used to come when Sarojakshi was alone also. He would ask, 'Saroja, will you cook chicken for me tomorrow?' 'What will you do if I say I won't?' 'I'll carry you to my room and order you to cook,' 'Oh is that so? Who gave you the authority to order me?', 'Why should anybody else give me. I myself have that authority!'. 'You keep quiet sir, only Appajappa has got that authority, not you!' 'Is it so? Here, I'll exercise my authority.' Lakkappa said, understood her suggestion, looked if there was anyone around, came near, held her hands firmly and said, 'Now, will you obey me or not?' and exercised his authority. Such self-confidence! Afterwards, he would order her. 'Come, Saroja, Let's go watch a film.' Then without caring what the neighbours would say, she would obey him, be a pillion rider on his motor-bike and go to films and other places. Did Appajappa beat me at least then? Sarojakshi one day told Lakkappa. 'You see if Appajappa comes to know of this, will he be quiet? Will he let us go scot free?' Lakkappa retorted, 'Who? Appajappa? Your husband? Do you think, he is not aware of this? He won't do anything. Don't worry!' Saroja felt it a disgrace to be the wife of a man who stayed passive even after knowing that his wife was having an affair and an even greater shame to continue to be his wife. And Lakkappa was a clever lover. However subtly she suggested or then openly asked, he was not ready to marry Sarojakshi or let her seek a divorce from Appajappa. This Appajappa was an obedient husband. If she said she would leave him, either he would blink his eyes obediently or would shed a few tears. When a child developed in her womb this Lakkappa withdrew. Was it with fear that she would establish authoritatively that the child was his? Or did he feel some shame for what he had done? Or did he think, she would insist she was impregnated by him and he ought to marry her? Sarojakshi thought, 'It was easy to do anything without risk with a woman who was married and was living with her husband. Whatever happens, there would be no responsibility. She did not know whether Appajappa knew this or though he knew he was too weak to take any action. Or Shashikanta might even be the child of Appajappa. How can it be said that he was fathered by Lakkappa? Sarojakshi reflected, unless stepping out of this limit or frame of marriage, a woman may not understand the actual form of family. After Lakkappa distanced himself with fear, Sarojakshi realised the truth that she had no alternative in life except to adjust with Appajappa. Her anger and indignation against Appajappa became less. It was true that she adjusted to him but could her mind be satisfied? Appajappa was never a man to fill her mind. He could only be pitied and not abused. For, how many days could films, storybooks, radio, film-hits divert her? For how many days could Shashikanta's smile keep her engaged? A child after its birth may be fodder for a year to its mother's mind. But could it fill up that inner vacuum? Can a child become a companion? Sarojakshi would attend to the lectures being conducted in Mysore, read poetry and serious novels. Appajappa was promoted as Forester and was transferred to Madikeri, Virajpet and Nagarahole and he stayed alone and would cook his own meals. Sarojakshi stayed in Mysore saying that it was not possible to get proper medical treatment for the child in those small towns. Appajappa, who had never contradicted her, agreed to this arrangement also. Yet she thought, except pity what other feeling could arise in her mind against that man. If she had wanted, she could have had the friendship of some men and could have enjoyed life. But she did not desire casual friendship. When Appajappa was transferred from Nagarahole to Kunigal, she felt bored with Mysore, felt more pity oozing out towards Appajappa and told him: 'Look here, fix a house in Kunigal. I too will come. There is a hospital there.' Oh, the sense of blessed relief on his face! There was no hardness on the face of her husband that could command the wife, 'Look here, if you do not agree to come and stay with me wherever I may be, I will kick you hard and break your bones!'

Sarojakshi sat holding a novel in hand. In Channarayapattana, she could not get literary works. Serious works of literature were still rarer. She remembered what she had understood by experience that it was an illusion to think that serious literature would fill the inner emptiness. She felt, serious literature turns the inner emptiness into a burning nothingness. It was really good that she could not get good books after she came to Kunigal! Except third rate films, nothing was available there. She would ruminate, if only there was work or job to occupy the mind from dawn to dusk, a woman like her could behave kindly with such a husband. Does a woman having an aggressive mind leave a passive husband free? Her mind gets angry howsoever she tries to control. Her anger makes him more and more helpless. Sarojakshi thought, if there was another companion, she could have behaved more cordially with her husband and could make him happier. If he too had another female companion, could he make his wife happier? Though this thought was strange, it flashed across her mind. She remembered, after Subbayya's acquaintance and friendship, her anger against Appajappa had subsided and she began to behave with him more tenderly. It was true, a sense of quietude had been born in her when she came nearer to Lakkappa. Then, how can that passion, that fills the void within, be a guilt? It was natural, that delight, comfort and happiness would be generated in a man or a woman in whom that void is filled. How could people, who lack inner happiness and delight in themselves bestow them on others? When the Conservator Subbayya visited Kunigal for inspection, he came to Sarojakshi's house for lunch. He was a Kodaga, a good marksman, a hunter. He was a strong superior officer who could exercise his authority. Sarojakshi thought, an officer must be like him. He had said, 'Saroja, you do not have the complexion, build of body and beauty, yes it is true. But compared to you all the beauties of Coorg are like food without spice or salt. You see Saroja, if I visit Kunigal frequently on the pretext of inspections, our department would get suspicious. Instead you come to Bangalore. If a room is fixed in a hotel, there will be no problem!' When Sarojakshi would say to her husband, I want to get some books from Bangalore. Please take care of the child! Oh how gladly and obediently Appajappa would agree. She knew that he would surely agree. She herself had doubted whether Shashikanta was the child of Lakkappa or Appajappa. Who could say Vaijayanti was not a Kodava girl by looking at her? In a way, Subbayya was a man who could reign and govern a woman. But Sarojakshi had understood his limitations within six months. In every matter he was straightforward and downright. In the very beginning itself, he had clarified regarding their relationship, what can be expected and what was not possible. He conducted himself in the way that could not stain his or her dignity. There was secrecy in all his actions. He was generous in bringing her a sari, jewels or any other articles. She did not ask him to promote her husband. Without Subbayya's effort, Appajappa would not have been selected so early for training and sent to Coimbatore and got promoted. But even once, he did not boast before her that he managed it. Sarojakshi reflected: what is this? Is this the only meaning of governance? How can people who do not completely dedicate themselves, govern? Subbayya did not totally offer himself; perhaps independent people may offer themselves. Sarojakshi analysed: officials will always maintain their limitation, even in love.

Sarojakshi got up and looked in the mirror at her cheek near the left jaw. The layer of the skin was peeling off. The red-skin inside was turning pale. She remembered that Subbayya did not give vent to his anger in this way even on a single day, did not scold her or use bad words. However, she pondered whether anger and blows would become hot, melt the hearts that were not moulded and unite them. Somehow, she felt Manjayya would become a true lover. He would become a companion of life, who could give all and receive all and melt away in complete harmony and oneness. Manjayya was a free man, not a government servant. He need not fear anything. He was a land owner. He had not got his contract hankering for it or as means of livelihood. It is said that his wife had left him or did he himself leave her? However he is an independent man. While she was attending to him, serving him food, snacks or coffee, her mind would completely offer itself to him. Her condition was completely clear. Appajappa maybe in the house or may not. Even if he was in the house, she could have told him. 'Some groceries are needed, please go and get it from the market. Don't be in a hurry to return. You like that cool lemonade, you know. Go to that Guru's factory and drink lemonade. Children too like it, take them also with you.' If she had said so, he would have obediently taken both the children along and gone off. She could have enjoyed the company of Manjayya. But Sarojakshi, after her two affairs did not crave for such a relationship. She needed something deeper, she needed real companionship. She had been dreaming that Manjayya would meet her expectations because of his respectful behaviour towards her – bringing fruits, flowers, his suggestive speech and his smile of self-confidence. She thought, if he had rushed stealthily into the kitchen, opened up his mind fully and said, 'You see Saroja, don't you think it is artificial to maintain distance when the minds are united?' she would have offered herself from the depth of her being. But instead, why did he behave in that manner?

However, her heart kept reassuring her that one day, he would surely come to her. Sometimes the doubt too would raise its head, whether it was the prompting of her heart or mere desire. She waited one week, two weeks, three weeks but he did not come. She was disappointed, thinking, he might never come at all. One day she felt curious to see his wife, who worked as a teacher in the same town. Although the reason and purpose of why she should see his wife or what she should know were not clear, desire to see her became irresistible within two days. Watchman Usmani had said: 'Manjayya's wife is a very beautiful woman with fair complexion. Oh, one must wash one's hands before touching her – good height and figure, sharp eyes, a sharp and straight nose.' Moreover

Sarojakshi had enquired about the background of Manjayya. One day at eight in the morning, Sarojakshi went to the girls' middle school and stood near the outside gate. Students and teachers came one by one and gathered. In the meanwhile, there came a woman. As soon as she saw her, she was sure it was Savitramma by the form, self-confident stance and the shadow of sadness. Sarojakshi called a little girl near her and asked: 'What is the name of that teacher?' The girl said: 'Savitramma miss.' Sarojakshi stood there till Savitri went inside the school. Somehow Sarojakshi felt her body break out in sweat. She thought, if this Manjayya who has left such a beautiful, self-confident wife for so many years does not feel any sadness, would he come in search of me. This thought exposed her purpose of coming here. She was depressed and returned home. But within two days, the depression subsided and there arose a positive outlook. She consoled herself thinking: if mere complexion, colour, height, figure and countenance, these characteristics were going to mould the personality of a woman, the same characteristics and qualities should mould the personality of a male also. Appajappa who has these characteristics lacks personality. It is well known that Manjayya left his wife seventeen years back. She does not exist for him. So Sarojakshi found another point to defend. That there was no question of comparison at all. Several times she tried to forget Manjayya. She would feel satisfied that she had really forgotten him when she diverted her mind in watching films, spending more and more time with her children, getting books from the high school through some of her acquaintances and reading them. But now, after she saw Manjayya's wife, he began to haunt her always. Her mind would be predominantly occupied by the feeling that Savitramma was her rival. Sarojakshi would console herself; how could she be a rival, when it had been seventeen years since he left her and there was no communication at all between them. Oh what madness possessed her! But Savitri's picture refused to vanish from her mind. She was ashamed when she was aware that Savitri occupied her mind more than Manjayya. Then she would condemn herself thinking she had fallen to the level of an ordinary woman.

One day Appajappa brought terrible news. He said, 'Manjayya has smashed the skull of someone and killed him, for he had entered his grove to steal coconuts. Police inspector Narayana Murthy, along with the S.I., Dafedar and PCs has gone to Bilikere, but Manjayya could not be caught. Sarojakshi shuddered, listening to this news. She could not clearly distinguish, whether the shudder was caused by the punishment Manjayya would get in court or by the cruel deed, the murder he had committed. The same evening, Watchman Usmani came with a load of firewood needed for her house. Sarojakshi enquired from him, unable to control her anxiety, 'Well Usmani, did you hear the news?' Usmani praised Manjayya heartily, 'You see madam, if there is a real man, it is this Manjayya. Is he a woman, wearing bangles, to tolerate and keep quiet if someone breaks into his grove and steals away coconuts? Oh! he has smashed the thief. He has the courage and valour to be the Chief Conservator.' Sarojakshi asked, 'He is not yet caught by the police, what will happen?' Usmani answered, 'He has a quicksilver brain, he's like mercury. He acts like a lawyer though he has no law degree. He sports a black coat too. Would that brain commit murder, without planning an escape route? Perhaps he is moving secretly escaping from the police to collect witness and evidence. After everything is ready, he may, on his own, go to the police station and say, "Look here I have come. Go to court, write whatever chargesheet you are going to." You need not worry, avva.'

Sarojakshi was calmed, but was not completely rid of anxiety. There was a fear, for it was not clear how events would turn out in court. She was eager to know what happened afterwards and what will happen further. But whom could she talk to? Appajappa did not have the intelligence to explain what turn Manjayya's case could take. Whom should she ask? How could she help Manjayya? In this turmoil, she did not get a wink of sleep and the whole night she spent tossing and turning. Appajappa was snoring heavily. In the midnight when there was a knock on the door, she at once asked, 'Who is it?' Before the word 'I' was completed she knew instinctively that it was the voice of a person familiar to her. She got up and opened the door. He spoke to her for five minutes and went away.

However, one point was clear in her mind; that her decision of asking Manjayya not to take Appajappa as a witness was right. She knew that this fellow did not have the intelligence to face the cross-examination even for a minute. She had enough confidence about her sharp intelligence, but could not do anything to save him. Along with the sadness that nothing struck her, no means to save him, the anxiety of what may happen was increasing day by day. One day she went to Hassan with Appajappa to see Manjayya, when the jail officials said, 'As enquiry is still being conducted, nobody would be allowed to visit him.' Her eyes filled with tears.

Manjayya was released and Sarojakshi sighed with relief. But he did not come to see her. She waited for a week, two weeks then for more than a month. Her mind could not think of anything except him. Her confidence – as tall as herself – that he would surely come, was sinking and contracting inch by inch with each passing day. She would be eager to ask her husband as soon as he came home, whether Manjayya had come to the office. But she was stubborn and did not want to ask him on her own. She had complete belief in her husband's nature. As far as her knowledge went, he would surely say as soon as he returned home, if Manjayya had come to office.

One day Appajappa returned from the office by three in the afternoon. He seemed to be exhausted and he had a long face. He sank on the chair and did not raise his head. Sarojakshi understood that her husband was in a state of dilemma: an inner urge to confess something to his wife and a fear to come out with it. She broke the ice and asked, 'How come you're back so early?'

Tears streamed from Appajappa's eyes. He said, 'I had not told you. I've been suspended. All over the taluk there were complaints that I take bribes. Four days back, the Deputy Conservator visited those seven or eight villages which had sent the complaints to conduct investigations. He has sent orders, "Until the enquiry is completed, you are suspended with immediate effect. You have to hand over charge to the Arasikere Ranger." He has sent the orders with the Arasikere Ranger who came and took over charge.' By the time he narrated this, a steady stream of copious tears flowed down his cheeks.

Sarojakshi could make out nothing. It was not a surprise if there were complaints about Appajappa taking bribes for it was a fact. But he neither pestered anybody for bribe nor did he threaten any harm if they refused to. In fact, he was a man without such capacity or strength. The whole system of bribe of the taluk was thought out and organised by Manjayya. Suddenly it struck her: he had told, he would teach her a lesson. He had done so by ensuring that her husband did not get his salary. Was it revenge, for not complying with his plea of sending her husband to commit perjury in the court and for saying what would happen to her family if the judge wrote in his report, 'This Appajappa, despite being a government servant committed perjury,' and her husband lost his job? Was it a challenge that, 'You see, even now I'll see that your husband loses his job?' While one part of her mind was engaged in this thought, another part was filled with contempt against her husband. A sense of guilt also was mingled with it. If she felt disdain for her husband who shed tears, another disgust was born in her mind towards that beast Manjayya, who perhaps never shed tears. Her husband sat in the chair, head downcast. He pressed his palms to his eyes and stopped the tears. She felt like consoling him.

But again there was contempt. In such situations, should a wife console a husband or should it be the other way round?

When at night, he was tossing on the bed unable to sleep, Appajappa asked his wife, 'Of late, I've not met Manjayya. He is well experienced in matters of court and offices. If we approach him he will surely save us. I can't think of any other way!'

Sarojakshi answered instantly. 'You're an officer. Manjayya is the contractor appointed by superior officers on the basis of your recommendation. Why should you take him to your superiors for your work?'

She had used the singular while referring to Manjayya. Appajappa remarked, 'What's this? Why are you using the singular for Manjayya and disrespecting him? How can you do so?'

'Okay. Let's call him "his highness" and show him royal respect. What I asked was, can't you go without him and mend these matters?' Appajappa clammed up. She was aware that her husband did not sleep for a long time. She too did not get a wink of sleep. She had not imagined that Manjayya would stoop to such vileness. She thought, if she had known this, perhaps her mind would not have turned towards him. But in a little while, she realised the strangeness and oddity of her mind. Why could she not dissociate him from her mind even after she knew the details about his conduct and character? She decided: If there was anything between them, it was only enmity. But again her mind got busy trying to understand itself, turned round and round and suggested: no, it was not possible. Only disdain, scorn, contempt. Contempt was natural. Vile, mean worm! He had decided to threaten her. 'I'll make your husband lose his job and cause you to starve.' Sarojakshi burnt with anger.

She was working in the kitchen in the morning. When she came out, her husband and his bicycle were not to be found. She asked Shashikanta who was doing his maths sums, 'Where is Appa?' He said, 'He got ready and went to office!' She at once understood and was furious. She was worried too, when he had voluntarily gone to Manjayya, surely that rascal would weave another web. Now she was furious, for if her husband had not informed her of his going to office, it was because he had gone to see that fellow. She bit her lip. No, he would never understand nor had he the manliness to manage. If he had that, why should she be ... before the sentence ended in her mind, her eyes filled with tears. Immediately she suppressed it. But little Vaijayanti who was in the kitchen asked, 'Amma why are you crying?' Sarojakshi snapped. 'Don't you have any lessons? Did you write the alphabet?' But Vaijayanti was not a girl to be scared off. She punched her mother and ran out. Sarojakshi was curious to know what trick Manjayya might have played, but that would be known only after Appajappa returned home. At the same time, she was worried if this stag would be caught in that hunter's trap. She knew Appajappa would never hide anything from her; he had no strength or sense for that. She realised that if she showed a little anger, he would change according to her wish. However a longing rose in her mind: a husband should be a pinnacle that a woman can raise her head and look up to, he should always be touching the open sky. Her mind fixed in that imagination and remained suspended in it. How beautiful that picture was! She tried to remember whether she had read this comparison in any poem or novel.

It happened as she had expected. Appajappa did not return by afternoon, but came back late evening around eight. He had a big, ripe jackfruit tied on his bicycle carrier, whose aroma was invading the nostrils from a furlong away. The fruit was from Manjayya's field. It was Appajappa's favourite fruit. Sarojakshi thought Manjayya had sent that to enthral him. Appajappa brought in his bicycle, put down the fruit and said in an apologetic tone, 'I had gone to Bilikere.'

Sarojakshi asked, 'Did he prepare milk kheer for lunch, or not?'

'Yes, who told you? Did Usmani come?'

Sarojakshi did not speak for a minute. Then said, 'Okay come, have your dinner. The milk kheer he offered before you left, would have digested by now, cycling that distance.'

Appajappa asked with surprise, 'What? Offered kheer before I started. Who told you? Usmani had already left by then!'

As the children were yawning, she first served them. They decided to cut the jackfruit in the morning. When only the two of them were having their dinner, Sarojakshi asked him, 'How much money did Manjayya want you to bring to fix things for you?' Appajappa said, 'What are you saying? Do you think Manjayya will take money from us? He only gives us. The superior officers swallow ships. Especially in the Forest Department.'

'Okay. How much did he ask you to bring to bribe the superiors?'

'Two thousand.'

'Can't you take the same two thousand, go to your superiors and get the work done?'

'What! Me!' Panic spread across Appajappa's face. 'What if they hand me over me the anti-corruption squad on the charge that I tried to bribe the officials?'

She said, 'What is the guarantee they will not hand over Manjayya to the squad on the same charge.'

'You see, Manjayya knows how to talk with them. He is smart.'

Sarojakshi felt contempt towards this man, her husband, rising inside her yet again. Somehow in this instance she did not feel any contempt towards Manjayya. But a rage was swelling within her that she must catch Manjayya and smash his head, with a cudgel or slice it off with a sickle. In this fight, either he or she must die or maybe both together. The mental picture fascinated her. Yes, both of them should fight and die together. She did not speak further. Finishing his meals, Appajappa went to the bedroom. It was always his duty to make the bed, adjust blankets and tie the mosquito net. Sarojakshi had never ordered him to do those things. He would do them on his own. By that time, she would finish off the kitchen chores. While in bed, Appajappa's mind was worrying on how to get those two thousand rupees. Finances were completely under the control of Sarojakshi. He did not know whether something was saved or not. It was the thirtieth day of the month and on the morrow he would not get his salary. Even if something was saved, it would be needed for the day to day household expenses. Appajappa was scared to ask his wife for her gold bangles or chain. He began worrying, 'If she refuses to give, what will I do? Sarojakshi was lying there picturing her fighting with Manjayya, blood pouring down their bodies, dying together. After midnight, Appajappa finally spoke, 'Unless we sell some gold, how can we arrange two thousand rupees?'

Sarojakshi did not speak. Appajappa knew that if he repeated the question, she would get irritated, so he kept quiet. But he was certain that she was awake and had heard his question. He kept quiet with the expectation that tomorrow or the day after, she herself would tell him what to do.

As soon as they woke up in the morning, the children demanded they cut the jackfruit. Appajappa looked at his wife. She said, 'Why did you have to take it just because he gave you?'

Appajappa stood for a minute as if he had committed a blunder and then tried to defend himself. 'Wasn't I bringing it earlier also?' When she told him to cut the fruit, he smeared oil on the sickle, cut the fruit into two halves, took out the fruit pieces from one half and brought the other half into the kitchen. She told him, 'Look, after breakfast cycle down to Bilikere and tell Manjayya, "You see Manjayya, if we have to arrange for money, we must sell gold or pawn it. We do not know any reliable jeweller. Please come, speak to my wife, take her to the shop and settle the business."'

Appajappa was beside himself with joy. He was elated that his wife had agreed so swiftly to his suggestion. She said, 'Do not speak a single word more than this. Perhaps he may come with you. If he does, I'll talk about this business. You will never understand it. While we are talking, you go out saying that you have some work in the market.'

Appajappa rapidly took his bath, lit incense sticks before the gods, ate roti, chutney and jackfruit, drank coffee and drove away on his bicycle.

He returned by afternoon itself. 'Manjayya has sprained his right leg. He can't walk. He said even pedalling the cycle was painful. I offered to take him doubles on my bicycle, but he said he could not sit on the carrier.'

'Was the leg swollen?'

'No. He said it was really paining. He told somebody to bring oil and got it massaged. I too massaged a little.' Sarojakshi did not react. She went into the kitchen.

Manjayya did not come even after a week. Appajappa asked his wife, 'What shall we do now?' Sarojakshi stipulated, 'I will spare some of my jewels for raising the money. But only on the condition that you yourself go and meet the superior officers and complete the job. There should be no middleman or mediation by anyone else.' Appajappa had no answer to that, so he became silent. As he had nothing else to do, it was difficult for him to while away time. He would search for some work, take the bundle of clothes to the tank, wash them, put them out for drying or take the broom and start sweeping the floor. Sarojakshi would be furious, because it was considered an insult to a woman if her husband touches the broom while the wife was at home. The more angry she was, the more obedient he would become. Her anger rose in proportion to his obedience. He would think that she was getting angry for his blunder of being suspended, and as if to compensate, he would be more submissive. One day Sarojakshi scolded him. 'You are born a male. I did not ask you to do household chores like a maidservant.' Appajappa began to think about the meaning of her words. Finally, he could not understand anything, had his breakfast, went away to have a walk in Market Street. He came for lunch, again went out and returned in the evening. He would sit or stand on the platform of any shop in Market Street, or near the taluk office and while away time. This became his routine. Sarojakshi did not object to it. She kept quiet thinking that at least she could avoid getting irritated looking at a man who sat at home like a woman in her periods in an orthodox household. One day while having lunch Appajappa said, 'I met Manjayya near the taluk office.'

'What did he say?'

'I invited him home. "Of late you are not coming at all, what is the reason?" I asked. But he said he had some work in Hassan and was on his way. I reminded him, I had requested him to come and finalise the matter of selling jewels and speak about it with you. "But that day you had sprained your leg," I said, "Please come and speak to her, collect money and help me in revoking my suspension. But he said jewellery was women's business and he could not be bothered about it and went away!"' Appajappa reported.

'If you meet him again, don't speak to him.'

'If you say don't speak to him, how can our work be done?' Appajappa insisted.

She controlled her anger. But a thing that struck her consoled her. Was there mere villainy in Manjayya's behaviour? Or was he scared of coming and meeting her? However, it was true, he caused this suspension only because of wickedness, because of the rage of a beast. 'See how I will teach you a lesson, I will see to it that you won't get even a fistful of rice.' But, even though she had sent the message to come and speak with her, he had not come. She understood it must be either out of shame or fear.

After several days, the hard cash they had with them was spent and she had no other way save selling pieces of her jewellery. As she was managing the household finances, she was not in a position to consult her husband. Though a suspended person was entitled to one-third salary, she knew that it would take months to be sanctioned. One day Appajappa learnt that it was Manjayya who had instigated the farmers to write a complaint against him. Manjayya had made thirty different farmers write complaints about a single man at one time. Duplicate of these complaints reached Bangalore also. As such Appajappa had to be suspended. Now, nothing could be done until there was a direction from Bangalore Head Office and the enquiry was conducted. Appajappa was shocked and surprised. He began introspecting, what injustice had he done to Manjayya! He came home, reported it to his wife. She said, 'How is it? Did you not know this earlier? You should have gone to the District Office and found out what the matter was.'

'How else should I have known?"

She said, 'Was it not enough? He did not come to our house, even when you asked him. He pretended that he had sprained his leg.'

Appajappa did not speak. He remembered that his wife was more intelligent.

The contempt she had till now against this villain turned into rage. His picture was always filling her mind in the form of rage. She longed to teach him a lesson he would never forget but she was restless not knowing the method. She knew, he would solve this problem if she herself would go to Bilikere and plead with him that he was competent. But she had to go and bow before him, had to say, 'There is no one except you to solve my problem,' she had to offer herself in the way he wished. She felt her body was on fire. Awareness then dawned clearly. She could outwit him only if she solved her problem without his help. Moreover she realised it was impossible to get the suspension revoked just by selling jewels and going to Bangalore. She thought, as this situation was created by her, it was her problem to solve. She knew her husband could do nothing except to put the entire load on her head and sit. One sleepless night, while she was thinking about this, Subbayya came to her mind. Immediately, she felt that she had won. She felt sad that this had not struck her all these days. She reflected, where might he be now? Wherever he might be, he would be in a senior post, he would surely recommend to someone and do the needful. Along with this belief, an uneasiness too took hold of her. There was no contact with him at all, after she became pregnant with his child, Vaijayanti. When Subbayya was transferred from Bangalore to Mysore, she was four months pregnant. Forgetting that?! Perhaps it was easy for him to forget that, anyway, was he not an officer? But she tried hard to forget him, finding solace in reading. And how difficult it was not to get perturbed while looking at Vaijayanti's face! Actually after seeing this Manjayya, the pain caused by Subbayya's memory was a bit subdued. Now her mind was hurt; she had to go to the same Subbayya and ask for help. She spent eight days agonising over it though she knew that there was no other way. Finally whatever money she had at home was exhausted and only fifty rupees remained in the bank. She decided to go and meet him. She told her husband, 'Enquire where Subbayya is now. Let us go and meet him!' Appajappa went to Hassan, returned in the afternoon itself and said, 'He had been to Dehradun as Superintendent of Training College. Now he has come to Bangalore as Deputy Chief Conservator.'

Sarojakshi said, 'Let us go to Bangalore tomorrow by the morning bus.'

Appajappa looked scared. He did not answer. When Sarojakshi again asked him, he said, 'What if he asks, why did you do such a thing?'

She said, 'I'll go in and speak with him. You wait outside!'

She requested her neighbours to look after the children until evening and the couple took the first bus to Bangalore. They reached the office in the forenoon, at eleven thirty. The officer was available. She remembered her past experience. If she wrote her name on a slip of paper and sent it in, immediately he would send for her. Or had he forgotten her after five and half years? No, Subbayya was not that sort of a person. People like Manjayya, who go in search of a hundred women may forget, but not Subbayya. Yet she felt her spirit sinking, felt uneasiness and shame, for she had to go and meet the person she had removed from her mind. Though she tried to avoid it, there was that old memory that was springing up the attraction. He must be nearing fifty now. She imagined his hair and moustache to have turned grey. She decided there was no use delaying, took a slip of paper from the peon, wrote, 'Sarojakshi, [Forester Appajappa's wife, Kunigal] and sent it in. Her husband asked, 'What did you write?' 'Keep quiet. I have written my name, what else.' She scolded him as if instilling courage in him. Within a minute, the peon returned and gestured her to go in. She told her husband to wait, entered alone through the half opened door, went around the wood-and-cloth partition screen and stepped inside. Subbayya stood up with desire and surprise. He stretched his hand, held her hand tightly for more than a minute and smiling squeezed her hand softly. He asked, 'Where are you these days? Please sit down!' It was the same friendliness of the past. His shining black hair, same black sharp Coorgi moustaches. She thought he must be using hair dye. She did not know how to begin. He had not changed much in those five years. He too held her gaze with a stare, not knowing what to talk. There was the painting of a tiger on the wall behind him. The tiger had occupied the complete wall. If seen absent-mindedly, it would seem so real, that you would get startled. To its left and right, two large paintings depicting dense forest scenes were strategically placed. He felt embarrassed for staring at her and repeated his question, 'Where are you now?'

'In Channarayapattana.'

'I had gone to Dehradun Staff College. I came here only last month. It was hectic. I thought of enquiring where you were and was planning to fix an inspection camp. If not how could I contact you? It will not be safe to write letters for it may reach someone else's hand.'

Still Sarojakshi looked dispirited. Subbayya asked her, 'Why are you so listless? Do you think, I am speaking so just because I saw you now? I swear, your memory haunted me even in Dehradun. But what could be done? Now, if it is Channarayapattana it is closer, only twice the distance of Kunigal. These days, there are many express bus services too.'

Sarojakshi's mind was deciding on the one hand not to reveal to Subbayya the purpose of her visit. But she could find no other way. By then the wall clock struck twelve. Suddenly she remembered her children whom she had left in Channarayapattana, especially the little daughter, Vaijayanti, this man's daughter, the man who was looking at her with eyes full of desire. He did not know whether it was a daughter or a son. When he was transferred to Mysore Sarojakshi was four-months pregnant. Subbayya also had accepted it was his. But he did not enquire whether the child was a boy or a girl. Perhaps with a sort of pride and embarrassment or perhaps he had completely forgotten the result of the days they spent together in Bangalore hotels. Sarojakshi felt, what Subbayya remembered was only the happiness, the delight of those days and the desire for happiness provoked by that memory. She scanned Subbayya's face silently. Vaijayanti's eyes, nose, eyebrows and cheeks completely resembled those of Subbayya; even the complexion. If Appajappa was smart, if he looked at Subbayya and remembered his daughter, surely the truth would flash. Even if it did strike him, he was not the type of man to take any action. He had sat with bowed head on the bench reserved for visitors. This memory made her sad. She had a strong urge to tell Subbayya, 'It was a girl child. She is running her fifth year. She is a true replica of you.' She killed the thought at once.

Subbayya asked, 'Why Saroja, why are you so dull? I think there is some problem. Tell me: Won't I solve your problem?'

'You see, there is a sandalwood contractor in the taluk. He has caused his favourite farmers to write a false complaint against Appajappa and the department has suspended him and there is no salary coming in. When Sarojakshi began narrating this, her mind felt light for it came out of the sphere of the relation between herself and Subbayya.

Subbayya asked, 'Tell me everything. What sort of a person is that contractor?'

'He has got enough of landed property, does not have any shortage for means of livelihood. Along with this, he works as a "foot lawyer" too. There are no courts and offices he does not know. It was this Manjayya who squeezed money from the farmers, saying it was to be given to the superiors. You know, Appajappa does not have the skill or strength for extracting money.'

After thinking for a minute, Subbayya questioned her, 'Did he by any chance have his eyes on you and try for you? And as you did not allow him leeway, is this his way of getting back?'

Suddenly she felt she was stabbed with a dagger. She thought this senior officer, who was trying to establish his past authority again on her, had entered her inner mind and was trying to bring out what was there. Within a second her eyes filled with tears thinking, did this man feel that she was such a cheap woman? Did he get me so easily? Then Subbayya got up, bent across the big table, held her shoulders, squeezed softly and consoling her said, 'No, Saroja, I did not ask this to cause you distress or to tease you. If we are clearly aware of the enemy's motive, the solution is easy. It was only for that reason that I asked this question.'

She thought: Yes, what he is saying is true. She felt a desire that she should tell him how Manjayya tried to overpower her and add some lies also. She should also tell Subbayya that as she did not give her consent to his suggestion that Appajappa should commit perjury in court in that murder case on Manjayya, he had instigated the farmers. Sarojakshi felt like telling the truth so that Manjayya would get suitable punishment. She was certain that it was not impossible to put his nose out of joint if officers of this cadre made up their minds. She was silent for a minute. Then she subdued that desire and said, 'See, why should I conceal anything from you? That Manjayya doesn't have any feeling of that kind. Once Appajappa had contradicted him by asking what authority he had to book a case, being only a contractor who looked after sandalwood trees. That fellow, so to speak, is a man who acts like a lawyer without a law degree and creates all sorts of disputes between persons and parties. That's why he has done it.'

Subbayya said, 'It is alright,' and pressed a button on the phone beside him. His assistant came in from the ante-room. The officer asked the assistant, 'Is there any report on Appajappa, Range Officer of Channarayapattana, Hassan district?'

'Yes sir, before you took charge here, his suspension orders had been already dispatched from our office.'

'Bring me the complete file of Appajappa.' Within a minute the assistant brought a big file, put it before Subbayya and went out.

Subbayya opened all the pages of the file, glanced at them and said, 'Yes, the matter of all the complaints is the same. Looking at the dates, it is obvious that all these complaints were written within the gap of mere four days. However, we do not know, how far these places are from each other. Anyway it is evident that these complaints are created in a fit of anger. If that Manjayya was really acting like a lawyer without having a law degree, he would have maintained the difference of two or three weeks between two complaints. These types of complaints are not unknown to capable administrators. Now you do one thing. Appajappa is sitting outside, isn't he?'

Sarojakshi said, 'Yes'.

Subbayya pressed the calling bell, told the peon to call in Appajappa. It took five minutes for him to enter. Even after coming in, he stood at a distance, deferentially, fear and respect blended in his stance. Subbayya questioned, 'What's it? What are these complaints about?' Appajappa did not open his mouth. Subbayya took out a sheet of paper, put it on the table and said, 'Now write this: "For the kind consideration of the respectful Deputy Chief Conservator." Subbayya made Appajappa write the application. Appajappa wrote it and signed, standing beside the table and bending down. Then Subbayya said, 'Okay, wait outside now.' Appajappa went out and breathed a sigh of relief. By that time, one of the persons waiting for interview with the officer had occupied the seat Appajappa had left and so he had to keep standing.

Subbayya once read the application and asked Sarojakshi, lowering his voice, 'Where are you staying?'

'We came here directly from the bus station.'

'Look here Saroja, tell your husband, "Your officer will help you. Some other records are yet to be searched. Service Register has also to be searched and examined. All these things are to be straightened up by the clerks. I must be here and be after them to complete these things. So, you go back to Channarayapattana and take care of the children. I'll be back tomorrow." By the by, how many children do you have?'

Saroja felt ashamed that her dignity was decreasing and he was pulling it further down. That last question, especially, made her still more trivial, she thought. Immediately she remembered Vaijayanti's face. She had an inner urge to tell him to see Vaijayanti: that she was his own replica. Didn't he remember, she was four-months pregnant when he was transferred to Mysore. She felt so angry that she was almost asking him, had he at least once enquired whether the child was a boy or a girl. But she simply hung down her head and sat.

He asked her in a soft voice, 'Do you have any problem?'

Sarojakshi said, 'Do you remember what you had told me once? Even while you are hunting a man-eating tiger, you won't kill it when it's sleeping; you won't hunt down a sick tiger or a wounded one. Do you still remember this?'

'Yes surely, there needs to be fairness even in hunting. There must be sportsmanship. We must give suitable opportunity to a rival. You see, what fulfilment is there in challenging and defeating a player who is down with sickness or fatigue?'

Sarojakshi said, 'Our friendship is not new, it need not be formed on new grounds. Just remember how old it is. But now, when I am in a sad plight and have come to you requesting help, if I spend a night with you, I feel it will be a body blow to my self-esteem. You too may get the same feeling any day in the future, wouldn't you?'

Subbayya felt as if caught in a trap. His face which was beaming with happiness from the very moment of Sarojakshi's coming into his office, turned pale. But within seconds, he regained his composure and said, 'Of course, of course, there is no question of exploiting at all. I am here to set right injustice wherever it is committed. Moreover, you know there is a government order that nobody, at any cost, should kill a tiger. That order also was passed at my insistence only. However strong an animal the tiger may be, it is a helpless animal before a man with a gun in his hand. Yes, both must meet on equal footing. I really appreciate your words. Friendship is important. How is everybody at home? You look weak. It is a long time since I have seen you. Take some tonic and nourishing food.'

Sarojakshi smiled, 'There is no salary coming in owing to this suspension. What sort of tonic can I afford?'

He assured, 'Don't worry. It will soon be revoked.'

She thought it fit that she should leave now and said, 'I need not worry at all, when I have so much confidence in you.' She got up. Subbayya bent down, held her hand and said, 'Surely I will do the needful.' She took leave of him.

The couple directly came to the bus station and they could catch a bus that would pass through Channarayapattana. They could get only separate sets. In a way Sarojakshi felt at ease because of this. She remembered her old days while she was shuttling alone on the same route from Kunigal to Bangalore and after a couple of days from Bangalore to Kunigal. She would get mad if she did not meet Subbayya at least once a month! Now not only was he distanced from her mind, but he seemed like a villain. She was surprised at the feeling that she thought this Subbayya was more of a villain than that Manjayya. Maybe, he may not revoke the suspension and may leave the file to rot. He might have decided that he would make her come again. These doubts filled her head. Appajappa was sleeping happily, perhaps with the consolation that his purpose of going there was achieved.

It was not that every woman Manjayya pursued had offered herself without resistance. As sometimes, even an expert marksman misses the target by just a fraction, it had happened with Manjayya also. But never before had he ever thought of revenge on anybody who did not consent to his advances. Till now he had taken his defeats sportingly. Besides, he had a sort of patience also, 'If not this woman, there will be hundred others, why should I bother?' This was the credo he lived by. But this time around, he had stubbornly gone round the villages, made Bochihalli Ningappa also go round and get farmers to write complaints against Appajappa, got their signatures, bore postal charges, and somehow very swiftly got Appajappa suspended. When he knew about the suspension order, he was elated. When the very next day Appajappa came to Bilikere seeking help, Manjayya thought Sarojakshi was defeated and had sent her husband in a peace-making effort. But the next day Appajappa came again and said, his wife had sent a message that she had to arrange money either by selling or pawning jewellery and for that Manjayya himself had to come. At that moment, though he thought it was an invitation by her to offer herself as a gift to the victor or to make amends for her impropriety, the very next moment he felt an immense shame. Though he was not aware of why or what it was at that moment, he felt terribly ashamed to face her and to speak with her. Her husband was suspended because of him. Appajappa had not known it or was not aware of it yet. Why should he be ashamed to go there? After all what had happened? Finally, it was I who had slapped her cheek and softened her, why should I feel insulted? It should be she who should feel it. Manjayya created all arguments that struck his pseudo lawyer's intelligence and tried to build a dam but could not prevent that flood of shame. He now began to understand the truth in Sarojakshi's opinion, that if he had depended on Appajappa's witness in court, it would have caused damage to his case. But at that moment, that too the swift manner in which she uttered, it seemed to Manjayya that she was scorning him. That memory was causing him more and more to burn in the fire of revenge. Somehow he evaded going to meet her feigning a sprain in his leg. Even after Appajappa went back, Manjayya's problem was not solved, but rather it was more intensified; he knew today or tomorrow it would come to light that he had caused the suspension. There would be a situation of seeing her face to face. What should he say then? 'Listen, you tried to exercise your authority on me, insulted me by your words so I did this to punish you,' but this firm answer was somehow becoming weak. If she asked smilingly, he was sure she would really ask and he had never experienced such quandary. 'Oh you please tell me which of my words insulted you. Didn't you yourself say in the end hundred percent of what I spoke was true?' What should he do then? After three or four days he brought to his mind directly the facts to trample down the original source of his shame. After all, what great beauty she was that he should fall for? Was it complexion, build or youth of sweet seventeen? But he remembered he had already several times thought about these factors and without getting any answer he had got frustrated. Then again he became aware that to push everybody into darkness, the brightness of her eyes alone was enough. Even while he lied down in darkness, he would feel the radiance of her eyes dazzling him as bright as a torch with a new battery. Sometimes he would get suspicious whether the slut knew some black magic or any mantras. But as Manjayya did not have even an iota of faith in such matters, the suspicion would not haunt him for long.

After three days, he found another way. He wondered at himself for not remembering the familiar and ever fruitful ways in the course of his experience. It was quite common that some woman belonging to the circle of his experience would haunt him. Whatever might be his efficiency in this field, it was not certain that he could get the woman as soon as he desired. She might have gone to another place or she might have been married, be staying with her husband and not in a situation to come out from home. She might be a nursing mother. If he had brought her from another place, she might have run away. In such contexts, to forget the woman who was haunting his mind, Manjayya would search a woman of the same kind and same age, of same dexterity and skill or he would teach her those skills, prepare her to be suitable to his taste and get service from her. Then the haunting woman herself would vanish like the scent in the blowing wind. Now also if he could find one like Sarojakshi. Yes, he realised her specialty. Looks of dark complexioned women with white in their eyes will naturally seem bright. Shining white teeth and earrings of white stones reflect in a dark complexioned face and enhance its brightness. Yes, he should search for such a one. He immediately got ready. He stuffed his pocket full of currency notes, went to Hassan, asked his old friend Puttamma to show him only a new girl. Puttamma called Kusumakshi and showed her to Manjayya in the evening. End of this girl's name was also an 'akshi' and she had the same sharp eyes. Yet a young girl of eighteen, Manjayya stayed the night with Kusumakshi at the back room in Puttamma's house. She had learnt skills and art of this trade directly from Puttamma. Manjayya felt she was top class. After all, what was Sarojakshi before this young girl! Manjayya consciously involved himself in the act and when he was at the peak, Sarojakshi vanished from his mind. He cheered himself, 'Bravo, well done' and engaged himself in it more and more. After all was over, Kusumakshi began to snore softly. Manjayya felt he was empty, wholly empty. Name of this person was not unknown to him. Either Kali or Boli or something and in this profession they call themselves Kusumakshi, Kamalakshi, Kanthamani or something else. This too he remembered. However, he didn't know why he felt anxious thinking what if Sarojakshi knows about his sleeping with this girl. But how could she know? By chance if she gets to know? Fear surfaced within him. Suddenly he got angry. How could she know? She questioned him so much, smilingly. How could she get the authority to taunt me in that manner, because I made an advance? If she liked she should say 'yes'. If not 'no.' Why all that coquetry? Had he asked her with how many she had slept? Again Manjayya got angry. Within half an hour, he cooled down. Actually, she might not have had any other man except her husband. If so, why did she refuse him? Then what was the meaning of such talk, full of love and affection, offering of food, snacks and that service of female companion, fanning him lovingly while he was eating? He could not understand anything, even in the company of this Kusumakshi whatever might be her real name. He felt like waking her up and asking, but *it* was snoring. Why should he disturb *its* sleep? If he wakes it up, it will think *for that* only he woke it up and will say *yes*. But he had no mind to mount again; his mind had turned towards Sarojakshi. He felt it disgusting to be lying down with it. It had rubbed its body with the Mysore sandal soap he had given, bathed, had jasmine flowers in its hair. Puttamma always keeps clean the room and bed, not a bug was there. Yet he felt everything disgusting and thought of getting out and going to the park near the bus stand, lying down or sitting on the stone bench. Why did he feel so? He felt like going to Channarayapattana, kick Sarojakshi so violently that her back was broken. He began to toss on the bed restlessly, bereft of sleep. Sarojakshi's words echoed in his mind: 'How many have you hunted down? Won't you tell me at least?' What authority had she to question me so? What was her specialty?

In the morning Kusumakshi asked his permission to leave. Manjayya did not feel like touching her again. He felt bored, gave some tips and permitted her to go. He got up, shaved, had a bath, took his handbag and came out. But he could not decide where to go. Many places like the lawyer's house, the bus stand, Santosh restaurant, the D.C. Office and the Superintendent's House came to his mind. He could not make up his mind. And when he went to Santosh restaurant, to have his breakfast and the waiter stood before him he did not know what to order as he remembered the non-veg delicacies Sarojakshi used to prepare. That waiter was known to Manjayya. He said, 'Bring what you think is best.' From Hassan, Manjayya came to Channarayapattana by bus, took his bicycle from the watchman of Travellers Bungalow and came down to Bilikere.

He thought of going to Channarayapattana and meeting Sarojakshi. But there was that impassable shyness. One month passed away in this manner. He was surprised to find the change that had taken place within him during this period. He was not feeling the desire to have any woman. He felt as if he had suddenly aged and old age had finally enveloped him. One day near the wet-lands, he met Channamma with whom he had developed friendship a year back. She asked him tauntingly, 'Oh what's it? It seems our Ayyaavaru has ordered for ochre loin-cloth?' She smiled. She was a clever conversationalist. Yet he did not like to invite her to the hut. She winked and said, 'What? Have you grown old, so soon, Ayya?' He said, 'Yes! Yes, I have become senile and my sap is dried up. But you are still dancing in heat.' And was about to give her two rupees. But she said, 'I didn't ask you for money. If you want I myself can give you some coins, here take it,' she put her hand in her small bag containing betel leaves, areca nuts and lime. Manjayya felt really insulted. But being aware that one should not get angry in such situations, he kept quiet.

After Appajappa got suspended, Manjayya completely stopped his sandalwood business. The Ranger of Arsikere had taken charge of this taluk and was coming here only once a week. Appajappa was suspended because of the complaints of bribe against him. These were not the reasons for Manjayya to stop his sandalwood business. Somehow he had lost the enthusiasm of going round the villages looking for the trees in which the core was ripe and to prepare suitable deeds. He would get angry at himself thinking that because of holding this damned contract, his work of pseudo-lawyer got neglected.

One day Bochihalli Ningappa came in search of Manjayya. He said, 'Look here Ayya, here is a letter of inquiry, please go through it.' That letter informed that the inquiry of the allegations on Appajappa was to be held at the Inspection Bungalow of Channarayapattana, Ningappa had to be present there, give a statement and had to present witnesses and documents in defence of his allegation. Ningappa asked Manjayya, 'You must tell me, what will they ask and what and how should I answer. Anyway you'll be there with me won't you?' Manjayya said, 'As a departmental man, if I too am served a notice, I'll come. If not, my coming there will be against the rules.' He evaded the issue. He did not feel like giving correct information and guidance to Ningappa and other farmers who had been instigated by him. It had been about three months since Appajappa got suspended.

There was no salary for four months and Appajappa too had not come to him after he had come with Usmani. Manjayya did not see him in Channarayapattana either, after he saw him once. Manjayya thought he could not defeat her in this matter. It was not difficult to prove the bribe if properly worked at the time of inquiry and the witnesses were correctly briefed. But he did not feel like doing it. Even if he proved it, he felt he could not win. When he had postponed three months hesitating to go and see her face, if he defeated her, after all, what might happen? Appajappa would be transferred or an increment would be stopped. But by this, Manjayya thought, his uneasiness would not be reduced. He advised whatever flashed at that moment to Ningappa and sent him away. He inferred other farmers too would have got such notices and they too would come looking for him. He thought the whole night, woke up in the morning, instructed Puradamma and Puttellayya what works were to be done at home and on the fields and left Bilikere.

Manjayya returned after a week. By the time he came back, an order from the Department was waiting for him! As Manjayya had instigated the farmers against a departmental official and had made them give false complaints, his sandalwood contract was terminated with immediate effect. He was directed to submit all official records and sandalwood in his possession to the District Office and receive a receipt for it, within seven days of his receiving the Order, failing which further action would be taken. Manjayya did not feel sorry for the loss of the contract. But he became restless. How did the tide turn against him? From whom could he know the details? He pumped air in his bicycle, rode to Sankenahalli handpost, met Usmani and from him he came to know what had happened: many farmers who had put their thumb impressions to the complaint, did not attend the inquiry at all. The Investigating Officer who came directly from Bangalore started cross-examining with pointed questions. The farmers who attended blurted out. 'What do we know sir? That contractor Manjayya told us and we thought it true and put our thumb impressions.' Only Ningappa bore the cross-examination till the end. At last, when the officer began to grill him further, Ningappa could not sustain anymore. He was forced to open up and tell the truth. He said, 'I instigated the farmers because a case was booked against me.' Inquiry, what an inquiry! A very strict and upright officer, a tiger of a man! Mallareddy is his name,' Usmani described.

Manjayya asked, 'What happened to Appajappa?'

'The Inquiry Officer decided that Appajappa was falsely implicated and was innocent and ordered his balance of salary to be released immediately. Besides he is transferred to Nelamangala. The order came by post four days after the officer conducted the inquiry and returned to Bangalore.' Usmani winked at Manjayya and continued, 'No, Sahib, it is impossible for the likes of you to defeat that woman. She had gone with her husband to the Deputy Chief Conservator himself. He is her old friend Subbayya.'

Manjayya got the shock of his life. 'Who told you?'

'Appajappa himself told me. I met him in the soda shop near the bus stand one day. I asked him, "'What's it sir? Why have you been so quiet? Shouldn't you do something?" You see Manjayya sahib, Appajappa is a departmental man. He is the master sanctioning our salaries. If he gets suspended and sits at home, won't we feel sorry? Then Appajappa said, "You see Usmani, yesterday we had been to Bangalore. We have submitted a petition to the Deputy Chief Conservator. We know that officer since a long time." Then, the third day after this, a notice was issued informing the date of inquiry. You understand the remaining matters.'

Manjayya was not aware of the changes that took place at higher levels of administration after Appajappa's suspension. Of course he had not tried to know. Now hearing the name of the Deputy Chief Subbayya, he felt as if he sank within and fell down. He asked Usmani, 'When did he come?' Usmani said, 'Two months back. We did not know.'

Manjayya directly came back to his place. He realised he could not save his sandalwood contract with any sort of petition. He submitted all the records, accounts and sandalwood to the District Office, paid five hundred rupees from his own pocket and got a receipt. Which meant that the relation he had with that department was cut off and his relation with her as well. Anyway she won, that slut who had taken such senior officers, tried to keep me in her possession merely toying with me. He tried to console himself thinking he too paid her back, made her suffer for four months without getting a salary. But somehow, he could not be satisfied. She always hurt him, drilling his mind and rushing inside. That Deputy Chief sahib has transferred Appajappa to Nelamangala because it would be nearer to Bangalore. Now, would that Sarojakshi condescend to look at me, however nicely I behaved? He struggled hard to come to terms with the situation, that there was no other way except forgetting her. But however much he struggled, he could not.

Now there was no fixed purpose or certainty in Manjayya's work as earlier. Household chores, agricultural works were running smoothly under the supervision of Puradamma and Puttellayya. Either he would always be lying down at home or would cycle to Channarayapattana, engage a room in the Travellers Bungalow and would lie down there. He would be pacing up and down Market Street and sometimes while away time sitting on the platform of any shop. When hungry, he would go to any hotel and eat whatever was available. When too bored he would return to his place. While he was engaged in such a routine, one day, as he sat on the platform of Chintamani's shop in the Market Street he noticed her. She, of his village, of Bilikere, that Savitri, was going with her bhaava, Satyappa of Mattikere. He wore white khadi dhoti and khadi jubba and she was wearing a synthetic silk sari with five inch border, shining earrings, golden chain and gold bangles and was speaking something with her brother-in-law. She held a plastic bag in her hand and he too held a large one. If anyone looked at them, one may surely think that they are husband and wife going together either for walking or marketing in Mysore and Bangalore. Manjayya thought, 'Oh how trim she looks!' But by then they passed him by. Manjayya was surprised: why was Satyappa there? Swelled with illness, with a long face, crying that he had no money for treatment, oh, when had Satyappa met him? Was it a month ago? Now it seems he is completely cured. Something flashed in him. Immediately suspicion raised its hood and hissed in Manjayya's ears: this Satyappa practised celibacy for all these years and it was I who made him taste life again. Manjayya suspected: now this Satyappa might be cajoling his sister-in-law, to draw her to his side, abusing Manjayya, and taking Savitri for walking, marketing, etc. He got up and followed them. They were inside Kantharajapura's hardware shop. She held some aluminium vessels and was choosing. Satyappa stood silently near. Manjayya walked away, taking care not to be seen by them. By the time he paced twenty steps a plan flashed to detect some more matter about Satyappa. Manjayya directly went to Dr Hasheem's clinic and said Salaam to the doctor. After enquiring about his welfare and other matters, Manjayya asked the doctor, 'You see doctor, I had sent a patient to you. Satyanarayanappa of Mattikere, Tiptur taluk. Did he get cured?'

'Oh, he was not severely affected. Within eight days it dried up. As a precautionary measure, I gave some extra injections and medicines.'

'Where did he stay after he left this clinic? You see, I had been out of town for one month and could not take care of him.'

'There was no problem. His sister-in-law who is a teacher stays in this place, she works in Kannada Girls' Middle School. She came and took him to her house and nursed him. I told him, fifteen days back, he could go to his place. Yet she has kept him here, so that he will get good nourishment. It seems he leaves for his place tomorrow. Satyanarayanappa had come here today morning. He had already paid his medical bills. Even though I refused, he brought fruits and flowers, along with two hundred rupees and gifted them to me. Good man, generous by nature.' Now it was impossible for Manjayya to sit there and continue the conversation with the doctor. He said, 'I just wanted to ask you about him,' and took leave. Not feeling like going anywhere, he directly went to his room in the Traveller's Bungalow and lay down.

He ordered meals to be brought to his room in the night. The next day also breakfast and lunch came to his room, but he did not feel like eating. But when the stomach demanded, he ate a little and pushed the plate to the corner of the table. Though Manjayya frequently visited Channarayapattana and it was not such a big town, he had seen Savitri very rarely, may be four or five times only. Part of the fort where she lived and the girl's middle school which was as if annexed to the fort were not places Manjayya frequented. In the past he had seen Savitri, but did not bother if she had seen him. No other thought would develop about her and fill his mind, for as soon as he saw her, the feeling that 'she is proud and egoistic' would envelop his mind, like a reflex action. When years were spent in this manner, the feeling of neglect and disinterest, that there was no relationship between her and himself, grew. Savitri had not clearly occupied his mind even when he requested her father to be a witness in his favour. But her memory began to haunt him from the moment he saw her and her bhaava together. Seventeen years ago, in the early days of their marriage, Manjayya remembered: Oh, that complexion, fair colour, build of body, features, that tautness, no nobody had it. She destroyed her own family by being haughty and arrogant instead of leading a happy family life. He was not aware of her friendship with anyone either in her school or in Channarayapattana town. If there was any such relationship, he thought, wouldn't he have known? But, Manjayya's mind got perturbed after he saw her with her bhaava yesterday. Taking that sick person who suffered from V.D. to her home, serving, taking care of him as a nurse, even when the doctor said he might return to his place, keeping him for fifteen days more, fie, fie. Manjayya's mind was overpowered by jealousy more than suspicion. But when he remembered what Naagi had said about Satyappa, he felt relieved! 'Ayyo Ayya, he can't do anything,' she had said and laughed jeeringly. Yet when it flashed they may not have 'that' one but the minds are mutually ... Manjayya's turmoil increased.

Sleep eluded him at night. He began to reflect, why did it happen like that to him. He had slept with so many women. Had he ever bothered whether she would take any other customer after he sent her away? Though he tried to console himself, somehow this was happening with Savitri. It was so with Sarojakshi also. Who was that fellow Subbayya, it seemed he was a Coorgi, did that bastard have Manjayya's features, handsomeness or did he have that manliness? If once, only once that Sarojakshi had tasted him, she would never be able to look at that Subbayya. Manjayya ruminated, 'Yes, really I made a mistake that day. I should not have let her free her right hand. I should have finished everything, at the first strike itself. I should have used my skills and should have subjugated her like a slave. Like a slave who says, 'Whatever you say.' He lied down imagining what would have happened if he had made the right moves, without committing that mistake on that fateful day.

The next day he woke up a little late. When he was bathing, an idea flashed. What an excellent plan! Manjayya said 'Bravo' and patted himself on his back. He quickly finished bathing, wore pressed clothes, without wasting time for coffee or breakfast, put on his chappals and walked out. His bicycle was at the room in the Travellers' Bungalow. He had heard Savitri lived in a small outhouse behind Kote Nanjappa's house. If there was much hullabaloo he could always say he was her husband and it would be finished. When he paced rapidly, Nanjappa's big house was locked. When he opened the gate, walked on the small path visible on the right side of the big building, he saw the door of that small house was open. He directly went inside, stood near the door. Savitri stood arranging notebooks of school children. When she turned and looked at him, she was startled and stood speechless. Manjayya came near her and said, 'Look here, I came to talk with you.' She did not know either what to talk or what to do. He started to speak, 'Look here, you see, certainly I am not responsible for the death of your father. Because, you know, he did not give witness at all. Let us leave that. I myself was about to invite you home, meanwhile your father died. So many incidents happened.' There was confusion on Savitri's face. She stood looking at the table not knowing what to speak or what to do and not able even to raise her head to look at his face. Without a second's delay, within the time of a blink, 'Savitri, listen to me, I want to talk to you.' Saying so, he closed the door, leaped near her and hugged her tightly in one embrace. He put his hand on her mouth, thrust his leg across her leg and tripped her, used a wrestling grip so that she would not be able to free herself and whispering, 'Listen to me, listen to me' and coaxing her, embracing her, Manjayya invaded her. He was careful not to repeat the mistake he committed with Sarojakshi. Even after the invasion was complete, he closed her mouth not giving any chance for her to shout and began to stimulate her with all erotic parts of his body. She was protesting, struggling to roll back, throw him down and squeeze herself out. When she realised it was impossible to free herself physically from that iguana-like grip, which went on tightening and tightening every moment, Savitri wearied and quietened. Then Manjayya intensified his lewd stimulations with the science of a libertine which he had mastered by the practice of so many decades and knew Savitri had begun to respond and participate in the act. He whispered in her ears: 'Look here, listen to my words' and aggravated her passion. When he was sure that her resistance was melted, he took off his hand from her mouth. He thought Savitri was conquered and that was enough for the day. He decided, hereafter she would be obedient like a bitch and released his grip and got up. Shame was overflowing from the face of Savitri. As soon as he released her, she turned her face to the other side, went into the bathroom and closed the door. Manjayya did not stand there even for a second, put on his chappals, half closed the door, came out, rapidly came round the big house, crossed the gate and that street, turned to the other street and swiftly reached the Travellers' Bungalow. The whole day the memory of Sarojakshi did not surface, in the re-established self-confidence that he was not defeated and would never be defeated.

One day at eight in the morning a young man of about twenty came to Ramakrishnayya's house. Ramakrishnayya had gone to work in the fields and grove. Sukanya was engaged in household chores. The young man's shirt was drenched with sweat. His face was coated with dust. He seemed to have come from afar. He recognised Sukanya, but she could not identify him. He took out a slip of paper from the pocket of his pyjamas, put it before her and said, 'I work in your warehouse, weighing goods, sewing bags, loading on wagons. My name is Puttaswamy. There is a wound on the leg of *saahukar*. It is not healing, it has opened up. Flesh, bone marrow inside are visible. *Saahukar* will not survive. So the clerk has asked me to tell you and your husband to come at once and gave me this letter. But I did not know the correct route, got lost, ended up in another village and at last somehow reached here. I left my place before dawn, at four.'

Sukanya read the letter. Whatever the boy had narrated was written in it. Sarthavalli Nanjappa worked as a clerk in Sukanya's father's warehouse from the early days of Nagappa's business, though he was paid a low salary. Whether he could not get a job elsewhere or did not like leaving the place he was used to, was not clear. Sukanya asked Puttaswamy, 'What sort of wound? How did it happen?'

He answered, 'You know avva, *Saahukar* suffered from diabetes. The pharmacist said, "Sugar patients suffer from such wounds. I am doing whatever I can. If he does not survive, it is not my fault." He said that in case of sugar patients, wounds don't get healed easily!'

Puttaswamy was very anxious to get back soon. The clerk had told him to return as early as possible for it was the day of copra auction. Sukanya started to make rotis quickly for Puttaswamy. She had to ask permission of her husband, how and when she could leave for her father's place. When her father accepted without the mildest of protest two thousand and five hundred rupees for keeping Ganesha in his home for his high school education, Sukanya did not know about her husband's attitude towards her father. It was not in Ramakrishnayya's nature to speak about people. He kept himself aloof as if nothing had happened. Sukanya could not alleviate her grief by speaking with such a person. She was not completely confident whether he would accompany her at the moment of her father's death. She did not know when he would return from the grove. Even when he left home to work in the grove, he would take a book on spirituality that he brought from Holenarasipura. He would never remember the time of breakfast or lunch when he sat reading it near the well in the grove. Sukanya went to the wall near the backyard, loudly called for Lakshmi of Honna's house. As soon as Lakshmi came Sukanya told her, 'Look here Lakshmi, please send your boy urgently to our grove. Let him run and say to Ayyavaru to come at once. Someone has come. Let the boy bring Ayyavaru immediately.'

By the time Puttaswamy finished his breakfast of rotis and chutney, Ramakrishnayya returned with rapid strides. There was a bound book in his hand. He had kept a peacock feather as a book mark. Puttaswamy who sat in the frontyard reported everything once again to Ramakrishnayya. Thus Sukanya was spared the difficulty of explaining it all to her husband. She gave that letter to him and went inside. Ramakrishnayya remembered that the clerk Nanjappa was the man who was moving about busily during Ramakrishnayya's wedding, was fawning and behaving with servility. After reading the letter, he went inside and asked Sukanya, 'Now, what do you say?' She did not say anything but just looked at his face. After a minute, he said, 'There is a bus to Channarayapattana at half past eleven. Let us go. I'll borrow some cash from Chalapathi Shetty. If we catch that bus, we may reach Tiptur before evening.' Sukanya felt a great relief. She came out and sent a message with Puttaswamy that they would reach Tiptur by evening. Puttaswamy asked Ramakrishnayya the correct route and rode away on his bicycle.

The couple requested Subbannayya's family to take care of the house, locked it, handed over the keys to them and left. They could catch the Channarayapattana bus. When they got down in Channarayapattana bus stand, Ramakrishanyya left Sukanya in the bus-stand and went to Chalapathi Shetty's shop. Sukanya felt neither sorrowful nor comforted. What it was, she could not understand. There was anxiety and eagerness. Her mind warned her that her father's death was certain. Suddenly a desire arose in her mind. Somehow Ganesha must be informed about his grandfather's illness and she must make him come directly to Tiptur from Hassan. She felt that when his grandfather is breathing his last, Ganesha must be there. But how could she inform him? If a letter was written from Channarayapattana, it is said, it would reach Hassan tomorrow. But she did not know Ganesha's address. Till now she did not have any opportunity to write a letter. How could she ask her husband? He might ask her, 'Why should the boy come running there, oh what relation is there between this grandson and that grandfather.' Sukanya got angry against her father. She asked the person who sat on the wall nearby, with a ticket book in his hand, 'At what time is there a bus to Tiptur?' He answered, 'There are two buses madam, one at half past three and another at five in the afternoon.' Sukanya was relieved thinking she need not worry if her husband was a bit late. Would that Chalapathi Shetty offer money without getting a promissory note written and signed? That's why he was late. Sukanya knew her husband's nature. He would not finish his conversation quickly, take the money and start. He would sit like an idol. How could he understand her anxiety. She was angry with him. She suddenly noticed someone who passed before her. Yes, he was of her own village, the weaver Thammanna. She guessed, 'He might have started for his daughter's house in Hassan, and is waiting for the bus.' She got up, went there and called out, 'Thammanna Shettare.' He turned back, could not identify her and kept staring at her. Then Sukanya introduced herself, 'Oh you might have forgotten, I am the daughter-in-law of Parameshwarayya of your village.' When the smile of recognition dawned on his face, she said, 'You see, my husband and myself will leave for Tiptur now by bus. We learnt that my father is severely ill in Tiptur and is counting his last moments. Our son is studying in Hassan. He has engaged a room in the street behind the temple of Anjaneya behind the house of someone called Kenchayya. Will you please inform him that his mother has asked him to go at once to Tiptur and that he should not delay for any reason? Will you please do it?' Thammanna Shettaru smiled showing he had lost two of his front teeth and asked Sukanya: 'How did you know I had started for Hassan?' She did not know what to answer. However, he assured her, 'Yes I'll surely inform your son. Today evening itself I'll convey this news. My daughter's house too is near that place,' and went away.

Ramakrishnayya and Sukanya could catch the three o'clock bus. By the time they reached Tiptur and went home, dusk was setting in. Only that clerk Nanjappa was at home taking care of the patient Nagappa. A small bulb was burning emitting a dim light. Nagappa was lying down on a bed on the floor in the hall. Though there was a white bandage, the wound had a foul smell. The patient had become really weak and emaciated. The clerk said loudly, 'Your daughter and son-in-law have come.' Nagappa heard it and he could understand it also. Ramakrishnayya went near his father-in-law and asked, 'How are you feeling now?' Nagappa moved his eyes, as if he understood. Ramakrishnayya sat for a while near the bed. Sukanya came, touched the hands of her father, held his arms and shoulders and shook. Tears dropped from her eyes. Her father's eyes too filled with tears.

She asked the clerk, 'What did the doctor say?'

'Please come inside. I'll tell you,' he said, took her inside and switched on the light. This also was a bulb of low wattage, which gave as much light as a kerosene lamp. The clerk lowered his voice so that his words should not be heard by the patient and said, 'You know that doctor Seetharamayya, don't you? It is he who is examining your father and giving medicines. He told him twelve days ago, to go to Bangalore, for diabetic patients suffer such wounds. Your father was fully conscious then. But he did not agree to the doctor's suggestion. Instead he said that this Seetharamayya wanted his doctor friends in Bangalore to make money out of him. Your father said he would cure himself with some native medicine, drank bitter-gourd juice and kept quiet. You see Sukanyavva, I too told him it won't do any good and forced him to act on the advice of the doctor. But you see, after all, I am his subordinate, how much could I force my master? Moreover, master would not pay Dr Seetharamayya's bills. So, he did not bother to come and treat the patient. Then your father sent for Nanjundappa who is a pharmacist in the government hospital, for his fee is cheap. He comes, bandages the wound, gives tablets and goes. Master thinks he will be cured by this treatment and keeps quiet. That pharmacist comes and bandages because your father is a big warehouse owner. He has not paid this pharmacist also!'

Sukanya too remembered having seen Dr Seetharamayya. When she was a little girl, he was famous as the best doctor in Tiptur. He had his clinic in Doddapet. Sukanya called her husband inside, narrated everything that the clerk told her before the clerk himself and told her husband, 'Please go to Dr Seetharamayya. Tell him, "whatever may be the expenses I'll pay it. Please come and treat my father-in-law." If you request him, he will surely come.' When Sukanya finished her words, a thought crossed her mind: if he says he will pay whatever maybe the amount, he should have it with him. She did not have any idea how much her husband had borrowed from Chalapathi Shetty. However, Ramakrishnayya, without uttering another word, started to go and the clerk Nanjappa followed, to guide him to the doctor's clinic.

The doctor's clinic was full of patients in-waiting. Yet, when the clerk Nanjappa went inside and informed Dr Seetharamayya who had grey hair and grey sideburns and who was clad in a white shirt, white trousers and black boots, the doctor called Ramakrishnayya inside. He asked Ramakrishnayya to sit in the chair in front of him and spoke, 'Warehouse owner Nagappa's son-in-law, you say, which place?' Ramakrishnayya answered 'Ramakrishnayya of Bilikere.' Immediately the doctor said, 'I couldn't remember instantly, that's why I asked. Bilikere Parameshwarayya is your father. I know he died repenting that he had committed perjury in court. Unfortunately I did not have an opportunity to meet such a person when he was alive. Now, please tell me the reason for your visit. It seems you have rushed here without even freshening up.'

Ramakrishnayya said, 'Please doctor, I have brought money with me. However much it may cost, I don't mind. But you must come and treat my father-in-law so that he may survive. My wife and myself will stay here and nurse him until he gets completely cured.'

The doctor said, 'You see, I didn't catch your name!' The clerk who stood there said 'Ramakrishnayya', and then the doctor continued, 'You see Ramakrishnayya I told him ten or twelve days ago that the treatment for such illness was not possible here. You go to Bangalore. I'll give you the name and address of the nursing home and prescribe the treatment to be given immediately. It was not the only reason that Nagappa won't pay bills; he was not a person to offer money. But we have no facility to treat such patients in this town. If it is in a big nursing home, all facilities would be present. There will be experts to treat different types of illnesses and they take money proportionately. But what I feel is, if it is already past twelve days,' he said, thought for a moment, opened his list of treatment, searched the date of twelve days before and said, 'Look here, even if you take him to Bangalore today itself, he will not survive. Now you go home. After examining all these patients, I'll come and see him. Do you know what I can predict? I can say only, within how many days he will breathe his last. You see, you may ask your clerk Nanjappa and confirm. This Dr Seetharamayya does not boast. If he examines a pregnant woman, he can predict that she would deliver on such date only. Rarely it may happen a day earlier or later. In the same manner looking at the condition of the patient, he can predict the exact date of his death also. That too may occur a day earlier or a day later. Isn't it Nanjappayya?'

The clerk nodded, 'Very true, very true.'

The doctor looked at his watch and said, 'Look here, now it is seven thirty. I'll examine the out-patients and come to your house around nine.'

Ramakrishnayya and the clerk returned home. The clerk informed Sukanya of what the doctor had said. Meanwhile Sukanya had searched the kitchen. This time there was not even one seer of ragi flour in the house. Except half a seer of blackened crystalline salt in a stone jar, all other tins, pots and vessels were empty. There was only enough firewood. There was a kerosene stove and a little bit of milk in a vessel. This old stove was not in this house earlier. Sukanya guessed it must have been brought by the clerk to boil milk and she confirmed it by asking him. She did not know for how many days they would have to stay there. Moreover, it was not possible to return, simply by seeing once and leaving him in that condition. Now, she had to write a slip for provisions like rice, pulses, tamarind, chilly, coconut and all other things needed, give the list to her husband, ask him to bring those. Both of them had eaten only one roti each in the morning as they were in a hurry. Now, her husband had to go to the shop, bring provisions, then she had to cook ... oh, how time consuming it would all be? Thinking thus, she felt anger against her father. By then her husband and the clerk returned. She conveyed the necessity of buying provisions to her husband. Ramakrishnayya said, 'Why buy provisions now and then cook? We can go to a hotel, have our food and come back or we may order food to be brought here.' He looked at the clerk. The clerk too nodded his approval. He gave some money to the clerk and said, 'You too have your meals here. Bring three meals and some milk for the patient.'

By nine the doctor came and examined the wound on Nagappa's leg. 'There are only twenty four hours left. Even if you take him to London on a flight, this will be the only result!' He got up. 'Be prepared to face the inevitable.' He picked up his bag and left. Sukanya warmed some milk and made her father drink it. Some of the milk went inside the patient's mouth. She said to Nanjappa, 'Look, today you go home and take rest. All these days you have been taking care of my father day and night.' Nanjappa said, 'Okay, you know our house, don't you? If there is any urgency, send for me. If bhaava comes with me, I'll show him my house.' Ramakrishnayya went with him, noted the location and returned.

The patient was lying down perfectly still. Though the breathing was fast, Ramakrishnayya knew it was not the breathing of the final stages. He explained it to his wife. He felt sleepy and was yawning. He had missed his afternoon nap. Besides, he was not used to the long distance bus journey on an uneven gravel road. The heaviness of food added to it, but his wife kept awake. He should not leave her alone with a dying patient and sleep. Thinking so, he sat leaning against the wall. There was nothing to do, nor was there anything to speak. In such situations Sukanya wanted to talk. She would feel that her husband should tell her something. He should listen to whatever she said. Say 'Yes it is so'. Except in such situations, when could they talk to each other? Was it not through speaking that they could get mutual consolation and courage? But Sukanya knew her husband's nature. Even after his father Parameshwarayya hanged himself on the branch of the tree before Shivaalaya, when his body was brought down and taken for cremation, even afterwards also, her husband did not talk, did not utter a single word. He kept as quiet as he was today. Some nights he did not get sleep. Except that, there was no word of remembering or praising his father, or showing gratitude for how lovingly he had brought him up. But his face would always be mournful. His mind and eye were turned inward. Even now they were so, in silent introspection. Though all these were manifested, nothing was being expressed through speech. Sukanya consoled herself, would such a person speak in this situation? She decided she must be awake, now and then must put a drop of milk in her father's mouth. Except that she had no other work. She must watch with vigilance when death nears. What could she do by watching? She should tell her husband, 'Look here, what's happening?' Life would end on its own. Then, she remembered there was a sealed copper urn with holy Gangajal from Kashi in the niche of the gods in the kitchen. The seal should be broken and a small spoon of Gangajal should be put in his mouth at the time of his death. As soon as she remembered, she went in and ascertained that the pot was there and told her husband, 'You must open the seal with the sickle.' He said, 'Yes, it should be done. Search a sickle and wipe out the dust from its edge and wash that copper spoon also.' Now Sukanya felt satisfied her husband had spoken to her sincerely. Besides, she now got the support of a clear purpose to keep herself awake. She got up, searched the sickle and copper spoon and washed them, rubbing mud, for there was no tamarind in the house, wiped them and kept them handy. Again she sat beside the dying patient. Sometimes the patient would half open his eyes. For the rest of the time his eyelids would stay closed. When his eyes were half opened, she would ask him, 'How are you? Look Appa, I have come, Sukanya has come.' She would shout in his ear. She would feel satisfied at the look of recognition dawning on his face. It was past midnight. Time seemed to crawl. She thought of some other reason to speak with her husband but nothing struck her, however much she thought. She too felt drowsy. Her back started to ache from sitting upright continuously. Her husband had the wall to lean on. But near the bed where she sat, there was no such support. She did not feel like moving away to the opposite wall to lean on it. She was angry with her husband.

By then footsteps were heard and there was a knock on the door. Sukanya thought it might be Nanjappa. Ramakrishnayya asked, 'Who is it?' Hearing the words 'It is I,' Sukanya knew it was Ganesha. She felt as if she had grown an extra pair of arms. She guessed that Thammanna Shetty had immediately informed Ganesha. At that hour what bus was there from Hassan to Tiptur? Getting up, she remembered having just heard the sound of the train's departure. Ganesha came in and said, 'Thammanna shettaru informed me. There was no bus service at that time. I started by the night train, came to Arasikere and came here by the mail train.' Ramakrishnayya did not ask, who sent a message through Thammanna Shetty or any such thing. He thought it unnecessary to enquire about a matter that could be understood, that had been understood. It was his method. Ganesha came near the bed of his grandfather, asked his mother, 'What has happened to *thatha*, amma?' His mother explained. Then she turned to her husband and said, 'You go, spread a mat and catch some sleep. Ganesha will keep me company.' Ramakrishnayya went to the inner room, took the mat, shook off the dust, spread it and lied down. After a while, Sukanya too leaned on the wall and began to doze off. Ganesha was asleep on the floor itself.

Sukanya woke up at daybreak, wiped the face of her father and made him drink some milk. Ramakrishnayya and Ganesha woke up and sat around. The clerk too came from his house and stood there. The foul smell of the wound in Nagappa's leg had increased and the pharmacist had to come and put a new bandage. Though the patient was covered up to his thighs with a sheet so that flies should not besiege him, after daybreak flies began buzzing around, attracted by the fetid smell of the wound. The stench of the shirt worn by the patient exceeded the filthy smell of the wound. While Sukanya was thinking of making her father sit, wipe his body with a wet cloth and change the shirt, Nagappa opened his eyes. There was panic and anxiety on his face. He muttered to himself as if he was asking for something. He raised his right hand with difficulty and groped near his side. Sukanya thought she could now speak to her father at least once and said, 'Look here Appa, what? What do you want? Do you recognise me? Your daughter Sukanya. I have come. Look here Appa, Ganesha is here. See, your son-in-law is also sitting here.' But these words did not reach the mind of Nagappa. Sukanya again and again called him and asked, 'Appa tell me, what do you want? What do you want?'

The clerk who stood near him, said, 'Master has tied the key of his safe to the sacred thread on his shoulder. Whenever he was conscious and remembered the key, he would grope for it and touch it. Now also he is looking for it.'

Ramakrishnayya moved near his father-in-law, raised the shirt which was stinking and had a rancid smell, searched the sacred thread which also had a rancid smell and detected a thick key. He carefully untied the knot, without causing damage to the thread, put the key in Nagappa's right hand. He did not utter a word. Nagappa held the key in his hand, weakly at first. Gradually he folded the fingers around it and tightened the fist. The hand that stood on the elbow without support, held the key firmly and became a fist and sank on to the chest. Gradually his eyes were closed. Panic and anxiety on the face decreased and a drowsiness that suggested solace, encircled him. Everybody noticed that.

Ramakrishnayya told his wife, 'Go and have a wash. Give me the matches, I will light the bathroom stove, for you cannot take a cold water bath. Sukanya got up and asked her husband who was lighting the fire in the bathroom, 'Will you get some groceries?' Ramakrishnayya said, 'Look what are you going to cook now? Can't we get something from a hotel? I will ask the clerk to bring idli and coffee. Let's see what to do afterwards.' The clerk had not yet washed his face. Ramakrishnayya told him, 'The milk you brought yesterday night is still fine. Go home, finish your bath and other routine. While coming back, bring milk and twenty idlis and chutney from the hotel.' Ramakrishnayya gave him money. Ganesha sat near the patient.

Ganesha sat near the bed of his *thatha* until Sukanya swept the house and she and her husband finished their bath. Ramakrishnayya swiftly washed his clothes, spread them out to dry and returned. Ganesha then went to take his bath. The patient had closed his eyes. The fist that held the key was on the chest. Sukanya washed her sari, spread it out to dry, sat near her father to make him drink some milk. She said, 'Open your mouth Appa, have some milk.' She tried to open his lips, but they did not open. She put her fingers between them to open them forcibly. They felt cold. She called her husband, 'Come here, see, he is icy-cold.' Ramakrishnayya came and examined. He felt the pulse of the hand that held the key in its fist. Life had slipped away hours back. Sukanya began to cry, 'The whole night we waited oh, alas we could not put Gangajal in his mouth at the time of his death.'

In a little while, the clerk came with a packet of idlis in a handbag and milk in a jug and stood still. After ten minutes Ramakrishnayya said, 'See, I am a stranger here, I don't know anybody or anything in this place. Please arrange for bearers, priests to conduct funeral rites, firewood and other things needed. Take this.' He took out money from his coat pocket, counted and said, 'Here is a hundred rupees, bring whatever is essential. If more money is needed, I'll give it.' The clerk left. Ramakrishnayya went into the bathroom, brought a few pieces of firewood, put it in front of the house and lit it, as a custom to let people know that death had occurred in the house. There was nothing to do until the clerk returned after making all arrangements for the funeral. Sukanya too sat quietly for she was released from the pressure of grief. She had already finished a bout of crying. Ganesha stood near the inner door. He did not feel like crying nor did he know what to talk. Even after two and a half hours passed, the clerk did not return. Everything had to be adjusted; everybody had to be looked for. At last around twelve, he came rapidly holding the bag with all the articles needed. The priest and four bearers followed him. There was no one else. The priest came in and asked, 'What's this, why haven't you folded the legs and crossed the arms? They would have become stiff by now.' He found fault with the people who sat there. 'It did not occur to me. Let's do it now,' Ramakrishnayya said, came near the corpse, looked at the key held in the fist, stood silently for a moment. Then he turned towards the priest and said, 'Will you please look after the work to be done outside? There is some family matter to discuss.' The priest went out. The clerk too left the place and began supervising the work of funeral bier. Ramakrishanyya closed the front door, bolted it, came back and asked his wife to take that key from the fist of the corpse. She looked at her husband's face. He repeated, 'Didn't you hear?' As if she understood, she bent down and tried to take the key from the fist of the corpse. But she could not take it, the corpse seemed to hold on to the key tightly. She tried to prise open the fingers slowly and skilfully and pull out the key. But the corpse did not loosen even a single finger of the tightened fist. Sukanya tried again. Realising that it was not possible to take the key by bending down, she sat beside the corpse, held her breath and began to open the fist. She held open two fingers forcibly. Then when she tried to create a gap by piercing her finger into the gap of remaining two fingers, the fingers which were opened swiftly came into the earlier position and Sukanya's fingers were trapped. She sweated and panicked. She looked at her husband's face. He encouraged her, 'Free your fingers.' She tried again. But the corpse did not leave the key. She called out to her husband, 'Come here and take it out from its fist.' But he stood rooted to the spot and said, 'You yourself must take it out.' She now called her son. 'Ganesha, come here!' Ganesha came near her. Mother and son tried together, opened up the fingers of the corpse and took the key successfully from the fist. Sukanya went to give the key to her husband. He refused to take it and said, 'I don't want it. You two go into the dark room in the cellar, open the safe. Whatever money you find there, stuff it into a bag and bring it here. It should be carried to the cemetery, put on the corpse on the funeral pyre and should be burnt to ashes along with the corpse.' Sukanya could not understand what he said. She stood still. 'Didn't you hear what I said?' Ramakrishnayya asked and wrested away that key from her hand and said, 'Look here Ganesha, go to the cellar, search the safe and all boxes, stuff all the money you find there into a bag and bring it. He held the key before his son. By then Sukanya's mind became alert, she loudly chastised her husband, 'What are you saying? Have you lost your mind? To think of burning money?' Her voice was so loud that it could be heard by people outside. Ramakrishnayya coolly but authoritatively said, 'Don't shout. There is a reason for what I am saying. Act accordingly.' Sukanya began to shout even more loudly. 'What meaning? When did you have any sense or reason?' Ramakrishnayya came near her, raised his hand, slapped her hard on the cheek and said, 'Will you shut up?' Sukanya shuddered. From the very day she left her father's house and went to her husband's house, till today he had never beaten her. She had heard that her husband, let alone his wife, would never beat any stray cattle that wandered into his fields. Her courage and resoluteness sunk by this unexpected blow she suffered now. Ganesha who stood near also got scared. Ramakrishnayya held the key before his son and ordered, 'Ganesha, do as I say.' Ganesha took the key and went in.

Ganesha knew about the dark room inside the cellar. *Thatha* did not have electric lights there. He had kept a lantern behind the door. He would light it, close the door, bolt it and only after that, he would climb down into the cellar and open the door of that safe. Ganesha had known this by the sounds he used to hear from outside. Today he searched for the lantern behind the door of the room which was totally dark even in broad daylight. Somehow he detected the lantern, took it to the bathroom, wiped its chimney and lit it. He went to the room, descended to the cellar and tried to open the lock. But it did not open. He turned and turned the key in vain. Then he remembered his mother had said, the lock would open if the key is turned some rounds to this side and some to the other. Ganesha began turning the key this side and that. Finally the lock was opened. He held the lantern and he saw in the light bundles of notes. He pulled out one bundle and counted. All were hundred rupee notes and each bundle contained hundred notes. He brought a gunny sack from outside, counted and stuffed the notes in that. There were totally sixty five bundles. His mind calculated the total in a minute applying mathematical formulae he had studied. He closed the door of the safe, locked and carried the bag. It was heavy. He never imagined that currency notes would be heavy. He brought the bag, put it beside the corpse and told his father, 'There is six and a half lakhs here!' His father raised his head and looked at the face of his son. After a minute he said, 'Did I enquire how much was there? Did I ask you to count it? You better understand. There should never be impertinence or unnecessary talking.' Ganesha grew pale. Sukanya sat leaning on the wall as if possessed by a spirit, without talking to anybody. There was a red mark of four fingers on her left cheek. Ramakrishnayya went out, opened the front door and said to the people waiting, 'Come in, the sun is already overhead, let us finish everything quickly.' Immediately all of them came in. It was difficult to bend and fold the legs and hands of the corpse though two people jointly tried to bring the corpse to the measurement of the bier. As others were disgusted to touch the leg which was wounded, Ramakrishnayya himself lifted it, pressed with great effort and folded it. After the rites that were to be performed at home were over, Ramakrishnayya held the pot of fire, called his son and said, 'Look here, there is that bag you know, you tie it, carry it on your shoulder and walk in front of me.' The priest asked: 'What's it?' Ramakrishnayya said, 'It's a family matter. Please proceed with the further rites.' The priest said, 'Is this boy your son? A son whose father is alive should not come to the cremation ground.' Ramakrishnayya replied, 'When I myself am telling him to come, it doesn't matter if he does. Now, please permit me to proceed with the rites.' Warehouse owner Nagappa's body was hoisted on the bier and his funeral journey started. Though it was winter, the sun was hot. There were only those eight people. Without any other relatives or friends and any crowd, the journey crossed the border of the town and reached the cremation ground at last. The pyre was arranged stacking firewood in an order. Ramakrishnayya called his son aside and said, 'Look there, the firewood is stacked. Remove one layer and spread the bundles of notes as you spread a bed and cover it with firewood as it was earlier. Let no one notice it!'

Ramakrishnayya performed all rites shouldering the responsibility and duty of a son. He tonsured his head and bathed in cold water. Finally, after all the rituals were over, the corpse was hoisted on to the pyre. When it was lit, firewood at the bottom began burning with a crackling sound. When the pyre which was arranged as a building was stirred, bundles of notes were seen. The priest asked: 'What is it?' Ramakrishnayya answered, 'I have put pieces of paper so that the firewood would burn properly.' The priest looked at Ramakrishnayya. Someone had to be present there until the skull was split. So, Ramakrishnayya, the doer of all rites, held a long bamboo staff and stood there. When there was black smoke, red and yellow flames and everything was being burnt, Ramakrishnayya took care that all the bundles of notes were burnt to ashes by pushing them into the fire. Then the skull split. After performing the necessary rites, all of them went to the stone well nearby to take bath.

After the corpse was taken away, the neighbour Ananthakrishna's family came, consoled Sukanya, sent their servant to clean and wash the house. They also brought food enough for these people. After her husband, son and the clerk returned from the cremation ground she served them and she too ate something. It was already evening and the sun was about to set. 'I don't want food or anything again at night. If you need money, you can take it from my coat pocket.' Ramakrishnayya told his wife, spread a mat, put a plank under his head and lay down covering himself with his dhoti. Nobody could know whether he was asleep or just lying down. Sukanya knew that since the day he had asked his father to give evidence in court in favour of Manjayya, her husband was not sleeping properly at night. Sukanya lit a lamp, put it in the place where her father breathed his last and inverted a basket on it. She and her son Ganesha were inside the house. There was neither bed nor blanket for anyone. Somehow Ganesha slept. But she could not. She was getting terribly angry. Oh, in their married life of so many years, for the first time, that too in front of their grown up son, her husband slapped her on the cheek, made her shut her mouth. She no longer wanted to sob or cry, but was getting very angry. She had slept barely a couple of hours the previous night, yet she could not get sleep now. She was awake for a long time at night. Train towards Pune had passed by, and the Bangalore-mail by which Ganesha had come went past as well. Sukanya remembered that the time in midnight would be known in Tiptur only by the sound of these trains. Along with this, the memory of this house after the death of her mother would follow, and the memory of her coming to father's house on her own. Yet what stupidity it was to burn to ashes six and a half lakh rupees. Thinking thus she gathered courage and decided to question her husband at any cost. 'Why did you do this stupid thing?!' A feeling of contempt followed this decision. After all what else can he do, he has already hit me once.

After all of them finished bathing Ramakrishnayya called his wife and said, 'Tomorrow after lifting the ash of father-in-law, let us leave for our place. Why should rice and other provisions be bought for only one or two days. Can't food be brought from the hotel? Or whatever you say.'

'What about rites to be performed next?' she asked.

'I am also thinking of that. Should it be performed here? You and Ganesha can leave for Bilikere. I will go either to Holenarsipura or to Paschimavaahini and perform the rites as all facilities are available there. Before that, I must go to Channarayapattana and borrow from Chalapathy Shetty another five hundred rupees. If you want to come to Holenarasipura, it is okay or whatever you say.' Sukanya felt emboldened. 'What's the matter? You are saying again and again "as you say" "as you say" why did you act so angrily yesterday?' Ramakrishnayya asked calmly, 'What did I do in anger?' 'You, who had never hit me, slapped me hard and the bundle of six and a half lakh …' Before she finished her voice choked.

Ramakrishnayya said, 'Look, Sukanya, you did not understand even in such a situation. Besides you began to shout, so that people waiting outside should hear it. That's why, to stop you I slapped you. But tell me, what could have I done with that paper except to light firewood?'

'What do you mean? What could we not have done with six and half lakhs? Don't we have a son? Are we not living? To who else should it have come except to us?'

Ramakrishnayya did not reply at once. It was his nature. Sometimes afterwards, he would speak a word or two and be silent. Now also he began looking at the big cross beam of Madras ceiling. Then he got up and went to the bathroom. Sukanya knew that if she would be standing there, her husband would come back and answer; if not, it would be many days later. So she stood there. Ramakrishnayya poured water in the bathroom, washed his hands and feet, gargled, came back, sat in the same place and began looking at that cross beam. After five minutes, he said, 'He did not say anything about it, to whom it should go, while living. He neither gave it to anyone while he lived nor did he say to whom it should be given and he did not write it up also.'

Sukanya argued, 'If children have to get father's property, should it be written? Should there be a will? When your father died, had he written that his lands should belong to his children before he died? Are you not enjoying it now?'

As usual, he became silent. Sukanya still stood there. At last he said, 'You see, Nagappa did not live like everybody. Why do you insist that I should speak about the nature of a dead man. He died holding the key tightly in his fist. There was no other way for me to send everything that the key represented except to send it with him.'

Sukanya spoke as if it was a counter statement, 'It could have been donated to charity or any religious work in his name.'

Ramakrishnayya, looking at the cross beam, but without delay answered, 'What authority do we have to donate in his name, that which he had not willed while living?' Sukanya did not reply. After a little while, Ramakrishnayya said, 'A man should not talk much but he must realise' and again became silent.

No other argument came to Sukanya's mind. But she was not satisfied either. She went on muttering to herself that her husband's act was senseless, always senseless and went in. The whole day and the night as well as the next day, she was in a turmoil. Without having any discussion it was accepted that her husband should go to some sacred place on a river bank and finish all the rituals and come back. Sukanya too wished to go with him.

Ramakrishnayya finished the rites of collecting the ash and came back. When the three of them were ready to return, the clerk Nanajappa was there. She called her husband inside and asked, 'With whom should we leave the house key?'

He stood brooding. 'Tell me fast,' she said but he did not reply. She still stood there. 'We will miss the bus,' again she said. Finally Ramakrishnayya said, 'We neither have the authority to give it to anybody, nor do we have the authority to keep it for ourselves. It would be quite proper if it is given to Ganesha and he be asked to go to the cremation ground and throw it away there.'

She looked at his face to know whether he was speaking with anger. No, his face was calm and collected as always. Anger rose within her again and she asked him in a quarrelling tone, 'If so, why do you perform his funeral rites spending your money?'

Ramakrishnayya did not delay his answer. 'You see Sukanya, when I have married a girl from the family without a male issue and happen to be the only son-in-law, is it not my duty to do it? By performing these rites and *shraaddha,* if the dead person is not liberated from the state of *preta,* he will be in a state of being neither here nor there. Don't they say so? If there is any other person to perform this rite, I'll not do it.' Saying this much he went out.

Sukanya stood there for two minutes and thought. At last, she called the clerk inside, gave the keys in his hand and said, 'Please take care of all things.' She followed her husband. Ganesha held a handbag and walked behind his mother.

Savitri was burning inside with rage, shame, humiliation and insult. She was a lone woman at home, raped by a vile lewd fellow. She thought of many options like, lodging a complaint, going to Bilikere and telling her brother to thrash that fellow ... no, none of these, she herself would go wherever he was, however strong he might be, stand in front of his house, take off the chappals from her feet and ... But all these would never cause shame to that scoundrel. Her rage was burning her, not knowing how she should take revenge about the rape she suffered. Law court, Village Panchayat or police, wherever she might go for justice or demand that he must be punished, Manjayya would hold his ground, 'Am I not her husband?' By this, he would shame her even further. The solution, by the evening of that very day, came to her mind at least fifty times: She should inform her brother or she herself should hide a dagger, go to him, even before he was aware what it was ... and if questioned in court, she should tell them why she did it. Was he waiting for that day, when Nanjappa and his wife would go to Hassan to attend a marriage and there would be nobody in the compound from morning till evening? Even if they were in the main house, how quickly he grabbed her with the speed of a tiger, without giving her an iota of chance to make even the slightest of sounds! When she remembered this, her decision to punish him with the dagger would get strengthened. Savitri could not teach in class that day. She could not gather strength to stand properly. She could not take food in the afternoon or at night. When she lay down sleepless, the memory of what happened in the morning came before her mind scene by scene and she condemned herself. It was true that he was a rake, a scoundrel who intentionally came and raped her. But she, who was protesting as far as she had physical strength, why did she gradually succumb to his provocation? Why didn't she have the wisdom and decision that he was doing all that only to melt her and she should not slip, should not be enthralled. She remembered, seventeen years ago, in his house when she was in her sweet seventeens, how he would ensnare her with the same provocations; oh that day also it was the same. Self-reproach started; what had happened to her wisdom. Where had her reasoning vanished? She felt more shame than humiliation. Her anger turned inwards. She started thinking what sort of punishment she should get. She thought of putting the dagger to herself, the dagger she had meant for him and this thought began to haunt her continuously.

After a long while, when it was close to dawn, she felt slightly sleepy. She gave herself to sleep thereby alleviating the turmoil of her mind. Though she woke up in the morning at her usual time, she was calmer thanks to the three hours of sleep she had. She woke up and freshened herself. While doing her household chores she remembered the many forms of lust that used to haunt her when she started living alone. In the beginning when she left his house nothing bothered her. But afterwards, like a dog used to eating leftovers, her mind would get lascivious remembering Manjayya's leftovers. His big house, that room, the cot and lewd drama reflected in the two big mirrors by the sides of the cot. But it would not take the form of any other man. For her, sex meant only him, only his form and figure. But to him it was okay even if it was a female worm. She tried to strengthen her resolve. She should trample down that desire, and being the daughter of Parameshwarayya, if she could not control at least that much, what meaning and what fruition was there in her life? Imbibing this thought, she tried to lessen that desire and gradually snubbed it out completely. No, it was a lie that she trampled down that desire completely. When he came to her father and asked him to give witness and said: 'You see, after I am acquitted, I'll beg your daughter for forgiveness, take her to my home and lead a respectful life.' Then, why did she silently give her consent for her appa committing perjury? She had assumed that after her father's death, her desire for sex was completely burnt to ashes. After that not even a single day the imagination of it had appeared, even in a subtle form. If so, why did her mind and body succumb to his stimulations and provocations? She blamed herself, 'Fie, you are a mean worm, with instincts only at the base, animal level.' Her blood began to boil and it turned to disgust, to loathing and self-contempt.

While returning from school in the evening, she remembered her bhaava Satyappa of Mattikere. When he was suffering from illness that caused disgust even physically, he accepted in his inner self that the mistake was his. He did not engage himself like her in self-reproach, but started analysing at which turn of his life had he selected the wrong path. She remembered then, how she had felt angry with him, as he was not reproaching Manjayya. That evening, and the whole night her mind compared the attitude of her brother-in-law with hers. Manjayya had stimulated Satyappa only vocally. But he provoked her physically, raped her; by applying his expert skills he made her participate in the act. She questioned herself, 'Was it wrong on her part to respond when he physically attacked her and produced continuous stimulation with electric power.' For a while, her mind sought the consolation of self-defence. Then she thought, her brother-in-law too would have felt so. While engaged in this comparison, her mind would find meanness and opportunism in such defence.

After four or five days of such reasoning, her mind started thinking: Why did Manjayya come all of a sudden in that manner? What was his purpose? He stimulated her weakness, caused her to fall into an abyss and not waiting even for a second, he ran away. Would he come again with such intention? He came, he ambushed and he struck her that final blow! Having undergone that experience once, Savitri decided she would never become a prey and succumb to him. She thought: it would be easy to swallow the prey when the purpose was not understood by the prey. But once it was understood, it would not be easy to vanquish the prey. She gained courage and willed that she would achieve the impossible. Yet the feeling that she was humiliated and had lost her self-esteem, was not alleviated at all. She developed an apathy towards food with the feeling that she had become a sinner, a fallen woman and had committed adultery. Sleep failed her regularly. She felt she could get some solace if she shared this with someone. But with whom could she? She had not spoken to anybody about her marital life till now. She would not speak about it when she came to this town to work as a teacher because of disdain against Manjayya and by realisation of her mistake in marrying such a person with stubbornness, not heeding the advice of her father and brother. After she spent about three years as a teacher, she developed a feeling that to speak about that matter would belittle her dignity. Even at Bilikere house nobody would raise the topic. Yet, several people in Channarayapattana knew about him. Who did not know about Manjayya who loitered on the streets of that town frequently and played the field like a dog in rut? Moreover, in that town there were many families which had relationships by marriage with Bilikere. But who was there to whom she could narrate the recent incident? And who was there who had the strength to hear and understand her agony and the depth of her fall? She remembered her elder brother. But she felt she should not cause him pain by sharing this. She visualised its result also, that if he knows about this, he would in all probability resort to the sword and sickle. Her conscience began to prompt her. Though her elder brother was extremely patient, he would surely take the sickle in hand, for the injustice caused by Manjayya, first to his house, his sister, then to his father, now again to his sister. Savitri decided not to tell her brother, imagining all the troubles of court. Then with whom could she share this? She realised, she could not confess it to her sister-in-law, as Savitri's pain would not melt Sukanya's heart. She decided not to reveal it to anybody, and just like her brother to keep everything inside herself, allow it to melt away in silence. But, when she went to bed that night, she remembered her Mattikere bhaava. It was already some time since he had gone back. She was curious to know, what he was doing and how he was re-building his self-respect. He had confessed his downfall not omitting anything. He had poured out his heart to her. Yes, she felt, it would be easy to confess only before such a person and he would understand. She thought both of them were sinners of the same kind, who were egged on and provoked by Manjayya and committed adultery. When this comparison rose in her mind, another thought rose, almost simultaneously. She was afraid whether she too had contracted that disease. She shuddered. All other comparisons and self-esteem were suspended now and this fear alone enveloped her mind. Even after midnight, she could not get sleep. It was already eight days since this heinous incident took place. But she had not felt any pain or burning. Her brother-in-law had the symptoms the very next day itself. Thinking that, she felt a sort of relief. After a while she had another supportive consolation that she had led family life with him for six months, then also Manjayya's conduct was the same. But she had not contracted any disease. However, she found a solution before it was daybreak. She decided to consult Dr Hasheem in the morning. He was a gentleman. She would overcome her shame and tell him about her staying alone. She would also tell him about Manjayya's nature, how he raped her and would ask him for some medicine as a precaution, although she did not suffer any pain or irritation at present.

She was a little afraid to go alone to a male doctor. But which woman could she take with her? If she took anyone with her, Savitri would have to tell them everything. When she had acquired such courage that she was capable of defending herself even if Manjayya himself came again, why should she be afraid to go to the doctor, that too, to such a good man. Without any shyness or getting embarrassed she told the doctor everything. He said, 'I know avva, what sort of a man Manjayya is. But I did not know that you were his wife. I think you are not affected with any disease. If even a trace of it was contracted, it would have shown the symptoms. However you take a course of six injections. Let me give you the first injection immediately.' Savitri decided to visit the clinic for another five days and be rid of this fear.

Four days later, Ganesha came to Channarayapattana in the evening. When he went to Bilikere, he would catch a direct bus to Bilikere from Channarayapattana bus stand itself. But when he went from Bilikere to Hassan, he would stay the night at his atte's house in Channarayapattana, would start by the first bus in the morning, reach Hassan and attend classes. Savitri would prepare breakfast for him and pack food enough for noon and evening. Along with that, she used to give him fifty, sixty, sometimes even hundred rupees for his expenses, for she thought a boy studying outside home needed money. Though Ganesha's visit to his atte was mainly for the money, she never understood that or thought about it. Besides, he too sometimes felt like speaking to her intimately. He would tell her about his college, strikes, lecturers who do not know how to teach and all such details of his student life and his chief role in all those activities.

Now Ganesha informed her of an important news – his Tiptur *Thatha* had passed away. He described all details about how he died and how he breathed his last holding the key of the safe in his fist, how the corpse held it tightly in its fist, the fist not opening however much his mother tried, the fingers of the corpse being stronger than iron and how he joined his mother, wrested the key adventurously. All this Ganesha enacted, laughed and ridiculed. But his atte did not laugh. She was listening to it seriously. Then Ganesha said that his father made him open the safe and burnt away six and a half lakhs of rupees along with the corpse. While describing this, Ganesha said that his father did so out of anger, for *thatha* had taken two thousand and five hundred rupees as expenses for keeping his grandson for three years.

Savitri did not know anything about it and asked, 'What is this story about two and half thousand?'

Ganesha said, 'You know Atte, I too did not know. Appa will not speak about anything with anyone. Even Amma had not told me. Yesterday after we returned to Bilikere, she told me everything and said. "Your father burnt away six and half lakhs to hurt me, only because of his anger."'

Savitri knew that her brother had sold his wet fields. She only knew that her brother had some loans. She had asked her brother: 'Why did you sell that land which gave you food, without informing me? I had some money with me. Besides there were the gold bangles and chain. You could have sold them and cleared the loans.' But her brother said, 'No, Savitri, it would not have ended there. Moreover, I being your elder brother, should give you. Instead, how can I take from you, you who are working hard for your livelihood?' He had not mentioned about paying his father-in-law. Savitri asked Ganesha. 'Tell me Ganesha, whatever your appa said when he cleared that loan – tell me whatever you remember.'

Ganesha narrated the whole incident. Sukanya's vow to Ranganatha Swamy of the Hill, Ramakrishnayya's prostrating before his father-in-law requesting him to take the money and free him from debt, offering the money to Nagappa and Nagappa asking his son-in-law to exchange an old note.

Savitri asked again, 'When your amma asked the reason for burning that six and half lakhs, what reason did your father give? When this happened you were also present, weren't you? Remember clearly and tell me everything correctly.' Ganesha reported the conversation between his Amma and Appa, in the correct sequence and said, 'Appa quoted some philosophy. "When he died holding the key in his fist, whatever that key involves should be sent with the dead person. What authority do we have to donate in his name, which he had not willed to give away while living?"'

It was not difficult for Savitri to understand her brother's mind, but it took a little time. Then she asked, 'Look here, Ganesha, do you also think that your appa burnt away that six and half lakhs because your grandfather took money as expense for your food? Don't you understand the meaning of dying with the key in a tight fist, though your appa explained in such detail?' Ganesha said a bit severely, 'That is different. Six and half lakhs! Is it to be scoffed at, Atte?'

Savitri did not feel like discussing further. She became silent. This silence of his atte seemed to Ganesha like the silence of his appa. But it was not quite as that of Appa. His atte usually spoke more freely with him. But she became silent. Ganesha felt that the brother and sister were of the same nature and felt a sort of embarrassment. In the night, Ganesha slept quickly. But Savitri could not. Her mind was filled with Nagappa's key, flames and ashes of those six and half lakhs. The humiliation, insult and disdain she was suffering vanished from her mind. Her conscience told her, as far as she knew, her elder brother had not done that with anger. She thought, such matters could be comprehended only in silence and nothing could be grasped by arguments and counter arguments, and she began finding deeper meaning in her brother's silence. She learnt that the further rites of Nagappa would be performed in Paschimavaahini and Ganesha would apply for leave and go there to attend the ceremonies. Savitri decided to apply for leave for four days and stay with her sister-in-law. It was natural for anybody to suffer intense grief. She decided to go to Bilikere the next day by four by the bus in the afternoon and offer her condolences to Sukanya and return next morning to Channarayapattana. She woke up early, prepared breakfast and lunch packet for Ganesha and gave him fifty rupees. She knew well what she gave him was extra money, without the knowledge of his father. It was just like a mother giving her children money secretly. Being his atte, his father's sister, she gave him money and Ganesha had this feeling from the beginning itself. But now for the first time, a question rose in her mind: how much of the inherent quality and culture of his father and father's father has descended in this boy of twenty years, the only son of her elder brother? Though the training she got as a teacher pulled her reflections towards the concept of heredity, education, environment and other things, this question began to stir her conscience.

Ramakrishnayya could get accommodation of a kitchen and a room in a choultry on the banks of the river Kaveri in Paschimavaahini, on a nominal rent. They did not need a place bigger than that. A priest agreed on contract to perform rites of four days for ₹500 inclusive of all expenses. There were only four persons from Ramakrishnayya's family. He would go to the river bank to perform the rites. Ganesha would go by bus, one day to Mysore and another day to Srirangapattana for sightseeing as he did not have any other work. Only Sukanya and Savitri were left in the choultry. Sukanya spoke with so much discontentment that she had never expressed earlier. Savitri could never imagine that her sister-in-law could speak in such a manner. Sukanya reproached, 'When his father died, he invited the whole village, arranged a *samaaraadhana* – a huge community meal for people, who had gathered in the weekly market place. But when my father dies, we have come here to Paschimavaahini as if to perform the rites of a pauper and send him to the other world.' Sukanya was not unaware that her husband had taken a loan of three hundred rupees when they went to Tiptur to see her bedridden father and now he had taken a further loan of five hundred from Chalapathi Shetty. Savitri also knew that. But Savitri kept quiet, thinking that she should not contradict her sister-in-law, for after all Sukanya was giving vent to her anger against her husband. If she could get any solace from it, let her do so, thought Savitri. Sukanya said: 'Didn't he burn six and a half lakhs? If only ten thousand from it were spent, all the rites and *samaaraadhana* could have been performed in his own house according to the dignity of my father. You see, Savitri, you do not understand that your brother has it in his mind to cause humiliation and insult to the warehouse owner Nagappa.' Not content still, Sukanya continued her tirade. 'It is true my father was a little tight in money matters. If you do not tighten your belt, can money be saved? Was it not for his daughter that he saved it? Instead of that, like this house, proclaiming, "I'll perform *annadaana*, I'll be hospitable," and cooking and cooking daily for all wayfarers, borrowing, selling paddy field that produced food ... Oh! what happiness or comfort did I enjoy becoming the daughter-in-law of this house?' When Sukanya spoke in that strain, Savitri had her answer almost at the tip of her tongue. But she stuck on to her decision of maintaining silence and thought her sister-in-law grieved owing to the six and half lakhs that was burnt with the corpse. Once Savitri too had thought that her brother should not have touched that money but he should not have burnt it either. Sukanya had continued, 'It is also true that my father did not give on his own, when he was alive. Didn't he know that after his death, all that would go to his daughter? He held the key tightly because when he was ill and unconscious either servants or the clerk might take away the key and rob the safe. If he was aware that his daughter had come, he would have given that key to her. He held it with the purpose of giving it to her. But he was not conscious at the right time. Was it his mistake? Who gave the authority to your brother to burn the money that my father earned and saved with so much of hard work? That too to a person who sold his wet-lands for livelihood, without having the ability to earn a single copper coin ...'

Savitri was about to answer, 'The duty which he is fulfilling now by tonsuring his head, borrowing money and performing rites to the dead person has given him authority to burn it also.' But again she remained committed to her decision and kept silent. Her silence enraged Sukanya more and more. Savitri was haunted by surprise and suspicion, whether her sister-in-law was the same one she had seen until then.

Rituals of the twelfth day were over, all the four of the family had finished their lunch. Rice, sambar and butter milk were brought in three vessels for them for their dinner. Some parched paddy grains, milk and two bananas were kept for Ramakrishnayya, for, taking meals after performing funeral rites was a taboo. The assistant cook and the priest left for Srirangapattana. Before leaving they said, it was *maasika* the next day and it was important that they should come before eight in the morning. Ramakrishnayya too went to Srirangapattana with them. Sukanya and Savitri laid down on mats. Ganesha was sitting on the platform, engaged in reading a film magazine he had brought from Mysore. Water in the river flowed monotonously with complete disregard for everything around.

Nanjappa, the clerk, came there from Tiptur. He held a handbag and an umbrella and was wearing a dhoti, shirt, and a black cap. He recognised Ganesha. 'Oh is it the choultry?' saying so, he came in. Sukanya felt contented and excited too. At least one person from her side had come to her appa's ceremony. Besides, she became enthusiastic thinking that Nanjappa might have brought some news regarding the warehouse business. She got up and welcomed him. Nanjappa narrated how he came there, sat on the mat and said, 'You see, I thought you must have gone to some sacred place on a river bank to perform the rites. To confirm the place you had gone to, I went to Bilikere, enquired from your neighbour Subbannayya and directly came here. I must return immediately. I have come here to inform you personally the matters concerning the business in Tiptur, for it is an urgent matter.'

Sukanya said, 'It is good that you have come. Please wash your hands and feet in the river. There is rice, sambar and buttermilk.' Nanjappa at once got up and went near the river. He freshened up by washing his hands and feet. As ten days were already over, defilement resulting from death was cleared. Besides as a daughter given in marriage to another family, Sukanya was in any case free from that defilement. She spread plantain leaf and served him food.

Nanjappa said, 'I'll talk while I eat, for I have to catch a return bus immediately. Where is bhaava?' he asked and looked here and there.

Sukanya said that he had gone to Srirangapattana.

He said, 'It is Okay. I had decided in my mind and came here to inform you even in the presence of bhaava. You call Ganesha also here. He is also very important in this matter.' Savitri went out of her own accord, sent Ganesha in, climbed down the steps, went to the river bank, walked down half a furlong and sat on a rock, the flowing water lapping her feet. Nanjappa began narrating. 'You see, I need not tell you anything about the nature of my master. Bhaava got angry, took out bundles of money from the iron safe and burnt them with the corpse. Can one get back the nose which is cut to spite one's face? Let us not talk about it now. Do you know what has happened in the warehouse? Accounts of the warehouse are in the bank. Who has the authority to sign in that book? You know this also. Your father didn't have only the money that was burnt to ashes. You know, generally merchants store money in iron safes, when it cannot be deposited in banks, or they will keep it somewhere else. Copra bags have arrived in the warehouse. If we are ready to purchase, more will come. Though it is not the season, some would still be remaining for sale. And the suppliers need money for disbursement to the farmers. Who should sign the cheques? If you produce suitable documents informing that as the proprietor of warehouse, Nagappa, is dead, all rights of his movable and immovable property would be transferred to you, Sukanya, his only daughter and legal heir. All accounts of the bank will then be transferred in your name. We have to pay the suppliers and collect it from the buyers. All accounts pertaining to it have been maintained correctly. You should know this also that *saahukaar* was a miser in spending money but he was a very strict and sincere man in accounts, weight, dates and rates of interest. That's why clients of our shop would never go to another shop. Even now it is so. I'll be there and I know all transactions. You, your husband or your son come to Tiptur. You can easily manage the warehouse. To build such a business needs at least twenty years and a bit luck too. What is the use if the warehouse which has built such goodwill is shut down? Besides, I too am not aware in which places master has purchased properties and how much did he have. All those documents may be either in the iron safe at home or in the bank locker. In my estimation, the value of these properties is more than ten lakhs. You must get all that registered as the heir to the deceased and transfer the *khata* to your name. It is not proper either to close the warehouse or to say that we have no money to clients. You see, a trader should never close his shop even for a day. He should never reveal even for a day that he has no money. Now these rituals are going on. If not you could have come with me today itself. Anyway, your husband may not agree immediately. But, is there any justice in ruining what should legally become a grandson's possession, only because your husband does not agree?'

Sukanya was enthusiastic and she became excited. It was a fact, she knew that her father had purchased lands in many places. She had never imagined that she could continue managing the warehouse business. She felt, now this Nanjappa had come like a God to favour her. Nanjappa said, 'But one thing, look here sister, when master lived he never paid us generously. He was paying me, who looked after so many things and worked hard, only three hundred rupees. To that Puttaswamy, who had come that day to inform you, master was giving only one hundred and ten rupees. I'll tell you now itself. I'll work honestly, instruct you, guide you in whatever matter you want and will manage the warehouse. But you should give me five hundred a month; and to Puttaswamy who looks after weighing, loading wagons and all other work, you must give two hundred and fifty rupees. To all other workers also you must give on par with what other warehouses pay. I'll go and tell them this, so that they should not leave here and join other warehouses.'

Sukanya nodded. By then he was finishing his meal having rice with buttermilk and said, 'I'll return immediately. When our master lived, it was lawyer Chandrashekarayya who was looking after all the legal matters. I'll inform him everything. He has to prepare all the documents by the time you come there. Besides, you decide in whose name the warehouse should be. Either it should be in the name of the husband, wife and son, or in the name of mother and son or only in the name of grandson. You make a decision and come. Because until it is decided and recorded, you cannot transact business with the bank.' He informed everything in detail and got up. He washed his hands and got ready to leave. 'Either through Channarayapattana or through Nagamangala and Belluru, I am sure to get a bus. I'll walk to Srirangapattana bus-stand,' he said, wore his chappals and walked out.

Sukanya became excited and restless. She thought their days of poverty were over. Love and affection towards her father swelled. She said to Ganesha who stood in front of her, 'You understand this, my son. Your grandfather saved the whole money for his daughter and grandson, by being tight-fisted in money matters. He had reasoned well that if he had given money and property earlier, these Bilikere in-laws of hers would waste everything by feeding wayfarers.'

Sukanya did not know what else to do. She removed the plantain leaf that Nanjappa had his meal on and cleaned the floor. She asked her son three times, 'Did you understand?' Meanwhile Ramakrishnayya returned holding a bag full of fruits. It was the special offering he brought to serve for the meals of *maasika* along with the dishes the cooks prepared. He put down the bag and sat leaning against the wall. Then Sukanya told her son, 'Your atte must be sitting on the bank of the river. Go and ask her to come back.' Within ten minutes Ganesha returned with Savitri. Sukanya explained everything that Nanjappa had informed her, with the introduction why she sent for Savitri. 'Savitri, come sit here. I'll tell before you why the clerk from Tiptur had come. You know, your brother slapped me hard on my cheek in front of our grown-up son, my father's corpse as a witness. I am sure now too he will hit me again. I sent for you, because, let him hit me now with you as the witness.'

Then, when there was silence, Ramakrishnayya did not speak. He sat looking out from the door, at the river which flowed in front of the choultry. The quality of disinterestedness and disregard that the river always had, was reflected on his face as well. Sukanya waited a long time to get an answer, got frustrated and told Savitri, 'Savitri, ask your brother to answer me.' She again waited. After a minute, Ramakrishnayya said, 'I did not know that people who cannot understand will not understand even if slapped. Nothing remains to tell or talk about. I should ask Ganesha a word or two.' He turned to his son and said, 'Look here son, think calmly and tell me. You see, the property of the dead will not become ours only by the fact that the government has transferred the right of succession. When it was not in the inclination and the culture of the soul of the warehouse owner Nagappa to make his will such that his property should belong to such a person or such an institution at least after his death, what sort of wisdom or reasoning exists in you joining his *praarabdha*? This would be a sort of theft. Theft equivalent to stealthily squeezing yourself into another's grove.'

Ramakrishnayya said these words looking at the face of his son and stopped speaking. But Sukanya immediately retorted, 'These Bilikere people need not teach my father the law, that after his death, his property would surely belong to his daughter. What sort of will should he have made? Should he have chanted mantras?'

Ramakrishna turned towards her and said, 'I asked Ganesha. Give him a chance to speak. I leave the final decision to you both.' He again looked at his son's face.

Ganesha felt embarrassed to meet his father's eyes. He felt uneasy, as if someone was spying on him, sitting inside those eyes. He turned his eyes towards the pillar and said, 'What can I achieve by simply getting a BSc degree?' Ramakrishnayya answered, 'You see, this is an irrelevant factor. It is like an argument that, because I do not have, I'll trespass into another's grove. If you feel BSc is not enough, you continue your study either in Mysore or Bangalore. I'll support you, even if I have to take loans.'

Savitri said enthusiastically, 'If you study for MSc I'll send you two hundred rupees every month.' But after realising the context, at once, she bit her tongue. She thought that her sister-in-law's burning eyes would be turned on her.

Ganesha answered, still looking at the pillar, 'Why should we give up everything because Tiptur Thatha was a miser? He did not spend either for food or for clothes. You are angry for he took two thousand and five hundred rupees from you as expenses for my stay there. You see you sold that paddy-field for eight thousand rupees. Let the warehouse come to me, with just one month's profit, I'll get you back that paddy-field.'

Ramakrishnayya did not speak again. The surprise and shock that he suffered inside were not revealed on his face. But it became unbearable to Savitri. However, she had determined not to talk again, after she bit her tongue. After saying that much, Ganesha felt embarrassed to stay there and went out, wore chappals that were near the door, climbed down the steps and turned towards the street at the bank side. Sukanya too came out and sat on the platform.

Sukanya could not sleep that night. Ganesha too was tossing and turning. Nobody knew whether Ramakrishnayya had slept. Her brother's words took Savitri's mind and intellect off to a different altitude and from that height, the humiliation she suffered from Manjayya and her feeling that she had fallen began to seem insignificant.

Her brother had gone towards the canal in the morning. Her sister-in-law and Ganesha were dressed up and ready as if for a journey. Ganesha held his mother's small trunk. Sukanya came near Savitri and said, 'You see Savitri, now the warehouse is closed.

We should go to a lawyer, get the court order and only then can we transact business, transfer bank accounts. Ganesha and myself will go to Tiptur right away. The clerk said that clients would go elsewhere even if there was a single day's delay. Though I am the daughter, there will be no work or participation of women in funeral rites. Your brother, who is the son-in-law, however, will perform *maasika* today and *Vaikunta* tomorrow. Ganesha has said that after we get the bank accounts in our possession, we should arrange for a community meal matching the dignity of my father, inviting the clients of the shop and all others in Tiptur. You too must come and attend. Savitri, you inform your brother to come directly, day after tomorrow, to Tiptur, after he completes the rituals here.' Saying this, Sukanya quickly walked behind her son.

The priest and the cooks who were coming daily, came in a little while. It was the day of the *maasika*, a very important day in the proceedings of '*shraaddha*' rites. Cooks began cutting the vegetables they had brought. The priest started arranging darbha grass and other things needed for rituals.

Ramakrishnayya returned. The priest said to him, 'You have a bath and be ready by eleven. I'll keep everything ready here, go home by bicycle and return. Other Brahmins too, who are to take part in the rituals, will come by then. However we cannot begin these rituals before noon.'

Ramakrishnayya came out and went to Savitri who sat on a step near the water and asked, 'It looks like both of them left for Tiptur today itself. I don't see her trunk and Ganesha's bag.'

Savitri simply said, 'Yes.' Somehow she felt it was mean and humiliating to report to her brother what her sister-in-law had told her. Now as Ramakrishnayya spoke, she got out of her humiliation and embarrassment. He did not speak again, but sat near the water, brushing his teeth. Savitri got up, climbed the steps and returned to the choultry. The priest would have noticed that the daughter of the dead person was not present that day. He would surely ask at least in the afternoon, where she was and while answering him Savitri thought she would be utterly embarrassed.

She said without being asked, 'There was some urgent work at my sister-in-law's father's place. Someone came from there, she left just now and will be back by tomorrow.'

The priest raised his head and looked at her. He said, 'No problem. There is no role for women in inauspicious rituals. But we cannot celebrate any auspicious function without them. Without them, work doesn't happen.'

Savitri thought it was true. However, she looked at the face of the priest to see if he was speaking ironically. She felt that he had spoken without any contextual meaning and only about the Shastra.

Only the brother and sister remained in the choultry that evening, the night and the next morning. Savitri thought it would be mean to speak to her brother about this matter. However, she knew the importance and understood her brother's mind. Now if she asked anything, it would simply be raking up the obvious. There was utter silence. Both were staying in the same place without talking: but she had the feeling that they had understood each other. Savitri had just gained special strength. There was no other work at night. Moreover, in that desolate river bank, it was the atmosphere of night as soon as the sun set. Both of them went to bed. Even after two hours, Ramakrishnayya did not get sleep. He did not even yawn and was simply tossing and turning. Savitri asked him, 'Annayya, when you burnt the currency notes, were you angry, for your father-in-law had taken expenses for the food of his grandson?'

He did not reply immediately. It was certain to her, he had heard her question. He explained after a while, 'You see Savitri, if I had had even an iota of such anger, I would not have done that. It is a different matter altogether whether that money reached Nagappa's *preta* or not. I have been doing these rites in his name since three days. But if you ask, whether the *pinda* that I am offering would reach his *preta* or not ... Have you seen it? What can I say? Is it not with the faith that it surely reaches him, that I am doing this? He searched for that key with so much of eagerness, anxiety and restlessness, held it tightly in his fist and died. What was the way to send with him *the thing* that key held within it? The Shastras say, that objects of *here* may be sent *there* through any one of the five elements, namely Earth, Water, Fire, Air or Space. At the time of cremation, Fire is the carrier. I sent the money through it. Nagappa's *preta* has agreed that his son-in-law has acted most suitably and is feeling happy. It should be analysed only from the point of that *preta*. All these practical or business ideas about what should belong to whom and what should not, according to government law, are rooted in selfishness.'

Ramakrishnayya said this much and was silent. Savitri did not ask him anything more. Savitri reflected: Her annayya was not criticising Nagappa with any yardstick of high-low, sinner or saint but he was viewing it all only with the limited duty of sending him what was his. She had the feeling that her annayya also was just like her father. When Annayya, the eldest son was twenty, Appa lost his wife. Now, her annayya, when his son Ganesha is twenty years of age, her sister-in-law left her husband and went away to her father's place to get the property. Perhaps her Appa and Annayya shared the same destiny. Would her sister-in-law return to Bilikere? No, she won't leave such a big business on the shoulders of her young son of yet immature mind. It was impossible that her annayya would go there. He did not go there even for a day when Nagappa was alive. For that matter, Nagappa too never invited his son-in-law. Will he go there now? All in all, her brother became lonely. Thinking that her brother did not have anyone to cook ragi-balls for him twice a day, her heart melted. Whatever kind of difficulties and pains he suffered, to be silent and not to reveal to anybody was his innate nature. But will there not be grief and agony within him? Savitri began churning these inside her. After some time, her annayya said, 'You see, I was the only one who had to perform those rites. And I alone had the authority to burn that money. Sukanya is arguing that it was wrong. If at all it was wrong, I have to earn that six and half lakhs, pay it up and get redemption from her debt. But even if I work hard, the whole of my remaining life, let alone six and a half lakh, I cannot earn even one tenth of it. When we think on business lines, interest should not be forgotten. If it is ten percent, it would be sixty five thousand interest per annum. Then interest on the interest earned and the compound interest will grow like fast spreading poison and I have to be drowned and suffering for many births in the well of her debt.' Ramakrishnayya said this and laughed loudly. Savitri understood that sadness, grief and pain were throbbing in that laugh. Or did he laugh jokingly without having any pain or sorrow? Savitri doubted. Her annayya had led twenty-two or twenty-three years of married life with Sukanya. Did he or didn't he know the nature of his wife? Or was there no opportunity at all for her to reveal her true nature? Savitri reflected, how was it that even the son turned totally opposite to the characteristics of his father's family.

She too did not get sleep. The question haunted her: Who would cook for her annayya? When he was a little boy he knew cooking. But how many years ago! It was not whether he knows how to cook or not. But a man at this age, living alone, cooking for himself, doing all domestic chores … Savitri felt sympathy. She got an idea. How about getting herself transferred to Bilikere? Then there would be someone to look after him. Yes, why shouldn't it be so? However, she should not be hasty. Her sister-in-law may stay for a couple of days in Bilikere and some days in Tiptur. Sukanya should not feel that because of Savitri's interference, her family was broken. Later she decided to wait for some months and think about that. She slept after well midnight.

The ceremony of *Vaikunta* and rituals were over by two in the afternoon. The brother and sister caught a bus at half past two and reached Channarayapattana by five. Ramakrishnayya directly took the bus to Bilikere, for it was already five days that the house had been locked. Savitri had to be present at school the next day, so she went home.

Savitri got sleep as soon as her head touched the pillow. When she woke up before dawn, she felt nauseous. She had not taken any food that could upset her stomach though for four days she ate food prepared for the ceremony. But, it was cooked purely and cleanly. Yet why did she feel this nausea? Thinking so she went to the bathroom and tried to retch it out; but it refused to come out, nor would it stay inside. When she began to think why it was annoying her so, she remembered that in this haste of ceremony she had forgotten that the date of her periods was already delayed by more than a week. Her whole being shuddered. Her mind, which was completely engaged in the manner of Nagappa's demise, rift between her brother and his wife and son, now all of a sudden, returned to the place where she had left it and began to visualise a more dreadful state. She was humiliated and raped. She had to undergo the torture of being jabbed by the doctor for six days, owing to fear of contracting the dreadful disease. Now, this. Savitri felt there was no end to the injustice that was brought upon her by him. She thought of putting her finger to the throat and retching out what was pressing inside to get some comfort. But she was afraid, if the loud sound of vomiting was heard by Nanjappa or his wife, that too in the morning. She sat for half an hour but could not retch out and again she came in and lied down. She didn't feel enthusiastic to get up and engage in the daily routine. She had no doubt about her being pregnant. If it was known, she ought to explain to everybody the rape Manjayya committed. But who would believe her? That villain would deny it to humiliate her more. Besides he may try to prove that there was no difference between him who goes in search of umpteen women and Savitri. She felt, oh! what sort of an existence does a woman have to suffer! An existence that has to shoulder the result of all injustice.

It took nearly a week for her to accept the situation she was in. It was certain that she was pregnant. But in whom could she confide? There was only her Annayya who she felt intimate with. If she told this to him, he was not a person to suggest any easy solution. He would surely tie Manjayya to a tree and grill him. Nothing else struck her. She began to feel it was utterly shameful to announce that she was helpless and had succumbed to rape. Yes this was also a sort of rape. He told lies to her. She was stubborn and married him – later there were many rapes – by him, she thought this was also one in that line. She decided against telling this to her Annayya. The solution that seems natural to anybody in such a situation struck her also. If allowed to grow for more days, it may become difficult to get it removed. She decided to go to a doctor, tell him what happened and end the matter. Which doctor should she consult? After reflecting the whole day, she remembered Dr Hasheem. He was competent, gentlemanly and a decent doctor. She believed, if she told him everything, it would never leak out and create a scandal. She should go to his clinic the next morning before other patients throng there. If it was him, she need not have to face the embarrassment of explaining anew. He already knew the injustice caused to her by Manjayya and had treated her by giving six injections. She had to request him: 'I'm faced with this now, doctor. Please help me.' The rest would be his responsibility. Savitri decided to meet the doctor, the next morning before eight.

That night suddenly there was an agony inside her which boiled and rose to the surface. She had not suffered such intense grief even after the humiliation and insult of rape she succumbed to. It was such a grief that urged her to sob convulsively. As far as she remembered, she had wept so uncontrollably only when her appa died. Long back, when she was yet a little girl, she must have wept so much when Seethakka died. Then, when standing outside the hut in the grove, she listened to Manjayya's foreplay of adultery and sport of sex, when she walked out on him and left his house, there was rage, disdain, feeling of revenge that burnt her so intensely that she thought of setting fire to everything, but she had not suffered such agony. It was a grief that could be calmed only by crying. But she could not weep loudly. Nanjappa's wife would immediately come. She would ask, 'Why are you crying child?' and put her hands on Savitri's shoulder and try to offer solace. Then the sobs would burst out more strongly and she would be forced to reveal the reason. Savitri folded the edge of her sari, stuffed it in her mouth and cried convulsively. That eased her grief a little and she went to bed. After a little while, the reason for her grief became clear to herself. Yes, it might be the result of rape, it might have been done by a scoundrel, but a new life was sprouting inside her. It was praying and appealing for protection, nourishment of her blood, flesh and milk. Restlessness of that new being inside was showing itself as morning sickness. In her thirty-fifth year, it had caused her life to sprout and had emerged as her own. Why should she kill it? That worthless scoundrel may move about proclaiming it was not his, let him. While that fellow who has mere falsehood as his capital has so much of courage, why should I, who possess strong truth, not be a brave woman? Who has the courage to deny this, standing before me? She felt consoled when the decision of bringing up her child took form in her mind. Crying stopped and the tears in the eyes seemed to be tears of peace and contentment. She did not feel like wiping them away. She imagined the whole night the pleasing sensation of that child growing day by day in her womb. She drew in her mind thousand pictures of that child being born, shouting joyously, beating its hands and legs as if it is flying skywards. The question whether it was a male or female, did not rise in her mind. Savitri recalled, if her appa had punished her in the manner which was impossible for his nature, he got so angry as to kick his daughter, he must have felt such an enormous grief that could turn the earth upside down. Though he advised her, she was so adamant. Even when Annayya scolded and explained everything, she was stubborn. It was a sheer obstinacy. Savitri again and again decided that she would save her child with the same stubbornness. The same decision came to her mind again for the hundredth time. She thought was it not enough to decide once? Why should she again and again try to make it firm? By the time the cock crew somewhere in the distance, a sort of contentment and comfort of a firm decision becalmed the turmoil in her mind and brought sleep to her body.

It was late when she woke up in the morning. She grew anxious, whether there would be a loud sound while retching out, though she resisted. Let there be a loud sound, today itself, I will be out with it, but somehow she felt she should not be rash in her decision. So, as she did daily, today also very carefully she completed the agony of vomiting, finished her household chores and went to school. By afternoon, her mind began to think in a different direction. Anyway this would be his child. Surely there would be resemblance either in eyes, nose or in brows or forehead. She should cause to write his name as father in the government records and in school and throughout its life. She should always be telling her child: your appa was a such a fellow. You should not become like him. She had to struggle her whole life with his memory. In a way, till now she lived without worrying. Now she felt why should she be burdened with so much of anxiety. Within one or two hours, this thought strengthened and got the upper hand.

While teaching the last hour of the day, she felt an urge to leave the class at once and go the doctor's clinic directly. Somehow she managed and remembered, the doctor had said when he treated her with injections, to come in the mornings as there would be a throng of people in the evenings. She decided to go to the clinic the next morning.

But while she cooked for herself at night, affection and love surged towards that unborn baby. No doubt he was a sinner, but being a mother, should she end its life before it opens up its eyes to the light of the world? The whole night she was haunted by the fear of this sin. The decision she took a hundred times the previous night, began strengthening again and again this night too. She felt, without that child no peace was possible, there was no fixed purpose, no meaning to her life. Deciding that she ought to save it she slept by dawn.

But by next morning another thought took root. Why did he come to her and do this? Had he any dearth of professional young girls or woman of that kind? He must have done this intentionally, perhaps he had planned to pester her and through that to have a hold on her. When this reason occurred and when she felt sure that except that, no other reason was possible, her rage for revenge recurred. She felt utterly disgusted by thinking to what purpose, to what *praarabdha* she should live defending herself, struggling lifelong with the child of that man, who did so much injustice to her and to her father, he who was the cause of her father's death too. As usual, the doctor's clinic would be crowded by the time she comes out from school. That day also while cooking, the same feeling filled her mind. A question arose in her mind: even if she got the child saved, could she bring it up without anger or regret? She could not get sleep even after dawn. She heard crowing of the cock and then heard the crows. When she opened her eyes it was already daybreak. Her eyes were burning and her whole body ached. She felt weak. She understood it was the result of four sleepless nights, got up at once, finished the job of retching out, bathed, had breakfast, packed lunch, changed her dress, locked the house and walked to the clinic.

The clinic was open. A boy was sweeping but the doctor had not come. Savitri sat behind the curtain in the place reserved for ladies. When the doctor came, luckily, there were no other patients. She sat in the place where patients were examined and conveyed whatever she had to in four or five sentences. The doctor thought for two minutes and said, 'You see, I don't have any experience of terminating pregnancy. Nowadays even so many unqualified people do it. Even nurses and pharmacists conduct this and earn money. But afterwards the patient suffers until her death. And you know another thing: after you treat such matters, you must shut your mouth, but these rural doctors do not have such loyalty. Even if you go to Hassan, they ask you about your place, relatives etc. So, you better go to a big place where nobody knows you. By the by, don't you have any male person as your relation? You may go with such a person and if he says, 'She is my wife, we have already two children and it is enough for us!' there will be no second word. If he requests to terminate it will be easy. In a good nursing home, a lady doctor, who has got MS in Gynaecology will treat this. You need not feel fear or shame. I'll recommend your case to a nursing home in Mysore, telling, 'The lady who brings this letter is sent by me.' Though it is a bit costly, the job is done without causing pain and with the help of anaesthesia. It is a job of only fifteen minutes. You must take a man with you. Now I remember, you have your brother-in-law and he knows well about you. You tell him what has happened and request him to go with you. Then there will be no problem. I will write a slip in his name. But you should not return by bus immediately after the treatment. You have to stay in the nursing home for two days. Until then I'll give you some tablets so that you may get sleep.' Who will get sleep in such situation, that too having this inside? Dr Hasheem had forgotten the name of Savitri's brother-in-law. He asked her, wrote Mattikere Satyanarayanappa, the address of nursing home, gave the slip and sleeping tablets to her.

Savitri felt calm and content when she came out of the clinic. Yes, what the doctor said was correct. Hassan and Channarayapattana, moreover, were known places. Mysore was far off and a big city. She thought she could get consolation if she spoke frankly with her bhaava. She went to school. She applied for one week's leave stating that she had some domestic work to attend to at her native place, gave the leave letter to the Head master, finished her classes and came home in the evening. She decided to leave for Mattikere the next morning by the first bus, get down at Mattikere Gate and walk five miles. It was twenty five years ago that she had been to that place. She came back from Mattikere to Bilikere after Seethakka's death and she had not attended Ramachandra's marriage also. She stuffed some saris and other requirements into a bag and went to bed. She got good sleep too as she had swallowed the sleeping tablet. When she was travelling, she thought: while she had decided to get rid of this because she did not want to have his memory or thought, with effort she resolved not to remember him with anger, disdain and disgust. Then she engaged herself in looking at the trees, plants and villages through the window of the bus.

She walked close to the village and enquired for Satyanarayanappa. She was told, Satyappa lived in the hut in his grove. She walked, asking people the way to the grove. It was no doubt the same path of lanes, tamarind trees and pits, lowlands, but now the whole place, without an inch of empty space, was converted into agricultural land. Her bhaava lived in a hut in the grove. One thing she had not known was the existence of three other huts in the grove; big huts, with men, women and children living there. There were twenty hybrid Sindhi cows.

All around the empty place in the grove, grass of special species was grown, chest high. Immediately Savitri understood it was the result of Satyappa's social upliftment work. After her brother-in-law explained, she understood the details. Her brother-in-law had brought in three families which did not have an inch of land. He had bought cows with his own money. Growing grass, looking after the cattle, milking cows – all these had to be done with collective effort. Twice a day, one of them had to carry milk by cycle to Tiptur and supply it to the hotels. The profit from the milk sale belonged to these three families. From this business, each family could save up to fifteen thousand per year. With four years of savings, they had to procure uncultivated land and make their own arrangement. Satyappa said, 'I have not attempted any large scale experiment. If it is successful, I'll try to develop dairy farming in our village. Besides, we should try to get a veterinary hospital to this place.' Satyappa explained his plan to Savitri. He continued, 'You see Saati, I have left half the lands to Ramachandra. I asked him to start such work. You need not have the trouble of carrying milk daily to Tiptur. I will send that with my people. But he got angry with me, stopped speaking to me, for I have taken half the property which he was enjoying. Besides, he concocts many scandals against me and spreads it.' Satyappa said and laughed. He explained his next programme also: 'Look here, after these three families become self-dependent, I'll bring another set of three or four such families.'

Satyappa began to cook. Savitri sat before the oven. He spoke while preparing rice, sambar and ragi-balls, 'I've stood guarantee for these cows and have taken loans from banks. My actual problem is not of money but how to reform these people. If I am not around, they steal coconuts from my grove. They mix water with milk, while on their way to take it to Tiptur and increase the quantity. It is difficult to drive home the fact that they can work and earn and there is no need for theft or lies. And that they would be ruined because of those. Sometimes I get so angry that I feel like driving away all these people. But I am working here, realising that fulfilment of karma yoga lies in bringing internal change in them, rather than uplifting them financially. Anyway, is it possible to reform them in five or six months, those who have been victimised by injustice for so many years and have not developed education and knowledge? I teach their children and am sending them to school also.' Satyappa poured out his thoughts.

Savitri felt there was a sort of fruitfulness in her bhaava's effort. While they were having their lunch, Satyappa asked, 'I am sorry Saati, I think you have not come all this way here without any purpose. I did not enquire about you at all, instead, I am telling you only about myself and my work.' Savitri's face turned crimson with embarrassment. But, however, as she had to tell him, she made up her mind and narrated everything. She began, 'You had to face agony once from Manjayya. The same sort of agony has occurred now to me also,' and explained the details. While listening to her, there was pain on his face but no surprise. After she washed the plates, cleaned the floor and sat on the mat he said, 'Hasheem is very decent and a respectable doctor. As he says it is better to go to Mysore, I'll come with you. But you think once again. Have you not taken this decision because you are afraid of society? Or out of disgust and disdain against Manjayya?'

Savitri answered, 'Bhaava, do you think I do not have enough courage to answer society, that is, to the twenty or thirty people known to me? It is true, I feel disgust, disdain, enmity and rage. But do you say I should feel all these against him only and should not let even the shadow of these fall on his child? You may be trying to become a Mahatma, but I don't wish for any such thing. Please start at once. If we reach Channarayapattana or Tiptur, we may catch a bus to Mysore from there.'

Satyappa said, 'Alright, the decision is yours. Let us go to Tiptur. I must get some money from there. I don't keep money in this hut. Do you know why? Someone among these might steal it and the rest of them won't co-operate in finding out who the thief is.'

'I have brought enough money with me. You need not take any,' though she insisted, Satyappa did not agree. Both of them walked five miles to the bus road. After they reached Tiptur, Satyappa went to the warehouse and got money. Savitri did not go near the warehouse. She had narrated about the death of Nagappa and about her sister-in-law and Ganesha coming to Tiptur. Satyappa took Savitri to a hotel, for which he supplied milk and asked her to be there until he came back from the warehouse.

After he returned Savitri asked, 'You could have got money from this hotel itself.'

Satyappa said, 'No, it is not like that. Accounts of milk belong completely to those families in the grove. I manage and look after the accounts, but do not touch that money.'

The afternoon bus from Tiptur reached Mysore at eight. They went directly to the nursing home. After the slip from Dr Hasheem was given, the patient was admitted immediately. The duty doctor said, 'Lady doctor will come tomorrow morning and treat her. Let the patient be here. Men are not allowed to stay at night. You make arrangement to stay somewhere else.' And then told a nurse to get the patient prepared the next morning for anaesthesia. Satyappa took his handbag, engaged a room in a hotel nearby. He was back at the nursing home next morning by six. While admitting her to the clinic, it was written, 'Savitramma, wife of Mattikere Satyanarayanappa, wishes to terminate her pregnancy.' When Satyappa came in the morning, a consent letter to administer anaesthesia to the patient was taken from Satyappa.

Without any complications everything was over and within twenty minutes Savitri was brought to the ward. In a little while she gained consciousness. When her bhaava touched her shoulder to console her she felt like crying and sobbed convulsively. After a little while, she felt drowsy and stopped crying.

After giving Savitri fruit juice in the afternoon, Satyappa went back to the hotel to have his meals. By the time he returned, Savitri was completely conscious. The effect of the anaesthesia had worn off but her face looked serious. She was lying down quietly as if reflecting on something. She did not even speak to her bhaava, when he came into the ward. He pulled a chair and sat silently. After half an hour of grave silence, she said as if she had decided right then, 'Bhaava, you take me also to the room in the hotel. I don't want to stay here.' Satyappa said, 'But Dr Hasheem said you should be in the nursing home for at least two days.'

'Let him say. You see, when you had been to the hotel to take your meals that nurse just told me, the lady doctor who conducted the abortion said, this woman has not given birth to even one child, but asks for removal of this conception as the children she has now are enough for them. She said, "the relation between these two seems strange. He has already crossed fifty, this woman is around thirty-four or thirty-five." That lady doctor seems to be loose-tongued. The nurse who was in the operation theatre told it to the other nurses and all of them, one by one, on some pretext or the other, come here, see me and go out. Didn't you notice anybody staring at you?'

Satyappa was disgusted with the behaviour of this lady doctor. He thought, people of our country, whether they belong to rural or urban area lie and behave unethically. Even educated professionals like this doctor are no different. Savitri was looking at his face. So he replied quickly, 'Let them come, let them see me also. Let us not get embarrassed. The main work for which we came here is completed. Stay here at least for two days and have proper nursing. Then let us stay for two more days in the hotel. After you are completely recovered, let us go by bus or taxi. But now, don't allow your mind to be disturbed by such talks.' After a minute he said, 'See Saati I have brought three families and established them in my grove, you know that. It seems my son Ramachandra himself said that his father, after tasting a woman, now has brought three women into his grove so that they can give themselves to him whenever he wants. When the son himself says so, would the rest of the villagers not believe it? What should I do? I keep quiet as if I have heard nothing!'

Savitri got angry against Ramachandra. She knew there was no falsity in her bhaava. Actually he is trying to understand the truth deeply. She thought, how lust for property and money eggs on the son to think so meanly about such an honest father!

When she moved to the hotel room, Savitri confided in him whatever was very intimate to her which she could not convey to any other. Satyappa too would analyse and support her ideas with his old experiences and sometimes he would show what was wrong in her arguments and thoughts. Savitri felt that till then she had not shared her inner feelings with anyone. He would lie down on the bed near the door and she on the bed near the window. When they were conversing, Savitri told him around midnight, 'You told me bhaava, that egged on by his provocation, you got maddened at this age and walked fourteen miles to Bilikere seeking him and also about the aftermath of that action. I too want to tell you one of my experiences. I know you are capable of understanding it with compassion. You are experienced enough to suggest to me the right path on which I should tread in the future. I hope you remember, we were talking for a long time in the night sitting in the shed in the backyard, when you had come to Bilikere to attend the funeral ceremony of Appa. Then you asked me,

"When Manjayya slapped that maidservant Kempamma so hard who was of his mother's age, you were disgusted at his cruelty. Though Kanchi was a thief, was it not sheer brutality and cruelty to murder him?! Yet, how did you agree to continue your family life with that cruel beast if he would be acquitted by your appa giving false witness? If you had not agreed to live with him again, Appa would never have committed perjury." You had asked me this question. Do you remember? Then I did not answer it. I was ashamed to answer it. After all, how familiar were we then? Now I feel I must answer your question. But I am also embarrassed.'

Satyappa encouraged her in the darkness, 'It doesn't matter. Tell me everything.'

'Didn't I tell you, he had given me abundant sensual pleasure for six months after marriage. After I came out of his house, it was just like starving for seventeen years. However, I controlled my mind. Yet whenever the desire for sex would arise, my mind would go to him. Except to have him, there was no other way out. My mind could never imagine any other man in his place. There were umpteen women for him, but even after I left him, he was the only man for me. When I was asked, I agreed that Appa commit perjury, thinking at least I have got an opportunity now and I may enjoy that family happiness again. This is the first shameful factor and the second is ...' Savitri stopped speaking.

Satyappa insisted , 'Tell me, don't conceal anything.'

She resumed, 'You know, Manjayya raped me, he gripped me so tightly as a wrestler, that I did not have any chance to speak, shout or wriggle out. He has that terrible knowledge of holding the pulse of women and how to pulsate it. Just as a whore has the knowledge that catches on the weakness of a man and makes him dance to her tunes, every adulterer masters the skill of making women dance to his tunes. Manjayya is that sort of a man. At the end of that rape, I was conquered, I grew weak and I participated too. And that fellow understood it. This defeat is the factor of my shame. If only I did not allow myself to be defeated, I would not have suffered such humiliation and shame. When you suffered from that disease, indirectly caused by Manjayya, I abused him, but you shouldered the whole fault and did not blame him. After I underwent this experience, I too thought that, firstly I must understand my weakness and ward it off. Without that, there is no use in simply calling him names – rascal, scoundrel, etc. It will be mere abuses.'

Satyappa did not answer at once. After five minutes, he said, 'I understand. There is nothing unnatural in it. Let us sit together tomorrow, think and find out a solution for this. Because this is a problem which will pester you in future also.'

Savitri did not speak again. He fell asleep after a while.

After both of them bathed, ordered breakfast and coffee from room service and the waiter took away the dishes and cups, Satyappa said, 'Look here Saati, you are just thirty-five and beautiful and are earning also. In big cities, it is said, women who are highly educated usually marry at this age. If you think seriously and decide, you may marry again. I'll search a groom. If advertised in papers, suitable grooms or their parents will reply. I'll give the advertisement with my name and address. I'll give dowry – a token amount of one and a quarter rupee and I will get the merit of *kanyaadaana*.' Saying so, he laughed. She too felt like laughing. It was a long time since she laughed and it eased her mind a little. After a while, Satyappa continued, 'You see, this is one solution. Or if you decide not to marry again, you involve yourself completely in some work like me. You cannot be satisfied by teaching some hours in a school, get a salary, cook for yourself and eat. It is quite natural that the mind drags us in many different directions. You know, we should never burden the mind with blames. You just think about this: what work we have entrusted to our minds? In what sort of cultivation we have engaged our strength of body, mind and intellect so that they should not get lazy? It is a pity, the mind cannot engage itself in such a way. You see Saati, a thought occurs in my mind. There is a village called Banjara Hatti near our place. There are lands surrounding the village. The government has given some concessions for the people who are backward. But how can these people be reformed, by merely giving concessions, free lands and the officials staying in Bangalore? In this village, theft and drunkenness are more rampant than in any other poor village in the area. There is a school of sorts too. Yet there is no education for children. The elders of the village feel happy if the teacher doesn't open the door of the school. The teacher also is of that kind. If you agree, I'll get you transferred to that place by requesting someone in the department. You may stay in that village or in my grove. It is only a distance of one and a half mile. I strongly feel you should stay in that village. Do you know what is the condition there? Unless education, cleanliness and dynamism are awakened in the parents, it cannot be strongly developed in the children. They cannot be reformed or developed until they are guided on the right path and made to be engaged in dairy farming, coir industry or sericulture. If they develop loyalty towards work, it would be easy to bring up children. Within ten years, the children of the village may be made to take the leadership of their village. In such a situation, to say "my duty is accomplished just by teaching children spelling and arithmetic in school, is a fraud." If you stay in Banjara Hatti, you may show a purpose, a goal first to school children and through them to the parents. You may teach writing and reading to grown-ups also in the evening. You will take a salary from the government for your livelihood. But your aim and purpose should be to reform and change the whole village and the people. It would not be possible unless you are one among them. However, I'll be around. I too work with the adults and teach them in the evenings. Just think, whether this is acceptable to you.'

Satyappa became silent. Then as if he had just remembered, he continued, 'Let me go get some soap. I've to wash my clothes.' He wore a shirt, put on his chappals and went out. He climbed down the steps, bought soap in the shop in front of the hotel, came back and said, 'Saati, please don't think that remarriage is not respectful. Before you decide anything try to understand what exactly you want.' He said so and picked up his clothes to be washed. Savitri came near took away the clothes from Satyappa and said, 'Bhaava, now I am quite fit. I can wash. Give it.' She picked up her clothes also. But Satyappa did not allow her to take away the clothes and said,

'You see, you are still weak. I'll wash your clothes also. There should not be any differences like male and female and it ought not to be there at all while nursing the patient.'

Satyappa and Savitri started for Channarayapattana by the morning bus, after staying two days in the hotel. After coming home with her, he told her that he would leave for his village by bus in the afternoon. Then Savitri said, 'Look here bhaava as it is written in the folk story, that the life of a great wizard lies in the parrot which is kept in seven cages that are inside seven caves in the middle of seven hills that are amidst seven islands beyond seven seas, your life too is in your grove. I've still three days leave and have not yet gained enough strength to work. If you stay, cook and serve me, I'll recover from this weakness.' Saying so she laughed. He looked at her face. There was peace and contentment without the weight of sorrow.

He remarked, 'What I cook will be food suitable only for a patient. Will you eat it?'

'If so, I'll cook. You serve me with your nectar-like hands. I'll eat it and recover fast,' she said and took his handbag quickly into the inner room and hid it, before he could understand what she was doing.

Satyappa stayed there for three days and left for Mattikere. Savitri experienced a feeling which she could not understand, but which filled her from inside, with a great sense of comfort that at last she got a person who could be a companion, with whom she could share her thoughts, worries, who could solve her problems and who could ward off her loneliness. She would always be remembering him. Manjayya, his injustice, rape, whatever he had committed, vanished from her mind. All those seemed to be incidents that had happened in some bygone days. She began recalling every word her bhaava had said and found new meaning in them. One day Satyappa had said, 'Your elder sister Seetha was such a good woman in every way. But she made one mistake, who can forgive that?' Savitri insisted, 'What mistake did my sister commit, bhaava?' He had said, 'Dying and leaving me behind, all alone.' When he spoke these words, his eyes shone with the memory of twenty-six years back. Now Savitri's mind filled with the memory. When Seethakka died, he had hugged little Savitri who was crying and he too was weeping. Savitri thought, how many years of difference there was between him and herself? Yes of nineteen years. Then, she was nine and a half, he was twenty eight and a half. Thus the mind which was wandering in the tunnels of inner conscience, within ten or fifteen days began to have clear form of memories, emotions and necessities. What if there is a difference of nineteen years? Did she not marry Manjayya though he was seventeen years older than her? There arose a supportive argument in the relationship between her bhaava and herself. Age was immaterial. Age was related to the body. She did not wish to have physical relationship and he too had experienced that, had suffered, felt disgusted by it and had transcended it. She thought, why shouldn't it happen? She had not thought at all about what might be her bhaava's thoughts regarding this, until her feeling strengthened further again in fifteen days. Now, when she reviewed her memory with this point of view, she did not find any such feelings or ideas in him. She was disappointed. While he had completely involved himself in the service of villages and village reforms, would he accept to lead a family life again? Had he not reached the state of mind that having a family was a binding? Her mind would engage in guessing, although he had never ever told that family meant bondage. Then, what might be his objection to become a family man again? She thought of telling him, 'You do your village service. You spend whatever is produced in your lands for that purpose. I have no objection. Get me transferred either to Mattikere or to any village nearby. Let us manage our lives with the salary I get. What other objection would he have? For eight days, these consolations and justifications filled her mind. Meanwhile she began feeling that even if they marry they should not have any physical relationship for it would demean both of them. How could she convey all these to him? Even if she conveyed it, if he said, 'Saati, your feelings and emotions are still immature. You are nineteen years younger than I. I've carried you on my shoulders, played with you as with a daughter,' thinking so her mind would lose its courage. Her mind got comforted, thinking that she had a support. But in the blind feeling of not knowing what was the form of that support, she lost her mental equilibrium. She felt like writing to him to come to her place once. But, by chance, what if he says he doesn't want all this? What next? In these anxieties she became passive. After a week's turmoil she wrote a letter to her bhaava, expressing all the emotions which were surging inside her.

The business of Lakkoo's shop in the weekly market place, which Manjayya had helped her set up, began flourishing. Although, Manjayya was with her and helped her initially in deciding what stocks should be brought from Channarayapattana and Hassan, what should be the amount of profit fixed on those stocks, Lakkoo soon learnt the secrets of the trade. From the beginning itself, she had mastered trading in coconuts. Now she started buying loose coconuts also. As she took coconuts instead of money and would give beedi, matches, coffee powder, soap and other articles of daily use, people who did not have ready money with them started coming to her shop. If it was coconut, she got it for only eight annas. After it was dried it became copra and she would get one and a half rupees for it. Along with this, she engaged a boy to look after the buffaloes and clean the cowshed and earned from the milk business also.

After she started the shop, she would sometimes get confused. If Manjayya was going to take her as wife after one year of Kanchi's death and they were going to live together as man and wife, why should she be sitting in the shop from morning till evening? She would question herself and once asked Manjayya also. He said, 'Look Lakkoo, you were a woman who always worked for your livelihood. Can you sit idle for one year? However, if you don't want to sit in the shop, okay, leave it. I'll look after you.' Lakkoo's self-respect was provoked by Manjayya's answer. She thought, why should she quit working and decided to continue her shop business. Kanchi, her late husband, did not know about business matters or accounts. As such she was the owner of whole transactions. But Manjayya, as she knew, was as clever as a serpent, would he give her the ownership? Somehow she felt her mind would be squeezed out if she would lose her independence in money matters. Sometimes she used to think, even after she started living with Manjayya she should not give up her shop business. Again an objection would raise its head: will that person allow me to be sitting in the shop, instead of looking after the vast property – grove, wet-lands and dry lands – he owns?

Yes, it was very rare for her to meet Manjayya or to have physical relations with him. He was not coming to Lakkoo's house openly because, as he said, he did not want this to be known to people now. He would come to her house in the thick of the night, after everybody in the village slept and leave before dawn or even earlier. If she asked him to come daily, he would say that he would not be in the village at all and she was not to go to his house. Manjayya had told her, their relationship should not be known to Puttellayya. Lakkoo could not leave her shop at day time. She had gone twice to his hut in the grove. But while crossing the main gate of the grove, if anybody from the village saw her walking towards the village, she would feel humiliated, thinking that she too was like those whores Naagi, Channi, Malli and Siddi who would sleep with Manjayya for money. So, one day she bluntly said, 'Look here, should a wife come to that hut in the grove to sleep with her husband? Hereafter I'll not come there.' Manjayya said, 'Yes, what you say is correct,' and recognised her reputation at once. Lakkoo felt happy but the opportunity of sleeping with him further decreased. When Manjayya would be at the village he would come to her shop, sit for a while and talk with her for two or three minutes. Their relationship reached this level. When the physical desire which was stimulated by him would madden her and made her hanker after it again, she would suggest through words. 'I too feel like it Lakkoo, come to Tiptur. Let's have fun, or let's go to Hassan and enjoy ... come.' He would agree as if he was ready. But how many times could she travel to those far off places, locking up her shop, leaving the buffaloes in the care of servants? So, she would try to control her desire. She would think, Manjayya is not at fault in this matter, it was only her mistake. But when Lakkoo knew that this fellow had not stopped sleeping with other women in the hut in his grove, she was enraged. She told herself, 'You see, I am not a wife to keep dumb if you still continue your lewd conduct.' When he came to her shop the next time, she directly asked him about this. Manjayya said, 'Lakkoo, is it proper to cut off suddenly relationships which are so many years old? They ask, why did you leave us. They are clever. They would think, he has formed some new relationship. They know about you and me. They will spread it in the whole village. Though they visit my hut, I have stopped physical play with them. You hear me, after getting a woman like Lakkoo, which fellow wants to sleep with other women?' Manjayya spoke evasively. Lakkoo had not gone through the widow's ritual of living together with a man before the villagers, so she could not hold his collar and question him. Manjayya continued, 'You see Lakkoo, Malli, Naagi or Siddi may come to your shop on a market fair day, when your shop is full of people and ask you, 'Hey Lakkoo, what authority do you have to prevent Manjayya from sleeping with us?' Then what about your respect? Those women are whores who do not care about what they speak. So, I must slowly untie myself from them.'

Seven or eight months passed and Lakkoo felt Manjayya would not have the ritual of living together with her. She got angry. At the same time, she herself had a rethink about such a relationship with a person like Manjayya. Meanwhile, her business too had flourished and her shop earned some reputation. She thought, if she could buy some more things, set up and arrange the shop, she could outdo Siddalingappa's shop, which was famous in that place. Siddalingappa was called *Saahukar*, a wealthy man, around the villages for his business was good. If she excelled him in business, people will call her also a wealthy woman, a *Saahukarti*. Manjayya nurtured her desire. He had an empty place, a field near her shop. He suggested he would build a shop there and they could jointly run a general store. Lakkoo said, 'You build the shop and give it to me. I alone will run the business.' He agreed without a second word and said, 'You see, your name itself is Lakshmi, Goddess of Wealth. I suggested so because if I do business with you, my luck will increase. Earn well and keep everything with you. It is enough for me if I could get two square meals a day.' While agreeing so generously, he suggested he would not undergo the ritual of marrying a widow. But she would get mad if she could not go to Tiptur on the pretext of selling copra and spend a night with him now and then. She had understood that it was not possible for her to live without him regarding that aspect. He would be generous enough to come to her house at night, though rarely.

Gradually two things occupied Lakkoo's mind: one, to develop her shop and be called a wealthy woman. The second was to enable her daughter Latha, studying in Hassan, to get as much education as she wanted to. Latha had completed sixteen years and was now running seventeen. She was the very image of her father Kanchi, the same facial features and build of body, sharp nose and sharp chin. She was not stupid like her father and Lakkoo was always proud of her daughter's intelligence. She would think that Latha should study in high school. Except from her mother, from where could she get such intelligence? Was it not she who gave birth to Latha? Though there was high school in Bilikere itself, Latha refused point blank to study in a village school and joined a school in Hassan and stayed at her aunt's house. Lakkoo too consented with affection, for her daughter could enjoy city life, see films, etc. Lakkoo also was born and brought up in Hassan. Let alone film, then she did not even have proper food. Coffee curing had not yet developed in Hassan. How small that place was then and how much it has changed! Lakkoo's elder sister worked in a coffee curing factory and her husband in a saw mill. Her elder daughter was married and had children. Only one of her sons seemed to be studying and all the others were tramps and lazy bones. When Lakkoo brooded about all this, she would remember her daughter eating ragi-balls and rotis in her aunt's house, though Lakkoo sent money regularly every month. She got an idea – would it not be better if Latha joined a hostel? She wanted to know how much it would cost. She asked Manjayya and knew it would be a hundred and fifty rupees per month. She decided to admit Latha to the hostel after extending the shop. However, she used to give money to her daughter without the knowledge of her sister and say, 'Don't keep yourself hungry in the afternoons. Go and eat idlis or dosas in a hotel.' When she could not go to Hassan, she began sending money through Manjayya.

In the beginning, Lakkoo was much troubled wondering whether Latha would agree to her mother living together with Manjayya. Lakkoo had told her daughter that her father had slipped down from the tree and died – the same version that she said in the court as a witness, and the daughter naturally believed her mother with heartfelt sincerity. She told her daughter not to come to Bilikere, not even during holidays, for the damned street whores concocted so many stories. Lakkoo had stressed and driven home to her daughter that if Manjayya had not helped, she could not have established the shop. Yet Lakkoo's mind was riddled with fear, whether her daughter would agree to Lakkoo's decision of living together with Manjayya. But she had found the solution to this too in her mind. If Latha did not agree, she would countermand, 'Who is going to pay for your education?' But now when she had reached the state of mind that this sort of relation was optional, she felt comfort, for she didn't have to face the problem of telling her daughter that she was marrying again. If she desired to be with Manjayya leisurely for a whole day, she preferred to go to Tiptur and never to Hassan, because it was the place where her sister and her family lived. Moreover it was the town where she had grown up. If somebody met her, or Latha got to know ... these fears haunted Lakkoo.

Yet Lakkoo decided firmly about one thing: if she could not have him as her living-together partner, she must keep him to herself alone – and not let him sleep with any other whore. Let the annual death ceremony of Kanchi be over, then she would not be afraid of any woman's words in the street. She would tell Manjayya to come in broad daylight. If he comes in the night, he should sleep there the whole night and should go home after daybreak. Latha would not come to this village, leaving Hassan. She thought what was the difference between Naagi, Malli and Siddi and her own self, if she and Manjayya keep their relationship in wraps. Finally if that fellow would not agree to this and still go in search of street whores, she decided to use her trump card and teach him a lesson. She would plan in her mind: in broad daylight, on the day of the market fair, she would catch him by his dhoti in front of her shop and ask him, 'Look here, if I had not committed perjury and saved you, you would have been hanged. Don't you remember what you swore by the village Goddess beneath the beech tree?' If he would still be stubborn, she would call for the Village Panchayat. Her decision to hold him and not let him wriggle out of her hold was strengthened. But that fellow was cleverer than she was, terribly clever and crafty. When this thought came to mind, she would get confused, not knowing what to do. For a moment she would consider becoming indifferent to him. But when she felt she might be cheated, her obstinacy not to let that happen would grow stronger.

It was one year since Kanchi's death. Lakkoo's resolve of having a firm hold on Manjayya grew. If it was formalised living together, it was okay. If not, he was not going to sleep with any other either. An obstinacy developed in her that either he must come to her home bravely or she should go to his home openly. She wanted to tell Manjayya her decision. But she could not meet him at all. He was always away in Channarayapattana, Hassan, Tiptur or somewhere else. When she asked Puttellayya, he questioned Lakkoo herself, 'Who knows, when will he come, where he goes ... Am I his master?' She tried hard to forget him thinking he was a dog going round villages, why should she insist on getting him and tying him to herself only. But sometimes suddenly she would get the courage and compulsion. She thought what did that fellow know about Lakkoo? She wanted to make him realise what stuff she was.

One evening it was already dark. Lakkoo closed the door of her shop, drew the bar and was securing it with the large padlock. The last bus from Channarayapattana stopped in the bus stand in front of her shop. After the passengers got down, six passengers waiting there got on the bus and it went away. Among the passengers who got down, a girl was coming on that side, holding a bag in her hand. Immediately Lakkoo knew it was Latha. She felt happy seeing her daughter. At the same time she was surprised for Latha had come all of a sudden. She asked, 'Have you got holidays Latha?' Latha said 'Yes' but Lakkoo saw the girl looked dull and pale. Even while they were walking, Latha lagged behind with bowed head, as if nobody should see her face. She was not matching her steps with that of her mother. Lakkoo wondered why and thought, perhaps Latha was feeling shy as she had come from the city to the village. Yet she had her doubts and thought were not girls from Hassan more courageous? By the time they reached home, Rudra was preparing to milk the buffaloes. Lakkoo had ordered him not to milk the buffaloes until she returned from the shop. After the milking was over, she would measure it and mix the amount of water needed, fill it in a big carrier with a measuring vessel and send it to the regular customers. After finishing all this, Lakkoo came in, but Latha still stood leaning on the wall. She had not even sat down, nor had she lifted her neck. The mother cajoled her and asked, 'Why are you standing like this, child.' But Latha did not speak. Lakkoo went near her daughter, put her left hand on Latha's shoulder, raised her daughter's chin with her right hand and saw her daughter's eyes were brimming. Again Lakkoo urged, 'Tell me avva, what happened,' but Latha did not speak. Then, she loosened herself from her mother's hold, said, 'I will tell you later,' and went into the bathroom. Lakkoo entered the kitchen. Though her daughter ate ragi-balls and rotis in her aunt's house daily in Hassan, Lakkoo did not want to serve her daughter the ragi-balls she had cooked in the afternoon, and kept rice on the boil. After freshening up, Latha, instead of coming near her mother, climbed the ladder and sat on the loft where the copra was spread out to dry. Rudra brought back the carrier after the distribution of milk. He put fodder and water for the buffaloes and went out after listening to the daily statement from his employer, 'Come early tomorrow. Don't say – I slept, and could not wake up early.' Then Lakkoo closed the door, climbed two steps of the ladder and called, 'Come down, Lathakka,' held her daughter's hand and pulled her down. There was no light on the loft. The bulb was burning in the hall downstairs. When the daughter was climbing down slowly, the mother held the ladder lest the ladder slip. Rice was boiling on the stove. When her daughter got down, Lakkoo held her daughter's hand, sat her on the mat, hugged her shoulders and pleaded, 'Please tell me my dear, why are you afraid to tell me?'

When her mother gently stroked Latha's head, she felt like crying again. But she decided to convey what she had to, controlled herself, looking at mother's face, she begged for assurance and said, 'Amma, you should not beat me, really Amma, I've not committed any mistake.'

'No, no dear, have I ever done that, beat you? You tell me what happened.' The mother's anxiety was rising.

Latha said, 'I have not got my periods.'

'Why did you do this? Who is that rascal?' Lakkoo held the face of her daughter and staring at her eyes shouted.

The daughter's eyes were fixed on the gaze of the mother. 'It's Manjayyaru. He said, he would marry me, made me believe him.'

'What! Did he seduce you too, telling that and making you believe it?! He is dodging me since a year telling me either he would marry me or he would start living together with me.' Though Lakkoo bit her tongue she could not take back the words or tear away her eyes from her daughter's eyes. The daughter could not understand at first. When she opened her mouth and said, 'Amma,' as though her jaws had locked, her mouth stood wide open and so were her eyes.

The rice cooking inside was burnt black. The fire in the oven died down. The eyes that were fixed on each other's eyes remained in the same position for some time. Filthy, disgustful shame erupted from inside both and spread like poison. They felt it was impossible for both of them to see each other in that birth. The daughter hung down her head, raised her knees and put her face between them. The mother as if blinded with shame got up and switched off the light. In that unbroken darkness, they could hide from each other. Whenever the daughter came home, the mother used to make her sleep in her own bed; but now both of them began to feel, forget sharing the bed, sharing the same house, or even the same world was disgusting and unthinkable. The mother, weary and sorrowful, laid down on the floor beside the wall. The daughter who had buried her head between her knees, slumped down on the mat. Latha had come there in the hope of confessing it all to her mother. She had imagined burying her face in her mother's lap, recounting all that happened to her, how she believed Manjayya ... But now, all such thought vanished. Looking at her mother' face brought a disgust akin to that while chancing to look at shit. Same was the case with Lakkoo. Without her being aware, her mouth on its own spoke out about Manjayya and herself sleeping together and made her worse than shit.

When she turned back, she felt sick and wanted to sob, to cry her heart out.

But if she cried, her daughter would know that her mother was there, so Lakkoo controlled her sobs with despair. The daughter felt like retching loud. But if she did that her mother would know that the daughter existed. So she controlled her vomiting with distress. The mother wanted to stretch her hands and legs. But, she folded them even closer, for if she stretched and they touched the daughter, she would become polluted by her mother's impurity. The daughter wanted to turn sides. She was afraid that the fire of disgust would erupt by the accidental touch. The whole night was suspended in the silence of darkness, a silence in which neither experienced even the rhythm of their breathing. Nothing was either heard by the ears or seen by the eyes.

Manjayya exulted for two days in the feeling of triumphing over Savitri yet again. Then, the same boredom set in. After winning over, what should he do? A thought flashed: it would be really fruitful if he could keep Savitri, who was defeated, in subjugation forever. But, subjugating her forever meant, he too should be in her control always. If not, would she comply? This contrary thought caused him to think that once was enough for the present. He was satisfied that he had taught her a lesson. She who had not cared a bit for him and thought of living independently. Along with it he felt proud, more so, for making her understand. Manjayya was a real man, better than that Mattikere fellow. He thought, did that Mattikere fellow have the courage to sport with her? If these thoughts were pestering him, along with these, Sarojakshi's memory began haunting him a hundred times more. That harlot would be further emboldened if she had booked the Deputy Chief himself. Manjayya felt the challenge rising in him that he should go another day, hold her and overpower her as he had done with Savitri. But, she would be very careful, as soon as she would see him, for he had already tried once and she would be prepared. Moreover an experienced woman would be quicker. When this thought came to mind, he would get discouraged. As such Manjayya was wandering around in Bilikere, Hassan and

Channarayapattana as if lost. Recently he would always be either in the Traveller's Bungalow of Channarayapattana or on the streets. He felt it difficult to stay at home in Bilikere as earlier and he felt bored. Meanwhile he heard of the death of the warehouse owner Nagappa of Tiptur. Immediately he thought of doing some mischief, interfering in the business of late Nagappa. He returned to Bilikere, took out the agreement of contract deed he had made with Nagappa, read it correctly and rushed to Tiptur. He showed it to lawyer Gurushanthappa and filed an objection. Manjayya had made an agreement with late Nagappa. He would supply to Nagappa's warehouse ten lakh copras every year. Nagappa should give Manjayya one anna per rupee in the total profit. It was the agreement. So Manjayya held that he had partnership in the warehouse. Now Manjayya claimed that the warehouse must be handed over to him. He asked the lawyer to file a suit to that effect. Gurushanthappa said, 'There is no point in this to win the case.' But Manjayya insisted, 'You see lawyer sahib, winning is not merely by the strength of law, but from the weakness of the opponent. Please understand this. If the son-in-law did not even touch the six and a half lakhs of his father-in-law's money and burnt it to ashes, he will never step in there. So there will be no claimant. Holding this one link and pulling it tightly, why not make this business come to me?' Manjayya challenged the lawyer, put a packet of notes on the table and the lawyer took Manjayya's signature on the petition. Manjayya thought that he would often be coming to Tiptur and could call Lakkoo also to come there and if he could get hold of the warehouse he could search in Tiptur, Turuvekere, Chikkanayakanahalli and other taluks. He felt excited and happy. But the whole thing turned completely against him though it was not totally unexpected. Nagappa's daughter and grandson demanded the authority of the warehouse transaction. The court immediately awarded an interim decision, granting the ownership of the warehouse to late Nagappa's daughter and grandson but recognised Manjayya's objections for consideration at a later date. It also observed that the agreement between the petitioner and the warehouse owner was only a contract on the basis of commission and not a contract of partnership. Even if it is thought as a contract of partnership, the petitioner has only the commission of one anna. Naturally, the daughter and grandson will have the portion of fifteen annas. As such, complete authority over the business is handed over to them immediately. If it was not decided swiftly, the clients will go away, the warehouse will have to be closed and there will be complete loss. So this has been decreed. The merits of Manjayya's petition would be enquired by the same court in course of time and decision will be given.' Manjayya got into the bus to Channarayapattana.

Manjayya's mind was again enveloped by boredom. He thought he should not have gone to court when a plan did flash but it was too late: he should have told Sukanya and Ganesha that he had an agreement with him made by late Nagappa. If he went to court, the decision would be in his favour. He should have threatened them and said they did not have experience in business. He would help them in warehouse business and should have entered into the business cunningly. He felt sad. But he knew Sukanya would never have believed him. What would be Sukanya's mind towards him? He felt listless thinking, why should he join with her? After all did she possess any beauty!

Manjayya thought, of late, his luck was on the wane. He was not successful in any of his ventures. While thinking thus, he felt somehow, if he once won over that Sarojakshi, his planets might turn for the better. But what should he do for that? Thinking about this, Manjayya stayed in Channarayapattana. He knew Appajappa had reported for duty in Nelamangala. Sarojakshi was staying with her children in Channarayapattana. For how long was she going to stay here? Manjayya thought, why shouldn't he take fruits and flowers and speak courteously with her and look for an opportune moment? It was already evening. He decided to execute his plan the next day and went for a walk in the street. He had only walked the distance of a furlong from the circle. By then a boy came from behind and asked, 'Are you Bilikere Manjayya?' Manjayya turned back. The boy said, 'Dr Hasheem is calling you.' Manjayya thought there must be something concerned with some patient who was known to him. When he went to Dr Hasheem's clinic, it was full of patients. Looking at him, the doctor said, 'Manjayya. I'm very busy right now. Will you please come by nine? I've something to speak to you about.' He then went behind the curtain where he examined the patients. Manjayya went out wondering what might be the matter.

Manjayya finished his meals in a hotel, went to Dr Hasheem's clinic at nine. There were no patients. The doctor said, 'I saw you walking in the street. At once I remembered and sent word with the boy. Please sit down. How is your health?' After Manjayya sat there, the doctor directly spoke to him. 'You know, that madam here is your wife. I did not know at all. It seems it is already seventeen years since you left her. She is a very decent and respectable lady. That day, when she was alone, you went and raped her. You may argue in court that as she is your wife, it cannot be considered a rape. When there is no relation for seventeen years, all of a sudden you go to her, while she is alone and forcefully had satisfied your desire and say it is not rape, whatever definition you give, court will sentence you. Do you know the law?'

Manjayya was rendered speechless by these words which were suddenly thrown at his face. When he was still recovering, the doctor continued, 'You see, though the law is in such a way, which respectable woman goes to court? This lady too won't go to court. But four or five days after you raped her, that lady came to me.

She asked me, with an enormous feeling of shame, whether she had contracted the disease, because her husband had touched her and told me what you did. However, there was no symptom of the disease. Yet as a precaution I gave her six injections. You see, what should be the value and dignity of the husband if the wife would be afraid she would be infected with disease if her husband sleeps with her?' The doctor looked at Manjayya's face. He seemed tongue-tied, the words corked from within. As if he did not notice it, the doctor continued to complete what he had to say.

'You see Manjayya, your story does not end there. You raped her that day, you know, now she is pregnant. Thirty-five years old, husband has deserted her and there is no one to take care of her. She works and earns her livelihood. If a woman could get a child, will she say she doesn't want it? But if she accepts that child, it would be as good as accepting relationship with him who begot it. So, to get rid of even his memory, that woman decided to terminate her pregnancy and came to me. I said, I don't do that and asked her to go to a nursing home in a big city and gave her the address. You see, if a wife decides to do away with the child for it reminds her of her husband, what sort of a man he must be? Think about it. It is too much and you have gone too far Manjayya ...' The doctor grew silent.

Manjayya felt someone had slapped him hard. Till now, nobody had told him this, that too, to his face. But as Hasheem was a doctor, he could not deny the facts. Though, at once he thought of defending himself by saying, that he was separated from Savitri because of her impertinence, he could not speak.

After a little while, the doctor spoke. 'You see Manjayya, I am a doctor. It is my duty to treat a patient with respect, talking with them happily and not scolding whatever sort of disease they are affected with. I treat the patients not taking extra profit, even if they are V.D. patients. It is reported, you say Dr Hasheem is just a

V.D. doctor. But you understand this Manjappa. Just because I treat this adultery disease also with a sense of duty, don't think that I approve of adultery.'

Manjayya felt reproached by the last words of the doctor. But no answer came to his mind. Moreover, he was cautious not to contradict or antagonise this doctor who could cure all V.D. diseases so easily. The doctor looked at his watch and said, 'Now it is time for me to go home. I've some work,' and got up. Manjayya felt relieved. He wished the doctor good night and came out.

While walking towards the Traveller's Bungalow, Manjayya blamed the doctor in his mind. 'Oh, this bastard preached me so much for I called him a V.D. doctor. His name is as such, who doesn't know it is his specialty? Everybody calls him by this name only. I too might have called him so. But which bastard might have carried my words to him?' Manjayya engaged his mind in this enquiry. But when he lied down alone in the Traveller's Bungalow, the decision of Savitri to terminate her pregnancy caused by him began to churn in his mind. Till now Manjayya had never thought about children and such things. Even now it did not bring sorrow to him, nor did it bother him that the child that would have been his was destroyed while it was still germinating. Fact was many women who had slept with him became pregnant, whether it was through him, or some other, there was no dearth of women who put the onus on him and said, 'It is yours.' That meant the responsibility and expense of terminating that was his. Besides, it made him proud also. Without neglecting their demand he had helped them for termination of pregnancy. That too was easy. Maniambal of Hassan was a trustworthy lady doctor. Fee also was fixed. She would never ask any objectionable question about, why, what, where, who, what is your name, etc. She was a strong and competent doctor who had achieved dexterity by experience and would finish off the job in two minutes and send away patients.

That Dr Hasheem told about a nursing home. Where might he have sent her? His mind was as if struck, when he reflected upon the possibility of Savitri still not going to the nursing home. His mind began turning and turning around Savitri's decision of terminating the child that reminded her of his relation and his character. That slut had disdained him. She had considered him a worthless fellow to be remembered. Not only she, all people of her family were so. It flashed across Manjayya's mind, as wind blows on fire. They won't talk. Mere silence. The sort of silence which stated clearly there is no relationship between you and me. Her father also lived so and her brother too. It seems he won't talk at all. When Manjayya remembered all this, he realised he did not win at all and felt that his thought that he had triumphed was a total lie. He could not sleep for a long time. A feeling of defeat, a sense of biting dust, haunted him. He tried to get rid of it, tried to motivate himself, to regain his arrogance.

Thinking this Manjayya is not a male if he is defeated, a sinking feeling consumed him. Somehow he was asleep by dawn.

When he woke up at about nine in the morning, he did not feel like getting up from bed. A sort of listlessness filled his mind. What was the point of getting up? He pondered: a pregnant wife should in all fairness come to her husband, must request him, instead, if she decides on her own .... what impertinence, arrogance it was! Or was it a lie that she had become pregnant due to him? Did she tell my name, impregnated by that Mattikere fellow? For, there was a husband, called Manjayya. He tried to ease his mind thinking that married women had this safety and security net. But this thought made his pride sink further, to the very depths and he discarded that idea with deliberate effort. It was true he had slept with her at that time. Moreover, didn't that Naagi tell? What could that worthless Mattikere fellow do? This ready confirmation followed. Has she already gone and terminated it?

How many days ago did she go to Hasheem? He too had not asked the detail. Even now if he went there, and she had not removed it – yes, not removed it .... His thought did not continue and got stuck there. If she said directly to his face, 'Yes, this child reminds me of you. I don't want to have that memory.' Then? Why did he go seeking her that morning? What beauty was she after all? That insolent slut! She was an old hag of thirty-five. Women are young and sappy only within thirty. Manjayya thought, hereafter he must make it a rule that he won't even touch a woman who had crossed thirty. He felt it was right. Another favourable idea too flashed from his decision. By this, he might be free from being haunted by that woman Sarojakshi. Yes, what might be her age? Thirty, thirty-one, thirty-two. Anyway if a woman reached thirty she is an old hag. So Sarojakshi is disqualified. When he thought so, he felt like getting up, washing his face and ordering coffee. But by the time he finished his coffee, he felt deflated.

It was fifteen days since he met the doctor. Manjayya couldn't be interested in anything. He could not get rid of the feeling that Savitri and Sarojakshi had defeated him. He decided to stay quietly in Bilikere, not bothering about all these, but within two days he felt bored. He went to Hassan to attend to some urgent work. But he did not meet with success in that work either. He thought, it would be alright within eight days, when he would come there again, and came to Channarayapattana. What could he do there? Oh! how many months, since he saw Kanthamani? He thought of going to her. But somehow he didn't want to either. He finished his lunch, went to the Traveller's Bungalow and lied down. He had a nap. By the time he woke up, his mind was filled with thoughts about Ramakrishna. Lawyer Gurushanthappa in Tiptur had said that the whole of Tiptur knew about how he burnt to ashes six and half lakh rupees of his father-in-law with the corpse. What did he achieve by burning money? Money exists only to buy pleasure. That Nagappa did not have the liberality of giving money and buying pleasure. All his business was stranded in simply hoarding money. At least if this son-in-law had spent it and visited Bombay and Bangalore ....

Oh, what kind of girls he could have enjoyed! What an amount of money! He could have enjoyed until he became old. Interest of that amount was enough, he could have used it and saved the principal amount also. He could have offered *tilodaka* to the *preta* of his father-in-law with faith and devotion, sitting on a cot in a prostitute's house and said, 'Look here, maava, you did not make your son-in-law happy when you were living. You too did not enjoy life. Look here, now I am enjoying, making up for both of us.' Imagining this, Manjayya uttered a guffaw. His mind felt comforted. He thought, 'I should have been the son-in-law of Nagappa. Oh, what a pity! What pleasure might that Nagappa's daughter have got by marrying such a boring Ramakrishna! This silence, this sanyasa, this foolishness of burning bundles of notes will only be in men who do not have enough sap in their organ. Manjayya began pitying Sukanya imagining she was suffering inside from hunger. But Manjayya's mind again turned towards Ramakrishna. He began to reflect, 'How can a person who fails to understand the simple truth that money exists only for exchanging, understand Vedanta.'

Likewise, Manjayya felt real sympathy for Ramakrishna who was rejected by his wife. Along with this, he felt pity for Sukanya also, for she left for her father's place thinking she could not have 'that' from husband, at least let this money, property be with her. Meanwhile somebody called out – 'Manjayya Sahib.' He got up and opened the door. Lo! there was Usmani. Looking at him, Manjayya got zealous. Usmani was a good talker, besides he would have got some interesting news also. Usmani was in haste. He had come without locking his bicycle, left outside. Usmani offered respects to Manjayya and said, 'Sahib, after you left there is no pleasure or lustre in the department. Now I'll make a move. Have to see the Ranger. The present Ranger Munirangappa is a very strict man. I came here to give you a message. I met that woman, your friend Appajappa's wife. She said that there are three vessels with you, which belonged to her. She asked me to inform you to return them. The Ranger in Nelamangala has not yet vacated the quarters. So, this woman is staying here, so that there would be no disturbance in her children's education. She told me: "Tell Manjayya to come home." Usmani winked knowingly.

'What? Usmani are you joking,' Manjayya said.

'No, no sahib. I swear on my mother. You see sahib, what happened, happened, why should friendship be cut off? Now, though her husband is transferred, even now I send firewood freely to her house. In the same way, why shouldn't you go to her house?' He said gravely and swiftly rode away on his bicycle.

Immediately Manjayya was afire. Oh, she has sent word that I had three vessels that belonged to her. He decided to go there and have a look. He got up at once, washed his face, combed his hair, wore pressed clothes and rode on the bicycle. It was four in the afternoon. Sarojakshi was reading a book sitting in the hall. When there was a shadow near the door, she turned to that side. Her face blossomed with excitement and she did not know what to speak. Her face seemed wrung with uncertainty and shyness. For a minute both of them did not know what to speak.

Then she said, 'You have left your bicycle in the sun, bring it inside or the wheels will be deflated.' He looked at her face. 'Yes, I am telling you only,' she said.

'I have to go back.'

'If you had to go back, why did you come here? Now, do as I tell you.'

Manjayya brought his bicycle inside, put it behind the door. She brought water for him to drink and asked, 'What would you like for snacks?'

'No, I don't want anything. I've just had my tiffin ...'

'Okay then, you will have your dinner here, I'll prepare your favourite dish. Tell me what do you prefer?' He again looked at her face. 'Why do you look at my face? How many days it is since I cooked for you. You stay the night here. I won't let you go, even if you want to.' Sarojakshi laughed freely. Manjayya felt emboldened and said, 'Oh, if it is so, I won't go.'

But, he did not speak anything further. Nothing struck her either. Sarojakshi went inside and returned after five minutes and asked, 'You always brought flowers and fruits when you visited us. How is it that you have come empty-handed today?' A frown creased his forehead at the lapse. Manjayya lowered his eyes. She went near him, held his face in her hands, raised it and said, 'Look here, you should not have the feeling that you have committed any wrong. Of course, what was it you did? You asked for love, when you did not get it, it is natural for men like you to get angry. I hope, by now you have understood that it was really good that Appajappa was not allowed to stand in the witness box. You did all that to teach me a lesson for I did not reciprocate your love. But the only mistake was, sitting on your anger for such a long time. Didn't you understand, when I sent word with Appajappa, that you yourself should come to sell the jewels? I thought Manjayya was very intelligent. If I had known you to be such a dullard, all this would not have happened. Tell me, why didn't you come? Why didn't you come until I sent a message through Usmani?'

'You see, that Ningappa provoked farmers, cooked up a case against me and caused the farmers to commit perjury. I am not bothered or feel sorry for losing that contract. I need not depend on it for my living. But I am really sorry, that you have misunderstood me. It was true that I got angry with you. I did slap you that day but I felt very sad afterwards. I too understood the risk of making Appajappa a witness. Complaint against Appajappa was not instigated by me. You must believe me,' he said and held her hand.

Sarojakshi too held his hand with the same tightness and stood silent for a minute. He was still not looking directly at her face. She said, 'You spoke with me that day informally. Do you remember? I do remember it very well. But why did you start speaking again in formal plural with me today?' Manjayya's face lit up a bit. Sarojakshi spoke, 'Of late, whenever I remember you, I imagine as if I am talking to you. Then, I think about you and talk about you in the singular. Not with any sort of disrespect. It comes to me naturally. Look here, when we are together, we must speak with each other in the singular only. If spoken in plural, it seems there is some distance between us. As per custom, a man must be elder to a woman. But friendship increases when we behave as if of equal age. So, it feels good to me when I talk to you in the singular. And you too should speak to me only thus.'

By then, the children had returned from school. Hearing the sound of their coming Sarojakshi, moved away five or six steps from Manjayya, came near the door and welcomed Vaijayanti with a voice full of affection. 'Ah, here comes my little one!' and patted Shashikanta's shoulder lovingly. The children came inside and were surprised to see Manjayya. There was a faded memory in their mind. It was after a long time this uncle had come. They went inside. Sarojakshi followed them and gave them snacks, came out and sat in the chair before him. Manjayya did not know what to talk. Sarojakshi recalled, she alone had been talking till then. But now she too could not think of a topic. When Shashikanta came out after eating the snacks, Sarojakshi called him and said, 'Shashi dear, will you bring a kilo of meat? Uncle has come today, let us cook a special dish for him.'

'Oh no, Amma. I have to go out and play!'

She cajoled her son, 'No dear, please bring it for me and then go and play. Don't you want pulao too?' and went in, brought the money and gave it to the boy. Vaijayanti went to the neighbouring house to play.

Sarojakshi was cooking inside. The children were playing on the street with other children. Manjayya sat alone in the chair in the hall. His mind was filled with the memory of the touch of her hand. She was the only one ... there was none to compare with her and she herself had asked him to stay the night there. This assurance filled his mind. His shyness lessened. Darkness was setting in. She came out, switched on the light and went inside. The children came inside, sat reading, doing their homework, near the pillar in the hall where Manjayya sat. He was looking at the children. The boy was handsome and that little girl was as charming and sweet as a girl he had seen in a film. The aroma of cooking permeated the whole house. Manjayya felt 'Santosh Restaurant' was useless before this. After some time Sarojakshi called the children into the kitchen and served them. Then brought him food on a silver plate and put it on the teapoy. She too took her meals sitting in front of him. She went in, put the children to bed, came out and said, 'Come on, come and sleep.' He looked at her face. She said quite naturally, 'Your bed is ready.' He got up and went inside. She closed the front door, bolted it, switched off the light and followed him. The children slept in one of the rooms. In the other one there was a large double bed, made of wood from the Forest Department with a comfortable mattress on it. A double sized mosquito curtain was strung across it. Everything was spick and span. There was a plate with folded betel leaves beside the cot. She closed the door of the children's room, came into Manjayya's room and closed the door of that room also and asked, 'Do you sleep wearing your shirt and coat?' He took off his coat and shirt, she hung them on the hanger, held his hand and took him inside the mosquito curtain, joined the edges of the curtain under the bed, rested her head on his lap, hugged him and said, 'See, that day you slapped me and went away. Was it possible to hit like that without any authority? It was so with me too. I too slapped you. Did you think I slapped you without having any authority? Realise this now. Your authority lies in me and mine in you. Do you know how much I remember you and yearn for you? Now tell me, why didn't you come?'

He bent down and embraced her but was tongue-tied. She cajoled him, 'Hey, why my Manju, speak, speak my lord.' He got excited. Immediately she said, 'Tut-Tut, you are a naughty boy, your mind at once flows towards that, when I want us to talk hugging each other. You must answer all my questions. I'll answer whatever you ask me. Come on, give me your hand,' she put her right hand in his right hand, squeezed and said, 'I promise you. You should not lie to me, I will not lie to you. That day, you remember? I had asked you how many women you had hunted?' I did not intend either to taunt you or blame you. Yes it was out of appreciation that my Manju was a real man, without that virility, no one could have hunted so many. Suddenly you flew into a rage and questioned me, "With how many did you sleep? Who fathered both your children?" You see, I am not angry for what you asked, but for the manner in which you did. Do you understand? You must say "Yes" if you do. It is not possible even to tell stories to children if there is no response. Without your response, is it possible to open my heart so as to pour it all into your heart? Come on, say "Yes." She looked at his face. Manjayya said, 'Yes, tell me.' 'No, not like that, it is not enough, you must say, "Hey you ought to tell me. I must hear. If you don't, I'll kick you, break your bones." Say so, will you say it or not?' She forced him.

He too got into the mood, 'Hey tell me, if not, I will break your bones.'

'If so, look here, there is no secret between you and me. You see, till now I've not mouthed to anyone what I have done. This is the first time. I will tell you. Later you must tell me your story. Do you ever realise, how much trust it needs if a woman decides to tell whatever she has done with another man? You must have known after having experience of so many women. My neighbours are aware of your coming here today, keeping your bicycle inside and staying here this night. Perhaps they know who you are and also what your reputation is. Many people know of your visits to that Kanthamani's house. Even so, if I have asked you to stay the night here and have kept you in my house courageously, tell me, from where did the courage arise? Tell me from where?'

'From love,' he said and kissed her for the first time.

'No, it is not possible from mere love. It is possible from trust. There is no meaning in love without complete mutual trust. You understand this. Come, let's talk together lying down, there should be nothing between us, no, not even clothes.' She herself took off all his clothes. Lying naked, he was embarrassed, his face was pale. She said, 'Hey, you are an old tiger who has bared hundreds of women and have yourself been naked before them. Why should you feel embarrassed in such a way? If you feel ashamed to be naked alone you take off my clothes too.' But he did not put his hands on her clothes. 'Aha, how shy is my little one!' She came near, kissed him, stripped herself naked and said, 'Did you see? You and I should always be like this, forever and ever, until our death. Come on lie down,' she said and pushed him down on the bed, hugged him tightly and said: 'This light pierces the eyes, doesn't it? I'll put it off, wait,' she pressed the bed switch and caused the room to go dark. He felt more comfortable. Then she spoke. 'Look here, I'll first confide my part of the story. Except Appajappa, I've experience of only two other men. Appajappa however, is my husband, so leave him out.' She slowly narrated the episodes regarding Lakkappa and Subbayya. She explained her meeting with Subbayya concerning her husband's suspension and told the intention of Subbayya in transferring Appajappa to Nelamangala. She further explained: 'I am not certain if Shashikanta is Appajappa's or Lakkappa's. But even before Vaijayanti was born I knew for sure she was Subbayya's and I had told him also. But, while speaking with me this time, it seemed he did not even remember it. Is it not enough for a woman to feel contempt against such a man? Would I have asked him to shoulder her responsibility? Or would I have demanded money or clothes for her from him? What could you call it, if you could not remember at all to ask whether it was a boy or a girl, what name did you choose, won't you show me – if all these never flash across your mind, what should you call it? Tell me what should you call it?' Sarojakshi stopped speaking. There was complete silence. For ten minutes she was on her own in that silent darkness, then suddenly she hugged him, held him tightly and resumed her narration. 'You see Manju, except these two I have not known any other man. Until I saw you, I did not have the concept of a real man in my mind. As soon as I saw you, my mind felt, yes he is a true man, pure male, do you know what eagerness I felt? To be with you, be with you forever. Oh. You do not have any dearth of women. There are hundreds. But you took so many days to become accessible to Sarojakshi. Now, tell me, what did you do all these days? Tell me everything. You must tell me honestly. I swear on myself. I told you all this, trusting that you will not judge me with any moral scale, just like that, I also do not weigh you with any scale. I am not interested in the details of hundred women. Of course, what is there in details? But why did you do all this? What started it all and when had these happened? What did you search for in those women? Did you see something new in me, something different? Yes, truth, you must tell me the truth only. Do you know why am I demanding it so forcefully? This evening you said it was Ningappa who instigated the farmers and made them commit perjury. I know it is a lie. You too know it. But why did you say so? What would I have done if you had openly said: "Yes, I wanted to teach you a lesson, so I did it! I would have appreciated your courage and accepted it. I would have surrendered to you. You need not tell that also. You have seen so many women, slept with so many. What didn't you get in them, which you saw in this Saroja? Tell me honestly from the beginning, I would like to hear.'

Manjayya reflected within himself. Yes, why was he going with so many women? What did he seek in each of them? As this Saroja asked, what specialty did he find in Saroja? Her questions began to prick his mind in the shape of a trident. But the answer eluded him. Saroja who had lied down quietly for long in the darkness said, 'You need not tell me now itself. Tell me tomorrow, the day after tomorrow, or at night, the day after, or any other day. There is no compulsion for you to leave for your place. There are Puttellayya and Puradamma, who look after your house and lands. There is a problem which I have to tell you. I am not telling this to put you in a dilemma. It is a fact.' She pressed her naked body to his, hugged as if she was squeezing him, kissed him deeply and said, 'Do you believe me? There is no moral or any binding on you. I'll tell you what my problem is: I'll shift to Nelamangala. Subbayya comes there. He asks me to go to Bangalore. Surely he will ask me to. He expects me to meet him in Bangalore. He is not to be blamed. When we were so friendly for three years, a sort of authority on each other developed. Could I go to him and ask him to revoke the suspension of my husband without that authority? If he was not there and there was another officer, could I have had the courage to meet him? He calls me to Bangalore. What should I do? Making my mind firm if I request him not to force me, he is not such a wicked person as to harm my husband. I am sure of it. But I need to rely on a man, the support of a man. My husband

Appajappa, six foot tall, holding a gun, can give me security in the wild forest. But he cannot emotionally support me. As such it is not possible for me to refuse Subbayya's friendship. But my mind is occupied by you. For me you are the man, the only man.' She came upon him, kissed him hard, brought her lips to his ears and breathed. 'Oh Manju, do you know what I feel? Why should I lie to Appajappa? He hears neither truth nor lies. Yet, living on his food, calling myself his wife, loving another person, why should I lead a life of falsehood? I'll come to your place, I'll cook for you, wash your clothes and in this way, did you understand 'in this way' means how? I will stay there serving you. I swear on you. But no other woman should enter the house I live. You call any woman you want to your hut in the grove. You may have any number of women you want in Hassan, Channarayapattana or in any other place. Why should I restrict a man who has the strength to reign. I will never feel jealous in this matter nor will I quarrel. You see, a woman like me will never feel as much of jealousy, suspiciousness, sense of sin or crime as that of a woman who stays in the restraint of a family, in the binding of a chaste woman. Coming to the responsibility of my children, it is I who gave birth to them. Appajappa is their legal father, isn't he? He manages their expenses. Do you know how much he has depended on me because I am with him and support him? I am bringing up my children with his salary. After I leave him and live with you, why should I raise my children with his earnings? I won't put the burden on you either. Ten years back I got a considerable amount from my grandmother's side. I invested it in the bank under a compound interest scheme. Now it has come to three times the original value. I'll get yearly interest enough for my children's maintenance and education. No, I won't put even an iota of burden on you. It is enough for me if you and I are together. You for me and I for you.' She said, spread the total weight of her naked body on him, lied down so as it should be comfortable. She did not talk again. He was listening silently. She felt tired of speaking continuously. She just closed her eyes and felt drowsy. Five or six minutes later, when she woke up, she said, 'Tut-tut, what a stupid woman I am. Desiring both of us to be happy, spreading a bed here, oh desire of such a long time. I spoke everything in one breath. What would I have lost, if I had spoken tomorrow? That's why it is said, women are not intelligent. Manju, my dear Manju, really you must scold me. You must say, "You stupid woman. I'll kick you and break your bones" and you must kick me too. Come Manju, come my lord,' she said and embraced him. As if she poured out all her emotion, she kissed him on the forehead, eyes, lips, chest, neck, navel and all other parts of his body. She made her touch as provocative as her imagination decreed. But Manjayya stiffened as though he was caught in frost. She called out, 'Manju, Manju,' many times, breathed warmth into him, gave him the heat of her body, but Manju did not melt. 'Why?' She put her lips into his ears and asked. He did not answer. After a little while, she said, 'Don't get upset Manju. If the mood does not cooperate, it is not possible for men. I understand. The mistake is mine,' she rolled over on to her side and lied down silently.

Again ten minutes passed. Then she said, 'Shashikanta usually wakes up once during the night and goes to the toilet. He may wake up, switch on the light and may come in search of me. I'll go and sleep in that room. You too get some sleep. Let's talk tomorrow after the children leave for school.' She got up and switched on the light. He felt terribly ashamed, pulled the blanket that was near his legs on his body. She wore all her clothes in an orderly manner, tucked the edge of mosquito curtain under the bed and went away. Sarojakshi opened the door of the other room and lied down with Vaijayanti, but could not get sleep. After a little while, Shashikanta woke up. She took him to the bathroom, returned and went to bed. Even after a long time, she did not get sleep. There was silence outside. There was silence inside the house too. The children were fast asleep. She heard the rustling sound of the bed from the room where Manjayya slept. She thought Manjayya was tossing and turning. She thought of getting up and going to that room, but felt a shrinking feeling within her. There was a suspicion in her that he won't open up like herself. While she was ruminating she heard the sound of the front door bolt being pulled. Immediately she got up, came to the hall and switched on the light. Manjayya was dressed up, was opening the door noiselessly. She felt a tremendous anger. But not showing even a trace of it, she smiled and whispered, lest the children heard, 'Hey why Manju, why are you sneaking out like this? Come here.' She bolted the door, switched off the light, held his hand, pulled him again in the darkness to the room with that big cot, where they had lied down. He followed her helplessly. As earlier she made him sit on the cot, stripped off his clothes in the darkness, pushed him down on to the cot, stripped herself, embraced him and asked, 'You see, I said whatever I had to. Now, you say whatever you want to, why are you so silent?'

Manjayya was silent. She held his face with both her hands, shook and asked, 'Manju, you must talk, the children will not wake up until daybreak, even if you light an atom-bomb-rocket. Do not get anxious. Please speak out your mind. Yes speak up. I do not insist that you accept whatever I asked. But I asked you only to make our relationship clear to ourselves. That is all. You see, you may guess why Subbayya has transferred Appajappa to Nelamangala. There are umpteen regular buses and city buses from there to Bangalore. It will be near and it is easy for me travelling to and fro from Nelamangala to Bangalore. But he is not a wicked man. He is not a person to harm my husband if I do not agree to his plan. Continuously for three years, he was very friendly with me. Besides he has given me such a lovely child as

Vaijayanti. Yet my mind is fixed on you. I feel disgust to sleep with him. It is more than a year since you hit me and went away. You might have forgotten. But I remember the name of the day, date and month also. It is said that a woman's memory is more precise in such matters. My Manju, this hand ...' she said, groped for his right hand, brought it to her lips, pressed it ten times to her lips so that the hand should become wet and said, 'which other hand has the authority to hit me except this hand? Hey hit me again, my little one. At least for fun hit me again,' she said, held his hand; struck herself on her cheek with it. He was as stiff as a rubber doll. She pulled him near and said, 'Let that be, you see I won't be a burden on you. I stayed here only with the purpose of meeting you. Appajappa will not compel me to shift to Nelamangala if I say it will be convenient here for the children to go to school or any such reason. Everything is as per my wish. I am the master here. If you feel any day, I am a burden to you, I'll write a letter to Appajappa to shift me to Nelamangala. Before that, one word, Manju. If you say "yes" I'll tell you. Say "yes." You must say "yes." If not see here,' she gently slapped his cheek and kissed it. He said 'Yes' in a feeble voice as if it was coming out of a cave. 'I feel shy to express it. But you are man enough to understand,' she said and laid her head on his chest. Manjayya was silent. 'You stupid Manju, should I tell you this also? Do you know how deep is my love for you? I don't know how it is with you. But I could not live even for an hour without remembering you. Within a month I am leaving for Nelamangala. I want to get a child from you within that period – as handsome and naughty as you. Give me such a son that when he grows up and attains youth, all women who look at him should melt down and fall for him. It is enough for me.' She held him tightly with her hands and legs and said, 'Manju, that's enough for me. Do you know, the symbol of love for woman is a child, like the man she loves. But not so with men. There is no such bondage for them.' She was aroused and began provoking him. But he was still passive and motionless. His spirit had dried up and sunk into the bottom of an abyss. For a long time, she had hugged him in the same manner. But gradually her power of stimulation came down. Suddenly she began sobbing convulsively. Tears filled her eyes, began to flow down on his shoulder and on to the pillow. He did not know whether he should console her. She herself moved away from him, put her face on the pillow, cried and cried as if it came pressing from inside her whole body. Then not caring for the sound, she opened her mouth and cried loudly eight or ten times as if it came coiling from inside. Then she became silent and grew calmer. She kept lying down for a while. Silence, complete silence. Manjayya it seemed had carried such silence which did not allow even the sound of breathing to come out. Some time passed. Sarojakshi suddenly put on the bed switch. A dazzling light that could blind the eyes spread across the room. Along with that light there was that piercing light of her eyes, teeth and earrings. Manjayya closed his eyes. He felt shy and pulled on him the blanket near his legs. Sarojakshi pulled away that blanket and threw it down from the edge of the mosquito curtain. She too sat completely naked on the edge of the cot and said, 'Men who do not possess virility brag more about their power. It is such kind of people who concoct stories about their power and spread them. Nature and looks deceive. From the day I saw you, my mind lied to me, created a delusion in me that you were really a manly man. Now, I am thoroughly disillusioned. Actually your wife must have left you because you do not have manliness, because you are impotent. As she happens to be a decent woman, she might not have mouthed it to anyone. Let that go. Get up, dress yourself, take your bicycle and get out. I don't want this relationship of deceit.' She took her clothes which she had thrown down the cot and went away into the room where the children were sleeping.

Manjayya was lying down as if he had no strength even to get up. He felt as if his whole body was paralysed. Every organ of his body, his hands feet, arms and thighs, had lost their power to follow his will. His mind had become a sunken heap like a thin sheet of paper drenched in water. He had not faced such a situation in his entire life. He continued to lie down. The light was burning. After a little while he suddenly got scared: if she comes again into this room! His nervous system was stimulated by fear. Suddenly he got up. He picked up his clothes from the floor, wore them swiftly, came into the hall and switched on the light. Within half a minute, he pulled the bolt, put on his chappals and pushed out his bicycle. He was afraid to look back, for she might have come and stood there. He forgot even to close the door. He mounted the bicycle and began pedalling furiously as though his strength, suspended till then, had all of a sudden bounced back.

One day at ten in the morning Lakkoo strode down the street and boarded the bus which stood before her shop and shouted as if she was ordering, 'Hey driver, start moving. Don't delay, make it fast.' Not only the driver and the conductor even the passengers in the bus were frightened. In her left fist she had clutched something like squeezed flesh and the blood stain on it was getting black. None could know what it was. The sickle in her right hand also was blood stained. Drops of blood were splashed on the pleats of her sari and were drying up. Many passengers in the bus were from Bilikere. Two of them asked, 'Oh Lakkoo, what is it?' 'Hey, who are you to ask me for explanation? Hey, you driver, take the bus directly to Channarayapattana police station and stop before it. If you turn it this side or that, I'll chop off your head with this sickle, look,' she said and raised the sickle. But she did not loosen her left fist. Whoever looked at her face thought Lakkoo had probably gone mad. The driver understood that she had committed some bloody deed and boarded the bus immediately. In such a situation, however, it was his duty to inform the police. Now she herself was demanding that he take the bus to the police station. So the driver hinted this to the conductor also, drove the bus directly to Channarayapattana without stopping for anybody to get down, or allowing anybody to get into the bus. All the passengers inside the bus were looking at each other, fear and anxiety writ large on all faces.

As soon as the bus stopped before the police station, Lakkoo got down with that thing in her left fist and the sickle in her right hand and rushed into the station. The constable at the door wanted to stop her and said: 'Hey, who are you? Stop, wait here.' But Lakkoo rushed inside shouting, 'Hey, go and call that inspector soon. I have not come here to wait. I've come to report.' Inspector Narayana Murthy stood up immediately as soon as he saw her. Lakkoo put the thing she had clutched in her left hand and the sickle in her right hand on the table and said, 'Hey, you Narayana Murthy, I've heard you are a strict man. I've not come here to utter any lies. First see this and understand what it is.' She said and sat on the chair as if she was his equal. The inspector bent down and peered at it closely. Oh, what Lakkoo had cut off and brought here, was the penis of a man. As she had held it compressed in her hand, blood had flown out from the cut part, hence its diminished size and distorted shape. Only from its front part was it possible to identify it. He looked at Lakkoo's face and recognised her. He clearly remembered that she was the same woman who one year back was a prosecution witness in the murder of her husband and in the witness box had cheated him, saved Manjayya and forced the judge to pass a stricture on him. He knew from the secret report of the police department about the relationship between Manjayya and her, her shop and all other details.

Narayana Murthy asked, 'Hey woman, whose is this? Why did you cut it off and bring it here?'

'You see inspector, this Lakkoo won't tell lies. It is, however, true that I once told a lie. Now you must take down whatever I say exactly, word for word, as I say it. If I ever have an evasive tongue or double-talk, not the judge or you, but I myself, look here,' she took up the sickle from the table, stretched out her tongue, enacted as if she would cut it off and said. 'I'll cut off my tongue. Hereafter, there will be only one word I speak and that is the truth. Pick up a sheet of paper and sit down. If not, I won't start.'

The inspector picked up a pen and a sheet of paper and began taking down her statement. 'That is Manjayya's. Thinking that he possesses a magic wand, if he puts it into both a mother and her daughter, what else should the mother do? So, I cut it off and brought it here.'

'That means he trapped you and had an affair with you and then, without your knowledge he seduced your daughter as well. And you came to know about this. Right?'

'Oh, really you are a clever one,' Lakkoo said and narrated, what came to her mind at that time. The relationship between Manjayya and herself and how he made her daughter believe him, seduced her and the result of his lust on her daughter.

The inspector took notes of what she said and asked her, 'Well, you see, Manjayya was such a strong man. When you held him and cut it in this manner, did he keep quiet? Did he not attack you? How did you cut it? Tell me in detail as it happened, step by step.'

Lakkoo began her narration. 'Today morning Manjayya was going to his grove. These days he doesn't stay for long in the village. It seems he came back yesterday evening. I saw him from my shop. I closed my shop, followed him and called 'Ayyare.' He stopped and asked, 'What's it Lakkoo?' I said, 'How could you forget the wife you have chosen to live together?' and smiled as if to show I was in heat. Then he said 'Come on, let us go to Tiptur.' I hung my head and said coyly, 'Instead of eating while hungry, should I wait until we reach Tiptur?' and then added, 'Anyway you're going to the grove, let me also come there. Somehow, he hesitated. He was never a bull that hesitated, when a cow came near. But I did not leave, I followed him, opened the grove gate and said, 'You go into the hut at once. If we are outside, someone from the nearby groves may see us.' He came along. I took him inside the hut. In the middle of the hut there is a stone pillar. I made him stand there, with his back to the pillar. Without any shyness, I embraced him, kissed him and pressed myself to him lustfully. I intoxicated him. I had pressed him to the pillar and hugged him tightly. You understand this inspector. I had thought it out and planned that I should act this way. And it happened so. I swiftly came behind the pillar. Even before he knew what was happening I pulled both his hands towards the pillar from behind. They were twisted near the shoulder. He shouted 'ayyayyappa' because of pain. I swiftly pulled off his dhoti and with one edge of the dhoti I tied both his hands tightly behind. With the other edge I tied his legs to the pillar. When I pulled his dhoti, his sickle fell down from his waist. This is his sickle. I knew he would take it with him, when he went to his grove. By chance if he had not brought it, see here ...' she said, pulled out a knife from her small pouch containing betel leaves, nuts, tobacco powder and lime and said, 'I would have cut it off with this. I had decided to cut off his penis. Hey, inspector you take down as I said. This Lakkoo does not say lies.'

The inspector asked, 'Did you cut it off at once?'

Lakkoo exclaimed, 'What are you saying? Do you think a judge awards punishment without trial and without making the criminal realise his offence? I told Manjayya, "You desired me, had relations with me and then you had relations with my daughter also. Is it right? Is it just? What should become of my daughter who is now pregnant because of you?" I cross-questioned him in every way possible and finally pronounced the judgement, 'You see, this is the punishment I award you. You are playing a double game with this magic wand you have, you now suffer the punishment.' After reading out the sentence of court, I held it in my left hand in this manner and cut it off, while he was crying, shouting, 'Oh Lakkamma, Lakkoo, don't do it, please don't. I swear on you. I fall at your feet, don't do it.' Then at that moment I had not thought of coming to the police station. Only after the job of cutting off was over, it flashed to me that such matters must be informed to the police. I felt, I was not a whore telling lies and moving stealthily like that Manjayya. So I clutched this in my left fist, held the sickle in my right hand and came running. The bus stood there before my shop. I got in, told the driver to take the bus straight to Channarayapattana police station and came here.'

The inspector asked, 'Okay, did you untie the dhoti with which you had tied him before you started from there?'

'Am I not saying that I came running as soon as I cut it off?' Lakkoo, weary of repeating the same thing, shouted angrily.

The inspector asked, 'Didn't you know that he would die there, if you do not untie the knots? Blood would flow continuously, if it was not stopped and proper medicines were not given.'

'Is that so?' Lakkoo opened her mouth wide and sat with mixed feelings of fear, surprise and anxiety.

The inspector immediately got up, ordered the constable. 'Get the jeep ready. We have to pick up the government doctor on our way and go to Bilikere. Lakkamma, get up. You too should come.' Two constables came running, held her arms and tried to take her towards the jeep. Lakkoo wrenched herself away forcibly from their grip and shouted, 'You sons of bitches, leave me alone. What am I, a thief running away, to hold me?' The inspector told the constables to let go of her. They left her hand. She got into the jeep and sat in the rear seat. Two constables along with another two sat beside her. All the passengers of the bus still stood there. The government doctor sat beside the inspector in the front, the pharmacist with his kit sat with Lakkoo and the other constables and the jeep rushed towards Bilikere. After crossing over the first canal, the jeep stopped at the main gate of Manjayya's grove. After Lakkoo got down, keeping her in front, all of them moved inside the grove. Lakkoo first entered the hut. The door was wide open. Soon she clapped and shouted, 'Oh God, oh Shiva, he is dead, ha, ha, ha, he is dead. Oh, so many crows, so stout, how could they see what was inside the hut? Yes that Yamadharma would have sent them. "You go, there is a corpse in such a hut. Go, bite it and eat,"' when she was speaking, all of them entered the hut and what they saw was gruesome. The corpse of Manjayya tied to the pillar was sunk and dangling. Blood had flowed down from the cut on to the rustling reed mat, had leaked on to the ground and had turned black. Crows were competing with each other at pecking the same spot and digging deep. But they had not touched their beak to any other part of the body.

The inspector thought of driving away the crows first. He said, 'Everybody come inside the hut through the door, stand in a corner, clap together and shout 'ha, ha, ha.' The crows flew out unwillingly. But they waited outside under the coconut trees. As soon as they saw the situation, they all understood that the doctor had no need to open his medicine kit. Yet they had to conduct a post-mortem of the body and write a report. They cut the dhoti with which the corpse was tied and brought it outside the hut. The doctor from Channarayapattana said, 'There is a government doctor in this place. Post-mortem comes under his jurisdiction. I came with you thinking, if at all there was life, let me treat him with first aid and immediately carry him to Channarayapattana. Then the inspector sent the constables along with the jeep to bring the Bilikere doctor, Patel and four important people of the village to be witness to the *Mahajar* and the relatives of the dead, if there were any. Till then nobody knew this news in the village. The whole village began gathering in the grove. Narayana Murthy was a person who acted swiftly. He quickly thought to whom should he hand over the corpse, as soon as the doctor began to cut the corpse. As he knew the background of Manjayya, he asked the villagers gathered there, 'To whom does the funeral rites belong? Or tell me who is going to perform it. You see, every corpse, whichever it may be – must get funeral rites performed according to its caste and custom.'

No one came forward. Then the inspector said: 'Is there nobody in this village related to the dead person or belonging to his caste? If nobody performs these rites, we police will burn the body. But first it should be recorded, that though it was enquired whether there were any relatives, nobody came forward to perform the funeral rites.'

When the inspector uttered these words, Patel Channegowda came forward and said, 'You see Inspector Sahib, there is one person who is a relative, Manjayya's brother-in-law Ramakrishnayya.'

'Manjayya married Ramakrishnayya's sister, but she left her husband due to his unfaithfulness. It is already seventeen or more years since she left him. Besides, to save Manjayya from going into jail, Ramakrishnayya's father went to give evidence in favour of Manjayya, repented for committing perjury and committed suicide. If things are so, will Ramakrishnayya come and perform funeral rites to such a relative? You do as per your rules and finish the job soon. We will put our signatures on the record.'

The inspector said, 'You fetch Ramakrishnayya here, in whatever way possible.' Then, the Patel went to the village by jeep.

By the time the doctor finished post-mortem and wrote the report, the jeep came back with Ramakrishnayya. Patel had told him everything. The Patel made his way among the crowd and took Ramakrishnayya to the inspector. The Inspector asked, 'Is this dead man related to you?' Ramakrishnayya did not reply. Patel had informed him what had happened here. Looking at his face, anybody could have told that a terrible conflict was going on inside him. It seemed his face was subduing emotions like anger, rage, disdain and disgust. The inspector again asked the same question, then Ramakrishnayya said as if he had come to a decision, 'Even if not related, any corpse even of a scoundrel or an outcaste should not be left without funeral rites. I will perform the funeral rites. Tell me what should I write and sign.' He turned towards the gathering, looked at everybody and at last identified the village priest Devarayya *Jois* went to him, took out money from his pocket, counted fifty rupees, held it before the *jois* and said, 'Take this. Quickly go to the village and somehow arrange for things needed and bring them here. As the body has undergone post-mortem and has become a lump, we need not build funeral bier for it and carry this bundle of flesh to the cremation ground behind the village tank. Anyway it is his grove. There is a pond also so there is water facility as well. Let us finish the rites here. In the backyard of my house, there are two big blocks of wood. But now there is no time to split it. Please ask, whether anybody may spare firewood from their house.' *Jois* took the money and went away. Puttellayya who stood there said, 'There is ample dry firewood, coconut shells and coconut fronds in the backyard of my master's house.' Ramakrishnayya said, 'If so run, put it in a cart and bring it here, run.' Puttelayya rushed out.

After completing his work, the inspector looked around and asked the constable who was near, 'Where is the accused women?' He said, 'She is sleeping in the hut sir. Two PCs are guarding over her.' The inspector went inside the hut and saw that Lakkoo had lied down on her back and was fast asleep on the rustling-reed mat. She was snoring loudly. Blood that poured down from the spot of Manjayya's penis was blackened and spread near Lakkoo's head. Without bothering about what was happening outside, she was sleeping in unperturbed calmness. The inspector asked, 'Since how long is she sleeping?' One of the constables said, 'A minute after the corpse was taken out, she said, 'I feel like sleeping. Don't make a noise,' and lied down. Soon she was asleep and began snoring. We are doing our duty of guarding as you had ordered us not to hold her by force.'

The inspector said, 'Now wake her up. Let her sleep inside the jeep.'

With great difficulty they managed to wake her up. At last she woke up and walked with the constables. The eyes of all the villagers gathered there were fixed on Lakkoo. But she was oblivious to their presence. She walked ten steps and called, 'Look here Narayana Murthy inspector.' The inspector came near her. She pointed to a coconut tree on her right and said, 'You see Manjayya had dragged the corpse of my husband beneath this very tree and put a stone under its head. I had given false witness that my husband slipped from the tree, fell and died. Do you remember? It is the same tree. That night I was at home. I had not gone to Tiptur or paptur or anywhere.' She then closed her eyes after cursing the constables: 'These have woken me up, while I was sleeping. Beat them with chappals.' She walked behind them with closed eyes, boarded the jeep, lay down on the long seat and was soon asleep. The inspector said, 'Do not wake her up. All of you somehow adjust and sit on the floor of the jeep' and the PCs somehow adjusted. None of the people gathered in the grove left that place. *Jois*, Puttellayya and others brought quickly whatever was needed. But it was difficult to protect the corpse, which was cut, from crows. Six people stood around shouting 'ha ha ha' and beating sticks.

Some of the youths gathered around were ridiculing and making fun about the cutting off of Manjayya's organ. Ramakrishnayya turned to them and shouted angrily, 'Are you not ashamed to speak like this? Do you know, the sin committed by a person settles in the mouth of the one who gossips about it?' All of them fell silent. In the presence of Bilikere villagers, Ramakrishnayya tonsured his head and lit the funeral pyre of Manjayya. When the fire began to burn, the crows flew away.

When the Patel called Ramakrishnayya, he was preparing to go to Channarayapattana. He had finished bathing, cooking and was just about to finish his meals. If the Patel was late by fifteen minutes, he could not have met Ramakrishnayya. He did not know at all about Manjayya's fate nor did he know that the whole village had gathered in his grove. Though the neighbours came to know about this incident and the men and children had gone to the grove, not able to suppress their curiosity, none had come and informed Ramakrishnayya. The elders had no mind to inform him on their own, for he did not show any interest in anything and never talked at all. Besides, he had suffered so much injustice at the hands of Manjayya. Moreover, people began to be afraid of him, when it was known to them through Tiptur people – though he had not told about it himself – that he had burnt to ashes, six and a half lakhs rupees of his father-in-law along with his corpse, that his wife and son had left him and had gone on to become owners of the huge property in Tiptur. Some people spread the rumour that he was a terribly angry man. Some whispered that he had gone mad. As such, his communication with people, which was very little earlier, had now completely stopped. He would go around his lands, cook his food once in a day and eat it twice. He would engage himself in reading books. After he finished them once, he would immerse himself in them a second time and lead the life of an introvert. Savitri came twice, stayed four days and went away. Even when she was there, he was a silent person.

Ramakrishnayya finished the funeral rites, came home, locked, gave the keys to Honna and went to Channarayapattana by the last bus. By the time he reached, the whole of Channarayapattana knew about Bilikere Manjayya's death, rather the manner in which his death occurred. When Savitri returned from school, Nanjappa's wife, of the main house had come to her house and gave her the news. Subbannayya's daughter Meenakshi had informed Savitri that after Manjayya was acquitted, relationship between Lakkoo and Manjayya had developed. Savitri too felt – if this scoundrel, having slept with the mother, bewitched her daughter also and seduced her, how else could the mother assuage the rage in her heart? Savitri's mind sunk down to the depths of despair. She had completely distanced herself from him. Yet a serious question filled her mind, 'Why had he become so?' She lay down on the mat not having any mood to cook food for the night. By then her brother came. When he took out the cap, she was surprised to see his head newly tonsured. 'Why, what happened? Why have you tonsured your head?'

'Manjayya died. As there was no successor to light the funeral fire, I lit it.' Ramakrishnayya did not elaborate further, but just leaned on the wall and sat down. After a little while, he said, 'See, however much wretched he might have been ... You take a bath. I will go to Paschimavahini, perform the rites from the ninth day and release his *preta* so that it easily reaches the next stage of the journey.'

Immediately an angry question arose in Savitri's mind: all along his life, that fellow had caused so much of distress and injustice to this family. Why should her Annayya perform all these rites for such a wicked man. But she knew, what her brother would say if she openly put this question to him. He would say, 'As there was no other heir, I did it.' It was so even with Nagappa of Tiptur. It is not known whether he felt disdain towards Nagappa. Perhaps not. About Manjayya, perhaps he did not feel anger. As such she understood that whatever she would speak, he would keep quiet and she went to take bath. After she bathed, patted her hair dry and came out, he said, 'According to pure orthodoxy, you have more defilement resulting from his death, than I have. So for ten days, I should not eat any food prepared by you. You may say, what belief is there in purity or impurity, after so much has happened. While

I have decided to perform his funeral rites and other rituals and ceremonies, why should this one be transgressed? While I believe in performing *Shraaddha* of my father, how can I say I don't believe in the ceremony of these people? So I'll go into the kitchen and cook. You stay here.'

She did not contradict him, not wishing to have any argument. Ramakrishnayya set the cooker for rice and sambar, lighted the stove and put the cooker on it with Savitri's guidance, sat near the door of the kitchen and said, 'You see Savitri, I had intended to go to Tiptur. Before that I wanted to speak with you also. The matter is this; Ganesha has become adept in warehouse business. It seems he is shrewder than his grandfather in deciding how much stock he should buy here and where and when he should send to Bombay, Kanpur, Delhi and other places. He has already earned one and half lakh rupees. It is said that there is no other merchant in Tiptur who runs his warehouse so intelligently, that too at such a young age. But, Ganesha has already started to keep the company of bad women. There is one woman he is going out with, the wife of the railway-wagon clerk Nallathambi and the other two are college girls. Sukanya came to Bilikere and said, 'Your son is going astray. Being his father, you should come and advise him. If you too come to Tiptur and stay there in that house, he will be afraid of doing such things. But I did not reply. She stayed for two days and returned. Now, except silk saris, she does not wear anything else. She will always be bejewelled. That is her pleasure. The day before yesterday, the warehouse clerk Nanjappayya came. Sukanya herself sent him. It seems Ganesha's amorous activities have increased. While studying in Hassan also he had such activities on a smaller scale. But now, when he possesses huge amounts of money, how to stop him? Many fathers of brides are asking for alliance. If we select a beautiful girl and arrange his marriage, he may come back to the right path. But if the father doesn't stay with them, how can the mother herself speak with the bride's people? Sukanya had asked, "Is it not your duty to help your son to be settled in family life – *gruhasthaashrama*?" Savitri, I being his father have a mind to complete this duty. But, do people who are once addicted to this, ever give it up even after marriage? I've my doubts. Is it fair to make someone's daughter a guinea-pig in our effort to try and reform him?? So, I have thought of going there and talking with Ganesha face to face. People with this habit tell lies very smartly. I feel, any personal or face to face talks will be one-sided. I started to come here to consult you on what could be done and then leave for Tiptur. But now, until the rites of Manjayya are over, I won't go.'

Savitri felt a deep despair gripping her when she learnt about the conduct of Ganesha. She was saddened by the thought: Oh, has another Manjayya been born in their family? She began cursing herself, thinking that this boy had been spending the money she gave him with affection for this purpose. Going with women? After some time her annayya ruminated, as if he explained the essence of desire, 'Kama, is the root, the source – it may take the form of property or manifest itself in the form of desire for the opposite sex. One complements the other.' Though Savitri could understand the background of the principle her brother was explaining, she could not grasp its depth in its entirety. Her mind was busy comparing Ganesha with Manjayya.

By that time, Mattikere bhaava came. Savitri understood as soon as she saw him that he had come after he got her letter. Satyappa's coming was a surprise to Ramakrishnayya. The cooker whistled its readiness. Ramakrishnayya enquired about Satyappa's welfare, went into the kitchen to cook some extra rice for the guest. Savitri asked Satyappa, 'Have you heard the news?'

'Yes, people were talking about it in the bus. I went to the police station to see and speak with Lakkoo. But they said, I could not see her without the permission of the inspector and was told if I come tomorrow at eight in the morning, I could get permission. A constable who was outside explained everything.' Savitri asked, 'Did you know Lakkoo?'

'No, I did not. But a woman in extreme rage has done this. Let us not discuss whether what she did was right or wrong. But who will assist her when she is in police custody? Who is the lawyer? How can she defend herself? I felt like helping her in whatever way possible. So I went there.'

Savitri was sad. See, her mind did not think the way her bhaava's mind worked. Ramakrishnayya sat still. After the rice was cooked, he served both of them and he too finished his meals. Satyappa washed the pots and pans and cleaned the kitchen, although Ramakrishnayya tried to dissuade him. These two lied down in the courtyard and Savitri in the room. Satyappa said, 'You see Ramakrishnayya, if you help Lakkoo, it doesn't mean you approve or defend her killing of Manjayya. See, you belong to the same village while I am a stranger. Please come with me tomorrow morning. Let us hear first, what happened. Besides we must enquire where that pregnant girl is. What is her psychological condition? What will her fate be? We must try and do something for her.'

These words of Satyappa instantly touched Savitri's heart.

Ramakrishnayya too felt that it was right. The next morning by eight, when these three went to the police station, the inspector permitted them to meet Lakkoo. Lakkoo was brought out from the room where she was imprisoned and they arranged a separate room to meet her. There were two benches in that room. Lakkoo sat on one bench and opposite her sat these three. The inspector ordered the constables not to stay there, sent them out and closed the door of the room from outside. But he sat eavesdropping outside the window. His plan was to collect information that could help in investigation by observing whether there was uniformity between Lakkoo's statement yesterday and what she would tell these people today. Would she speak of any new matter or will these people reveal something that would help the investigation?

As soon as she saw Savitri, Lakkoo herself began speaking, 'Oh, what's it avva? Did you think of me as your *co-wife*? But I tell you the truth. Listen, I was jealous looking at you and thinking you were my rival. I really wondered why does Manjayya love me, leaving such a beautiful wife. I believed in the beginning – what he told me – you did not do any farm work, that's why he left you. However, I thought to myself, being the wife of a man with so much of lands, why should she work in the fields.' Looking at Lakkoo, they could understand that she was in an abnormal state of mind.

Then Satyappa asked, 'Lakkamma, please tell us, how did your relation with Manjayya start? What happened in between? How and why did you cut off his organ? What else did you two talk before you chopped it off ? Please tell me everything because I must find out the truth. We want you to be acquitted. So I will go to Hassan and engage a good lawyer to handle your case. You need not worry about money however much it is going to cost.'

'Hey, why or what lawyer do I need? Lawyer is needed for liars. Manjayya needed a lawyer because he was a liar. You see, even if you engage a lawyer, I'll speak only the truth. I will say to the judge, 'Yes your honour, I held it like this and cut it off. You know, no lawyer can make me tell lies.' Lakkoo laughed loudly.

Satyappa said, 'Well tell us how did all this happen. Now did you have your breakfast?'

'Yes, you know, this Narayana Murthy is a real gentleman born to his father. He saw to it that I had my dinner last night. Now there was idli, dosa and coffee for breakfast. Yes I am full.' And Lakkoo began her narration: Kanchi trespassing into Manjayya's grove, stealing bunches of coconuts, Manjayya's coming to her house, his innuendoes and double entendres, then she herself sending Kanchi to Manjayya's grove and every other detail. The inspector who hid himself near the window outside learnt more details than the previous day. But there was no material difference between what she said yesterday and what she was narrating now. Lakkoo was reporting in such a way that it seemed difficult to ascertain whether she was narrating the events to those three or telling them to herself. Once in the middle of her reporting she said, 'You see Avva, your appa committed suicide by hanging, for he spoke only one lie with his tongue. If so, how many times should this Lakkoo be hanged? I'll say to that judge, "hey you record it thus."' Then she resumed her narration. She did not chop off his *capital* immediately. She first tied Manjayya to the pillar in that hut. She asked him, 'Whether you marry me, make me your wife or not, it is immaterial. But after you slept with me, how could your mind agree to sleep with my daughter also?' When I asked him whether it was right and just, he said, 'I swear on you Lakkoo, really I'll marry her. Please leave me,' I said, 'You wretch, what dharma is it to marry the daughter after sleeping with her mother?' Do you know what he said? 'Do you know dharma better than Parameshwarayya?' I said, 'Why do you drag his name here? He is a godly man.' 'Yes, that's why, just as he agreed, you also agree.' I asked, 'To what did he agree?' Manjayya said, 'You see, I had slept with Parameshwarayya's wife Janakamma. Then she was thirty-five and I was twenty-two. Nobody had an inkling of this. One day Parameshwarayya himself entered from the back door and saw us. I did not stay there a second and ran away. Afterwards that woman fell down into the deep water near the camel rock of the village tank. She did not slip and die. She was terribly scared of her husband and died. Nobody knows about this, but Parameshwarayya knew this. Even then, did he not marry off his daughter to me? If it is was not dharma, would he have done so? Like him you too marry off your daughter to me. All my property will be possessed by the child born to her. He swore on God. But do I trust him? I said, 'Hey, Manjayya, Parameshwarayya's dharma is his own. My dharma is mine,' and held it in my hand and cut it off. From there I myself came to this Channarayapattana police station ...' she continued.

Though the three of them at once felt in their minds that Manjayya was a liar, he could create any lie convenient for him in any context, after a minute, the minds of Ramakrishnayya and Savitri recollected the manner of their mother's death. When Amma died she was thirty-five, Ramakrishnayya was a nineteen year old youth studying in Hassan. Everybody said that Amma had gone on the camel-rock to wash clothes, slipped, fell down into deep water and died. That month, after her periods, it was said, mother had gone to bathe there. But that time after her periods, she stayed for seven days in a separate room and father was cooking food. Would anybody after periods sit for seven days in impurity without taking bath? And would any woman who wants to bathe go to that camel-rock, around which waters were eighteen feet deep? These questions began rising in Ramakrishnayya's mind. He pondered. Appa and Amma loved each other. Yet after her death, Appa did not speak even a single word about her. Before that, Appa was not so silent. After that incident, he became a total introvert. Manjayya had started philandering from his seventeenth or eighteenth year itself. When Amma died Manjayya was twenty-two. These details came to Ramakrishnayya's mind and began to take form. Savitri's memory too went into the dim corridors of the past; and she vaguely remembered: I was still a five year old girl. As soon as the day broke, I would run out either to Subbannayya's house or to the enclosing wall of Gangadhareshwara temple. Amma always scolded me – your feet will never stay at home.

Manjayya used to come to our house now and then and would talk with Amma affectionately. He was nearly of Annayya's age. Several days before Amma's death, if he came, he would come by three in the afternoon. Appa would have gone to the grove after his lunch. Seethakka's school would be over by five. I was staying at home. Amma would remind me of playing and would say, 'Look here. Rangamani and Sharada are playing in the enclosure of the temple. You too go and play.' She would give copra pieces and jaggery, send me away and I would rush out dancing. Only from this much, could one believe what Lakkoo told now? After mother's death, Manjayya did not step into our house. We were not grown up enough to question why. My vague guess is that, perhaps, Appa must have prohibited him from coming to our house, for Manjayya had already gone astray and the grownup girl Seetha would be alone at home. But how can I believe with only this much, what Lakkoo says. By then Savitri remembered how her appa who had never raised his hand to beat a cattle, oh with what cruelty he kicked her, when she insisted, she would marry only Manjayya! She thought, only for the reason that his daughter insisted on marrying a profligate, a person like her appa would lose all his restraint and culture and repeatedly kick his daughter so cruelly. Really Appa had completely lost his self-control. When Savitri remembered all these incidents, she felt she was swooning. She looked at her annayya's face. At once she knew that though he sat silent, he was boiling inside. Savitri collapsed on the bench. If her brother had not held her immediately, she would have fallen on the floor and got hurt. Ramakrishnayya got up and made her lie down on the bench. Satyappa got up and began fanning her with his towel. But Lakkoo went on speaking as if she did not notice anything.

'Yes, my daughter erred. It was the age and she committed a mistake. After such an error, it is natural that she is ashamed to show her face to her mother. I also committed wrong. It was my age that caused me to. But after committing such a wrong, I feel ashamed to show my face to my daughter. You see, if it is known that both of them had committed this offence with the same man, can the mother and daughter see each other's face? But she did not know about my relation and I was not aware about hers. But, knowing fully well that he was playing this game with both mother and daughter, should not he be sent to Yamadharmaraya for trial? Oh, Lakkoo will not see her daughter's face in this life. I'll fold my hands and request the judge, 'Listen to me honourable judge. Give me the punishment of hanging or put me in jail until death. But do not acquit me and give me the punishment of looking at my child's face.'

Savitri regained consciousness. Her annayya held her hand, helped her get up and took her out of that room. Satyappa remained with Lakkoo. When she came out and stood in the sun, Savitri felt that she had come into this day-to-day world. But all buildings, trees, roads which were familiar to her were looking as if they were painted with the colour black. Her annayya's words, 'Come, let's go home,' seemed to her like an order. If not, she would not have known what to do. She followed him. After they reached home, he leaned on the wall and sat in the courtyard. Savitri went inside her room and lied down. A feeling of entering into a cave enveloped her. A sense of terrible shame that she had not suffered ever, at any situation, began wringing her insides. She felt the strong support she possessed till now had sunk from beneath her feet and vanished and she had fallen into an abyss. Although she thought of blaming her mother, 'That woman called Amma ruined my life,' Savitri could not give form to those words clearly in her mind.

By then Annayya came and sat near the door of that room. His face was grave and hard, more serious than it had ever been.

A sort of obstinacy and hardness had turned his face into stone. Yet in a lowered voice he asked, 'You see Savitri, it was not the age for you to understand anything. It is said that Amma sat seven days in the room where she used to sit during her periods. Moreover, which woman will go to camel-rock, to wash herself after her periods? And after her death, Appa did not talk about her one single day. Before that, he was not so reticent. After this he became totally silent. These are the factors I remember. Do you have any other memories?'

Savitri felt as if three stone blocks fell on the head of a person who was already at the bottom of a well. She looked at her brother piteously as if she was pleading with him not to speak about anything. But he was expecting some aspects of her memory and was looking at her face. Her face was swollen as if from the rage boiling within her. After a little while, she said, 'You see Annayya, let us not test or analyse any more. Do you know how much strength the character and conduct of a mother gives to her daughters? Oh, I will never get the strength to stand straight hereafter.' She pulled the sheet around, covered herself and lied down.

Ramakrishnayya sat silent. He was now confident that nothing was left to probe or to make certain asking anybody, even Savitri. He felt there was silence inside his mind. Suddenly he felt, the only wise way left to him was to be totally silent. For a long time, he sat there. He knew, Savitri too had lied down silently. It was impossible for her also to get sleep. So he got up noiselessly, gently, closed the door and walked out. Stepping on the dusty road, he crossed the border of the weekly market place and began walking on the tank bund. Three-fourth of Channarayapattana tank was full of water and the waves were lapping about noisily. This tank, this water were both similar to that of Bilikere. But here, neither was there the camel-rock, nor such deep water as around the camel-rock. These similarities and contrasts came to his mind. Then he began to think about his appa and meaning of silence of his appa flashed across his mind. Did he become silent? Or did he become still? Yes, it was true he became still. Passive. What happened was not known to anyone. He did not tell anybody. Oh, how much he might have boiled with agony within? His silence was not born out of peace. With this understanding, Ramakrishnayya stood in the sun imagining the turmoil his father suffered in his heart since thirty years until he committed suicide. Waves of reddish water of the tank were forcefully dashing, dashing and dancing in vain in their effort to get rid of their unrest and discontent. Ramakrishnayya felt his appa too might have been continuously dashing inside himself and breaking. When Savitri insisted on marrying only Manjayya, he kicked her, for the unbearable agony and pain inside expressed itself as anger, but why didn't he reveal the truth at least then. If only Appa had said this, Savitri's infatuation would have been burnt, destroyed. Why didn't he tell me at least calling me separately? Was it generosity of protecting the honour of the dead? Or not to hurt the feelings of the surviving? If he had confided with anyone, his burning, that turmoil inside him would have been cooled. Oh Appa, Appa, why didn't you tell the truth? What was the reason for keeping it trapped within you? Ramakrishnayya stood there gazing at the blue sky. In the vast blue expanse, agony, pain and grief were burning in noiseless silence. In that burning desolate altitude, he spotted some birds. When he concentrated his sight, was it a crow? While he was looking, crowing 'ka, ka' two or three crows attracted his attention. They were flying over his head. Ramakrishnayya had tonsured just yesterday and the bald head was burning in the hot sun. Attracted perhaps by the red wound caused by the barber's razor, those crows were waiting to peck at his head. He had not brought even a towel to cover that wound. Ramakrishnayya said to himself, 'Appa, it is already one year since you committed suicide. Can't you come at least in the form of *preta* and inform why you hid the fact from me and Savitri?' He spoke the same words again and again. The top of his bald head and the wound were burning. Feeling it was impossible not to cover the wound, he took off the shirt and covered his head. His mind flew towards Manjayya. He remembered that this cruel irony of fate was not known to him the previous day, when he decided on his own, to tonsure his head and perform funeral rites of Manjayya as he had no one to perform it. He performed it with detachment, without weighing sins and merits of the dead person however vile that person might be. But now even those rites began to seem hollow and meaningless. While the corpse of Manjayya was burning, the *Jois* Puttabhatta said to Subbannayya who stood beside, 'You see, they are brothers-in-law, it is just like the relation between brothers. He has the duty to perform and so he is doing.' These words reached Ramakrishnayya's ears. Now, he remembered it and the meaninglessness of his deed increased still more, when he could see another dimension of his deed ... In people's view, any type of detachment will still be glued with relationship.

Ramakrishnayya stood in the sun for a while. He thought of bathing in that cool water. He had not brought even a towel with him. Doesn't matter, he could sit in the warm sun to dry himself. He took off his dhoti and shirt, stepped into the water in his under-pants, and plunged. Then came up and sat on a rock nearby. Looking at the spread of water, he felt like swimming. He loved swimming very much. Somehow, of late, he did not go swimming in the Bilikere village tank. Oh, what an elevated feeling he used to get, when he stepped into water where there was no noise of people washing clothes and then swimming noiselessly and lie floating on his back! He brooded, why did he give it up? When he sent Ganesha to study in his grandfather's house agreeing to that woman's stubbornness, no, no, there was no connection between that and this. He felt it was his own mistake. For a while, his mind thought about those incidents. Then he came out of the water, arranged his dhoti and shirt, put a stone on them so that they should not fly away in the wind, then plunged into the water again and began swimming. He felt tired, until he swam for a little distance. Then he began floating on his back. He was delighted as if he had entered a different world. All of a sudden, a similarity between his father and himself flashed to him – if his wife had not drowned in the water and died, would Appa have accepted her? Would he have lived with her? With these inquisitive questions, answers too flashed: no, she herself released Appa, in a way she pitied him. He felt it strange thinking so. But a correction followed: She did not die with an intention of releasing her husband. And this Sukanya also, he thought, by going to Tiptur had released him, he felt this was also true. But the question began haunting him: did Appa really get his freedom by his wife's death? Did I get freedom by Sukanya's going to Tiptur?

When he moved far away from the bank and reached the inner part of the tank, the dashing of waves lessened and floating was easy. Waves were not hitting the eyes and nose. He could have maintained balance even if he lied down motionless and would not have drowned. While he was staring at the sun beyond the sky with his open eyes, he remembered: this was the second day and tomorrow there was the rites of collecting the ashes of Manjayya. Along with this memory, he felt such a disgust as if he had touched shit. But he began to control his mind. Did he not suppress his disdain and perform funeral ceremonies of the Tiptur merchant? He found a way in this precedent. But an objection stood that these two were different relationships. He thought, what we call relationship is either absurd or a lie. If I had realised this, I would not have performed the funeral rites of Manjayya. Then a question stood out in his mind: but after doing that, how could he back out or retreat from performing the subsequent ceremonies? While he was floating, unable to decide anything, suddenly his mother's memory floated in his mind. It was the memory of thirty years back and the picture was faded and drenched in that span of time. Instead of mother, Savitri's face and eyes, which were like that of her mother, came before his mind. He was in a state of mind that could understand nothing. Why was she so adamant to marry that Manjayya? Why did Appa beat Savitri so as to cripple her? Perhaps mother's blood or mind found a canal to flow. Savitri's picture came before his eyes. At once he felt like reaching the bank, rushing home and kicking Savitri, breaking her bones so that she should die. Thinking so he began kicking the water continuously and drifted away floating. As he kicked the water so swiftly as if he had become mad, his legs started aching. When he changed into standing posture and looked yet how far away the bank was, he realised that he had swum in the opposite direction and the Tank Bund was still far away. He was ashamed to have swum in the water without any aim. To give the legs some rest, he turned and floated on his back. By then he had already swum beyond the centre of the tank and the waves were almost nil. Everywhere there was silence. There was balance in the swimming too. After the throbbing of blood in his body decreased, he felt peace inside and outside. After a long time another thought came to mind. He said to himself: 'By doing the ceremonies, I got rid of the disgust I felt for the Tiptur merchant. Now by completing the ceremonies of Manjayya, which I had already started, I must get rid of the disgust against him. Is it not to clean our minds, we have to perform rites – the karmas? All these, anger, reproach, disdain and disgust have to be washed, wiped and dried ... And this thought took root firmly in his mind. Suddenly he felt, oh how late it was already. With the memory that he had left Savitri alone at home, he became aware that she would have more grief.

After a little while, Satyappa too came out of the police station. When he said he would come again Lakkoo asked, 'Why, what work do you have here?' After coming out, he met the inspector and asked, 'You see inspector sir, there is nobody who would help Lakkoo to get a lawyer. If it is my district I would have known the most competent, reliable and intelligent lawyer to engage. You please guide me.'

The inspector said, 'You see, there is one Malali Venkataramayya in Hassan. He is very intelligent and competent also, but his rates are very high. Of course, we police do not like him. But while observing this case it seems there must be a good lawyer to handle the defence. Being a prosecution inspector, I should not speak much about this matter.' Satyappa appreciated the inspector's point of view. He too had heard about Malali Venkataramayya and knew it was he who had saved Manjayya. So, he directly walked to the bus stand and boarded the Hassan bus.

While the bus was moving, Satyappa did not have any illusion about the business that was to take place between the lawyer and himself. He started village courts as a solution to lawyers, courts, stamp fee, bus charges and expenses for false witnesses. But now he came to the decision through his experience of what happened when justice is sought in villages; that these courts were better. He enquired someone in the bus-stand about the lawyer, was told that generally the lawyer would be at court at the time and went to court. There he came to know that Malali Venkataramayya would attend court for big cases or on the final argument day and all other work would be handled by his juniors and Malali would be at home. Satyappa went to the lawyer's house in an auto. The auto driver, on the way, spoke about the Malali lawyer, with wonder, awe, respect and admiration. 'Oh, yes, sir, you cannot find such a brave lawyer. Not only in our Hassan, you see, people from Chikkamagalur, Shimoga, Tumkur and Mandya come to persuade him to present their case and request him to go there. Even if a man has committed murder in front of the judge himself, comes to this lawyer, narrates whatever he has done truthfully and surrenders before him, you take it from me, he is saved. If this lawyer begins his cross examination in court, police people, doctors, everyone will piss in their pants, in the witness box. He would not touch a murder case for less than fifty thousand. Where are you from sir? What sort of murder has been committed?' The auto driver gave further details about the lawyer.

Malali Venkataramayya, now, did not stay in his old house, which was big and spacious. He had rented it to the government and had constructed a palatial building in the new extension and lived there. Yes it was really a palace like building, with a big garden around. There were cement benches, flower plants and trees and a badminton court also in the garden. Satyappa paid the driver and walked into the house, sat in the place meant for visitors. An assistant came out and asked Satyappa to wait. He waited and waited for a long time. But nobody called him in. He asked the assistant who came out again. He said, 'I've told the boss your name and the job you have come for. You see, our M.P. and five M.L.A.s are talking inside about an election case. After they come out, I'll tell you.'

At three, all the six came out. On their faces also the feeling of awe and respect for the lawyer was visible. Then the lawyer went inside to have some snacks. After half an hour, the assistant sent Satyappa into the lawyer's chamber. The desk-table and the chair Malali Venkataramayya used cost fifteen to twenty thousand rupees. And who can evaluate the sofas and other furniture in the office? There were volumes and volumes of huge law books in nearly twenty five book cases – panelled into the wall. It was such a display that would intimidate or stupefy the client who entered the chamber. Satyappa saluted the lawyer, introduced himself, sat in a chair before the table and started from Manjayya's murder. Then the lawyer said, 'Oh, is that the same Manjayya? When I read in newspapers of Hassan today morning, I thought it must be him only. Last year in that case of murder in the grove, I had saved him from being sentenced. Now the wife of he who was murdered then, has done this to the fellow – yes, yes, yes. I know everything. I don't want unnecessary details. Just tell me the main points.' When Satyappa went on narrating, the lawyer was clearing in his mind some points that seemed simple; the accused is psychologically unfit to sustain the trial, when she committed murder her mind was not in her control; witness … Certificate of a psychiatrist stating even now her mind is disordered, even now she is obstinate that she tells only the truth in court and that itself is a proof to show that she is mentally deranged; point of guilty conscience that she committed perjury in her husband's murder case, she did cut off his penis in an abnormal state of mind, the man who had cheated mother and daughter and had slept with both of them. But with no intention of killing him, of course she did not have that intention at all. But the lawyer did not openly say anything to Satyappa. After Satyappa completed his narration, the lawyer said, 'You see, this is a very complicated case. Roots of this case will have spread in many places. We have to search for them and win the case. Although you belong to Tumkur district, you must have known this Malali is never defeated and showed his right hand spreading all fingers. Satyappa could not clearly understand, whether it was five or fifty.

He said, 'Please tell me clearly.'

The lawyer said, 'Fifty.'

Satyappa said, 'Look sir, I am not in any way related to this accused. I don't even know her. I am an agriculturist belonging to the lower middle class and I believe in the principles of Mahatma Gandhi.'

The lawyer did not get angry. He moved his right hand in a circular motion towards his thousands and thousands of books and said, 'You see these law books cost lakhs and lakhs of rupees. My assistants and myself must search in them for every case and gather points, what other courts have decided on certain matters. If you want a lawyer who handles your case without taking any fee, one fourth of the population of this town is there. Anyway, you pay up thirty thousand rupees.'

'Sir, I am here to fight for justice with a sense of duty.'

'So, do you intend to get justice by exploiting me?' the lawyer asked as if cutting with a knife.

'No Sir, I am not asking you to handle the case without fees. I know you too have establishment expenses. I have come here with an intention of helping a helpless woman, but my strength of paying is one part of that. I plead with you to notice this factor while fixing your fees. I am well aware that for your intellectual acumen, it is not enough even if I give one lakh,' Satyappa said very mildly but firmly.

'If so, pay me twenty five and bear the extra expenses. Alright, see, you do not on your own terminate the pregnancy of that girl. You inform it to the police, get a certificate from the government district surgeon that the girl is so many months and days pregnant, get his consent for abortion and only after that, you get it done. If not, important evidence will be lost. You bring that girl here, alright? Now I am busy. You come here the day after tomorrow. I will once again make that Narayana Murthy sweat profusely,' he said and got up. Satyappa understood there was no further scope for bargain regarding the fees. He took leave of the lawyer and came out.

As it was an extension in the outskirts of the town, Satyappa could not get an auto. He walked to the bus stand and took his meals in a hotel. By the time he reached Channarayapattana, it was 8:00 pm. He was not aware that the bus had already reached

Channarayapattana, for his mind was immersed in the thought about the money he had to arrange. If full twenty-five thousand was to be given to the lawyer, at least another five thousand was required for other expenses. How to adjust such a large amount? If he engaged an ordinary lawyer and not Malali, what could happen to Lakkoo? He got down from the bus and walked to Savitri's house, but the house was locked. Where must they have gone? He remembered he too had not told them that he was going to Hassan. When he enquired in the front house, he was informed that the brother and sister had left for Bilikere by the last bus. When he knew they had not given the key, he came to the main street. His bag was in Savitri's house. Forgetting that also, why did they leave suddenly for Bilikere? Satyappa thought perhaps to meet Lakkoo's daughter Latha. After two minutes he remembered – how Savitri had lost consciousness in that police room. Did she take it to heart? Whether Ramakrishna believed it or not, Savitri surely had felt giddy and swooned. But Satyappa could not get an answer as to why did they go to Bilikere. It was already half past eight and there was no bus to Bilikere. He decided to reach Bilikere on foot. Within five minutes he went to a hotel, got four idlis and chutney packed to eat on the way and started. He knew the bus route. It was two and a half hours long journey by walk. Within half an hour there will be moonlight. He walked on.

While on the way, his mind thought about what Lakkoo had said that too what Manjayya had told her, to save his life about the relationship between himself and Saati's mother. Nothing was taboo for a person like Manjayya. Satyappa had not known what sort of woman Saati's mother was. If judged by the characters of these two daughters, Manjayya's words about the mother was a sheer lie. What proof, what evidence was there, except that Manjayya told this after so many years in the context of saving his life? Satyappa thought, Saati by nature was intensely emotional. After the moonlight appeared, the road became clear and he could see the sky, the land, the trees and guess from his memory where he was. Now he felt that Saati herself must have forcefully taken Ramakrishna back to Bilikere. He became eager to reach Bilikere swiftly. He had seen that camel-rock in the tank of Bilikere. Seetha had shown him that place from where her mother had slipped and died. Not only that she had cried and prevented him from swimming there. Satyappa too had a suspicion in his mind; why would women, let alone to wash clothes, go to such a place for bathing? When he felt hungry he ate the idlis while he kept walking and it was 11:15 pm when he reached the outskirts of Bilikere. Instead of directly going home, he turned towards the village tank. He justified himself that he could have a look at that vast stretch of water in the silvery moonlight, but his inner anxiety did not alleviate. Looking around he went near the tank, reached the camel-rock, gazed at the clear water of that deep spot in the tank. He stood there for a while gazing at the expanse of water mildly shimmering like a silver plate and returned. While he was coming towards the edge of the sluice from the village, he noticed at a distance, someone coming this way. He swiftly turned to the left and hid himself behind a tamarind tree. He saw it was a woman. With firm steps, without turning this way or that she was coming as if drawn towards the fixed goal. Satyappa's suspicion was confirmed. Yes it was Saati. He hid himself until she walked forward. Satyappa thought; let her go first and stand on that rock. She would understand the meaning of his words when she reaches the brink of death. Before that, whatever I say won't enter her head. She would again come on the same road seeking death. He thought, anyone who commits suicide, would always stand still for three to four minutes before committing the actual deed. Savitri walked forward. Satyappa left his chappals at the foot of the tree and tiptoed slowly towards the tank. Savitri crossed the sluice, climbed on the tank bund, stepped in and stood on the camel-rock. Satyappa followed her closely. He was confident, even if she fell into that deep water before he reached her, he could swim and pull her up. She stood like a statue on the rock. Satyappa understood that she was in her final moment of thought and it was the last moment which would concretise intense frenzy and emotion into action. In a soft voice he called 'Saati'. It didn't seem like she heard it. Again he called 'Saati' a bit louder and went near her rapidly. By the time she turned back he had neared her and they had to stand facing each other. Satyappa did not touch her. He did not grab her. He stood there simply looking at her face. She had surpassed the state of surprise and frustration and stood still like a statue. Satyappa said, 'Sit down Saati, you can go ahead and drown yourself after talking to me.' His words did not seem to enter her ears. He stretched his hands, held her shoulders, made her sit down and sat in front of her. There was an expanse of shimmering, attracting white water behind her and to her left. To the right side also there was water spread to a little distance and there was the wall of the outlet of the tank. Still Savitri was not aware of her bhaava, sitting in front of her.

Satyappa started speaking, 'Look here Saati, in the morning you and Ramakrishna went home. I heard completely what Lakkoo said. Her mind is turned from normal condition and has stood fixed in a totally different mould. Who is going to engage a good lawyer for a woman in that condition? I went to Hassan and have fixed Malali Venkataramayya. Twenty five thousand is needed as fees for him and five to six thousand for extra expenses. Thinking how to arrange that amount, I came to Channarayapattana, but by then you two had left for Bilikere. Now I came here on foot. It suddenly flashed to my mind why you came to Bilikere and it further struck me that you would surely come to this spot. Do you know how? You know, I had decided to commit suicide. Then

I had thought of ending my life in the place where I committed the sin. First I thought of hanging myself in the hut of Manjayya's grove. Likewise, it is in this place that you became fascinated with Manjayya. And it is in this same place your mother lost her life. As such it struck me that you would surely come here. So I was frightened: what if you had fallen into the water before I came here? I came almost running, stood here, looked at this deep water in the moonlight and was returning. Are you listening?'

Savitri did not speak. But Satyappa was aware that her consciousness, her sense, was turning to this world and his words were entering her mind. For a while, he was silent. Then he said, 'I don't know whether you would have done what Lakkoo did. If you had known it earlier, would you not have done it? Now, tell me is it not your duty to protect her from punishment? Totally thirty thousand rupees are needed. I will arrange as much as possible. Will you give the balance? Or we can use some of your jewellery. We can sell it and get the money.' Savitri was silent. Satyappa asked again, 'Tell me Saati, will you give the money? I know you will.'

Savitri put her hand to her neck, pulled off her golden *Maangalya* chain, took off her gold bangles from her hands, and collecting everything held it before him. He received the jewels and said, 'I knew Saati, you would surely give. If we sell it, we may get fifteen to twenty thousand. If I keep these in my pocket, they may fall off when I bend down,' saying so, he held the edge of her sari, put the jewels in it and tied three knots. She sat silently. After sometime he asked, 'It seems Lakkoo's daughter Latha stays in this village. She is a young girl. I don't know what she might have done by now and who is consoling her. Both of us should go and take care of her.'

Savitri now spoke as if she came to her senses and knew what he said. 'Bhaava, I understood your plan. You tied those jewels in my own sari. That means I should go with you and sell it to a jeweller. I don't want to take that responsibility. Anyway I am going to die and didn't desire to die wearing gold on me. It did not occur to me to remove it at home and come here. At least let these be useful to Lakkoo. That's why I took them off and gave them to you. Please take them,' saying so she began untying the knot.

Satyappa held her hand and said, 'It will not be a virtuous deed if you give them with indifference and with the attitude, "anyway I am going to die, why should I bother what happens to these." You yourself should come. Sell them and give the money. Not only that, you must go to court and support her. Please understand.'

Savitri turned her head and looked at his face. He was gazing at her with firm eyes. Then all of a sudden she began sobbing. Now, Satyappa gained confidence. She said, 'Bhaava, I very well remember the woman, who was called my mother. I was only five when she died. Afterwards, when I was ten or twelve many people of our street would say, "You are the spitting image of your mother, eyes, nose, eyebrows, chin, everything. She herself is born again. You see Annayya also for many days called me Ammayya. I was feeling proud then. But now ..." she said and at once got up and turned towards the water.

Satyappa too got up with the same swiftness, held her arm and said. 'Listen Saati, listen to what I say. That woman is your mother and she is my mother-in-law. What Lakkoo said might be true or it might be a lie concocted by Manjayya. Even if it is true, I will not show any disrespect to my mother-in-law. Tell me one thing. Hereafter, will your annayya stop performing your mother's annual ceremony?'

She said, 'No, I think he will not stop. You know, he took over the burden of performing the funeral rites of Manjayya. I asked him: "Will you perform other rites even after knowing this?" He answered, "Yes I will do. Whether it is mother or father, if they have committed any sins it is their responsibility. But, because of that if we give up performing *Shraaddha*, it would be lapse of duty on our part. As there was no one else to do, I performed Manjayya's funeral rites. He who has done funeral rites must do other ceremonies also. How can I now escape from my duty, because I came to know there was an illicit relationship between him and my mother? It is my duty to help that *preta* pass into the next world. To judge its virtues and sins is the duty of Yamadharma."'

Satyappa held Savitri's arms, pulled her down and said, 'You also must think like him. Come, sit here, I'll tell you.'

She protested, tried to escape from his hold and said, 'No, no bhaava, don't force me, I don't want to live, I must die.'

He asked, 'What will you gain by dying?' She did not know any answer. He asked her again. 'Tell me, what will you gain? You ought to answer me. If you convince me, I'll not stop you.'

Savitri said, 'You are clever and are asking me questions which I can't answer and are making me tongue-tied.'

'No, Saati, it is not any sort of cleverness. I too had sat on the tree with the noose around my neck. Before I jumped down, this question rose in my mind. There was no answer to that. Instead, there will be hundreds of things to do if I lived.'

'I know what you are going to say.'

'I don't speak about village reform now. The first task is to take care of Lakkoo and her daughter. The second one is something you ought to do. Only you can do it. You do not know what is happening in Tiptur. Do you know, Ganesha is already becoming a mini version of Manjayya? I know this for I frequently visit Tiptur. A Manjayya in your house! Oh Parameshwarayya's son Ramakrishnayya has begot a Manjayya in his house! I did not have the strength to reform Manjayya. It needed the presence of a great Mahatma to reform such a person. Unfortunately there was no such Mahatma in these surroundings. If there was one, Manjayya need not have died in such a way. Ganesha is still young and he can be reformed. You must go to him, hold his hand, make him sit alone near you and describe the plights and hardships you experienced by marrying Manjayya and ask him whether he too would like to become like Manjayya. You know Saati, the effect or change that would occur by your narration and advice, would not happen with his father Ramakrishnayya's advice. Do you understand?'

'Yes,' she said.

'What did you understand?'

'Ganesha's mind melts more by my advice and my describing my hardships than his father's words!'

'Not only that, Ramakrishna's way of life is that of *Nivritti*. He can give up anything. He can detach himself from anything. Even after what Lakkoo said, he decides to perform the *Shraaddha* of Manjayya. Is it possible for ordinary people to burn to ashes six and a half lakhs, without any anger and regret?! Oh to whom is it possible? That is his power. But, people, looking at such persons get scared and move away from them. They won't come near. Can you influence people without getting near them? It is so even if you have to win over your son's mind. You see, gradually I have taken Ramachandra into confidence and am explaining to him in a friendly way. Let it be. Another thing. Legally you are Manjayya's wife. All his property and assets belong to you. The key of the iron safe, which was in the girdle, worn around the waist of the corpse is in the custody of the police. There might be silver, gold and many other valuables in the safe. There are so many wet fields, dry lands and grove. What will you do with all those?'

'Please, bhaava, don't try to create desire or greed in me. While I have come out with so much of disgust away from him, I don't want to even touch his property.'

'Look here Saati, you are speaking just like the sister of Ramakrishna. You don't touch it and suppose you sign a legal document saying you have no connection with that property. Then the government will take it over. What happens then? The government auctions all the property and buys a small aircraft for the luxury of some ministers. What good is achieved by it? What I say is, you should not touch even a single paisa of that money. You must earn your livelihood by your salary only. You must use Manjayya's money for the welfare of people. There is that hut in his grove, you had described, do you remember? You had narrated the sin and lies he committed there every day. You must start a philanthropic institution in the same place. If you commit suicide because of fear or shame, or frightened by sin, then that suicide will triumph over your greater strength. Sit down, there's still more to discuss. I am feeling tired standing as I had to walk two miles in Hassan and eight miles from Channarayapattana.'

Savitri sat down. Satyappa sat in front of her and said, 'You see, both of us should meet Lakkoo's daughter and speak to her. She may speak with you more freely than with me. It seems Manjayya had told her that he would cause to abort the child in her womb. That's why she was scared and came to her mother. Suppose, now she says, 'No I do not want to get my child aborted. I will give birth to it and bring it up.' Then something must be given for her livelihood and for the upkeep of the child. It should also be given a share of Manjayya's property. A Mahatma may be born from an abject sinner. If a suitable atmosphere is created and good education is provided, that child may become a great person. Whether to save the child or not, should be decided by that girl Latha. You have all this work to do. Besides, do you know why I came? I received your letter.' He looked at her face. He knew from the reaction on her face that her memory had shifted to that matter. Then he said, 'Now you have so many responsibilities to shoulder at Bilikere. Moreover, you yourself have written everything very clearly. You have decided not to have physical relationship. When that has been decided, whether we marry or not it is immaterial. But, it doesn't mean that I don't need you. You don't know how often I remember you and how much I depend on you. You have complete authority over me. Let us decide gradually, what we should do in the future. Get up, let us go home. Ramakrishna may get worried and come searching for you.'

'No, I had slept in my room, closing the door. I closed the door and came out.'

'Doesn't he know the front door or the backdoor is not bolted from within?'

Savitri became aware of her mistake. It was visible on her face in the moonlight. Satyappa said, 'Is it not my karma to struggle with such a stupid woman?' and laughed. The stiffness on Savitri's face lightened ever so slightly.

Niyantru, oh, how difficult it is to be a pure witness – *Shuddha Saakshi* – simply to be knowing and incapable of saying anything, doing nothing and rectifying nothing? The witness doesn't have the power even to stop injustice that is happening or that will happen. If only it was possible for me to inform Latha what sort of a man this Manjayya was, she would not have suffered such a plight. While my son Ramakrishna himself was pleading, supplicating and searching for me in the sky, "Appa, Appa, why didn't you tell me? What reason did you have to hide it, restrain it in your inner most being?" I could not answer him. Oh, *Niyantru*, I have understood your law. A person has power to say, to do, to stop and rectify anything as long as he exists in that world: how could all that be possible in the state in which relationships are crossed over? Aren't all these different kinds of relationships? However, I must limit my thoughts and observations to the purpose for which you sent me back to that world in invisible form. *Niyantru*, I'll inform you first the chief factor. The accusation of Manjayya that by appearing as a witness in court I harmed him more than helping him is true. If the witness stammers, falters before the judge and stands still as if he lost consciousness, the value of that witness will not only be dismissed, it will be detrimental. Actually he was acquitted with Lakkoo's witness. He has given the same reason to justify his not taking Savitri to his house to lead a family life. But, *Niyantru*, truth and untruth of my words should not be decided by results. I had not gone to Tiptur on that Saturday, nor had I seen Manjayya. But it was enough for the loss of gravity of my life. Then, I was not aware that man has an inner mind. I had known that only whatever I consciously knew as mind, was the real mind itself. Then, I began brooding, did I decide to commit suicide afraid of infamy or disgrace? Why didn't I commit suicide inside the inaccessible cave of a mountain, desolate shore of an ocean or in the centre of a desolate forest? Did I hang myself in the place with the desire where all the villagers should see and all people should accept my truthfulness and say "see, he sentenced himself with such a punishment just because his tongue uttered a single lie?" Is this also a sort of proclamation? *Niyantru*, now I am finding clues that the truth that proclaims itself will have a powerful root of falsehood.

But it is true that I committed suicide for I felt no support for life after the loss of truth. But, *Niyantru*, I feel like telling you, why I accepted truth as the sustenance of my life. As far as I remember, knowingly I never told a lie. This was imbued in me from the very beginning. After I witnessed the adultery of my wife, the difference between falsehoods began to manifest itself clearly in my mind. I felt certain that a man would either seize truth or lies and there was no middle path. Then, I was forty, my wife was thirty-five. She was a mother of five children, two dead and three alive. The son was nineteen, daughter was fifteen. The last girl was only five. I was happy and contented with my family. I was leading my life happily cultivating my lands, feeding guests and being contented with what I had. I had never suspected my wife, for suspicion means, finding lie in a relationship. Which husband of normal mind suspects his wife who is suitable and helpful to her husband and affectionate with the children? Every day after the guests had their food and I too had finished my lunch with them, I would take rest for a while and then go to the grove. I would work until the sun set and the birds returned to their nests and then return home. One day when I went to the grove after my lunch, a worker asked me for advance payment of twenty rupees. He begged that he needed the money urgently, for his wife was sick. I went home to bring the money and pushed the front door. It was bolted from inside. I never used to call out loudly. Thinking she might be washing dishes in the backyard, I pushed the wicket gate of the backyard and went behind. She was not there. I thought she must be sleeping, let me not wake her up and stood still for a moment. I had to give money to that worker, for his wife was sick. I thought of a plan. It was possible to remove the latch that was put on the back door, slowly with a finger. At night we would use the bolt or fastener. I removed the latch with my finger, came in, went directly inside. I did all this silently for she should not be disturbed in her sleep. With the same silence I pushed open the door of the room and went in. And alas, what did I see! She, of thirty-five years, who had given birth to five children and had saved three, my wife, was indulging intensely in the physical act with Manjayya who was only a little older than her son. How pale she became when she saw me! How that Manjayya got up like a lightning, after getting a little space, how he pushed me and ran away! All these details are now unnecessary here. This incident totally pulverised me. You see *Niyantru*, trust is the mainstay of relationship. Truth is the fundamental principle of trust. What support or what justification would be revived in the life of a man in whom these two have been destroyed? The seventh day after this happened, my wife drowned in the deep water of the village tank and died. But I had to continue living to bring up the children and help them stand on their feet. What support could I rely on to live? Is it not natural for a man to practise with special care and attachment, that from which he was deprived of? So, truth became my supreme sustenance. But, *Niyantru*, you must not think that I would not have got hold of truth if I had not undergone such a shock. It is not possible to possess or hold anything new which was not naturally in you and develop it into supreme good. *Niyantru*, it is not my purpose to have a discourse on truth and untruth!

'What did you ask her afterwards?' The *preta* immediately recognised that this emotionless and authoritative voice was that of *Niyantru*.

'No, I did not ask her anything. I took the money and went back to the grove. I can't describe the pain, agony, distress and disappointment I suffered. I firmed up my mind and came home. My fifteen year old daughter Seetha was cooking. She said that her mother was in periods again after fifteen days. My wife sat in the separate place set aside for women in periods. I did not turn that side. My daughter was cooking. My son was studying in Hassan. Another daughter of five years was playing in our house and in the neighbours' houses. Three days passed, four, five, six and then seven. As usual, a woman in periods should go to the village tank, bathe and purify herself. But, my wife did not go out. It seemed, she ate only half of what her daughter served. I did not ask her why. Nothing remained between us either to ask or to say. From where could I get words which were not there at all? I did not scold or admonish her even with a single word, nor did I show my face to her. After seven days were over, the eighth morning, at dawn it seems, she said to her daughter Seetha that she would go to the village tank to have her purification bath. By daybreak, two or three people came running and told me, 'Your wife had gone to take bath on the camel-rock, slipped, drowned and died.' The question 'Was I the cause of her death?' haunted me. Really, it never came to mind that she would act in such a manner. I was completely absorbed in my own agony and worry. Then I decided on one thing. What could be achieved by destroying the reputation of the dead woman and the respect her children had for their mother? Moreover, what authority did I have to destroy that respect? As such, just like truth became the sustenance of my life, silence too became my nature.'

The voice of Chitraguptas intervened, 'You decided in your mind to reveal this truth when Savitri insisted on marrying Manjayya.'

'Yes, I had decided to tell her. But she was a stubborn girl. Even knowing full well the history and character of Manjayya, she insisted on marrying him. There was no use saying it again and again. If I had revealed this truth, I certainly could have averted it. But from the revelation of this truth, what an amount of pain she and my son Ramakrishna would have to suffer? Was it proper to destroy the respectful memory the children had in their minds about their dead mother for the last twelve years? This question haunted me. If Savitri marries Manjayya and ruins her life, it is her responsibility: but I decided not to reveal the truth. But, then it did not occur to me that to conceal truth was also a sort of mental imprisonment.'

The *preta* narrated this much and kept quiet. There was total silence. It expected that *Niyantru* might question about something. After a little while, *Niyantru* said, 'You want to tell something. Say what is in your mind.'

'There are only two points, *Niyantru*: I committed suicide with an illusion that the problem would be solved by it. A person while living may go anywhere, think whatever he wants, but the mind of a person who commits suicide will adhere itself to a singly inescapable situation and become limited. Now I am feeling that had I lived, I could have found several possibilities that could be performed as atonement. The second point is: Janaki, my wife, sat with bowed head for seven days in the place set apart for women in periods. Then, I feel, I was totally absorbed in self-pity and self-absorption of the pain of my shattered trust. I did not bother a little to understand, why she did so. I did not try to understand what was happening to her. If I had tried to understand and spoken openly with her, perhaps she too would not have committed suicide. My suicide may be considered as escapism. But now, I am feeling that at least one part of her sin of committing suicide might have been attributed to me. My lord, *Niyantru*, I later reflected – why was my wife attracted to Manjayya, who was her son's age? I could not find an answer. Even now, I desire to know the reason. You gave me the special power to enter into the minds of the characters of that world and know what happens there. But Janaki is here. I do not know in what condition she exists and you know everything. You yourself tell me, why she did so?!'

Niyantru said, 'I will summon Janaki's *preta* here. You ask her face to face.'

Parameshwarayya's *preta* showed its reluctance or disagreement through its silence.

The voice of *Niyantru* asked, 'Why, are you not interested to know? Have you no desire to know?'

'No, not like that my lord. She lost that life thirty years ago, feeling it difficult to face me. All the shastras proclaim that in Yamaloka there is punishment after trial. By now she must have already suffered enough of that punishment. Now being face to face with me might be an extremely fierce punishment than the one you sentenced her with. I agree that punishing is your duty. But why do you use me as the tool of punishment?'

'No, you have completely misunderstood. You see, it is the way in the human world to use one as a tool for punishing another. But in this Dharmaloka, each one is responsible for his own punishment. Likewise, each one is the creator of his own happiness. Iron crows, cauldron of boiling oil, burning oven, frying pan – all these are only mythical creations of man's world. You can see her and listen to her words, for your understanding only. But you will not be visible to her. She will not be aware of your being here. Do you agree?'

'Yes my Lord, it is your grace.' After saying this the *preta* experienced being transferred from its place. But it did not get confused by this strangeness of change of place as it had by now understood, that place, region and space were totally different here. It stayed quietly. A *preta* appeared before the centre of Parameshwarayya's sight, a thing only a ball like *ichhaa-pinda*, of thumb-size without differentiated parts as eyes, nose, mouth, hands and legs. Parameshwarayya's *preta* did not know whether that new *preta* moved by itself or it was a feeling created by movement of space. That *preta* was looking simply at itself.

The voice of *Niyantru* questioned the newly arrived *preta*, 'You have been distanced from your past life for such a long time and you have undergone a part of the punishment. I have summoned you here for eliciting fresh information. Are you going to answer yourself instead of the Chitraguptas?'

'Yes my Lord.'

'Your name was Janakamma. You were thirty-five years old when you died. There were grown up children. You developed physical relationship with one Manjayya who was nearly your son's age. Why did you do so? Did not your husband have the potency to satisfy you?'

Janakamma's *preta* did not reply at once. After a while, the voice of *Niyantru* ordered. 'It is possible for me to know everything from the Chitraguptas. I have already known it also. But to test you, whether you have reached the level of telling the truth at least now, I am asking you. Tell me quickly.'

'Yamadharma, if the judge of that human world had asked this question, I could have told "yes my husband did not have the potency to satisfy me" and I could have earned sympathy of the law. But as you are well aware of everything, I cannot tell that. My husband was potent enough. I did love him too. I knew he too loved me and was affectionate towards me.'

'Yet, why did you desire to sleep with Manjayya?'

'*Niyantru*, you know the answer to this question. But you too cannot give any solution. By then Manju had already slept with several women. He used to come to my home calling me "Atte, Atte." I thought he was a suitable groom for my daughter Seetha, but as he had already gone astray and was a profligate, I decided not to put forward the proposal. But, what happened? If I begin to explain the reason, it would be like commenting. So, I will narrate the incident itself. I used to go the village tank to wash clothes. One day, the steps of village tank were crowded with people who came to wash clothes and there was no vacant place. So I went to that camel-rock. I knew that even if I slipped a little, there was a deep whirlpool. But I justified myself that I was not going to step down for bathing and there was no danger if I merely washed the clothes. I took courage. After washing clothes there one day, I got attracted to the place and went there every day to wash clothes. Besides, deep waters will always be clear. There was no anxiety of water being sprayed on me from other's clothes and I could raise and beat my clothes as forcefully as I wanted, without bothering if water would splash on anybody. One day when I was washing clothes, Manjayya came there swimming. I turned and saw. His graceful physique was seen beneath the surface of small waves of clear water as if a painting was being modified or metamorphosed in a dream. It took me almost a minute to identify him as Manjayya. He came near the rock and tried to climb it and sit there. Losing his grip, he slipped into the water. I don't know whether he did actually slip or pretended to. At last he stretched his hand and said, "Atte, hold me a little, my arms are completely tired." He was panting. I pitied him and stretched my hand. He held my right hand with his right hand and climbed on to the rock easily. But even after climbing over, he continued to hold my hand. I tried to pull my hand away, but he tightened his grip. He tightened his grip so much that I could not pull out my hand, and he said, "If you leave, what shall I do alone?" I got angry, shook off my hand, but he did not leave my hand then also. He looked at my face, stared as if he would enter into me through my eyes. Then he said, "Anyway, we have held each other's hands. Now I take your leave. Other people should not see us like this, is it not so?" He jumped down into the water head first. After a long time, he got out of the water stood and turned towards me. I got really very angry. Again I decided not to marry off my daughter to such a fellow. I rinsed the clothes and returned home. The whole day the hand he squeezed was aching. I would touch that right hand again and again with my left hand. I thought of not going to that camel-rock to wash clothes the next day. But I could not give up the attraction of that clear water whirlpool. Yes, I went there, and had decided, "Let him come, I will teach him a lesson." But he did not come that day. By the time I finished washing clothes, I felt like looking at the waves on the water, and was thinking "He has not yet come, why hasn't he?" It seemed as if I was seeing in the vagueness of the wave his picture-like graceful body which modifies in the dream. Oh Lord, *Niyantru*, you must have understood what happened inside me by then. The third day he came swimming in the same manner, and stretched his hand and said. "Please hold a little." I scolded him: "Tut-tut, you shameless scoundrel." But I had scolded him so softly that nobody should hear. "My hands are tired, don't delay please," he stretched his hand. I held his hand, helped him to climb on the rock. *Niyantru*, I need not describe to you the violence of waves that rose from inside me and dashed in front, behind and around my whole being. You are aware of everything. He came swimming in the same manner for still two days more. Then one afternoon around three, he came to our house. He knew very well that nobody would be there at home during that time. I was scared. My mouth said no, pleaded and beseeched. But he had that terrible power of understanding the mind. He said, "Why do you say no, when the minds are united?" I did not initiate it myself. But I did not have the power either of mind or of body to resist or prevent him. He was omniscient in that matter. Till then I was dedicated to my husband and that day I lost my sanctity. The whole day I grieved. He came the next day also and another day also he came. Then I reflected, I am a housewife with husband and children, where would my relation with him end? Nothing was known. But I had no power to give him up. He had become a power which pulled me, surpassing my intellect, mind and will power. Some pull inside which was unknown to me thrust me towards him. You see *Niyantru*, is it right to make me responsible? I was swept away caught in the flood that overpowered me.'

The voice of *Niyantru* asked, 'Did you have any thought of leaving your husband and marrying Manjayya?'

'Oh, how was it possible? What was Manju's age? What was my age? Moreover, if I did that, what about the future of my children? I had thought about all that. Nothing else was possible. So, I decided to meet Manju as many times as possible, seeking a safe time and both of us had decided that he should come by three in the afternoon. Oh, *Niyantru*, I ask you a question. Who created in me such an insatiable desire? Who created Manju? Doesn't he have any responsibility at all?'

Meanwhile another *preta* started coming there. One looked at the other. The newly arrived *preta*, within a moment recognised the *preta* which was there earlier and spoke, 'Oh Janakamma, are you here?'

'Oh Manju is it you?' This *preta* was excited. 'Why do you address me in the plural? Are you angry, for I left you there and came away? Don't you think the difference of age is a lie, once we love each other and are united?'

'Well, Janaki, are you here?'

'Oh Manju, when did you die? From what illness?'

'No, I didn't die. I came here in search of you. That day your husband came unexpectedly, do you remember? I escaped, thinking that if I stayed there your husband would catch me, call the neighbours and witnesses and evidence would be created. That was over. Then why did you jump into that whirlpool in the village tank, without telling me, or asking me what to do? I searched and searched for you, cried and cried, burnt in the fire of your separation. Finally I was wearied of that world and came here so that I could at least meet you.'

'My Manju, I knew, how much sorrow you would feel for me. I know you will sacrifice everything for my sake. Oh, how many times you had whispered in my ears with extreme intensity, "Oh Janu, I'll do anything for you." The agony I feel when it comes to my mind would be a crore times terrible than this punishment of Yamaloka.' Saying so Janaki's *preta* sank on the floor, rolling down, tossing and turning and started crying, shedding hot and continuous tears as scalding as steam.

'What he says is a lie.' Another voice was heard. The *preta* by its experience understood that the humble but precise voice was that of the Chitraguptas. The voice of Chitraguptas asked, 'If you were grieving so much for her, why did you marry her daughter, by begging and pestering and all sorts of stratagems? You hear this Janakamma, this Manjayya married your daughter Savitri by begging and beseeching. He then left her and ruined her life. Now he is telling you lies.'

Janaki's *preta* asked, 'Did you hear it Manju? Did you do so?'

Manjayya's *preta* answered, 'Chitraguptas may know only the external incidents. How could they understand the inner mind?

You see Janu, I was swimming in that whirlpool of camel-rock, searching and searching for you. Was it not there that we first met and held hands? There I found Savitri. Your own form, your own eyes, nose, forehead, eyebrows and chin. I thought I was blessed, for my Janaki who was drowned in the whirlpool had come up again for me. Then I asked, begged her and married. But later I understood I was bewitched by external form and beauty, I thought I had been cheated. My Janaki was totally different. To me, who had experienced her intimacy, this Savitri's company became intolerable. So, I left her. Yes dwelling on your memory I left her.'

Janaki's *preta* began crying with grief, more loudly with a sense of blessedness.

Chitragupta's voice spoke, 'What he says is a lie.' The voice of *Niyantru* awarded the decision, 'Here what Chitraguptas speak is the only truth.'

Manjayya's *preta* rolled on the floor and humbly requested, 'The honourable court of law should listen to my appeal. In the court of human world, the statements of professional witnesses are not believed. But here, you are purely depending on such professional witnesses, like Chitraguptas. If you follow such method how can an innocent, guiltless accused like me, get justice?'

For a while, there was silence. Then the voice of *Niyantru* was heard, 'Do not heed his words. You continue your report.'

'My Lord, it is only an external incident that this Manjayya is murdered. Actually it is a suicide.'

But Manjayya's *preta* protested, 'No, No, I was never a coward to commit suicide.'

Chitragupta's voice continued without minding the protest of Manjayya's *preta*, 'After coming out of the house of a woman called Sarojakshi, this person nearly hundred times told himself in extreme anger that he ought to cut off his organ which failed and humiliated his whole being. It was the focal point of his ego, his active principle. After three days, a woman named Lakkoo cut off its external form. Then there is another quality of suicide. Now, whichever being whether man, woman or any male or female animal enters into his grove, immediately they will be in heat. Cows, as if they have gone mad, rush in search of bulls; the bulls if they do not have access to cows, try to mount other female species like buffaloes, donkeys etc. You need not tell anything about dogs; this belief is developed in the whole village. A person called Satyappa tried to start a rehabilitation centre, a righteous place for destitute women. But the women who came there were possessed by abnormal physical desires. Even the male workers who came to work there are suffering from the same complaint. Men who are impotent or lack potency have started believing that wandering, at least stealthily during nights, in this grove, might enhance their potency. Proclamation is also one of the aims of suicide. This has not been achieved as successfully as this Manjayya. As such, we beg you, your honour, considering his purpose, his power of determination and all the aftermath of that his death must be treated as suicide.'

The report of Chitraguptas was still being continued. But by then, it seemed the scene was changed. The *preta* of Janakamma had become invisible. The newly arrived *preta* too vanished. Only the *preta* of Parameshwarayya remained as if falsehood and truth were brandishing swords. Its mind was dulled and got confused. After a while it asked:

'Lord, what is the root of lie? Is there no end to it?'

TRANSLATOR'S NOTE

When Bhyrappa's *Parva* was published thirty-five years ago, critics hailed his treatment of the *Mahabharata* for demystification of the epic. But, soon after he published his *Saakshi*, they were baffled by his introduction of myths like Yamadharma, Yamaloka, Chitraguptas and pretas, in a social novel. Bhyrappa replied: 'I am neither for removal nor for retaining and creating myths. As an artist my aim is to explore different levels and dimensions of truth; myths are only means to achieve this.'

In this novel the *preta* of Parameshwarayya is presented before Yama. Yama gives a special privilege to the *preta*: 'In my court usually *pretas* are not given an opportunity of submitting a report of their lives because they are prone to lie to escape punishment. Chitraguptas who always dwell inside every human being record his or her behaviour, report in my court and that is final. But since you have punished yourself by committing suicide for perjury, I consider you have a strong tendency to stick to truth. So I give you the privilege of making a report on yourself.'

According to Vedanta a person grasps truth only when his consciousness becomes completely pure. *Saakshi* can be called a metaphysical novel dealing with the problem of truth and falsity, without solving which, the problem of other values and disvalues of life cannot be analysed.

Bhyrappa devises a unique technique of presenting the incidents of this world in the frame of magic realism of yamaloka. The thumb-sized *preta* of Parameshwarayya is the narrator here, reporting to Yamadharma. Fusion of myths, philosophy and psychological insight into human passions at their worst and at their heights gives an aura to the structure of the novel. The first chapter of the novel, pregnant with the author's motifs reminds one of the exposition scenes of Shakespearean plays. The word *saakshi* has spiritual undertones throughout the novel. As a study of evil and preoccupation with *purusharthas, Saakshi* is a unique fiction the like of which has not appeared in any Indian language.

I am grateful to the author for permitting me to translate into English, a classic like *Saakshi*. My special thanks to Arjun Bharadwaj for his help in preparing the manuscript and typesetting it.